CREATION MYTHS OF PRIMITIVE AMERICA

Jeremiah Curtin in the Ruins of Palenque,
Central America.

CREATION MYTHS

OF

PRIMITIVE AMERICA

JEREMIAH CURTIN.

BENJAMIN BLOM   New York/London

First Published 1898 as
CREATION MYTHS OF PRIMITIVE AMERICA
IN RELATION TO THE RELIGIOUS HISTORY
AND MENTAL DEVELOPMENT OF MANKIND
Reissued 1969 by
Benjamin Blom, Inc. Bronx, New York 10452
and 56 Doughty Street, London, W.C. 1

Library of Congress Catalog Card Number 68-57187

Printed in the United States of America

DEDICATION

❦

To

MAJOR J. W. POWELL,

Director of the Bureau of Ethnology, Smithsonian Institution,
LL.D. of Harvard and Heidelberg :

Sir,— You lost your right hand in fighting to save American unity ; but though the hand went from you its cunning remained, with the power to plan and to execute.

The same kind of impulse that sent you to the field of battle to serve the country and the world, sent you to the field of science to serve as a geologist and an explorer in the majestic region of the Colorado, and finally brought you to found the Bureau of Ethnology.   Through your labors, combined with those of the men whom you have associated with you, the world has learned more of the great primitive race of our country than it learned from the discovery of the continent till the day when the Bureau was founded.

I beg to inscribe this book to you as a mark of my respect and friendship.

JEREMIAH CURTIN.

Steamer " Germanic,"
on the Mid-Atlantic Ocean,
   October 21, 1898.

CONTENTS

Contents

INTRODUCTION

INTRODUCTION

❦

THE creation myths of America form a complete system; they give a detailed and circumstantial account of the origin of this world and of all things and creatures contained in it. In the course of the various narratives which compose this myth system an earlier world is described to us, with an order of existence and a method of conduct on which the life of primitive man in America was patterned.

That earlier world had two periods of duration, — one of complete and perfect harmony; another of violence, collision, and conflict. The result and outcome of the second period was the creation of all that is animated on earth except man. Man, in the American scheme of creation, stands apart and separate; he is quite alone, peculiar, and special. Above all, he belongs to this continent. The white man was unknown to American myth-makers, as were also men of every other race and of every region outside of the Western Hemisphere.

Described briefly and by an Indian, the American myth system is as follows: " There was a world before this one in which we are living at present; that was the world of the first people, who were dif-

ferent from us altogether. Those people were very
numerous, so numerous that if a count could be
made of all the stars in the sky, all the feathers on
birds, all the hairs and fur on animals, all the hairs
of our own heads, they would not be so numerous
as the first people."

These people lived very long in peace, in concord, in harmony, in happiness. No man knows,
no man can tell, how long they lived in that way. At
last the minds of all except a very small number
were changed ; they fell into conflict, — one offended
another consciously or unconsciously, one injured
another with or without intention, one wanted some
special thing, another wanted that very thing also.
Conflict set in, and because of this came a time of
activity and struggle, to which there was no end or
stop till the great majority of the first people — that
is, all except a small number — were turned into the
various kinds of living creatures that are on earth
now or have ever been on earth, except man, —
that is, all kinds of beasts, birds, reptiles, fish,
worms, and insects, as well as trees, plants, grasses,
rocks, and some mountains ; they were turned into
everything that we see on the earth or in the sky.

That small number of the former people who did
not quarrel, those great first people of the old time
who remained of one mind and harmonious, " left the
earth, sailed away westward, passed that line where
the sky comes down to the earth and touches it,
sailed to places beyond; stayed there or withdrew
to upper regions and lived in them happily, lived in

agreement, live so to-day, and will live in the same way hereafter."

The American system, as we see, begins with an unknown great, indefinite number of uncreated beings, — in other words, of self-existent personages or divinities. Those divinities were everything at first; there was nothing except them, nothing aside from them, nothing beyond them. They existed unchanged through untold periods, or rather through a duration which would be periods were there a measure by which to divide it. They lived side by side in perfect concord, in the repose of a primeval chaos of quiescent mind which presents a most remarkable analogy with the attenuated, quiescent, undifferentiated matter which, according to the nebular hypothesis, filled all points of space in the physical universe before the first impulse of motion was given to it.

At last this long period is ended, there is mental difference among most of the first people, character is evolved and has become evident; rivalries, collisions, and conflicts begin.

The American creation myths, as far as we know them, form simply a series of accounts of the conflicts, happenings, and various methods by which the first world was changed into the world now existing. This change was effected in various ways. In the myths of certain tribes or nations, it is mainly by struggles between hostile personages. One god of great power and character overcomes a vast number of opponents, and changes each into some beast,

bird, plant, or insect; but always the resultant beast
or other creature corresponds in some power of
mind or in some leading quality of character with
the god from whose position it has fallen. In certain single cases opponents are closely matched, they
are nearly equal in combat; the struggle between
them is long, uncertain, and difficult. At last, when
one side is triumphant, the victor says, " Hereafter you will be nothing but a ―― "; and he tells
what the vanquished is to be. But at this point the
vanquished turns on the victor and sends his retort
like a Parthian arrow, " You will be nothing but
a ―― "; and he declares what his enemy is to be.
The metamorphosis takes place immediately on
both sides, and each departs in the form which the
enemy seemed to impose, but which really belonged
to him.

There are cases in which the hero transforms
numerous and mighty enemies indirectly through a
special wish which he possesses. For example, a
certain myth hero brings it about that a large company of the first people are invited to a feast, and
while all are eating with great relish he slips out
unnoted, walks around the house, and utters, as
he goes, the magic formula : " I wish the walls of
this house to be flint, the roof also." Next moment
the whole house is flint-walled, the roof is flint also.
After that he says, " I wish this house to be red-
hot." It is red-hot immediately. His enemies
inside are in a dreadful predicament; they rush
about wildly, they roar, they look for an opening;

there is none, they see no escape, they find no issue. Their heads burst from heat. Out of one head springs an owl, and flies away through the smoke-hole; out of another a buzzard, which escapes through the same place; out of the third comes a hawk, which follows the other two ; out of a fourth some other bird. Thus the action continues till every head in the flint house bursts open and lets out its occupant. All fly away, and thus the whole company is metamorphosed. Each turns into that which his qualities called for, which his nature demanded ; he becomes outwardly and visibly that which before he had been internally and in secret.

The hero in the above case could not wish his opponents metamorphosed directly, he could not wish this whenever he pleased or wherever he met the great company ; he had to induce them to enter the house, which he turned by his wish into flint and then heated. When the moment of terrible anguish came on them, the true nature of each of those people grew evident; each head burst open, and out sprang the real person.

All those of the first people whose minds had been modified, who, so to speak, had grown specialized internally, who were different from that which they had been to start with, were forced to change also externally, and could not escape or avoid that great power whose shadow was approaching; their destiny was on them, and they felt it.

In the Wintu system, one of the two which are set forth in this volume, nearly all changes were effected by Olelbis; but there are examples of agents with other means. Tulchuherris turns old Tichelis into a ground-squirrel at the climax of his perfidy. He changes Hawt, the porter at the dangerous river, into a lamprey eel, whose children are to be eaten by Indians in the future. Old Sas, the false and vain chief in Saskewil, is beaten by his son-in-law, and receives his present form of sun and moon at the end of a long and bitter struggle, in which strength, wit, and keenness use the very last of their resources.

There are cases in which some of the first people are so modified mentally that they are conscious of what has happened within them. They are ready for the change, they are willing to undergo it; but there is no immediate occasion, no impending struggle in which an opponent could have the chance to transform them. These people transform themselves by the utterance of a wish, and produce their own metamorphoses. There are still others who know, as do all, that a new race is coming, that they will be changed when it comes unless they are changed some time earlier. They know that they must be changed as soon as they see the new people or a sign or a mark of their coming. These unchanged first people, few in number comparatively, attempt to escape; but their attempts are vain, their efforts are useless. In the distant east they see smoke from the fires of the advancing new people, the Indians of America, or hear the barking of the dogs of this people, and that instant they receive the forms which are due them. Others escape for a season and hide in dark places; but the Indians go everywhere, and the metamorphoses continue till the career of the first people is ended.

I have in mind at this moment a representative picture of this last group of persons who were unwilling to be metamorphosed and strove to avoid the new race, the inevitable Indians. They had no desire to see men, and they fled to all sorts of lonely retreats and remote forest places. At a certain point on the Klamath is a rough mountain slope which rises abruptly from the water; far up, well toward the ridge, about seven-eighths of the way from the river to the summit, is a bulky high stone which seen from a distance looks much like a statue. Close behind is another stone, somewhat smaller, which leans forward in the posture of a person hastening eagerly. Both are white and shining; they have the appearance of quartz rock. These were two sisters hastening, rushing away to escape the coming change. When they reached the points where they are standing at present, the foremost sister looked toward the east and saw smoke; the second did not look, but she heard the distant barking of dogs which came from the place where the smoke was; both were changed into stone that same instant.

With the transformation of the last of the first people or divinities, which was finished only when the Indians or some sign of them appeared in every remote nook and corner in which a remnant of the first people had taken refuge, the present order of

things is established completely. There are now in
the world individualities of three distinct sets and
orders. First, that small number of the first people
whose minds had never changed, those gods who
withdrew and who live in their original integrity and
harmony, who retired to places outside the sky or
above it; second, the great majority of the gods, who
have become everything in the present world save
and except only Indians. This cycle finished, there
is a new point of departure, and we meet a second
group of myths concerning the existent world as it
is now with its happenings, — myths containing
accounts of conflicts which are ever recurrent, which
began before all the first people were metamorphosed, conflicts which are going on at present and
which will go on forever; struggles between light
and darkness, heat and cold, summer and winter,
struggles between winds which blow in opposite
directions, — in fact, accounts of various phenomena
and processes which attract the attention of savage
men more than others because savage men are living
face to face with them always.

This second group contains a large number of
myths, many of them exceedingly beautiful and, so
far as they are known, highly pleasing to cultivated
people. Unfortunately few of these myths have
been given to the world yet, for the sole and simple
reason that comparatively few have been collected
from the Indians.

The first cycle of myths — that is, those which refer
to creation, in other words to the metamorphoses of

the first people or gods into everything which is in the world, including the world itself — is succeeded by another in which are described the various changes, phenomena, and processes observed throughout nature.

In this second cycle, as I have just stated, light and darkness, heat and cold, opposing winds, heavenly bodies appear as heroes and leading actors. For ages the reverence, sympathy, and enthusiasm of primitive men have been given to those heroes, and are given to them yet, by every tribe which preserves its ancient beliefs and ideas.

In this cycle is one small group of myths which to the Indian is very sacred, a group which in many tribes is revered beyond others. This group associates the earth with the sky and sun considered as one person, or the sky and sun considered as distinct from each other. To these are added one, and sometimes two personages born of the earth. In the simplest version of this myth the earth maiden through being looked at by the sun becomes a mother, gives birth to a great hero, the chief benefactor of Indians. This hero gives the race all gifts that support existence, and it is through him that men live and prosper. Under whatever name he appears this benefactor is really that warm light which we see quivering, waving, and dancing above the earth in fine weather. He is the son of the virgin earth, of that mother who has never known a consort save the one who looked from the height of heaven on her.

The lives of the first people are described in creation myths, and presented as models upon which faithful Indians are to fashion their lives at all times and places. All institutions of primitive man in America were patterned upon those of "the first people." Every act of an Indian in peace or in war, as an individual or as a member of a tribe, had its only sanction in the world of the first people, the American divinities.

There was not on this continent one institution, observance, right, or custom which was not god-given, theoretically. The Indians of America always acted in a prescribed manner on a given occasion, because the gods of the world which preceded this had acted in the same manner in similar conditions and circumstances.

No people could be more religious than those of this continent, for there was no act of any kind in life during which they were free of religious direction. The source of this religion is in the myths, and in the explanations concerning them given by wise men, — in other words, by sorcerers.

What shall we say of this Indian system, and what is its value?

The first to be said is that it is complete, and for every Indian believer well-founded and symmetrically developed. In the primitive religion of America there is no speculation, all is simple statement; there are no abstractions, qualities are always connected with persons.

Indians believe that the whole immense body of

myths was delivered to them by the first people in one place or another. Among the Iroquois there is a detailed account of how myths were told to an ancient chief and an assembly of the people on a circular open space in a deep forest. On this space was a large wheel-shaped stone. From beneath this stone came a voice which told the tale of the former world, told how the first people had become what they are at present.

Day after day the chief and the people came to the stone, sat, and listened till the whole cycle of tales was narrated.

On the Lower Klamath is a very old, immense tree, which has given an account of the first world and people. This tree itself is one of the first people metamorphosed; no one knows what its age is. Sorcerers go to it yearly, hold converse, put questions, receive answers. Each year a small stone is added to a pile in which there are thousands of pebbles, apparently. This pile stands near the tree; no one is permitted to count the stones in it. The pile is sacred; once a stone is placed with the others, it must stay there forever.

This sacred tree has told tales of the first world, — the tales known to Weitspekan Indians and revered by them.

On the Upper Columbia is a great rock which resembles an elk somewhat. This rock is also an oracle, one of the first people; like the round stone of the Iroquois, it has told of the first world, and its tales all belong to the Shahaptians.

The Indian system has its plain and clear revelation; for believers it has tangible and undoubted connection with the world which preceded the present one. Its narratives explain how in one place and another the first people revealed the tale of the world's transformation.

For the Indian this is all-satisfactory. He has a system which is perfect, extensive, rich in details, full of interest, — a system which gives proofs of its origin through testimony delivered by divinities. It was revealed to the wise men, the worthies, the patriarchs of his race. What more could he wish for? What more could he ask? Nothing. The wisdom of his nation is more valid, more reliable than the witness of his own senses. His eyes and ears might be deceived by tricksters, but not by the truth delivered to great men among his own people, preserved by them sacredly and passed down to others.

This is the position of the Indian. He believes in his own system fully. How are we to relate ourselves to that system and its contents? What should we think of it? How was it conceived, how developed?

We do not believe in an Indian first world nor a previous people turned into animals, plants, insects, birds, fish, and reptiles. We have no ancestors who founded that system; we possess no traditions that came from it, no beliefs that are based on its teachings, no faith in its sorcerers, no dread of their workings. Any statement as to how the Indian system was conceived and how it was developed is very different in character from a statement of what the Indian system is externally and on the basis of its own story.

In presenting the system from the purely formal side we are dealing with simple facts, which we collect and range in order. Once we possess these ordered facts, we have the externals of everything Indian,— not only religion, but medicine, politics, social life. We might stop there and say, This is the system. But from our point of view we are forced to go further, we must seek explanations. We form no part of the Indian assembly of believers, we have no faith in their system except to show us what the Indian mind is; hence we are forced to ask how the Indian founded his religion and evolved it, we are forced to look for its origin and meaning. We give no credence to his tale of revelation; we are certain that he himself — that is, his race — began the system, that it was developed from insignificant beginnings, and increased through lengthy periods till it reached its present form and fulness. We have not the details of how he acted, but we know where the myth-maker had to begin, and we see what he has effected.

The physical universe was for myth-makers of the old time in America the same in principle that it is for us to-day, the visible result and expression of unseen power and qualities. The difference between us and them is determined by the things that we see and the way in which we apprehend them.

What did the ancient myth-makers say of this universe, and what interest or value has their statement for us at this moment?

The primitive men of America saw before them forests, plains, deserts, mountains, lakes, and rivers of various sizes, from the smallest to the greatest; they lived in climates varying from the coldest and most inclement to the hottest and most difficult of endurance. They saw around them on all sides a world far more hostile than friendly, — a world of savage beasts, wild creatures, poisonous reptiles, deadly insects. Each creature, every plant had its own fixed and settled character, its own aim and object. Whence came beasts good for food or clothing; whence others dangerous to life, beasts to be slain or avoided? Whence came trees and plants of various kinds and uses? Whence came sweetness in the maple or bitterness and poison in another tree? What is the origin of corn, and why do poisons grow to kill as corn does to nourish? Whence came the rattlesnake, and whence the salmon? Because of these questions myths appeared, and those myths gave answers which received full faith and credence, — answers on which was built a theory of how this world arose, and what the true and proper scheme of life was.

The myth-maker looked at the universe around him, and saw throughout every part of it individualities having qualities, desires, and passions in varying degrees. He observed these individualities, and gave a detailed account and history of how this world arose. He gave this history by projecting existence into a past which was remote and passionless. Out of that harmonious past he evolved the present world and its order by describing in the past world the play of all those passions, desires, and appetites which he saw at work in life around him. Such was the method employed in producing the American creation myths. The task required much time, long observation, careful thought, and no small constructive power. These creation myths with the next, which I have mentioned already and called action myths, are the great result of mental toil and effort in the old time on this continent. In these two sets of myths the Indian has told what he thinks of the universe.

When Europeans came to this hemisphere, the American myth system was unbroken and perfect. There was no second order of thought here. The continent was untouched by foreign conquest or ideas. The inhabitants had lived in mental isolation, in absolute freedom from every outside influence. Human history has no second example of a single system of thought developed over such a vast area. Inhabited America extended at least nine thousand miles from north to south, more than one third of the earth's circumference and considerably more than the earth's diameter. This territory where broadest was at least three thousand miles from east to west, both in North and South America. Over this immense portion of the earth's surface with its endless variety of soil, climate, scenery, and conditions of existence, a single system of primitive philosophy was developed with a fulness and a wealth of illustration which could find no parallel in any other place. The result of all this is that we have in America a monument of thought which is absolutely unequalled, altogether unique in human experience. The special value of this thought lies, moreover, in the fact that it is primitive, that it is the thought of ages long anterior to those which we find recorded on the eastern hemisphere, either in sacred books, histories, or literature, whether preserved on baked brick, burnt cylinders, or papyrus.

The American system, which gives us a circumstantial account of the beginning of all things, is as far reaching as the nebular hypothesis, or as that theory which gives a common origin to man and all sentient existences.

Primitive man in America stood at every step face to face with divinity as he knew or understood it. He could never escape from the presence of those powers which had constituted the first world, and which composed all that there was in the present one. Man's chief means of sustenance in most parts were on land or in the water. Game and fish of all sorts were under direct divine supervision. Invisible powers might send forth game or withdraw it very quickly. With fish the case was similar. Connected with fishing and hunting was an elaborate ceremonial, a variety of observances and prohibitions. Every man had a great many things to observe as an individual, a great many also as a member of his tribe or society.

The most important question of all in Indian life was communication with divinity, intercourse with the spirits of divine personages. No man could communicate with these unless the man to whom they chose to manifest themselves. There were certain things which a man had to do to obtain communication with divinity and receive a promise of assistance; but it was only the elect, the right person, the fit one, who obtained the desired favor. For instance, twenty men might go to the mountain place, and observe every rule carefully, but only one man be favored with a vision, only one become a seer. Twenty others might go to the mountain place, and not one be accounted worthy to behold a spirit; a third twenty might go, and two or three of them be chosen. No man could tell beforehand what success or failure might await him. The general method at present is the following, the same as in the old time : —

Soon after puberty, and in every case before marriage or acquaintance with woman, the youth or young man who hopes to become a doctor goes to a sacred mountain pond or spring, where he drinks water and bathes. After he has bathed and dressed, he speaks to the spirits, he prays them to come to him, to give him knowledge, to grant their assistance. The young man takes no food, no nourishment of any sort, fasts, as he is able, seven days and nights, sometimes longer. All this time he is allowed no drink except water. He sleeps as little as possible. If spirits come to him, he has visions, he receives power and favor. A number of spirits may visit a man one after another, and promise him aid and co-operation. The eagle spirit may come, the spirit of the elk or the salmon, — any spirit that likes the man. The spirit says in substance, "Whenever you call my name I will come, I will give my power to assist you." After one spirit has gone, another may appear, and another. A man is not free to refuse the offers of spirits, he must receive all those who come to him. As there are peculiar observances connected with each spirit, the doctor who is assisted by many is hampered much in his method of living. There are spirits which do not like buckskin; the man to whom they come must never wear buckskin. If a man eats food repugnant to his spirit, the spirit will kill him. As each spirit has its favorite food, and there are other kinds which to it are distasteful, we can understand easily that the doctor who has ten spirits or twenty (and there are some who have thirty) to aid him is limited in his manner of living. Greatness has its price at all times, power must be paid for in every place. Those for whom the spirits have no regard, and they are the majority, return home without visions or hope of assistance ; the spirits are able to look through all persons directly, and straightway they see what a man is. They find most people unsuited to their purposes, unfit to be assisted.

This preparation to become seers or sorcerers

among Indians is of very deep interest. I have
given a considerable number of details on the subject
in notes to " Kol Tibichi." The spirit of any plant,
any star, or other personage in creation may become
a man's attendant. In our popular phraseology,
this is called his " medicine."

In a Modoc myth the morning star is the attendant of the sun. According to this myth the sun
is destroyed every day physically, is consumed into
a heap of ashes ; but as the sun has an immortal
golden disk in his body, a disk which contains his
whole existence, he can never perish. This disk
remains always in the heap of ashes. There is a
condition, however, incident to the sun's resurrection : he must be called. Every morning some one
must rouse him, as a hireling is roused to his daily
labor. The morning star has that duty, and will
never be freed from it. While the sun exists, the
morning star must call him. At the summons of
the star the golden disk springs from the pile of
ashes, the sun is renewed completely, and goes
forth to run his race till consumed again in the
evening. Here we have the Phœnix rising from its
ashes daily instead of once in five centuries.

The system outlined in the myths contained in
this volume is that of the Wintus and Yanas, two
stocks of Indians whom I shall describe somewhat
later.

The Wintu system is remarkable for the peculiar
development of the chief divinity, Olelbis, called
also Nomhliëstawa.

The word " Olelbis " is formed of three etymological elements : ol, up ; el, in ; bis, dwelling or sitting, — dwelling on high. Nomhliëstawa is formed also of three elements: nom, west ; hliës, to hurl ; and tawa, left-handed. Both names are epithets, and the Wintus have forgotten who or what their chief divinity is ; at least I have not been able to find a man among them who could give information on this subject. Olelbis lives in the highest part of the sky ; with him are the best of the first people. From his beautiful house, Olelpanti Hlut, he sees everything on earth, and seems more real and familiar than any divinity connected with other tribes. He is certainly more effective in management, more active than any divinity of other Indian stocks, so far as I know.

Olelbis disposes of the first people, except in a few cases, and he retains with himself whomsoever he likes. He sends to the earth and transforms those whom he thinks more useful below than above, and gives the example of a single ruling divinity which, without being all-powerful or all-wise, is able, through the knowledge and services of others, to bear rule over the world in all places and everywhere.

The two old women, the grandmothers, are interesting persons, counsellors of the chief divinity, rainmakers, wise with a knowledge of people of whom Olelbis is ignorant, at least professedly. These old women have been turned into a stone which has a spongy appearance and looks like the inside or porous portion of bones which are without marrow.

The great majority of Wintu metamorphoses are effected by Olelbis. The only exceptions are those of Sas, Hawt, and Tichelis, transformed by Tulchuherris, and certain changes such as those of color produced at the great musical contest given by Waida Dikit. When each played on a flute at that contest till he had done his best, till he had lost breath, then he changed color. Though the Wintu system differs much in detail from others, it agrees perfectly with all bodies of mythology on the great point, the main principle, metamorphosis. Through metamorphosis, all things have become what they are; through revelation it was learned that the metamorphoses took place, and in what way they took place. We must not consider the final act as the whole; the change had been in process for a long period, and the final words from opponents in conflict, the commands of Olelbis, the decisions of personages who changed themselves at the approach of Indians, or at signs of their coming, are but the very last act, the final incident, the official ending, so to speak, of an immensely long career in each case.

Of course there is no true information in the American ethnic religion as to the real changes which affected the world around us; but there is in it, as in all systems like it, true information regarding the history of the human mind. Every ethnic religion gives us documentary evidence. It gives us positive facts which, in their own sphere, are as true as are facts of geology in the history of the earth's crust and surface. They do not tell us what took place in the world without, in the physical universe, they had no means of doing so ; but they do tell us what took place at certain periods in the world of mind, in the interior of man.

The term " ethnic religion " needs some explanation, perhaps, before we go further. An ethnic or primitive religion is one which belongs to people of one blood and language, people who increased and developed together with the beliefs of every sort which belong to them. Such a religion includes every species of knowledge, every kind of custom, institution, and art. Every aboriginal nation or human brood has its gods. All people of one blood and origin are under the immediate care and supervision of their gods, and preserve continual communication and converse with them. According to their own beliefs, such people received from their gods all that they have, all that they practise, all that they know. Such people, while their blood is unmixed and their society unconquered, adhere to their gods with the utmost fidelity.

The bonds which connect a nation with its gods, bonds of faith, and those which connect the individuals of that nation with one another, bonds of blood, are the strongest known to primitive man, and are the only social bonds in prehistoric ages. This early stage was the one in which even the most advanced group of Indians in America found themselves when the continent was discovered.

On the Eastern hemisphere, where there were so

many races quite distinct and different from one another, the conquest of one race by another, or the conquest of a number of races by one, was frequent and had a great influence on thought and on religion. The influence of one religion or system of thought on another was sometimes considerable, as the intellectual influence of Egypt on Greece, and sometimes great, as that of Greece on Rome.

The influence of the physical conquest of many by one was immense politically and socially, as in the case of Rome, which subdued Greece and, together with Greece, all that Alexander had conquered in Asia and Egypt. With the ruin of Carthage, Rome destroyed the ancient thought of Phœnicia, which was closely akin to the earliest Hebrew, and one of the most important among Semitic nations. With the conquest and assimilation of Transalpine and Cisalpine Gaul, the whole ancient fabric of Keltic thought on the continent gave way, and its chief elements were lost soon after.

The last of the ethnic religions of Europe, and one of the most valuable, that of the Lithuanians, continued in perfect condition till the fifteenth century, when it was ended through bloodshed and violence. This last of the systems of primitive Aryan thought in Europe passed away leaving slight traces. We know the names of some of its divinities; we know that it resembled the Slav, but was more developed, that it had sacred serpents and priestesses who guarded the holy, unquenchable fire ;

but, to the great regret of men of science, we have only small fragments of the system, brief and meagre accounts of it.

If we look closely into the religious history of the Eastern hemisphere, we shall find the position to be approximately as follows, —

In the oldest of the inscriptional versions of the "Book of the Dead" on the walls of pyramids, we find the religion of Egypt advanced far beyond the first stages of development. Though animals, birds, reptiles, and insects occupy a prominent position in Egyptian religion, it is not evident why they occupy that position. There is no inscription or book to inform us. The earliest stage of Egyptian religion is lost to us. Egyptian priests, when reproached for the national worship rendered various animals, birds, reptiles, and insects, creatures that were vile, useful, clean, or unclean, as the case might be, were unable to give a cause for the worship. They were unable for the reason that the mythologic account was unknown to them, or had been lost or was unconsidered; whatever the reason, neither papyrus nor inscription explains it.

The chief gods of priestly Egypt answered exactly to the Indian divinities of the second class of myths in America, those which I have called action myths. Among these the sun and the earth were very prominent. Of the earliest gods of Egypt, those which answered to the "first people," or divinities in American creation myths, we find no account thus far. If we had that account, it would explain why there are animals, reptiles, and insects in Egyptian religion.

In Greece those portions of the earliest mythology which were not lost were obscured. The ancient creation myths were either misunderstood, or were unknown to the educated at the period from which the first literary monuments have come down to us. Hesiod arranged and shaped Greek mythology to suit himself and his audience, so that it is quite impossible to learn from that author what the primitive myths of Greece were. If brought before him, he would doubtless have looked on them much as a certain French Algonkin and Iroquois scholar of Canada looked on the myths of America. The man had an extensive knowledge of Algonkin and Iroquois words, but an utter contempt for Indian thought, and no real knowledge of it whatever. When I mentioned Indian mythology, he exclaimed : " Mais, Monsieur, c'est quelque chose d'absurde."

No doubt the earliest creation myths were well known throughout rural Greece among the illiterate, but there was no philosopher of that day who knew their value. There was no man to consider them.

Roman mythology, as well as Greek, suffered from literary treatment, and it is only by collecting detached fragments and facts of primitive thought throughout the whole field of classic literature that we are able to get at something beyond the official religion of polished society in Greece and Rome.

From the wreck of ancient Keltic and Teutonic thought much has been saved on the two islands

of Ireland and Iceland. With this, together with
the American system and the mythologic inheritance
of the Slav world in Eastern Europe, we shall be
able perhaps to obtain materials with which to explain
the earliest epoch of Aryan thought, the epoch
which corresponds in development with the world
of American creation myths. In that case we shall
gain a connected view of Aryan speculation and its
methods from those early beginnings when there was
no passion or quality apart from a person, when
symbols, metaphors, and personifications were in the
distant future. The whole problem is to connect
the thought of this continent with that of the rest of
mankind, but especially and above all with the
Aryan and Semitic divisions of it.

It is to be regretted that Semitic beliefs of the
primitive period have not come down to us more
numerously; for example, those of the Phœnicians,
the earliest Hebrews, and other kindred nations.
Fortunately the Arabs, the most poetic of the race,
the knightly members of it, have given us in their
history one fact of great value. Just before the
establishment of the new religion by Mohammed
there were in Mecca more than three hundred
Arabic divinities, animal, vegetable, and mineral.
We can hardly doubt that the pre-Mohammedan
Arabic system of religion was the one which on a
time belonged to the whole Semitic race, different
among some divisions of it in details, of course, but
substantially the same everywhere. This statement
of the Arabic condition contains a fact of immense

significance.   It points to a system exactly like the American.   The pre-Mohammedan Arabic was the most splendid and important survival of primitive religion in any historic race on the Eastern Hemisphere.

It is proper here to explain the position of spirits in the Indian systems.   All the first people are conceived as having bodies as well as spirits.   When we speak of a spirit appearing to a sorcerer or " doctor," it is understood that that spirit has left its body temporarily and will return to it.   There are no spirits without bodies save an exceptional few who at the time of the metamorphosis of the first people lost the bodies which had belonged to them in their primal condition and received no new bodies at their fall.   This loss of bodies was inflicted as a punishment.   These desolate disembodied spirits wander about now in mountains and lonely weird places.   Uncanny in character, they are seen rarely, and then only by sorcerers.

A good deal has been given to the world of late on mythology by able writers who with good materials would attain good results ; but as the materials at their disposal are faulty, much of their work with all its cleverness is mainly a persistent pouring of the empty into the void.

We have seen attempts made to show that real gods have been developed by savage men from their own dead savage chiefs.   Such a thing has never been done since the human race began, and it could never have been imagined by any man who knew the ideas of primitive races from actual experience or from competent testimony. The most striking thing in all savage belief is the low estimate put on man when unaided by divine, uncreated power. In Indian belief every object in the universe is divine except man. Divinities have an immense range of power, there is an incalculable difference between the greatest and the smallest of them, — some have inconceivable strength and knowledge, while others are measurably weak and of limited intelligence, — but all belong to one category, all are divine, all are extra-human.

Vegetable gods, so called, have been scoffed at by writers on mythology. The scoff is baseless, for the first people were turned, or turned themselves, into trees and various plants as frequently as into beasts and other creatures. Maize or Indian corn is a transformed god who gave himself to be eaten to save man from hunger and death. When Spanish priests saw little cakes of meal eaten ceremonially by Indians, and when the latter informed them that they were eating their god, the good priests thought this a diabolical mockery of the Holy Sacrament, and a blasphemous trick of Satan to ruin poor ignorant Indians.

I have a myth in which the main character is a violent and cruel old personage who is merciless and faith-breaking, who does no end of damage till he is cornered at last by a good hero and turned into the wild parsnip. Before transformation this old parsnip could travel swiftly, but now he must stay in one place, and of course kills people only when they eat him.

The treasure saved to science by the primitive race of America is unique in value and high significance. The first result from it is to carry us back through untold centuries to that epoch when man made the earliest collective and consistent explanation of this universe and its origin.

Occupying this vantage-ground, we can now throw a flood of light on all those mythologies and ethnic religions or systems of thought from which are lost in part, great or small, the materials needed to prove the foundation and beginnings of each of them. In this condition are all ancient recorded religions, whether of Greece, Rome, Egypt, Chaldea, Persia, or India.

Through amazing ability of primitive man on this continent to retain, or perhaps through his inability to change or go forward, he has preserved a system of thought already old at the time of the first cuneiform letters and of the earliest statements on stone or papyrus. And the discovery of this system of ours coincides almost with the moment when America after a century and a quarter of free political activity, and of intellectual labor unexampled in fruitfulness, takes her due place as a World Power, and enters into intimate and searching relations, not with Europe alone, or one section of mankind, but with the whole human race wherever fixed or resident.

JEREMIAH CURTIN.

WASHINGTON, D. C., U. S. A.,
    October 11, 1898.

OLELBIS

CREATION MYTHS

OF

PRIMITIVE AMERICA

☙

ÓLELBIS

PERSONAGES

After each name is given that of the beast, bird, or thing into which the personage was changed subsequently. Names on which accents are not placed are accented on the penult. Names of places are explained in the notes. Kiemila and Herit mean "old" and "young," respectively; they are applied to male persons. Pokaila and Loimis are applied to females; the first means "old," the second "young."

Bisus, mink; Chálilak, goose; Chuluhl, meadow-lark; Dokos, flint; Hau, red fox; Héssiha, tomtit; Hilit, house-fly; Hlihli, white oak acorn; Hus, turkey buzzard; Kahit, wind; Kahsuku, cloud dog; Kaisus, gray squirrel; Kar, gray heron; Karili, coon; Katkatchila, swift; Katsi, chicken-hawk; Kau, white crane; Kiriú, loon; Klabus, mole; Klak, rattlesnake; Kuntihlé, fish-hawk; Lutchi, humming-bird; Mem Loimis, water; Mem Tulit, beaver; Min Taitai, sap-sucker; Móihas, bald eagle; Pákchuso, the pakchu stone; Patsotchet, badger; Poháramas, shooting star; Sas, sun; Sedit, coyote; Sosini, a small web-footed bird; Sútunut, black eagle; Tede Wiu, a small bird; Tilichi, a water-bird; Tilikus, fire drill; Titchelis, ground squirrel; Toko, sunfish; Tórihas, blue crane; Tsárarok, kingfisher; Tsaroki Sakahl, green snake; Tsurat, woodpecker; Wehl Dilidili, road-runner; Wima Loimis, grizzly bear; Wokwuk, a large bird, extinct; Yilahl, gopher; Yoholmit, frog; Yonot, buckeye bush.

THE first that we know of Olelbis is that he was in Olelpanti. Whether he lived in another place is not known, but in the beginning he was in Olelpanti (on the upper side), the highest place. He was in Olelpanti before there was anything down here on the earth, and two old women were with him always. These old women he called grandmother, and each of them we call Pakchuso Pokaila.

There was a world before this one in which we are now. That world lasted a long, long time, and there were many people living in it before the present world and we, the present people, came.

One time the people of that first world who were living then in the country about here [1] were talking of those who lived in one place and another. Down in the southwest was a person whose name was Katkatchila. He could kill game wonderfully, but nobody knew how he did it, nor could any one find out. He did not kill as others did; he had something that he aimed and threw; he would point a hollow stick which he had, and something would go out of it and kill the game. In that time a great many people lived about this place where we are now, and their chief was Torihas Kiemila; these people came together and talked about Katkatchila.

Some one said: "I wonder if he would come up here if we sent for him."

"Let us send for him," said Torihas; "let us ask him to come; tell him that we are going to have a great dance. To-morrow we will send some one down to invite him."

Next morning Torihas sent a messenger to invite Katkatchila; he sent Tsaroki Sakahl, a very quick traveller. Though it was far, Tsaroki went there

---

[1] That is, in the Upper Sacramento Valley.

in one day, gave the invitation, and told about Torihas and his people.

" I agree," said Katkatchila. " I will go in the morning."

Tsaroki went home in the night, and told the people that Katkatchila would come on the following day.

" What shall we do ? " asked they.

" First, we will dance one night," said the chief; " then we will take him out to hunt and see how he kills things."

Katkatchila had a sister; she had a husband and one child. She never went outdoors herself. She was always in the house. Nobody ever saw the woman or her child.

When Katkatchila was ready to start he told his sister that he was going, and said to his brother-in-law : " I am going. You must stay at home while I am gone."

The sister was Yonot. Her husband was Tilikus.

Katkatchila came to a hill up here, went to the top of it, and sat down. From the hill he could see the camp of the people who had invited him. He stayed there awhile and saw many persons dancing. It was in summer and about the middle of the afternoon. At last Katkatchila went down to where they were dancing, and stopped a little way off. Torihas, who was watching, saw him and said, —

" Come right over here, Katkatchila, and sit by me."

Olelbis was looking down from Olelpanti at this moment, and said to the old women, " My grandmothers, I see many people collected on earth ; they are going to do something."

Katkatchila sat down and looked on. Soon all the people stopped dancing and went to their houses. Torihas had food brought to Katkatchila after his journey. While he was eating, Torihas said to him, —

" My grandson, I and all my people have lived here very long. My people want to dance and hunt. I sent one of them to ask you to come up here. They will dance to-night and go hunting to-morrow."

Torihas stood up then and said, —

" You my people, we will all dance to-night and to-morrow morning we will go to hunt. Do not leave home, any of you. Let all stay. We will have a great hunt. Katkatchila, will you stay with us ? " asked he. " I shall be glad if you go and hunt with us."

" I will go with you," said Katkatchila. " I am glad to go."

They danced all night. Next morning, after they had eaten, and just as they were starting off to hunt, the chief said to his people, —

" I will send my grandson with Katkatchila, and some of you, my sons, stay near him."

Some said to others : " When Katkatchila shoots a deer, let us run right up and take out of the deer the thing with which he killed it, and then we won't give it back to him."

" Do you stay with him, too," said Torihas to Kaisus, who was a swift runner.

The whole party, a great many people, went to Hau Buli to hunt. When they got onto the mountain they saw ten deer. Katkatchila shot without delay; as soon as he shot a deer fell, and Kaisus, who was ready, made a rush and ran up to the deer, but Katkatchila was there before him and had taken out the weapon.

He killed all ten of the deer one after another, and Kaisus ran each time to be first at the fallen body, but Katkatchila was always ahead of him. When they went home Kaisus carried one deer, and told of all they had done, saying, —

"Now you people, go and bring in the other deer. I don't believe any man among us can run as fast as Katkatchila; he is a wonderful runner. I don't know what he uses to kill game, and I don't think we can get it away from him."

That night Hau spoke up among his friends and said, "I will go with Katkatchila to-morrow and see what I can do."

A great many of the people talked about Katkatchila that night, saying, —

"We do not think that he will ever come to us again, so we must all do our best to get his weapon while he is here."

Katkatchila was ready to go home after the hunt, but Torihas persuaded him, saying: "Stay one day more. Hunt with us to-morrow."

Katkatchila agreed to stay. Next morning they went to hunt. Hau went among others, and stayed near Katkatchila all the time.

On the mountain they saw ten deer again. Katkatchila stood back to shoot. Hau was ready to spring forward to get the weapon. The moment the weapon was shot, Hau ran with all his strength, reached the deer first, took out the weapon and hid it in his ear.

That moment Katkatchila was there. "You have taken my flint!" cried he. "Give it back!"

"I have not taken it," said Hau. "I have nothing of yours. I have just come."

"You have it. I saw you take it," said Katkatchila.

"I took nothing. I only put my hand on the deer's head."

"I saw you take it."

"No, you did not. I haven't it."

Katkatchila kept asking all day for his flint, but Hau would neither give it back nor own that he had it. At last, when the sun was almost down, Katkatchila turned to Hau and said, —

"I saw you take my flint. It would be better for you to give it back to me, better for you and very much better for your people. You want to keep the flint; well, keep it. You will see something in pay for this, something that will not make you glad."

He left the hunt and went away in great anger, travelled all night and was at home next morning.

Torihas's people went back from the hunt, and Hau with the others. He went into the sweat-house, took the flint out of his ear and held it on his palm. Every one came and looked at it. It was just a small bit of a thing.

"When I took this," said Hau, "Katkatchila got very angry; he left us on the mountain and went home."

All the people stood around looking at the flint in Hau's hand.

"You have done wrong, you people," said Patsotchet. "Katkatchila is very strong and quick; you will see what he will do. He has great power, more power than you think, and he will have vengeance. He will make us suffer terribly. He is stronger than we are. He can do anything. You will see something dreadful before long."

"Now, my people," said Torihas, "come into the sweat-house and we will see what we can do with that flint."

All went in. Hau went last, for he had the flint. He held it out, showed it again, and said, "I took this because you people wanted it."

They passed the flint from one to another; all looked at it, all examined it. One old man said: "Give it to me here, let me see it." He got it in his hand, and said: "Now all go outside of the sweat-house."

This was Hilit Kiemila. They went out, leaving him alone. Patsotchet kept on repeating, "Katkatchila is angry, he is malicious; before long we shall see what will happen."

As soon as Hilit was alone in the sweat-house, he began to rub the flint with his hands and roll it with his legs (Hilit was turned afterward into a house-fly, and that is why house-flies keep rubbing their legs against each other to this day). He wanted to make the flint large. After he had rolled and rubbed the flint all night, it was four or five feet long, and as thick and wide. He let the block fall to the ground and it made a great noise, a very loud noise; people heard it for a long distance. Hilit went out then and said, —

"Go in, all you people, and look at that good flint."

They went and looked. It was almost daylight at the time, and each one said, —

"Well, I don't know what is best to do; perhaps it would be best to send this off. It may be bad for us to keep it here; bad for us to have it in the sweat-house or the village."

They did not know who could carry the great block, it was so heavy. "Perhaps Patsotchet can carry it," said they.

Torihas went outside and called Patsotchet, saying: "Come into the sweat-house a little while. You come seldom; but come now."

Patsotchet left his house, which was near by, and went into the sweat-house.

"What are you going to do?" asked he. "It is too late to do anything now. I have known a long time about Katkatchila. He is very strong. He will do something terrible as soon as daylight comes."

"Patsotchet," said Torihas, "you are a good man. I wish you would take this big flint and carry it far away off north."

"I don't want to take it," said Patsotchet. "It is too heavy."

Torihas went to Karili, who lived a little way off, and said: "Come into the sweat-house. I wish to talk with you."

Karili went in. "Take this block," said Torihas. "No one is willing to carry it away, but you are strong. Carry it north for me."

Karili took up the flint, but when he had it outside the house he said: "I cannot carry this. It is too heavy. I am not able to carry it."

Torihas called in Tichelis, and said: "My uncle, will you take this north for me?"

"Why will not others take it? Why are they unwilling to carry it?" asked Tichelis. "Well, I will take it," said he, after thinking a little; and he made ready.

"Take it and start right away," said Torihas. "Daylight is coming. Go straight. I will go, too, and when I am on the top of Toriham Pui Toror I will shout, and show you where to put the block."

Tichelis put the flint on his back and hurried away with it.

When Katkatchila reached home he told his brother-in-law, Tilikus, and his brother-in-law's brother, Poharamas, and Yonot, his sister, how his flint had been stolen.

It was just before sunrise. Tilikus and Poharamas went out in front of the house and swept a space clean and smooth; then they ran off to the east and got pine as full of pitch as they could find it. They brought a great deal of this, split some very fine, and made a large pile there on the smooth place.

Just at this time Torihas's people were in his sweat-house talking about the theft. "Nothing will happen," said most of them; "old Patsotchet is always talking in that way, foretelling trouble. We will dance to-day. Tichelis has carried that thing far away; all will be well now."

Yonot, Katkatchila's sister, had one child, a little baby which she called Pohila (fire child). The woman never left the house herself, and never let any one carry the child out.

"Now, my sister," said Katkatchila, "bring your child here; bring my nephew out, and put him on that nice, smooth place which we have swept clean; it will be pleasant there for him."

She brought the boy out, put him on the smooth place. Poharamas was on the southeast side all ready, and Tilikus on the southwest side. As soon as Yonot put down the baby, they pushed pitch-pine sticks toward it. That instant fire blazed up. When the fire had caught well Poharamas took a large burning brand of pitch-pine and rushed off to the southeast; Tilikus took another and ran to the southwest. Poharamas, when he reached the southeast where the sky comes to the earth, ran around northward close to the sky; he held the point of his burning brand on the ground, and set fire to everything as he ran. When Tilikus reached the southwest, at the place where the sky touches the earth, he ran northward near the sky. The two brothers went swiftly, leaving a line of flame behind them, and smoke rose in a cloud with the fire.

After the two had started Yonot snatched up

Pohila, and as she raised the boy a great flame flashed up from the spot. She ran into the house with her son, and put him into the basket where she had kept him till that morning.

Torihas's people had begun to dance. Some time after sunrise they saw a great fire far away on the east and on the west as well.

"Oh, look at the fire on both sides!" said one.

"It is far off, and won't come here," said another.

"I feel the heat already!" cried a third.

Soon all saw that the fire was coming toward them from the east and the west like waves of high water, and the line of it was going northward quickly. The fire made a terrible roar as it burned; soon everything was seething. Everywhere people were trying to escape, all were rushing toward the north. By the middle of the forenoon the heat and burning were so great that people began to fall down, crying out, —

"Oh, I'm hot! Ah, I'm hot!"

Torihas made a rush toward the north, and reached the top of Toriham Pui Toror. When he saw the fire coming very near he called out to Tichelis, who was struggling along with the great block of flint on his back, —

"Go ahead with the flint! Go on, go on, the fire is far from here, far behind us!"

Tichelis heard the shouting, but said nothing; kept going northward steadily. When he was northeast of Bohem Puyuk, he saw the fire coming very fast, a mighty blaze roaring up to the sky. It was coming from the south, east, west. Tichelis could go no farther; there was no place for escape above ground; the fire would soon be where he was. The flint had grown very hot from the burning; he threw it down; it had skinned his back, it was so hot and heavy. He ran under the ground, went as far as he could, and lay there. Presently he heard the fire roaring above him, the ground was burning, he was barely alive; soon all blazed up, earth, rocks, everything.

Tichelis went up in flames and smoke toward the sky.

When the brothers Tilikus and Poharamas had carried the fire around the world and met in the north, just half-way between east and west, they struck their torches together and threw them on the ground. The moment before they joined the burning brands two persons rushed out between them. One was Klabus and the other Tsaroki, who had carried the invitation from Torihas to Katkatchila. They just escaped.

The flint rock that Tichelis dropped lies there yet, just where it fell, and when the Wintu people want black flint they find it in that place.

Poharamas and Tilikus ran home as soon as they struck their torches together.

Katkatchila had a little brother. He put the boy on his back, and went beyond the sky where it touches the earth in the south.

Yonot, the mother of Pohila, took her son and went behind the sky; her husband, Tilikus, went with her. Poharamas went to Olelpanti. He flew up to where Olelbis is.

Olelbis looked down into the burning world. He could see nothing but waves of flame; rocks were burning, the ground was burning, everything was burning. Great rolls and piles of smoke were rising; fire flew up toward the sky in flames, in great sparks and brands. Those sparks became kolchituh (sky eyes), and all the stars that we see now in the sky came from that time when the first world was burned. The sparks stuck fast in the sky, and have remained there ever since the time of the wakpohas (world fire). Quartz rocks and fire in the rocks are from that time. There was no fire in the rocks before the wakpohas.

When Klabus escaped he went east outside the sky, went to a place called Pom Wai Hudi Pom. Tsaroki went up on the eastern side of the sky, — ran up outside.

Before the fire began Olelbis spoke to the two old women and said: "My grandmothers, go to work for me and make a foundation. I wish to build a sweat-house."

They dug out and cleared a place for the sweat-house the day before the world-fire began. Olelbis built it in this way: When the two women had dug the foundation, he asked, —

"What kind of wood shall I get for the central pillar of the house?"

"Go far down south," said the old grandmothers, "and get a great young white oak, pull it up with the roots, bring it, and plant it in the middle to support the house."

He went, found the tree, and brought it.

" Now, my grandmothers, what shall I do next? "

" Go north and bring a black oak with the roots. Go then to the west, put your hand out, and there you will touch an oak different from others."

He went north and west, and brought the two trees.

" Now," said Olelbis, " I want a tree from the east."

" Go straight east to a live-oak place, you can see it from here, get one of those live-oaks." He brought it with the roots and said, —

" Now I want two trees more."

" Go to the southeast," said they, " where white oaks grow, and get two of them."

He went and got two great white oak trees, pulled them up with the roots, brought them with all the branches, which were covered with acorns.

Olelbis put the great white oak from the south in the middle as the central pillar ; then he put the northern black oak on the north side ; he put it sloping, so that its branches were on the south side of the house ; over against this he put a southeastern white oak sloping in like manner, so that its head came out on the north side. The western oak he planted on the west side, sloping so that its branches hung on the east side ; then he put up the two white oaks from the southeast on the east side : six trees in all. The top of each tree was outside opposite its roots ; acorns from it fell on the opposite side. Olelbis wished to fasten the trees firmly together so they should never loosen.

"Stop, grandson," said one of the old women. "How will you bind the top?"

"I have nothing to bind it with," answered Olelbis.

She put her hand toward the south, and on it came humus koriluli (a plant with beautiful blossoms). She took it with roots, stem, and blossoms and made a long narrow mat, the stem and roots all woven together inside and the blossoms outside. "Here, grandson," said she, "put this around the top of the house and bind the trees with it firmly."

He did this. The binding was beautiful and very fragrant. He wrapped it around the trees where they came together at the top of the house inside.

The two old women made four very large mats now, one for each side of the house. They wove first a mat of yosoü (a plant about a foot high, which has no branches and only a cluster of red flowers at the top). When they had finished it they told Olelbis to put it on the north side of the house.

"Now, my grandmothers," said Olelbis, "I want a cover for the east side."

"My grandson," said each, "we are sorry that you are alone, sorry that you have no one to help you in building this house. Now take this mat and put it on the east side."

They gave him a mat made of the same plant that was used for a binding to hold the top of the house.

"I want a cover now for the south side."

The old women put their hands to the east, and a plant came to them a foot high with white blossoms, of very sweet odor. A great deal of this plant came, and they made a mat of it. They put all the blossoms outside. The mat covered the south side.

" Now, how shall I cover the west side ? "

" We have the covering here already, made of kintekchi-luli " (a plant with blue and white blossoms).

They put that mat on the west side, the blossoms turned outward.

The old women gave him all kinds of beautiful plants now, and flowers to form a great bank around the bottom of the sweat-house. All kinds of flowers that are in the world now were gathered around the foot of that sweat-house, an enormous bank of them ; every beautiful color and every sweet odor in the world was there.

When they went into the sweat-house, the perfume was delightful. The two old women said then :

" All people to come in the world below will talk of this house, and call it Olelpanti Hlut when they tell about it and praise the house on high."

Olelbis said : " I want to lay something lengthwise on each side of the door. What shall I get ? "

The two said : " We will get sau " (acorn bread made in a great round roll like a tree-trunk).

They got sau, and put a roll at each side of the door ; these rolls were put there for people to sit on.

Olelbis walked around, looked at everything, and said, —

" I want this house to grow, to be wide and

high, to be large enough for all who will ever come to it."

Then the house began to extend and grow wider and higher, and it became wonderful in size and in splendor. Just as daylight was coming the house was finished and ready. It stood there in the morning dawn, a mountain of beautiful flowers and oak-tree branches; all the colors of the world were on it, outside and inside. The tree in the middle was far above the top of the house, and filled with acorns; a few of them had fallen on every side.

That sweat-house was placed there to last forever, the largest and most beautiful building in the world, above or below. Nothing like it will ever be built again.

"Now, my grandson," said the old women, "the house is built and finished. All the people in the world will like this house. They will talk about it and speak well of it always. This house will last forever, and these flowers will bloom forever; the roots from which they grow can never die."

The world fire began on the morning after the sweat-house was finished. During the fire they could see nothing of the world below but flames and smoke. Olelbis did not like this.

"Grandson," said the old women, "we will tell you what to do to put out that terrible wakpohas. There is a very old man, Kahit Kiemila, and he lives far north toward the east, outside the first sky. He stays there in one little place; he is all alone, and always in the same place. Tell him what to do, and he will do it. If you don't like the fire and smoke down below, tell the old man to turn his face toward you, to come this way and to bring with him Mem Loimis. He sits with his head between his hands and his face to the north, and never looks up. The place where he sits is called Waiken Pom Pui Humok Pom."

The first person who came to Olelbis on the day of the fire was Kiriu Herit. He came about daylight.

"You have finished the sweat-house, my nephew," said he.

"I have," said Olelbis, "but we are going to have trouble, and do you, my uncle, go up on the west side of the sweat-house, look around everywhere, and tell me what you see."

Kiriu went to the top of the house and looked. Soon another man came and said, "My brother, you have finished the sweat-house."

"Yes," said Olelbis, "and do you, my brother, go up on the east side of the house, stand there, and call to Kahit."

This was Lutchi Herit. Two more came and saluted Olelbis. "Go into the sweat-house," said he. These were the two brothers, Tilichi. A fifth person came, Kuntihle, and then a sixth, Sutunut, a great person. Lutchi kept darting around, looking toward the north and calling: "Kahit cannot take me! Kahit cannot take me!" Kahit was getting angry by this time, and thinking to turn and look at Lutchi, for though far away, he heard the noise of his darting and his calling. "That old Kahit may come out, but he cannot catch me!" called Lutchi, as he darted around, always watching the north.

Now Olelbis called Lutchi and Sutunut, and said: "You, Lutchi, go north, pry up the sky and prop it; here is a sky pole and a sky prop." Turning to Sutunut, he plucked a feather from each of his wings and said : " Go to Kahit in Waiken Pom Pui Humok Pom; tell him to come south with Mem Loimis. She lives not far from him. Her house is in the ground. And tell him to blow his whistle with all his breath. Put these two feathers on his cheeks just in front of his ears."

Lutchi went quickly. No one could travel as fast as he. He reached the sky on the north, raised and propped it. Sutunut gave the message to Kahit, who raised his head from between his hands slowly and turned toward the south. Sutunut put the feathers in his cheeks then, as Olelbis had commanded.

One person, Sotchet, who lived just south of Kahit, spoke up now and said, —

" Go ahead, Kahit. I am in a hurry to see my father, Olelbis. I will follow you. I am drinking my mother's milk." (He was doing that to bring great water.) His mother was Mem Loimis.

"Come with me, Mem Loimis," said Kahit to Sotchet's mother. " When I start, go ahead a little. I will help you forward."

Olelbis was watching, and thought, " Kahit is ready to start, and Mem Loimis is with him."

Olelbis made then an oak paddle, and hurled it

to where Sotchet was. Sotchet caught the paddle, made a tail of it, put it on, and went plashing along through the water. Not far from Kahit lived an old woman, Yoholmit Pokaila. She made a basket of white willow, and finished it just as Mem Loimis was ready to start. In the same place was Sosini Herit, just ready to move. In one hand he held a bow and arrows, with the other he was to swim.

Olelbis saw all this, — saw and knew what people were doing or preparing to do. " Grandmothers," said he, " Mem Loimis is ready to move. Kahit is ready. All the people around them will follow."

The great fire was blazing, roaring all over the earth, burning rocks, earth, trees, people, burning everything.

Mem Loimis started, and with her Kahit. Water rushed in through the open place made by Lutchi when he raised the sky. It rushed in like a crowd of rivers, covered the earth, and put out the fire as it rolled on toward the south. There was so much water outside that could not come through that it rose to the top of the sky and rushed on toward Olelpanti.

Olelbis went to the top of the sweat-house and stood looking toward the north. Sula Kiemila and Toko Kiemila had come that morning. " Take your places north of the sweat-house," said Olelbis, and they did so. Olelbis saw everything coming toward him in the water from the north, all kinds of people who could swim. They were so many that no one could count them. Before he had built the sweat-house, the two grandmothers had said to Olelbis: "Go far south and get pilok, which is a tall plant with a strong fibre, and make a cord." He did so, and twisted a strong cord from pilok. Of this he made a sling. He put his hand to the west, and kilson came on it, a round white stone an inch and a half in diameter. He put the stone in the sling, tied the sling around his head, and kept it there always.

He took this sling in his hand now, and stood watching ready to throw the stone at something that was coming in the water. Olelbis threw with his left hand. He was left-handed, and for this reason was called Nomhlyestawa (throwing west with the left hand).

Mem Loimis went forward, and water rose mountains high. Following closely after Mem Loimis came Kahit. He had a whistle in his mouth; as he moved forward he blew it with all his might, and made a terrible noise. The whistle was his own; he had had it always. He came flying and blowing. He looked like an enormous bat, with wings spread. As he flew south toward the other side of the sky, his two cheek feathers grew straight out, became immensely long, waved up and down, grew till they could touch the sky on both sides.

While Kahit flew on and was blowing his whistle, old Yoholmit lay in her basket; she floated in it high on the great waves, and laughed and shouted, "Ho! ho!"

"How glad my aunt is to see water; hear how she laughs!" said Olelbis. And he gave her two new names, Surut Womulmit (hair-belt woman) and Mem Hlosmulmit (water-foam woman). " Look at my aunt," said Olelbis again. " She is glad to see water ! "

As Yoholmit was laughing and shouting she called out, —

"Water, you be big ! Grow all the time ! Be deep so that I can float and float on, float all my life."

Olelbis was watching everything closely. Sosini Herit was coming. He held a bow and arrows in one hand and swam with the other. He was next behind old Yoholmit.

" Look at my brother, Sosini, look at him swimming," said Olelbis. When mountains of water were coming near swiftly, Olelbis said to the two old women, " Go into the sweat-house." The two brothers, Kuntihle and Tede Wiu, went in also. Olelbis stood ready to use his sling. When Yoholmit was coming near, he hurled a stone at her. He did not hit her. He did not wish to hit her. He hit the basket and sent her far away east in it until the basket struck the sky.

When the water reached Toko, it divided, went east and west, went no farther south in Olelpanti. At this time Olelbis saw a hollow log coming from the north. On it were sitting a number of Tede Memtulit and Bisus people. Just behind the log came some one with a big willow-tree in his mouth, sometimes swimming east, sometimes swimming west. He slapped the water with his new tail, making a loud noise. This was Sotchet, the son of Mem Loimis. Olelbis struck the log with a stone from his sling, and threw it far away west with all the Memtulits on it except one, which came to the sweat-house and said, —

"My brother, I should like to stay with you here." This was Tede Memtulit.

"Stay here," said Olelbis.

Next came Wokwuk. He was large and beautiful, and had very red eyes. When Kahit came flying toward the sweat-house, and was still north of it, Olelbis cried to him, —

"My uncle, we have had wind enough and water enough; can you not stop them?"

Kahit flew off toward the east and sent Mem Loimis back. "Mem Loimis," said he, "you are very large and very strong, but I am stronger. Go back! If not, I will stop you. Go home!"

Mem Loimis went back north, went into the ground where she had lived before. Kahit went east, then turned and went north to where he had been at first, and sat down again in silence with his head between his hands.

When Mem Loimis and Kahit had gone home, all water disappeared; it was calm, dry, and clear again everywhere. Olelbis looked down on the earth, but could see nothing: no mountains, no trees, no ground, nothing but naked rocks washed clean. He stood and looked in every direction, — looked east, north, west, south, to see if he could find anything. He found nothing. After a time he saw in the basin of a great rock some water, all that was left. The rock was in Tsarau Heril.

"My grandmothers," asked Olelbis, "what shall I do now? Look everywhere, there is nothing in the world below but naked rocks. I don't like it."

"Wait awhile, grandson," said they. "We will look and see if we can find something somewhere. Perhaps we can."

On this earth there was no river, no creek, no water in any place but that water at Tsarau Heril. This was the morning after Mem Loimis had gone home.

Now a person came from the east to Olelpanti, Klabus Herit. "My uncle," said Olelbis to Klabus, "I am looking all over the world below, but can see nothing on it. Do you know any place beyond the sky on the north, south, east, or west, where there is earth?"

"I know no place where there is earth," said Klabus.

Soon another person, Yilahl Herit, was seen coming from the west. When he came up, Olelbis asked, —

"My uncle, do you know of earth, or trees, or people in any place beyond the sky?"

"I do not," answered Yilahl. "But are you all well here?"

"We are well and unharmed," answered Olelbis.

"How did you come here? Which way did you come? Where did you stay that the world fire did not burn you?" asked Klabus of Yilahl.

"I will tell you," said Yilahl. "When the fire began, I went west, I went under the sky where it touches the lower world, I went out to the other side. The fire did not go there. There is earth now in that place."

"My uncles," said Olelbis, "I want you both to go down, to go west, and get that earth for me."

"I will go," said Klabus; and turning to the two old women he said: "Give me two baskets, very large round baskets."

The old women made two very large baskets. Klabus took these and went west with Yilahl. As soon as they started Olelbis took a great sky net (kolchi koro), and it spread out; it reached to the ends of the sky in every direction; it was full of small, fine holes, like a sieve. He spread it out in Olelpanti; put it under his sweat-house. It is above this world yet, but we cannot see it.

Klabus and Yilahl went west to where the earth was. Klabus dug it up and filled the baskets quickly; went to the north side of the sweat-house and threw the earth into the great net, then hurried back and brought more earth and threw it on the net. It went through the net and fell down here, fell on the rocks in this world like rain.

Klabus hurried back and forth very quickly, carrying one basket on each arm. He was going and coming for five days and five nights; fine earth was falling all this time, till the rocks were covered, and there was plenty of earth everywhere.

Yilahl gave no help. He went down the first time with Klabus, showed him the earth, and stayed there, but he did not help to carry earth or to dig it.

When Klabus had covered all the rocks with good earth, Olelbis told him to rest.

"Go west and tell Yilahl to help you," said Olelbis to Klabus the next morning, after he had rested. "Tell him to work with you, fixing the earth which you have thrown down. Go, both of you; make mountains, hills, and level country; arrange everything."

No fire was visible anywhere; every bit had been quenched by the flood which came in after Lutchi propped up the sky. Yilahl came out into this world below from under the edge of the sky in the west, and Klabus came out from under it in the east. Both met and went to work. Yilahl made the small hills and fixed the rolling country. Klabus raised the great mountains and mountain ranges. There was nothing but earth and rock yet; no people at work only these two, Klabus and Yilahl.

Olelbis stood watching and looking; he looked five days, found no fire in any place. Next day he saw a little smoke in the southwest coming straight up as if through a small opening. Olelbis had a Winishuyat on his head tied in his hair, and the Winishuyat said to him, —

"My brother, look; there is a little fire away down south; a woman there has fire in a small basket."

This woman was Yonot, the mother of Pohila, who had gone back to live in her old house.

"My brother," said Olelbis, turning to Tede Wiu, "do you see that place there? Go and bring fire from it."

Tede Wiu went quickly to the place where Olelbis had seen the smoke. He found a house, and looking through a crack he saw the glow of fire, but not the fire itself.

Tede Wiu stayed five days and nights watching. He could not get into the house where the basket was. That house was closed firmly, and had no door. At last he went back to Olelpanti without fire.

"I should like to catch the fish which I see jumping in that southern water," said Kuntihle, "but we could not cook fish if we had it, for we have no fire."

"You would better go yourself and try to get fire," said Olelbis.

Kuntihle went and watched five days. He could not get into the house, and no fire fell out. He went back to Olelpanti.

"We need fire," said Olelbis, "but how are we to get it? Go again and try," said he to Tede Wiu; "watch till fire falls out, or go in and take some."

Klabus and Yilahl were at work yet.

Tede Wiu went, crept under the house, watched five days and nights, stayed right under the basket in which Pohila was. On the sixth morning, very early, just at daybreak, a spark of fire fell out. Tede Wiu caught the spark, ran off quickly to Olelbis, and gave it to him.

They had fire in Olelpanti now, and were glad. Neither Yonot, the mother, nor Tilikus, the father of Pohila, knew that fire had been carried away to Olelpanti.

Klabus and Yilahl were still at work making the mountains and valleys, and had almost finished.

Now that there was fire in Olelpanti, Kuntihle said: " I will go and see that fish. Tilitchi, will you come with me? "

Tilitchi went. Before they started Olelbis gave them a fish net. They caught a fish, and went back, dressed, cooked, and ate it.

" This is a good fish," said Olelbis. " How did it get into that water? That pond in the rock is small and round; there is no water to run into it. Grandmothers, what shall we do with this pond and the fish in it? "

" We will tell you," said the old women. "Go to the west under the sky, break off a strip of the sky, bring it here, and make a pointed pole of it."

Klabus and Yilahl were just putting the top on Bohem Puyuk; all the other mountains in the world were finished.

Olelbis went west, got the sky pole, and pointed one end of it. He stuck the pole down at the foot of Bohem Puyuk, drew the point of it along southward, making a deep furrow. Then he stuck the pole far north, and made a second furrow to join the eastern end of the first one. There was no water in either furrow yet, and Olelbis said, —

" Now, my grandmothers, what shall I do next? "

" Take this grapevine root," said they. " Throw it to the place where you thrust in the pole at the foot of Bohem Puyuk."

He threw the root. One end of it went into the

mountain, the other hung out; from this water flowed.

"This will be called Wini Mem," said the grandmothers. "The country around it will be good; many people will go there to live in the future."

The grandmothers gave a second root, a tule root, and Olelbis threw this far up north, where one end stuck in the ground as had the grapevine root, and from the other end flowed Pui Mem — there is much tule at the head of Pui Mem to this day.

Olelbis took his sky pole again and made deep furrows down southward from Bohema Mem, large ones for large rivers and smaller ones for creeks. Water flowed and filled the furrows, flowed southward till it reached the place where Kuntihle found the first fish; and when the large river reached that little pond, fish went out of it into the river, and from the river into all creeks and rivers.

When the rivers were finished, and water was running in them, Olelbis saw an acorn tree in the east, outside the sky. He looked on the north side of the tree and saw some one hammering. He hurled a stone from his sling, struck down the person, and sent Tilitchi to bring him. Tilitchi brought him.

"Of what people is this one?" asked he of the old women.

"He is of a good people," answered they. "Put him on the central pillar of the sweat-house; we call him Tsurat."

Tsurat was only stunned. When Tsurat was taken to the central pillar, he climbed it, stopping every little while and hammering. The sound which he made, "Ya-tuck! ya-tuck!" was heard outside the sweat-house, — a good sound; all liked to hear it.

Olelbis saw on the same tree another of the same family. When he was brought, the old women said, "This is Min Taitai; put him on the ground east of the fire" — the fire was in the middle.

Min Taitai began to talk to himself. They could hear two words, " Wit, wit!" (coming back, coming back).

Olelbis stunned a third person, who was brought by Tilitchi. The old women said, "He, too, is of a good people, he is Hessiha; let him be with Min Taitai, and put a basket of red earth and water near them."

Min Taitai talked on to himself, " Wit, wit!"

"Who is ' Wit, wit?' " asked Hessiha.

"Sas" (the sun), answered Min Taitai, " was going down, and now he is coming back; that is who ' Wit, wit ' " is."

"Who is coming back?" asked Hessiha.

" Sas is coming back."

" Sas is not coming back, he is going on."

(In winter Sas goes down south, and in summer he comes back north. Min Taitai was saying Sas is coming back, up north. Hessiha thought he was saying Sas has gone down toward the west, and now is coming back east without setting.)

" Wit, wit" (coming back, coming back), said Min Taitai.

"Cherep, cherep!" (going on, going on), said Hessiha.

Soon they came to blows, began to fight; when fighting, Hessiha took red mud from the basket and threw it. Min Taitai took mud, too, and threw it at Hessiha. Both were soon covered with mud and water.

Clover, beautiful grasses, and plants of all kinds were growing around the sweat-house in Olelpanti. The whole place was a mass of blossoms. "Now, my grandmothers," said Olelbis, "tell me what you think. All that ground below us is bare; there is nothing on it. What can we do for it?"

"My grandson, in a place southeast of this is a house in which people live. The place is called Hlihli Pui Hlutton [acorn eastern sweat-house place]. An old man lives there. Send Tsurat to bring that old man to us."

"I will," said Olelbis; and he sent Tsurat, who brought Hlihli Kiemila, who had lived all his life in that eastern sweat-house. When Olelbis looked at the old man, he said to Tsurat: "Go to the world beneath us with Hlihli. Carry him all over it, — north, south, east, and west."

Hlihli was like an old worm-eaten acorn outside; inside he was like meal or snuff, and when he moved this inside sifted out of him. He had a daughter, Hlihli Loimis, and she had many sons.

Tsurat carried Hlihli all over the world, and when he had carried him five days little oak bushes were springing up everywhere from the dust which fell from him. They took seeds of clover growing around the sweat-house in Olelpanti and scattered them; clover grew up in every place. Olelbis threw down all kinds of flower seeds from the flowers blossoming in Olelpanti.

A little way east of Olelbis's sweat-house lived Sedit. At the time of the fire he ran through under the sky in the south and went up on the sky to Olelpanti. He stayed there with Olelbis until the fire and water stopped. Then he went east a short distance, and made a house for himself. During the great water Sedit caught Wokwuk, and afterward built a house near his own for him.

There was a big rock east of Sedit's house. Olelbis saw Chuluhl sitting on this rock, and he said, —

"My brother, I have put clover on the earth. I want you to go down there and stay with that clover, stay with it always. The place is a good one for you." This place was Tokuston on Pui Mem. "Take this pontcheuchi [headband made of dew], wear it around your head, wear it always, guard the clover, put your head among its leaves, and keep the grass and clover wet and green all the time. I will take that rock from near Sedit's house, and put it down on the earth for you." (The rock stands now about fifty miles above Paspuisono. It is called Pui Toleson — rock leaning east.)

Wokwuk at the time of the great water lost the middle and longest finger on one hand; it went far north, and after a time became a deer, and from that deer came all the deer in the world after the fire. When Kahit and Mem Loimis went east on the way home, Wokwuk lost a small feather from above one of his eyes. It went west and was turned into the beautiful shells tsanteris. He also lost two neck feathers. They went west and became kalas, and from that came all pearl shells. He lost the tip of his little finger. It went west and became the Wokwuk bird down here. He lost some spittle. It went east on the water and turned to blue beads, such as people wear now around their necks. Wokwuk lost a small bit of his intestines. It went south on the water and became mempak; from that come all mempak (water bone). He lost a piece of his backbone. It went east on the water and became an elk, and from that elk came all elks.

One day Sedit said to Olelbis, when all were telling Olelbis what they were going to do: "Grandson, I am going to take off my skin and let it go to the world below."

"Do so," said Olelbis.

Sedit took off his skin as he would a coat, and threw it down to this world.

"Now there will be Sedits all over down there," said he.

While Olelbis was gathering into Olelpanti all the people from every place outside this sky above us, Min Taitai and Hessiha were disputing and throwing red mud at each other.

Olelbis gathered people from every side till he had gathered them all at his house. They were there in crowds and in thousands, singing and talking inside and outside, everywhere in Olelpanti.

One morning Olelbis said to the old women, —

"My grandmothers, I cannot tell what to do nor how to get what I want, but far west of here is a ridge that stretches from the south to the north, and on that ridge people of some kind come from the south and hurry north; they do that every day; they go north along that ridge, and I do not know what kind of people they are. When they are on the top of the ridge, they run north very swiftly. As soon as Klabus and Yilahl finished the level ground and the hills and mountains in the world below, these people began to travel along the ridge in this way, and they have been going north ever since."

"You do not know those people," said the old women, "but we know them, the Katkatchila brothers know them; they are Kahsuku, the cloud dogs, the cloud people. If you wish to know more about these cloud people, ask the elder Katkatchila; he knows them; he lives far west at this time; go and ask him, go yourself."

Olelbis set out next morning early, and just before he reached Katkatchila's house in the west he came upon some one who was stooping and looking toward the south. It was the elder Katkatchila, who was watching the cloud people.

"Stop, my brother," said Katkatchila, "and watch with me."

The two looked along the ridge toward the south — it was before sunrise then — and they saw

a person come a little way in sight, then turn and
go back. He did not come nearer because he saw
Olelbis. The cloud people are very timid; they
can see a long distance, and have a very keen
scent. When he saw Olelbis, this one ran away
home.

"My brother," said Katkatchila to Olelbis, "we
have been watching here to drive back these cloud
people. We have watched night and day, I and
my little brother. My brother is near the eastern
slope of this ridge which runs north and south;
he stays there and watches."

"What do you mean by cloud people?" asked
Olelbis; "what kind of people are they? I have
seen only the head and neck of one; what I saw
looked well, seemed good. I wish you, my
brothers, would catch one of these people, if you
can."

"How is it that you do not know these people?"
asked Katkatchila. "You ought to know them;
you have seen every place, every person, everything; you ought to know these people. I will
tell you how they came. My sister and I made
the great world fire; we made the wakpohas because Torihas and his people stole my flint. I
was angry. I told my sister to put her baby
outside the house. We put pitch-pine around
it, and fire blazed up from the baby. When the
fire was burning all over the earth and there were
great flames and smoke, a big water and a strong
wind came; the water filled the whole world with
steam, and the wind drove the steam and smoke

from the great fire, and carried them far off to the south, where they became a people, — the cloud people. These people are red or white or black, all of them, and they are going north always. They have good heads and long necks."

" I should like to stand near some of these people and look at them," said Olelbis.

" I do not like to see them go north," said Katkatchila. " My brother and I are here trying to drive them back ; but they go north in spite of us. My brother is on the other slope over there to frighten them back ; but they turn to the east a little and go around him."

" Bring your brother here," said Olelbis.

Katkatchila brought his brother, and the two said, —

" These cloud people are very wild ; we cannot go near them. But we should like to drive them back or catch them."

" Go west, my brothers," said Olelbis, " and get something to stop that gap on the east where the cloud people pass you and go north. Stop that opening on the east, and stop the western slope also, leaving only a narrow place for them to go through. Get yew wood, make a very high fence with it, and stop the eastern slope."

They brought the yew wood and made a very high fence on the eastern slope, and then one on the west, leaving only a narrow gap open.

" Go to the east now," said Olelbis, " get katsau, which is a strong, fibrous plant, and make strings of it. Make a rope of the string and set a snare in the opening of the fence across the western slope to catch those cloud people."

The elder brother was on the ridge near the western slope, and the younger on the ridge near the eastern slope. The brothers made the snare and set it on the western slope. Both watched and waited for the clouds to come.

"Now, my brother," said Olelbis, when he saw this work, "watch these people well, frighten them into the trap, and I will go back to Olelpanti."

Next morning early the two brothers were watching, and very soon they saw a great many cloud people coming. Both brothers were lying flat on the middle of the ridge, so that the clouds could not see them. The clouds watched closely. They came to the place where they had always turned east to go past little Katkatchila; they ran against the fence and could not pass. They turned and went toward the west to pass northward along the central ridge; but when both brothers stood up, the clouds rushed to the western slope and fell into the trap.

Olelbis saw this and said: "Now, my brothers are driving them in. I must go and see!" And he ran off quickly.

"Oh, my brother," said the Katkatchilas when he came, "we have caught one cloud. All the rest went through the fence. They broke it — we caught one; the others burst away."

Olelbis looked at the cloud and said, —

"This is a black one! They broke down the fence and ran away! They are a strong people."

"Now, my brother," said the elder Katkatchila, "we will skin this cloud, and you may have the skin. We will give it to you."

"I shall be glad to have it," said Olelbis.

They stripped the skin from the cloud, and, when giving it to Olelbis, the elder one said, "You must tan this carefully."

"Make another fence," said Olelbis, "but make it stronger. You will catch more of these people."

"A great many clouds have broken through our fence to-day and gone north. Others went before we made the fence. We shall see these people by and by," said Katkatchila. (He meant that clouds would stay in the north and become another people; stay there always.)

Olelbis took the skin, turned toward home, and travelled on. He was rubbing it in his hands, tanning it as he went. The brothers put the body in a hole and buried it, not caring for the flesh. They wanted only the skin.

Olelbis went along tanning the skin of the black cloud, and he walked around everywhere as he tanned. He went away west, then north, then south, then east. At last he came home with the skin well tanned. He spread it and stretched it smooth. The two Katkatchila brothers had not been able yet to catch another of the cloud people, but they were working at it all the time. After Olelbis spread the skin on the ground, he took it up and said to one of the old women, —

"My grandmother is always cold; let us give

her this skin;" and he gave it to her. Each of the two old women said,—

"My grandson, we are glad to have this skin. We shall sleep warm now."

"I must go," said Olelbis, "and see my brothers drive in more of the cloud people." And he went.

"We cannot catch these clouds," said the older brother; "they go through our fence, they escape, we cannot catch them; they have gone to the north, they will stay there and become a new people. We have caught only one, a white cloud. Those that have escaped will become a new people; they will be Yola Ka" (snow clouds).

The Katkatchilas stripped the skin from the white cloud and gave it to Olelbis. He went around north, south, east, and west, tanning it in the same way that he had tanned the black skin. After he had tanned it well he spread the skin, stretched it, straightened it; then he gave it to the other grandmother.

Both old women were glad now. Both said: "We shall sleep warm at night now all the time."

Next day the two brothers caught a third cloud, a red one, but they kept that skin for themselves. They did not give it to Olelbis, because he told them to keep it. We see this skin now often enough, for the brothers hang it up when they like in the west and sometimes in the east.

"Now," said the two old women, "we have this white skin and this black one. When we hang the white skin outside this house, white clouds will go from it, — will go away down south, where its people began to live, and then they will come from the south and travel north to bring rain. When they come back, we will hang out the black skin, and from it a great many black rain clouds will go out, and from these clouds heavy rain will fall on all the world below."

From that time the old women hang out the two skins, first the white, then the black skin, and when clouds enough have gone from them they take the skins into the sweat-house again; and from these two skins comes all the rain to people in this world.

"The cloud people who went north will stay in the northwest," said Olelbis, "and from them will come snow to people hereafter."

All this time the people in Olelpanti were singing and talking. Any one could hear them from a distance. Olelbis had brought in a great many different kinds of people, others had come themselves, and still others were coming. After the tanning of the two cloud skins a man came and took his place above the sweat-house door, and sat there with his face to the east. This was Kar Kiemila. Right after him came Tsararok, and took his place at the side of Kar. Next came Kau; then the two brothers Hus came, and Wehl Dilidili. All these people in the sweat-house and around it asked one another, —

"What shall we do? Where shall we live? We should like to know what Olelbis will do with us."

"You will know very soon where we are going,"

said Toko and Sula. "Olelbis will put us in our places; he is chief over all."

Next morning Olelbis said: "Now, my grandmothers, what do you think best? What are we to do with the people here? Is it best for them to stay in Olelpanti?"

"Our grandson," answered the old women, "send all that are not needed here to the lower world; turn them into something good for the people who are to come soon, — those fit for this place up here. The great people, the best ones, you will keep in Olelpanti, and send down only a little part of each of them to turn into something in the world below and be of use to people there."

Olelbis called all who were in the sweat-house to come out, and he began to send them to their places.

To Kar he said: "Go and live on Wini Mem. Be a gray heron there; that is a good country for you." (Before white people came there were many of these birds on that river.)

To Toko he said: "Go to Kawiken on Pui Mem. Be a sunfish and live there always. You, Sula, go to the south of Bohem Puyuk on Wini Mem. Be a trout, and live at Sulanharas."

To Torihas he said: "You will be a blue crane," and to Chalilak: "You will be a goose. You both will have two places to live in, one in the south and the other in the north. You will go north in the spring and live there all summer; you will go south in the fall and live in the south all winter. Do this always; travel that way every year."

To Kiriu he said : " Go and live along the water. You will be a loon, and you will go up and down great rivers all your life."

To Katsi he said : " You will be a fish hawk, catch fish and eat them, live along rivers."

Olelbis plucked one small feather from the neck of Moihas. This he threw down and said, " Be an eagle, and live on high mountains." All bald eagles on earth came from that feather, but the great Moihas remained above with Olelbis, where he is now.

From Lutchi Olelbis plucked one feather, threw it down, and said : " You will be a humming-bird. Fly around in spring when the green grass comes and the trees and flowers bloom. You will be on blossoms and dart from one to another everywhere." Lutchi himself stayed in Olelpanti.

Olelbis pulled a feather from Kau, threw it down, and said : " You will fly along rivers, be a white crane, and live near them always." The great Kau stayed in Olelpanti with Olelbis.

From the elder Hus brother Olelbis plucked a feather from the right side, sent the feather down on this earth, and said, —

" You be a buzzard down there, and in spring go up on Wini Mem and look for dead salmon and other fish along Pui Mem, Bohema Mem, and other rivers, eat dead salmon and other fish. When people kill a snake or something else which they do not like, you will go and eat the snake or other dead thing. The Wintu, the coming people, will feed you always with what is dead."

Tilitchi had been sent for three persons, and now he brought the first.

"Who is this?" asked Olelbis of the old women.

"This is Dokos," said they; "he is bad."

Dokos was placed a little northeast of the sweat-house. He sat looking toward the west. Tilichi brought in a second and third person.

"Who are these?" asked Olelbis.

"These are both bad people," said the old women. "These are Wima Loimis and Klak Loimis."

"Put them with Dokos," said Olelbis. After he had called all the people out of the sweat-house to send them to their proper places, Olelbis had put something on their teeth to make them harmless.

"Come here, Wima Loimis," said Olelbis. "I have something to put on your teeth so that they may harm no one."

"I want nothing on my teeth," said Wima Loimis. "If something were put on them I could not eat." He asked again, but she shook her head, saying: "I want nothing on my teeth, I could not eat if anything were put on them."

"If she will not come, come you, Klak Loimis." Klak Loimis would not go to him.

"Why not come when I call you?" asked Olelbis.

"My sister Wima will not go. She says that she could not eat if her teeth were touched. I want nothing on my teeth. I am afraid that I could not eat."

"Very well," answered Olelbis, "you, Wima,

and you, Klak, want to be different from others. Come, Dokos, I will touch your teeth."

"My sisters, Klak and Wima, want nothing on their teeth. I want nothing on mine. I am angry at my sisters; my heart hates them. I do not wish to be good. I am angry at my sisters. I will be wicked as well as they." Then turning to his sisters he said: "After a while people will employ me against you whenever they are angry at you. Whenever you bite people or hurt them, they will call me to fight against you, and I will go with them. I will go into your bodies and kill you. Then you will be sorry for what you have done to-day. Olelbis asked you to be good. He wants you to be good, but you are not willing. I will be bad to punish you."

When the two women heard these words they cried, and Wima said, "Well, my brother, we can put something on our teeth yet."

Dokos placed his head between his hands and sat awhile in that posture. Then he straightened himself and said, —

"You two have talked enough; you would better stop. You are not like me; I am stronger than both of you, and I shall be so always. You, Wima, and you, Klak, will hate people only, but I shall hate all living things. I shall hate you, hate every one; kill you, kill every one. I want nothing of any one. I want no friend in any place."

"Well," said Olelbis, "you go as you are."

"I will go first," said Dokos.

"Go," said Olelbis, "to Koiham Nomdaltopi, be flint there, and spread all around the place. You, Klak Loimis, will go to Klak Kewilton, be a rattlesnake there, increase and spread everywhere. I will send you, Wima, to Wima Wai Tsarauton; you will be a grizzly bear there. After a while a great family will come from you and spread over all the country. You will be bad; and, Klak, you will be bad, but, Dokos, you will be the worst, always ready to hurt and kill; always angry, always hating your sisters and every one living.

"You, Klak, and you, Wima, when you see people you will bite them, and people will take Dokos to kill you, and Dokos will go into your bodies, and you will die. Wima, you will be sorry that you would not let me change your teeth. You, Klak, will be sorry. You will bite people, and they will kill you because you cannot run away from them. Your dead body will lie on the ground, and buzzards will eat it.

"Dokos, you will go to your place and increase. People will go there and get you to kill your sisters and others for them, and when you have pleased them and killed all the people they wished you to kill, when they want you no longer, they will throw you down on a rock and break you to pieces, then you will be nothing. You will be dead forever. Now go!"

To all those who let their teeth be made inno-cent, Olelbis said: "You will go to where I send you, — one here, another there." And he gave their places to all. To some he said: "After a

while the new people will use you for food," and
to the others he said: " The new people will use
your skins, and you will be of service to them,
you will be good for them."

The first person taken up to Olelbis's sweat-
house was Tsurat; and now Olelbis spoke to
Tsurat last of all and said, —

" Pluck one feather from your back."

Tsurat plucked it.

Olelbis threw the feather to the earth and
said, —

" The place where this falls will be called Tsurat-
ton Mem Puisono. This feather will become woodpeckers, and their place will be there. Their red
feathers will be beautiful, and every one will like
their red scalps and will use them for headbands.
The woodpeckers will be also called Topi chil-
chihl " (bead birds).

All people that were good on this earth only, of
use only here, Olelbis sent down to be beasts,
birds, and other creatures. The powerful and great
people that were good in Olelpanti and useful there
he kept with himself, and sent only a feather or a
part of each to become something useful down here.
The good people themselves, the great ones, stayed
above, where they are with Olelbis now.

OLELBIS AND MEM LOIMIS

OLELBIS AND MEM LOIMIS

ONE character in this myth is of great importance in actual Indian belief, the Hlahi or doctor, the sorcerer. The position and power of the Hlahi are explained at length in the notes to this volume. Sanihas Yupchi, the archer of Daylight, is Tsaroki Sakahl, the messenger sent by Torihas to invite Katkatchila to hunt; he appears also as the friend and messenger of Waida Dikit, who assembled the world concert in which Hawt proved the greatest musician.

PERSONAGES

After each name is given that of the beast, bird, or thing into which the personage was changed subsequently.

Hubit, wasp; Hus, buzzard; Kahit, wind; Kaisus, gray squirrel; Kiriú, loon; Kopus, small-horned owl; Kuntihlé, small hawk fishes in muddy water; Kut, unknown; Lutchi, humming-bird; Mem Loimis, water; Móihas, bald eagle; Pákchuso, the pakchu stone; Patkilis, jack rabbit; Pori Kipánamas, another name for Kopus Sútunut, black eagle; Sánihas, daylight; Sotchet, beaver; Toko, sunfish; Tsaroki Sakahl, green snake; Tsárorok, fish-hawk; Tsudi, mouse; Tsurat, red-headed woodpecker; Winishuyat, foresight; Wokwuk, unknown.

ONE evening a woman came to Olelpanti. Her name was Mem Loimis.

"Why are you here?" inquired Olelbis; "and from what place have you come?"

"I have come from my home in the earth to ask if I may live with you. I have come from the north."

"You may live here," said Olelbis; and she stayed there. She lived with Olelbis, became his wife, and had two sons: the first was Wokwuk, the second Kut.

Kut was still small, when one day the woman went out a little to one side of the house to get something, and a man came to her and said, "Come with me — come right away!" And he took her, took her quickly, took her toward the north, to the place where Kahi Hlut is. This man was Kahit, and Kahi Hlut was his house.

Olelbis knew not where his wife had gone; he knew not which way she went; he had not seen her going out and had not seen her afterward. He inquired of every one who lived in Olelpanti. All they knew was that she had gone west a little way to get something.

For five years after the woman was carried away the people in Olelpanti had no water to drink. This woman had given them water, and now some one had taken her, and without her there was no water.

"I cannot tell what to do without water," said Olelbis. "I don't think my children can live without water. I don't know what yapaitu likes my wife and has taken her."

The people in and around Olelpanti talked a great deal about Mem Loimis.

"I don't know how we are to live now," said Toko Kiemila to Olelbis. "Some one has taken your wife away. I cannot live without water much longer."

Another man who lay inside the sweat-house at the west end, an old man, stood up and said, —

"I do not know what people are to do without water. I do not know how you, Olelbis, are to

live without it. I cannot live unless I have water.
I am very dry. Why do you not try to get water
again? There is a man in Hlihli Pui Hlutton
whose name is Kopus. You can see his house
from here. He is a great Hlahi. He sings and
dances every night. Let him come here to sing
and dance. Perhaps he will be able to bring water
back to us."

The old man who said this was Hubit. He was
suffering from thirst so much that he had tied a
belt of sinews around his waist and tightened it till
he was nearly cut in two.

Olelbis went to the top of the sweat-house and
spoke to all the people.

"We must send for this Hlahi," said he. "Let
him come here to sing and bring water back to us.
Some of you young men who walk fast must go for
him to-morrow."

That night they talked about the person who
should go. One said to a second, "You walk fast;
you ought to go."

"I do not," said the second; "but you walk fast.
You are the person to go."

And so they spoke one after another, till at
last Lutchi said, "I cannot walk fast, but I
will go."

Early next morning he went out to the top of
the sweat-house and said, "I am going!" and he
shot away to the southeast.

He found the old Hlahi. He had not finished
his night's work yet. This Hlahi was Kopus
Kiemila.

"Old man, you must stop awhile," said Lutchi.
"Olelbis lost his wife, Mem Loimis, years ago.
He has two children, and he and all the people
are very dry; they are thirsting, they are dying
for want of water. He wants you to come and
see if you can tell us what to do to bring water
back to Olelpanti. Olelbis will give you five
sacks of acorns for your pay. You must sing
five nights for these five sacks. They are old
acorns."

"I will do that," said Kopus. "I will go with
you."

Lutchi returned to Olelpanti with Kopus, who
was called also Pori Kipanamas, which means a
man wearing a headband of fresh oak leaves with
two green acorns thrust in on each side. His face
was painted with acorn mould. A great many
people were waiting there, all very dry, very thirsty,
— all hoping for water.

"I sent for you to come," said Olelbis, "and
you must hlaha[1] five nights. All my people, all
my children, are dry. I am dry myself. I lost
my wife five years ago. I don't know where she
went, and we have no water since she left us. I
want you to sing and to dance. I want you to
find out where my wife is."

When night came, Olelbis gave a pipe filled
with tobacco to Kopus and said, "Now you must
hlaha."

Kopus smoked, became tunindili, — that is, possessed. A Tsudi yapaitu came to him and began

[1] Hlaha means, "to perform as a Hlahi, or doctor."

to chant. The yapaitu, speaking through Kopus, said, —

"I have looked all around the world, I have looked everywhere; every smell has come to my nose, every sight to my eyes, every sound to my ears, but to-night nothing comes to me. I cannot see, I cannot hear, I cannot smell." And he stopped.

"I am going to dance the spirit dance," said Kopus. "Who will sing for me?"

"Let these two Tsudi girls sing," said Olelbis.

Hubit was lying on the east side of the sweat-house, and he said, —

"Make haste, you two girls, and sing for that Hlahi. I am nearly dead, almost cut in two, I am so dry."

He had tightened his belt a little that evening. Kopus danced all night, and the two girls sang for him.

"I have not found out which way that woman went," said he, next morning.

He danced five days and nights, and then said: "I can tell nothing. I know nothing about this woman, Mem Loimis."

Every bola heris [1] that was lying inside the sweat-house was terribly thirsty. One old man got up and said, —

"What kind of a Hlahi have you here? What kind of a Hlahi is Kopus? He is here five days

---

[1] Bola means "to tell one of the creation myths;" bolas means "one of the myths;" bola heris is an actor in any of them, a personage mentioned or described in a creation myth.

and nights and can tell nothing, knows nothing. If you wish to learn something, bring a Hlahi who has knowledge of water."

"This old Kopus knows nothing of water," said Toko. "Old Kopus is a good Hlahi for acorns and for the Tsudi and Kaisus people; that is all he is good for. I know this Kopus well. Get a Hlahi who knows more than he does."

"You bola herises tell us," said Olelbis, "who is a good Hlahi for water, and we will get him. Look at my children; they are almost dying of thirst. Tell us where their mother, Mem Loimis, is."

"Oh, daylight, come quickly; be here right away! I am almost cut in two I am so dry. Oh, daylight, come quickly!" groaned Hubit.

No one mentioned another Hlahi. So Olelbis talked on, —

"All the people said that Kopus was a good Hlahi. That is why I got him; but he is not a good Hlahi for water. Now we will get Sanihas Yupchi, the archer of daylight, who lives in the farthest east, he is the son of Sanihas. He is small, but he is a great Hlahi. Lutchi, you must go now for Sanihas Yupchi. Here are one hundred yellowhammer-wing arrows for him, all red, and many others."

Lutchi went to the east end of the sweat-house, danced a little, sprang onto the sweat-house, danced a little more, and then whizzed away through the air. Lutchi travelled all day and all night, reached the place about daylight next morning, and said to Sanihas, —

" Olelbis sent me here to ask your son to come and hlaha for him. He sends you all these five hundred arrows made of kewit reed and one hundred yellowhammer-wing arrows to come and hlaha."

" You must go," said Sanihas to her son, " and I will follow you. Olelbis is a yapaitu himself; he ought to know where that woman is, — he thinks that he knows everything; but you go and hlaha, and hear what your yapaitu tells you."

Sanihas Yupchi started, and was at the sweat-house in Olelpanti next morning just as the sun was rising. He went into the sweat-house, and Olelbis gave him many things.

" Give me tobacco," said Sanihas Yupchi. " I am going to hlaha."

Olelbis gave him a pipe with tobacco; he smoked it out and was not possessed. Olelbis gave him another pipeful, and he smoked it out, but was not possessed. He smoked out ten pipefuls, and then people said, —

" I am afraid that the yapaitu will not come to him."

He smoked twenty more pipefuls, still he was not possessed; then twenty more, did not hlaha.

" He is no Hlahi," cried people on all sides; " if he were, the yapaitu would have come to him long ago."

" The yapaitu he is waiting for does not live near this sweat-house; he is very far away," said Toko. " Give him more tobacco."

They gave him five pipefuls, then four, then one

more, — sixty in all; after that a yapaitu came to him.

"The yapaitu has come," said Olelbis. "I want you to look everywhere and learn all you can; my children are nearly dead from lack of water; you must tell where Mem Loimis is."

Sanihas Yupchi began to sing, and he said, "I will have the spirit dance to-night; the two Tsudi girls may sing for me."

He danced twenty nights and days without saying a word, — danced twenty days and nights more. The two Tsudi girls sang all the time. Then Sanihas Yupchi sat down, said nothing; he had found out nothing.

Again he danced five days and nights, then four days and nights, then one day and one night more. After that he sat down and said, —

"I am going to speak. The place of which I am going to tell is a long way from here, but I am going to talk and let you hear what I say. Did any one see which way this woman Mem Loimis went?"

One person answered: "She went west a short distance to get something. That was the last seen of her."

"Was anything the matter with that woman?" asked Sanihas Yupchi. "Does any one know?"

"Yes," said Olelbis, "she was with child."

"Well, while she was out, a man came to her and took her away with him, took her far north and then east beyond the first Kolchiken Topi, where the sky comes down, where the horizon is; he took her to the place where he lives, and he lives in Waiti Kahi Pui Hlut. His name is Kahit, and after he took her home they lived pleasantly together till her child was born. Kahit did not claim that child as his. After a while Mem Loimis grew angry at Kahit, left her child with him, and went eastward, went to the other side of the second horizon. She stayed there awhile, and gave birth to two sons, children of Kahit. Then she went farther east to a third horizon, went to the other side of that, stayed there, is living there now. The boy that was born when she lived with Kahit was Sotchet. Sotchet's father was Olelbis. When the child grew up a little, Kahit said to him: 'Your father lives in Olelpanti.'"

Sanihas Yupchi told all this, and said to Wokwuk and Kut, the two sons of Olelbis, —

"Your mother has gone a long way from here. Mem Loimis is far from you. She is very far east. If I were at home, I could go to her quickly, but I am here. Now you must go and see your mother. In the far east you have two brothers, Kahit's sons. When you have passed three Kolchiken Topis, three horizons, you will see them, and they will know you. The way to your mother and brothers is long. That is what my yapaitu says to me — my yapaitu is the Winishuyat of Patkilis."

Sanihas Yupchi was Tsaroki Sakahl, a great person.

Wokwuk and Kut, the two sons of Olelbis by Mem Loimis, went away east. Patkilis's Winishuyat, the yapaitu of Sanihas Yupchi, said that he would go and help them till they had passed the second horizon. They did not see him. He was invisible.

They travelled one day, came to the first horizon, and passed that; then travelled a second day, reached the second horizon, and passed that. The yapaitu, Patkilis's Winishuyat, told them then how to pass the third horizon, and, having given every useful direction, went back to Sanihas Yupchi.

Sanihas Yupchi was waiting all this time in Olel-panti. Olelbis's elder son, Wokwuk, had tied the hair on top of his head with a young grapevine and thrust a chirtchihas bone through it—his father had given him this bone at starting. With this bone he was to raise the sky. He put it under the edge of the sky and raised it. When he and his brother had passed through, the sky came down with a ter-rible noise. When they had passed the third sky, they could see far east. Everything was nice there and looked clear, just as it does here at daylight when all is bright and beautiful. After going a short distance they saw two boys coming toward them. Soon the four met.

" Hello, brothers ! " called out the other two.

"Who are you?" asked Wokwuk. " How do you know that we are your brothers? "

" We know because our mother talks about you always. She told us this morning that we must go out and play to-day. ' Perhaps you will see your brothers,' said she to us ; ' perhaps they will come, we do not know.' You have come, and now we will go to our mother."

When they reached the house, on the third evening, the two sons of Olelbis stood by the door while
Kahit's two sons ran in and said: " Mother, our
brothers have come!"

Mem Loimis was lying at the east end of the
house. She was lying on a mem terek, water buckskin; her blanket was a mem nikahl, a water
blanket.

" Well, tell them to come in."

The brothers went in. Mem Loimis rose and
said, —

" Oh, my sons, I think of you always. I live
far away from where you do, and you have travelled a long road to find me." She spread the mem
terek on the ground, and said: " Sit down here and
rest."

" My mother," said the elder son of Olelbis,
" my brother is very dry. We have had no water
in Olelpanti for many years. Did you think that
we could live without water?"

" I could not help your loss. What could I
do?" said Mem Loimis. " I was stolen away and
carried far north, and from there I came to this
place; but your father is my husband. He knows
everything; he can make anything, do anything,
see everything, but he did not know that I was
here. You shall have water, my children; water
in plenty."

She held a basket to her breast then and took
water from it, as a nursing mother would take milk,
filled the basket, and gave it to the boys. She
gave them plenty to eat, too, and said, —

"You boys are all my children. You are sons of Mem Loimis. I am here now; but if there should be disturbance, if trouble were to rise, my husband Kahit would come and take me away. He told me so. Some day my husband Olelbis will know his son in the north who is living with Kahit. Some day my husband Olelbis will think of me; he may want me to come to him, he may wish to see me."

Wokwuk and Kut stayed five days with their mother, then one day, and after that one day more. Sanihas Yupchi, who was dancing and chanting in Olelpanti continually, said after the boys had gone:

"Get me a suhi kilo" (a striped basket).

Olelbis got him the suhi kilo, a little basket about two inches around, and very small inside. Sanihas Yupchi put it in the middle of the sweat-house. Nine days more passed, and Sanihas Yupchi was dancing all the time.

That morning Mem Loimis said to Kut, the youngest son of Olelbis, —

"Your uncle Mem Hui, an old man, who lives at the first horizon west of Olelpanti, is dry. He is thirsting for water. Take water to him. Your elder brother will stay here with me while you are gone."

Sanihas Yupchi had danced fifty-nine days. On the sixtieth evening Mem Loimis gave Kut a basketful of water for his uncle in the west.

"Go," said she, "straight west to where the old man lives. When you have reached Mem Hui with the water, I will go and see my son Sotchet

in the north. I hear him cry all the time. He
is dry. I will carry him water."

She gave Kut, in a net bag before he started, ten
gambling sticks cut from grapevine. She tied the
bag around his neck, and said, —

"Son of Mem Loimis, you will be a bola heris;
you will be a great gambler."

Kut was a very quick traveller, and could go in
one night as far as his brother in many nights and
days. He started. There were holes in the bottom of the basket, and as he went over the sky,
high above the top of Olelpanti Hlut, the water
dropped and dropped through the holes in the
basket, and just before morning one drop fell from
the basket which Kut was carrying, and dropped
into the basket which Sanihas Yupchi had placed
in the middle of the sweat-house at Olelpanti.

No one saw the water come, but in the morning
the little basket was full; the one drop filled it.

"Now," said Sanihas Yupchi, "I have worked
as Hlahi all this time, and that drop of water is all
that I can get. You see it in the basket."

The little basket in Olelbis's house that the one
drop filled stood there, and Olelbis said, —

"Now you are dry, all you people in this sweat-
house. You are thirsty, you are anxious for water.
Here is one drop of water. We do not know who
will drink first; but there is an old man on the
west side of the sweat-house crying all the time,
crying night and day, for water. Let him come
and look at it." He meant Hubit.

Hubit stood up, came, looked at the basket and

said : " What good is this to me ? There is only a drop there. It will do me no good."

" Drink what there is ; you talk so much about water," replied all the others, " that you would better drink."

" That drop can do no good to any one."

" Well, take a taste, anyhow," said Olelbis ; " it will not hurt you."

" I don't want a taste, I want a drink," answered Hubit.

" Take a drink, then," said Olelbis.

Hubit began to drink. He drank and drank, took his belt off about the middle of the forenoon, put his head on the edge of the basket and drank from morning till midday, drank till two men had to carry him away from the water and lay him down at the upper end of the sweat-house.

Though Hubit drank half a day, the water in the basket was no less.

Kiriu Herit drank next. He drank long, but did not lower the water. After him Sutunut drank till he was satisfied ; then Moihas drank all he wanted.

" Let all come and drink. When each has enough, let him stand aside," said Olelbis.

Tsararok drank, and then Kuntihle drank ; then Hus and Tsurat ; after them the old women, Pakchuso Pokaila, the grandmothers of Olelbis, drank ; then Toko ; then Kopus drank. But the people murmured, saying, —

" Kopus is no Hlahi ; he ought not to have any of our water. He is only good for acorns."

The two Tsudi girls, who had sung so long, drank very heartily.

Lutchi lived outside, east of the sweat-house; they called him to drink. He took one sip and went out. Lutchi never liked water.

Now Sanihas Yupchi, who had brought the water, drank of it; and last of all, Olelbis.

When all were satisfied, and Toko had gone back and lain down in his place north of the sweat-house, the basket was put near him; and ever after Toko had water in abundance, and so had every one.

There was plenty of water ever after in Olelpanti for all uses; but if Sanihas Yupchi had not brought it, all might have perished for want of water.

"I will go home now," said Sanihas Yupchi, after he had drunk. He wished well to every one and went away.

When Kut was carrying the basket westward, every drop that fell made a spring, — wherever a drop fell a spring appeared.

NORWAN

NORWAN

THIS myth, which recalls the Helen of Troy tale, is extremely interesting both as regards personages and structure. At present I shall make but few remarks, and those relating only to personages. Hluyuk Tikimit, quivering porcupine, known here as Norwan, is the cause of the first war in the world. The porcupine in American mythology is always connected with sunlight, so far as my researches go, and Norwan is connected with daylight, for she dances all day, never stops while there is light. Her title of Bastepomas, food-giving, is also significant, and would help to show that she is that warm, dancing air which we see close to the earth in fine weather, and which is requisite for plant growth. We have another "light" person in this myth, Sanihas, who is light in a generic sense, daylight generally and everywhere. The root Sa in Sanihas is identical with Sa in Sas, the Wintu word for "sun." Sa means "light" and Sas "for light," *i. e.* for the purpose of giving light. Sanihas is the light which is given.

In Bastepomas, the title given by Olelbis to Norwan, the first syllable ba means "to eat," bas means "for to eat" or food, tep means "to give," and tepomas "she who gives;" the whole word means "she who gives food."

Chulup Win Herit, the great chief, the white, pointed stone who lives on the bed of the great eastern water, the ocean, the husband of Sanihas, has a counterpart in Tithonos, the husband of Eos or Aurora, in classic mythology. Both had beautiful wives, and were visited by them nightly in the bed of the ocean. Chulup's tragedy is somewhat greater, for he is caught by Wai Karili and pounded into bits near the present Mt. Shasta, while Tithonos is only changed into a cricket. Eos, the Latin Aurora, was considered as the whole day by most poets, and Sanihas in Wintu mythology is the whole day, all the light that Sas gives.

There was a reason why Norwan preferred Tede Wiu to Norbis, but we can only infer it at present. The present Wiu bird is brown, and has no significance in this connection, but there was a red Wiu, the bird into which the Tede Wiu who fought with Norbis was changed. That he was a person who might be preferred by Norwan, herself a special form of light, is evident when we consider the immense importance in European tradition of the robin-redbreast and of the red-headed woodpecker among Indians.

That Norwan, food-giving light on the earth, was worth fighting for, is evident.

PERSONAGES

After each name is given that of the beast, bird, or thing into which the personage was changed subsequently.

Bisus, mink ; Boki, sturgeon ; Búlibok, a small nighthawk ; Chali Dokos, obsidian ; Chati Wai Halina, pine-nut bug ; Chir Chuma, sucker ; Cho, blackbird ; Chuchu, dog ; Chulup Win, a pointed rock ; Chutuhl, a small bird that goes in flocks ; Dokos, flint ; Dokos Hilit, flint fly ; Hamam, the longest black feather in the tail of the black vulture ; Hau, red fox ; Hawt, eel ; Héssiha, tomtit ; Hlihli, acorn ; Hluyuk Tikimit, quivering porcupine ; Ho, polecat ; Hokohas, mud turtle ; Hus, turkey buzzard ; Kahi Buli Pokaila, wind mountain old woman ; Kahit, wind ; Kaisus, gray squirrel ; Kar, blue heron ; Karili, coon ; Katsi, chicken hawk ; Kaukau, white heron ; Kawas, basket ; Keli, flint from which knives are made ; Kichi Not, a kind of arrow ; Kíchuna, a small bird that frequents rocks ; Kilichepis, —— ; Kiri Hubit, a kind of wasp ; Kobalus, a shell ; Koip, a small bird which calls "koip" ; Kopus, a small night-owl ; Kot, diver ; Kóyumus, a flint of mixed colors ; Kukupiwit, crooked breast ; Nomdal Lenas, streaks in the west ; Nomel Hiwili, a bird with white-tipped wings which comes down with a buzz very quickly ; Nom Sowiwi, —— ; Nom Toposloni, west fir bark ; Norbis, dwelling or sitting in the south ; Nórhara Chepmis, heavy south wind with rain ; Norpatsas, southern fire sparks ; Norwan, —— ; Notudui Ulumus, he stoops and picks up stones ; Pai Homhoma, he buzzes in the manzanita ; Patkilis, jack rabbit ; Puiké Tsumu, a deep red flint ; Saiai Not, hollow arrow ; Saias, white flint ; Sánihas, daylight ; Sau, acorn bread ; Sawe, mixed white and blue flint ; Sedit, coyote ; Séhinom Chábutu, chicken hawk ; Serin Dólite, small bumblebee ; Siriwit, whirlwind ; Sútunut, black eagle ; Tede Wiu, a small brown bird about as large as an English sparrow ; Tenek Not, a kind of arrow ; Tidok, ant ; Tsánteris, a kind of shell ; Tsotso tokos, a small very adhesive burr ; Tsudi, mouse ; Tsuini, a kind of small fish ; Tubuk, —— ; Tuichi kelis, feathered head net ; Wai Charatawa,

——; **Waida Werris,** polar star ; **Wainom Yola,** northwestern snow;
Wai Hau, northern red fox ; **Wai Not,** northern arrow; **Wik,** small
night hawk ; **Wai Karili,** northern coon ; **Vʹul Wuhl,** linnet ; **Yipokus,**
black fox.

A T a place east of Pas Puisono a woman came
up out of the earth. Her name was
Hluyuk Tikimit. She had another name, Pom
Norwanen Pitchen. We call her also Norwan.

She appeared before the present Wintu people
came out of the ground, at Tsarau Heril.

" I am in this world now," said Norwan to herself. " I will look around everywhere to see from
what places people are coming."

She lived alone in her sweat-house, which was
called Norwan Buli Hlut, remained in the house
and danced during daylight.

Olelbis looked down at this woman and said, —

" This is my sister, who has come up before the
new people on earth. I don't know what she will
do yet."

When Olelbis was building his sweat-house in
Olelpanti, he cut a piece from a white-oak tree, and
this piece rolled down outside the sky to the lower
world, where it became a people in Nor Puiken, in
the southeast, and that people were there before
the present Wintus came out of the ground at
Tsarau Heril.

" My dear sister has come up before the Wintus,
and will be with them hereafter," said Olelbis. " I
have not settled yet how her work is to be, have
not made her ready for it."

He put his hand toward the southeast then, and took yósoü (a plant that has a red blossom). He gave this plant to Norwan, and said, —

"Take this, my sister, and when you dance use it as a staff. It will have a blossom on the top which will be blooming always."

He reached southeast to the same place, took a small bird, plucked a feather from each wing, gave the feathers to Norwan, and said, —

"My sister, thrust these through your hair, just above your forehead, one on each side. These feathers will begin to sing in the morning early; you will know by them at what time you must begin to dance."

He stretched his hand again to the southeast, and took buri luli, which is a little red blossom that grows in spring on a plant about a foot high. He gave the blossoms to Norwan and said, —

"Roll this in your hands, crush it, put the juice on your face, and make your cheeks red."

Olelbis turned then to his grandmothers, who were standing near by, and asked if they had acorns.

"We have," said they. "We have plenty."

Olelbis took a handful, gave them to his sister, and said, —

"When you shell these acorns, rub them between your palms and hold your hands open; blow the dust which scatters; you will see it rise high into the trees, and acorns will come on them."

It was on the first morning after she had come to Norwan Buli that Olelbis gave Norwan the staff, feathers, blossoms, and acorns. On the second morning very early the feathers began to sing; then flocks of birds of their kind came flying toward the sweat-house, and Norwan heard a voice far up in the sky calling to her, and saying, —

"My brother's daughter, you have come upon earth before the Wintu people, and are dancing. When you dance you must not look toward the west, nor the north, nor the south, but turn your face and look toward Hlihli Pui Hlutton in the southeast, the place from which your staff and your paint came."

While this man was talking, Norwan looked up and saw him sitting with one leg crossed upon the other. He was holding a handful of white-oak acorns in his hand, and was sitting over the door of the sweat-house in Olelpanti. It was Kar Kiemila.

"Now, my brother," said Olelbis to Hessiha, who lived with him in Olelpanti, " I think it is best for you to go down to our sister and stay with her. Live with her always. When your feathers drop away or are pulled off hereafter, they will become like you, and there will be hessihas on the earth everywhere. Our sister will tell you what to do. You will stay with her, never leave her. The people will call our sister Bastepomas, because she is the food-giving woman. When you see anything, let her know; when you hear anything, tell her; when you want to do anything, ask leave of her."

Hessiha went down to live with his sister. Next day he saw a woman coming from the east and going west. He told Norwan, and she said, —

"Watch which way she goes, my brother. Perhaps she will come to us here."

He watched. She came straight to Norwan Buli.

"My younger sister," said she to Norwan, "I came out in the east, but I don't like to live there. I have left that place, and am going far away to the west. In the evening look westward, a little after sunset, you will see a red, yellow, and white person, Nomdal Lenas Loimis. I am she. I shall look nice. That is the kind of person that I am. I shall live in the west always, and you will see me there as streaks of colored light. I will turn my face to the east every evening on pleasant days, and all the Wintu people will say when they see me, 'Winis Nomdal Lenas Loimis'" (look at Nomdal Lenas Loimis).

"Very well," said Norwan, "I am glad to hear what you say, my elder sister."

Nomdal Lenas went off to the west. She was an immensely large woman with a big face, her hair was cut across her forehead, and this made it look beautiful. She was the first woman in the world who cut her hair in that fashion. Her face was painted in streaks of red, yellow, and white.

Next morning Hessiha saw another woman coming from the east. She stopped at Norwan Buli, and said, —

"My younger sister, we came upon this earth at the same time, before the Wintu people. I am going to the west a little distance. I came out in the east, but I did not like the place there. I am going to Bohem Buli. I will stay there and live on the north side of the mountain. I will be a mountain woman. My name is Kukupiwit Pokte."

She went to Bohem Buli.

Norwan danced always during daylight, never stopped in the daytime, never rested till evening.

Norbis Kiemila, the white oak which rolled to the southeast, looked toward the northwest and saw Norwan. "I see my wife on this earth," said he.

One evening Hessiha and Norwan were in the sweat-house, and Hessiha said,—

"My sister, I have heard news to-day from Norbis Kiemila. He says that you are to be his wife."

She said nothing, and Hessiha talked on : "My sister, I heard a man say that he would come to see you. He lives at Sonomyai — he is Sedit, Sedit of Sonomyai."

"My brother," said Norwan, "what are you telling me?"

"I am telling you, my sister, what I have heard. Sedit is coming."

"Why does he come? I don't like him. He has a bad breath."

Next morning Norwan rose and began to dance.

"My sister," said Hessiha, that evening, "I hear that a man is coming from Chanahl Puyuk, a good man. His name is Kaukau Herit. He is coming to see you."

"Why does he come here?" asked Norwan. "His neck is too long, his legs are too long."

"Well, my sister, I have heard that a man who lives far away west is coming to see you, Kobalus Herit. He is a good man. He lives at Nomken Kobalus Waimemton."

"That man has a crooked nose," said Norwan, "and a crooked mouth. I don't like him, he is all twisted."

Next evening Hessiha said, —

"There is a man who lives at the same place as Kobalus Herit. He wants to see you. His name is Tsanteris Herit."

"That man has a hollow breast," said Norwan. "I don't like him."

"A man from the far north is coming, Keli Herit."

"I don't like him," said Norwan; "he has a bad odor. He smells like the earth."

"A man from way down south, Bisus Herit, is coming to see you."

"Oh, I don't like him; his legs are too short; he eats bony fish."

"My sister, a man is coming who lives a short distance south of us, Tede Wiu Herit."

"I don't like him; he has too much breast; it sticks out too much."

"My sister, Katsi Herit, is coming."

"I know him," said Norwan. "He is too quick-tempered: he gets angry too easily."

"Chati Wai Halina Herit is coming to see you."

"I don't like him; he smells of pitch always.

"I must go now for wood; we have no wood this

evening," said Norwan, and she went out to bring some. She brought an armful, and while going to the same place for a second bundle she heard some one coming. A man took her by the arm. She turned, and saw Sedit of Sonomyai dressed beautifully. She pushed him away and ran home. Sedit did not follow her.

Next morning early she went out, and looking at one side of the door saw two stones lying there, and a hooked stick four or five feet long, called lakus, used to pull a limb of a tree toward you. She broke the stones to pieces, broke the stick, threw the pieces in the fire, and burned them. She knew that some man had put them there and intended to come. That night she was lying on the south side of the sweat-house and her brother on the north. It was dark, and they heard some one coming toward the house. The stranger came in, sat down behind Hessiha, sat with his head between his hands; his hair was sticking out, and looked as though it had never been combed. Norwan looked at this person, never took her eyes from him, but said not a word, and he said nothing. After a while he stood up and walked out. While going he threw something toward Norwan. It fell near her, and she picked it up. It was a small net bag half full of mice. She threw it after the stranger. He was Chati Wai Halina.

When morning came, Norwan took a bundle of brush, went to where the visitor had sat, swept the place clean, and threw fresh earth on it.

The next night they heard some one walking
outside. Soon a man came in. He had a quiver
in his hand made of deerskin. He looked around
and went over behind the place where Norwan was
lying and sat down. She lay there looking at him.
After sitting awhile he lay down, stayed all night,
and went away just at daybreak. This was Norbis
Kiemila.

In the early morning before dancing she built a
fire outside and sat down at it. That same morning Hessiha saw a man coming toward them, coming
from the southeast. When he came to where Norwan was at the fire, he sat down. His name was
Serin.Dolite. He wore a bunch of fresh leaves on
each side of his head. He had a second name, Pai
Homhoma.

" My sister," said this man, " I have come because
my uncle sent me to tell you that the people at
Hlihli Pui Hlutton finished talking yesterday, and
they are going to have a great feast and a pleasant
time. 'Tell my niece,' said he, 'to come and
dance with us.' My uncle is Kopus Kiemila. He
is named also Pui Uhlukyo. He is a Hlahi. He
sent word to Norbis two days ago, and he sent word
to Kaukau Herit. He has sent word everywhere.
There will be a great many people in Hlihli Pui
Hlutton. He has sent word to Sedit, who lives
at Sonomyai, and to Katsi Herit, who lives opposite
Pas Puisono, and to Kobalus Herit and Tsanteris
Herit and Keli Herit and to Tede Wiu Herit, who
lives at Koï Nomsono, and many others. He
has sent to your brother Waida Werris. Waida

Werris may come; he may not. Kopus Kiemila
wants you to come surely."

"Very well," said Norwan, "I will go to-
morrow."

Serin Dolite was satisfied and went away.

"Now, my little brother," said Norwan to Hessiha that night, "I am going away to-morrow.
You will stay here, I hope. I shall be glad if
you stay at home and take care of this house."

When she rose in the morning, she stretched her
right hand toward the southeast and got buri luli,
which are very beautiful red flowers. She put her
hand there a second time, and to her hand came
hawe luli, pure white blossoms, for clothing. A
third time she put her hand out, and hluyuk luli,
which are the star flowers, came on it. These she
put around her head as a garland, and made shoes
of the same flowers. Then she took her staff
yósoü.

"My brother," said she, when dressed, "I am
ready to go."

"My brother's daughter," called Kar Kiemila
from Olelpanti when she was starting, "go and
dance. I will sit here and look at you." Sweat-
house doors look toward the south usually,
but the great one above, made by Olelbis, on
which Kar Kiemila was sitting, had its door in the
east, because Olelbis took most of his beautiful
things from the southeast, and he could look down
in that direction from the door of his house in
Olelpanti. The door in Hlihli Pui Hlutton was
toward the west, because from that door they could

see the great house in Olelpanti. The house built by Olelbis was the best in all the world, above or below. Kopus Kiemila's house was second to it, and the best in the lower land.

Norwan went at the time appointed, and Hessiha stayed behind at Norwan Buli. When Serin Dolite brought the invitation, Norwan made him promise to meet her on the road.

"You must come," said she, "to give me news before I reach the sweat-house."

Just at the edge of a place called Pui Toror, Serin Dolite ran out and met Norwan.

"Oh, my sister," said he, "Kopus Kiemila sent me to say to you to come quickly, to hurry. The people from every place are there now. All those have come of whom I told you, except Norbis and your brother Waida Werris; they have not come yet. Besides others, Boki Kiemila from Hlop Henmenas has come. You must hurry as much as you can, and come quickly."

When he had given the message, he rushed back and left Norwan to travel at her own pace. She went along the top of Pui Toror, and came to a spot where she heard much laughing and talking. Soon she saw a large crowd of children playing. The ground was smooth, — no rocks, no grass, just level land. When she came up, the children said to her, —

"Our elder sister, we want to see the dance. We want to go to the sweat-house, but we have nothing to wear; we have no clothes and we can get none."

The girls were all of the Tsudi people, the boys, Patkilises. Norwan looked around and saw at some distance a great many sunflower leaves.

"We took leaves like those," said one of the boys, "and tried to put them on as ears, but we could not make them stay."

Norwan stretched her hand southward, and gray fog which rises from water came on it. She put this fog on a Patkilis boy to wear. She stretched her hand to the east, and red and yellow feathers came to it. Of these she made ears for that Patkilis boy. She put her hand south and found willow catkins, white ones, and made a tail and put it on the Patkilis boy. She gave him shoes made of the catkins. When that one boy was dressed, she said, "Let all the others be like this one;" and that moment all Patkilis boys were like him.

Now she took acorn mould, green and brown, put it on one of the Tsudi girls. She took yósoü leaves from her staff (the leaves are like mice ears), and put them on the girl for ears. She took more acorn mould, rubbed and rolled it out like a little stick, and made a tail. When one Tsudi girl was dressed nicely, she said, "Let all the others be like this one;" and that moment they were like her.

"Now, sister," said they, "we are ready."

Norwan started, and all the Tsudi girls and Patkilis boys went with her. When they came to the door of the sweat-house, they looked around and saw that all the trees were full of fresh, beautiful acorns; the top of the house was covered with them. There were piles and piles of acorns inside and around the sweat-house, and a little way off a great many trees were loaded with fruit.

From Olelpanti they could see down into Hlihli Puihlutton. All persons who had come were inside. Norwan looked in and saw many people, all looking toward the door.

"See Norwan coming," said they. "She is beautiful, — oh, she is beautiful!"

Kopus Kiemila was on the south side, near the door. He had five sacks of acorns near him. He was singing over them, singing about health and soundness. When he saw Norwan, he said, —

"Come in; come in, my brother's daughter. You are one of the last. All have come but two."

She went beyond Kopus to a seat. A young woman who was sitting near rose and said, —

"Come, my sister; come and sit with me."

This was Hlihli Loimis. Her brother Hlihli Herit stood always on top of Kopus's house and called, "Hai! Hai!" which means "Come! Come!" and beckoned with his hand for people to enter.

Norwan sat down at the south side of the door, and all the Tsudi and Patkilis children took their places behind her.

"You are almost the last to come," said Hlihli Loimis. "Look at the north side of the house. See how many people are there. See the light; that is Kaukau Herit. He is white and shining; light beams from him."

"Now," said Kopus, "all you people from the

north, my sons-in-law and my daughters-in-law, make ready to dance."

The northern people rose at his call and danced. Kaukau Herit danced. When he rose and moved, it was as when a light is brought into a dark place. He danced five times and sat down.

"Now, my sons-in-law," said Kopus, "sit back and look on. My sons-in-law from the west, you will dance now; dance you, Katsi Herit and Sedit of Sonomyai, and dance you, my daughters-in-law."

The western people danced; Sedit, Boki, all danced. While they were dancing, they dropped beautiful shells. These shells fell from them as snow falls from the sky, and the whole floor was covered with shells, just as mountains in winter are covered with snow.

" Now sit back and look on," said Kopus. The western people sat down.

" My sons-in-law and my daughters-in-law," called Kopus to the southern people, " make ready to dance."

The two Tede Wiu brothers from Koï Nom-sono were to lead the southern people in the dance. Kopus called five times; the southern people did not move. Then the elder Tede Wiu made a step and stopped; when he raised his foot to take a second step, all began to dance. Both brothers carried a load of mempak on their arms, and each had a flint knife. As they danced they attached long strings of mempak to one side of the house higher than a man's head; they extended the strings to the other side and tied them there. They stretched mempak in this way from side to side as they danced, and from end to end, lengthwise and crosswise; then they danced under it. The beautiful strings were shining in every color just above their heads. The music, the mempak, and the dancing were so beautiful that all were delighted; all people were glad; they could hardly sit still and look on.

The brothers danced up to where Kopus was sitting, took strings of shell and mempak from their necks and heads, and put them down before him; next they put down their two beautiful knives. When they had done this they danced away to the other end of the sweat-house, and then danced up again to where Kopus was.

Norwan rose and began to dance without knowing it. She could not help dancing. Every one looked at her. She danced with the two brothers, danced away to the other side of the house with them. Only after a time did she see that she was dancing.

The two brothers sat down; she sat with them. Then the three stood up and went out.

They had just gone when Norbis came in. He was splendidly dressed, wore mempak, had a garland of fresh young leaves on his head, and on the top of it mempak. He sat down and asked some one near by, —

" Where is my wife ? "

" Norwan has gone with the two Tede Wiu brothers."

" I don't believe that ! " said Norbis.

He sprang up, went around, and asked others. All said, " She is with the Tede Wiu brothers."

At last Norbis went out, taking his people. They had gone into the house, but had not danced. They followed at his call. He went swiftly to the northwest to overtake the two brothers.

The dance was at an end. All started home. Daylight was near.

The two brothers did not go to Norwan Buli Hlut, which was farther north than Koï Nomsono. They kept the woman at their own house till morning. When they reached home each of the brothers said, —

" My people, be ready for a great hunt at daybreak."

When daylight came the elder brother said, —

" Come, my people, we will eat together. You must all eat with me this morning."

While eating they heard shouts on the west bank of Bohema Mem, and soon they saw two men running toward them, — men finely dressed, with plumes on their heads. The men crossed the river, and came to the house of the Tede Wius. They were the Wul Wuhl brothers.

" We are here to tell you," said they, " that Norbis is very angry. He has roused all his people, and they are coming. He has sent us to tell you that he is beyond the Bohema Mem waiting for you. Norbis asks you to send out that woman to him."

The brothers said nothing.

"If you give her, he will go home; if not, he will fight with you."

"We cannot give her," said the elder Tede Wiu. "We did not go to the dance for her; we did not take her away from it. She came with us of her own will. If we give her away, she may come back right away to us. She can go where she likes, but we will not give her to any one."

The two messengers took this answer to Norbis.

"I believe this man will come against us," said each of the brothers. They went into the house and brought out elkskin armor.[1]

"Come, my people," said the elder, "take these, put them on."

They brought out more and more armor of untanned elkskin, and the people began to make ready for battle. It was not long till they saw two other men coming. These did not cross the river. They stood on the western bank and shouted, —

"Be ready! Prepare for battle! Norbis asks you to come to the river and cross. We will fight you on this side."

When the brothers heard this, their people put on the elkskins and hastened. The brothers left Norwan in their house, and bound it outside with mempak. The whole house was covered with mempak; no one could get out, no one could go in, they thought.

This done, the brothers crossed the river with their men. They looked down toward the south, and saw Norbis with his people moving along on

---

[1] Untanned elkskin was formerly used as armor by the Indians.

the western bank of Bohema Mem, and they extended as far as the eye could see.

"There are none there but Norbis and his people," said the Wul Wuhl brothers; "they are not all like him, but they are all his people."

The forces met, and both sides began to fight at once, and fought stubbornly. Norbis drove the Tede Wiu brothers to the edge of the water, but they rallied at the river bank and drove back his forces. A second time Norbis pushed them to the river; a second time they rallied and drove him back, drove back all his people. They fought all day, each side driving the other in turn. It was a hard and bloody battle; many were killed on both sides. Neither won, and both were very angry. When night came the Tede Wiu brothers said, —

"We will stop for to-day. If you wish to fight to-morrow, we will meet you here."

"I will meet you here," answered Norbis.

The Tede Wiu brothers went home. They found Norwan where they had left her, fastened in with mempak. That evening, when all were assembled and were talking, the elder brother said:

"My people, if they want to fight to-morrow we will fight with them."

He called a messenger then and said, —

"Go you and tell my brother Sehinom Chabatu to come and help me, and to come early in the morning. Go also to Waiti Nomken, a place on the upper Bohema Mem, to two women Kawas Loimis; let them know that we are fighting. On this side of their house lives Chir Chuma, a lame

man; let him know. Opposite Pas Puisono lives
Katsi Herit. Tell him to come early to-morrow.
A short distance from Tsarau Heril lives Wik
Herit. Tell him to be here. These are all great
men, and each will bring his people. There is a
man who lives at Kilichepin Kenharas. Kilichepis
is his name. Tell him to come with his people.
There is a man who lives at Sudi Sawul. His
name is Tuichi Kelis. Tell this man that I expect
him early with his people. All these big men will
help us greatly."

Norbis sent messengers to his friends. They
went southeast, south and southwest. He sent
southeast to Saias Saias Herit and south for Hus
Herit. He sent for Karili Herit; for Tcutuhl
Herit.

Next morning about daylight the friends of the
Tede Wiu brothers came. All came who had been
called, each bringing his own people. Friends came
to Norbis in the same way; none of those invited
failed on either side.

When all Tede Wiu's friends had come, the
elder brother confined Norwan as on the first day.
He bound the house all around with mempak.
They started then, and crossed the river with many
people. Chir Chuma had come. He was so lame
that he could not walk, and had two men to carry
him. These were the two Siriwit brothers (whirlwinds). (The whirlwinds were people at that time.)

The Siriwits carried Chir Chuma on two sticks.
He sat on the sticks. One brother held the sticks
behind, and the other in front. They moved

around with great speed, and travelled as easily on water as on land. When the two brothers had crossed the river, they saw two more lame men, one coming from the north, Chali Dokos: he was carried by Wainot Herit. The other was Sawi Herit; he was coming from the west, carried by Kichinot Herit.

After Tede Wiu's forces had crossed the river, the Wul Wuhl brothers came from Norbis, and said, —

"There are many people coming from the south with Norbis to-day. You will have a heavy battle."

Sehinom saw the southern people coming, and said to the elder Tede Wiu, —

"My brother, I will be with you all the time. I will guard you."

Three of Tede Wiu's men, Wik Herit, Tuichi Kelis, and Kilichepis, said, —

"We will go together. We will go to the eastern side, near the river, and take our people with us."

When going they turned to the Wul Wuhl brothers or Norbis's men, and said, —

"Tell Saias Saias Herit, Koip Herit, and Tsutsu Herit to come toward the river. We will fight them there."

"I will," said the elder Wul Wuhl; and turning to Chir Chuma, he said: "There is a man with a net coming from the south, Karili Herit; he will fight with you."

The Kawas sisters came now on Tede Wiu's side, bringing food, elkskins, and arrows for their brother, Sehinom Chabatu. They did not go where the fighting was, but stood back in the rear a little. Now Wai Charatawa came to Tede Wiu's side. He was a very small man and left-handed, but a great chief, a brother to Sehinom and to Wik Herit. He had his hair tied up and fastened in front with a long bone sharp at one end.

Norhara Chepmis came to help Norbis on the southern side.

Before the struggle began Norbis sent a message to the brothers, asking, " Are you willing to give up that woman ? "

They refused.

" Now, my people," said Norbis, " we are going to fight. I have done what I could to persuade these brothers to give up Norwan, but they refuse, and we are going to fight a second time."

At this moment Kiri Hubit came from the south, a strong man. He went to the east side to fight. He had only one arrow without a point.

When all these forces met, there was a terrible uproar.

" Now," cried Wul Wuhl, " a man from the south is coming; he is small, but brave and quick-tempered, a terrible fighter. He will strike on the left flank. His name is Nor Patsas Herit."

Yipokus Herit, who lived on the northeastern slope of Bohem Puyuk, was to be on the field at midday ; he was the one to fight Nor Patsas. His weapons were ice and snow.

Just at this time Norwan found a weak place in the mempak and untied it. As soon as she was out she went home to Norwan Buli.

When ready to meet, the two armies saw a very big woman coming from the northwest: an old woman, Nom Toposloni Pokaila. She was carrying on her back a great basket, as big as a house. This basket was full of pounded fir-bark, which makes the skin itch terribly and almost blinds every eye that it touches.

A man came from the northwest to the southern army, and said to Wul Wuhl, —

"Tell your man Norhara Chepmis not to engage in battle; let him stand aside and look on. I will do as he does." This man was Wainom Yola Herit. "If he fights on the southern side, I will do the same on the northern."

Wul Wuhl gave the message. Norhara drew back, and Wainom Yola did the same.

The two armies stood opposite, each looking the other in the face, each waiting for the other to begin.

At this moment the Siriwit brothers left the ranks on the east, the left wing of the northern army, and went careering around with Chir Chuma on two sticks. Now Nor Patsas, the small peevish southern man, saw Chir Chuma (the Siriwits were invisible), and could contain his wrath no longer. He ran at the lame man with all his might. When just in front of Chir Chuma, he struck the ground with his brand, and one hundred people, as passionate and peevish as himself, sprang up around him. But Chir Chuma rode right over Nor Patsas. The Siriwits knocked him to one side, rushed across his men, trampled, beat, and killed them.

The Siriwit brothers went some distance along the front rank, then turned back and rushed to where Nor Patsas had fallen. He was on his feet again, and dashed a second time at Chir Chuma. When just before the enemy, Nor Patsas struck his brand against the ground, a hundred men leaped up around him; all sprang on Chir Chuma, but the two brothers scattered and trampled every one of them.

Nor Patsas was raging. He had never been so angry in his life till that day. He turned and rushed at the northern army. He struck the ground once, twice, three times with his brand, and three hundred raging men were there around him. A battle began on the left northern wing, fierce and very bloody. Nor Patsas found no one to match him till Chir Chuma returned. The Siriwits were somewhat tired, and went more slowly while Chir Chuma fought with Nor Patsas. Chir Chuma had a red flint, called also sucker flint. With every blow of this he killed fifty and sometimes sixty people. When Nor Patsas gave a blow, he killed as many, and every time he struck the ground with his brand a hundred warriors sprang up to help him.

The fight begun by Nor Patsas with Chir Chuma brought in the two armies. Both sides fought desperately, but no one could conquer Nor Patsas till Yipokus came at midday. He rushed at the peevish, passionate warrior with weapons made of ice and snow. In the heat of battle water flowed from them and killed Nor Patsas, quenched the life in him. The southern army was pushed back, and driven a long distance down the river.

In the middle of the afternoon they rallied, turned on the pursuers, drove them to the field where they began in the morning, and were driving them farther, when Nom Toposloni ran past, and, throwing her crushed bark with the wind, filled many eyes with it and almost blinded them. She brought disorder to the southern army.

Norbis, afraid of being beaten, was ready now for anything. He called in Norhara Chepmis, who ran swiftly from the southwest with his warriors. A mighty storm of wind swept forward with Norhara. He struck the northern army fiercely. Wainom Yola, seeing this, rushed at the southern force with all his people, and they were so many that no man could count them. They were as swift as arrows. A roaring wind went with them.

Wainom Yola cut right through the southern army, and, turning, rushed toward Norhara Chepmis and his warriors. These two with their armies fought hardest of all on that day. In half an hour very few were left alive on either side, and those left were so weak that Norhara Chepmis and Wainom Yola were hardly able to lead them from the field.

There was not a man in the forces of the Tede Wiu brothers or Norbis who was not covered with snow and drenched with rain; all were shivering and nearly dead.

No one wished to fight for a long time after that day.

Norbis went home to the southeast without Norwan, the woman he called his wife; and when the Tede Wiu brothers went back to their house in the evening, they found that Norwan had escaped to Norwan Buli.

This was the end of the first battle on earth. None gained anything, and many were killed. Later there was another battle among the first people, and afterward many among the Wintus when they came up.

After Norwan had been at home awhile she said one day to Hessiha, —

"My brother, I did wrong. When I think of it now, I see that I did wrong. I understand all to-day. I see that if I had not danced with Tede Wiu, if I had not gone home with him, there would have been no fighting, no trouble in this world. If I had gone with Norbis at the dance, there would have been no battles, there would have been no killing; but I did not want to go with Norbis. I do not know why; but in some way I did not like him. I was dancing with Tede Wiu, and sitting with him, and going away with him before I knew what I was doing."

Sehinom Chabatu, after the close of the first great battle, went home and lived on Wini Mem five years before any trouble came to him. While helping Tede Wiu in his fight with Norbis, Sehinom killed Saias Saias and Chuchu, two of the best men among Norbis's forces.

All the southern people talked of these two, and told how they had died. A great man, far off in the southeast, heard of this. He was chief of the two when they were living, and his name was Chulup Win Herit. He was a slender, strong person. When he had heard the whole story, he said, —

"I have never liked fighting, I do not like fighting now. I have never gone to war, but I am going to war now. Norbis attacked Tede Wiu, he fought with him. Norbis has shown me what fighting is, and I am going to fight now."

Chulup inquired everywhere to discover who had killed these two men; he wished to be sure. All people said everywhere, "Sehinom Chabatu did it."

It was really Chir Chuma who had killed them. But Chir Chuma was under Sehinom Chabatu, and the blame was put on Sehinom.

They talked it all over, talked a whole night, and Chulup sent this message to Sehinom, —

"I should like to see you, I want you to come to Miol Tapa, near Puidal Pom. I will meet you there. If you want to fight, I will fight with you at that place."

The messenger was Tsotso Tokos Herit. While Chulup was instructing his messenger, Sehinom's grandmother was talking to him. This grandmother was a very old woman, Chir Pokaila; she was called also Kahi Buli Pokaila. She knew what was happening far away in the east, and what was going to happen soon, though nobody had told her: she knew with her own mind.

"My grandson," said she, "you have been fighting, you have been at war, and people will talk much of you. My grandson, you will hear something very soon. You must do what is best, take care of yourself. I will tell you what to do : when you go hunting or fishing, never go toward the east. Go north, west, and south, but never go east; the people in the east are talking of you. My grandson, I did not know that you were going to do the things that you have done. When I was rearing you and you were a baby yet, I told you how to hunt and fish; no more. I did not think that you would fight and strike down strong people. But there is a woman at Norwan Buli who brought all this trouble into the world; this fighting began for her, and now it will continue always and everywhere; there will never be an end to fighting in this world now. This place where we are living would have been good but for that woman. Now, from this time on, all these trees, mountains, rocks, all people in this world, will be bad and will hurt others. (This means that people will use stones, sticks, and everything to fight with when they are angry.)

"Now, my grandson, you must do as I tell you. My brother lives near by, he lives at Kahi Buli, his name is Kahit. Go and see him every morning early. And there is a man who lives a little farther away, up at Waitami. He is your brother. Go and see him every evening. He is a great man, he can do everything. His name is Katsi Herit. My two sisters live at Waiti Nomken. They have been in the war and have seen all the fighting. They are the Kawas Loimis sisters.

"My grandson, we cannot live as we used to live. We must live differently. I am getting very angry. We cannot eat, we cannot sleep as in the old time. When you went to war you killed two great men, two of the best men. Long, long ago Chulup, a great chief, went far away east, and has lived there since that time. He is going to come soon to see you. Take care of yourself; be on your guard. When he started east Chulup went to the edge of the great water and went under the ground to it, he went through the ground, and he lives in the east now on the bed of the great water.

"I will tell you what is going to happen soon. I am getting angry, and when I am angry you will feel a cold wind coming from the north. That wind comes because I am angry."

When Sehinom Chabatu went south, he was young yet, not grown; and now, when his grandmother knew what was happening in the east, she was instructing him. The place where they lived was Dau Paki Olel, a mile higher up than the mouth of Wini Mem.

One morning Sehinom Chabatu called all his people together. The old woman knew that some one was coming, and that day Tsotso Tokos came. He was sent by Chulup. When the old woman knew that he was near, she went into the house, brought out a quiver full of arrows, and hung it on a tree. Then she got a tuichu kilis, which is a net faced with white down, put it on her head, took the quiver, and ran some distance from the house, and rushed about in great fury. She acted like some one who is going to fight. People watched her.

"What is the matter with that old woman?" asked one person of another.

After a time she came back and sat down. A few minutes later a man was seen running in from the east, and soon Tsotso Tokos was at the house.

"Sehinom Chabatu," said he, "I am here to tell you what Chulup says. He says that he is growing angry; that he wants you to go to Miol Tapa to-morrow; that he will meet you there; that he has his men with him. He has gathered many people. He will wait for you at Miol Tapa."

When Tsotso Tokos had said these words, he went away. The old woman rose and said, —

"My grandson, do not sit long. Rise up. That of which I told you, a while ago has happened. I told you that trouble was coming. Send word now to the two Tede Wiu brothers. Send word to all your friends. Tell them to come quickly to help you."

Sehinom Chabatu sent a message to the Tede Wiu brothers, and a second one to the northwest, a third to the north, and a fourth to the southwest. In the north he sent to Sau Herit and to Kichuna Herit, to Hokohas Herit of Puidal Pom. Hokohas's people wore elkskin armor at all times; to Koyumas Herit, and to Puike Tsumu, a great chief, though lame. He sent to all who had been with the Tede Wiu brothers in the first war.

All came, and still others joined them. Among these was Cho Herit, who had a great many people. Sehinom's grandmother was terribly excited. She danced madly and ran around everywhere; she danced that night and the next day. The second morning all came very early to join

Sehinom's forces. The first came at daybreak, and one people followed another the whole day and the next night.

Chir Chuma, carried by two Siriwit brothers, came. Wai Karili, who lived on the south bank of Wini Mem, came. All his people had nets. Bulibok came from Bulibok Puyuk, and when the people on the road sat down to rest, he went ahead and called out, —

"Shoot at me, all you people! I want to see what kind of person I am going to be."

All shot at him. He sat still, but no one could hit him. And Kaisus Herit from Puidal Pom went ahead too, and asked all to shoot at him. A great many tried, but no one could hit Kaisus Herit.

Tichelis from Penehl Kente came, bringing his people.

"You are my brother," said he to Kaisus; "we will go together."

One Sedit came from Buli Puiwakat, and another from Sonomyai.

When all the people had assembled at Sehinom's, Wik Herit picked up dead coals and blackened his face. "I want to see fighting," said he. "I am a brave warrior. I want to fight;" then he puffed and strutted tremendously.

Nomel Hiwili, who lived at Waiel Nomeltos, came, bringing his people.

"My brother," said he to Sehinom, "I am not very strong, I cannot do much, but I will go with you and do what I can."

When they went to the place where the battle was to be fought, a messenger came and said, —

"Saiai Not Herit is coming to see you. He has no heart, and all his people are without hearts. Saiai Not wants to fight with you. Kichuna from Kinwinis Pom and Hamam Herit from the east wish to fight with you. All these people are at Memnom Kalai now, not far from here."

At this time they saw some one coming toward them from the east. This was a second Chir Pokaila. She was from Pokaitin Mem. When she came up she said to Sehinom's grandmother, —

"My sister, we will help our grandson, and if he is killed we will mourn over him together."

"It is time to move now," said Sehinom.

"We will be in the centre of the army," said the Tede Wiu brothers, and they took their places. Wai Karili went to the south wing of the northern army, and all his people with him. They went up on a level mound, and from there saw people coming on both sides, from the north and the south, as far as the eye could see. They came on like a great water, rolling forward. The people were in number as the grains in two clouds of sand. The two armies approached each other gradually.

Sehinom's grandmother, with her sister, was in front of the northern forces. She engaged the enemy first, and fought fiercely. She had arrows of kopus wood, pointed with Chirdokos, all made by herself. The northern army faced the east, and the southern the west.

Chir Chuma, carried by the Siriwits, came to help his two sisters. All three had the same kind of arrows. They killed fifty and sixty at a shot, and these three gave victory to the left wing of the northern army.

On the right flank of the northern and left flank of the southern army were good men, and there was hard fighting. On the northern side was Wai Karili with his people, having nets to catch the enemy. Then Hokohas and his forces, all dressed in elkskin armor; next Kaisus and Tichelis, with many people. Between Tichelis and the centre was Kichuna. On the other side, opposite Kichuna, was Hamam, who had sent word to Kichuna that he would meet him on the field. Opposite Sedit of Sonomyai was an unknown chief, but a very great fighter.

Wai Karili, Hokohas, Kaisus, and Tichelis with their forces were met by Hawt and Tsuini, whose people outnumbered those of the four chiefs opposed to them. The Hawts used solid blue rocks as weapons. They hurled them with great force, breaking the armor of Hokohas's people and tearing the nets of Karili's men. The Tsuini people threw smaller stones from slings in great showers at the people of Tichelis and Kaisus.

The battle raged with fury on that flank till evening. Many were killed on both sides, and of the chiefs Hamam and Sedit of Sonomyai fell. Neither side had the victory when night came, though Hawt and Tsuini were gaining a little.

In the centre were the great chiefs of both armies.

There Chulup, supported by Saiai Not, Tenek Not, and Tubuk, met Sehinom Chabatu and the Tede Wiu brothers.

In the morning Chulup began the fighting, and cut into the centre.   In the middle of the forenoon he had gone half-way through Sehinom's people. But Sehinom forced him back, and at midday Chulup was where he had begun in the morning. Sehinom advanced now, and tried to cut through Chulup's people.   He had gone more than half-way when Chulup rallied, pressed around him, pushed him back, and at sundown had rushed forward among Sehinom's warriors.

Just at that time Sehinom saw in the field behind Chulup a tall and very beautiful woman.   She was Chulup's wife.   Her name was Sanihas.   Sehinom Chabatu ran quickly to this woman, and led her to his own camp, while Chulup was struggling with the Tede Wiu brothers.   The sun was down now. Night had come.

Chulup dropped back to his own place.   He had lost his wife and gained nothing.   Both sides went from the battlefield and made camp-fires. You could see the two lines of fire running north and south, but could not see either end of them.

Chulup rose at daybreak next morning, rushed to Sehinom's camp, and after a sharp and short fight took his wife back before sunrise.   Both sides were very angry and fought hard.   At midday the southern forces had the advantage in the centre and the southern flank, and would have beaten Sehinom Chabatu but for his grandmother, his uncle, and his

aunt. The two women and Chir Chuma, carried
on two sticks by the Siriwit brothers, had beaten
everything in front of them.

At this time the centre and flank of the northern
forces had suffered much. Wai Karili left the fight;
he was angry.

"I will do something better than this," said he.

Taking his net, he went off to the southeast, and
never stopped till he was at the edge of the earth,
and had found the opening through which Chulup
passed when he came out on land or went back to
his home on the bed of the great eastern water.
He laid the net across the hole, thrust the middle
of it in deeply, covered what was left outside, and
waited in hiding.

At noon, when Sehinom Chabatu was hard pressed
and the enemy were pushing his people from the
field, his grandmother, aunt, and uncle, with the
whole army behind them, fell upon the rear of
Chulup's forces. The struggle began anew, and
from then till sunset was fought the hardest battle
of the world up to that day. At sunset they had
to stop, for there were few people left on either
side, and those were so tired that they could fight
no longer.

Each side left the field without saying a word to
the other.

Chulup sent his wife Sanihas home by another
way, and went himself to the passage where Wai
Karili was hiding. He went into the opening.
Karili drew the net, closed it around Chulup, and
tied it firmly. He put it on his back then, and

carried Chulup to Tehi Buli, some distance east of Bohem Puyuk. There he taunted him, saying :

" Now, Chulup, you did not take me, but I have taken you. You are not going to kill me, but I am going to kill you. Who is better, you or I ? " Then he killed him, and pounded his body fine.

When Sehinom Chabatu went home his grandmother said to him, —

" Now, my grandson, you are becoming a strong man ; you know how to fight, but men who fight do not live long. I have never told you to fight, but from this on you will see fighting. You must keep awake, my grandson. You must rise early, you must not sleep long ; some day you will hear news, some day something will happen."

After that Sehinom Chabatu brought the tallest yellow pine from beyond Dau Paki Olel, stripped all the bark off, painted it white, black, and red. The people danced around this pole, danced two days.

" We will go home now," said the Tede Wiu brothers, " but perhaps something will happen later on."

Then Dokos said to Wik Kiemila : " We have had all this fighting, we may have more fighting yet ; people may come to attack us, to kill you or me."

" My father-in-law," said Wai Dokos to Wik Kiemila, "we have killed a great man, Chulup Win Herit. I think now that we shall have much trouble ; he was the chief of many people ; they will attack us."

After this talk all went home. People lived in peace for two years.

"I will go and sleep in the sweat-house," said Sehinom Chabatu one night. He went. There were many in the sweat-house, and a greater number outside. Usually Chir Pokaila knew everything; but this night the old woman did not know that trouble was coming, she was in her own house asleep.

The door of Sehinom's sweat-house was on the east, and he was sleeping on the north side. Just before daylight some of the men lying outside woke up, and some in the sweat-house were awake, but none had risen yet. All at once they heard an uproar, a crowd of men shouting.

When the people around the sweat-house heard this shouting, they took their arms and ran forward. All inside the sweat-house rushed to the door, and as soon as they were out strange people killed them.

Sehinom Chabatu remained in the sweat-house. Chir Pokaila was taking bow and arrows to her grandson, but when she reached the door she was killed.

Chir Chuma, who lived near by, came when he heard the uproar. He was carried by the Siriwits, and went around fighting here and fighting there, killing many.

Sehinom, in the sweat-house, heard some one outside asking, —

"Is this Sehinom Chabatu's house? I cannot find him. He is not among these people. Perhaps this is not his house at all. I should like to see Sehinom Chabatu. If he is brave, he will come out. I am Sutunut."

Others cried, "I am Hus!" "I am Chutuhl!" "I am Koip!" "I want to see Sehinom Chabatu!"

All the people outside were killed now, except Chir Chuma. The Siriwits had carried him home. Sehinom Chabatu was left in the sweat-house. It was about the middle of the forenoon when all were killed, and the strangers set fire to the sweat-house. There was a log at each side of the door for people to sit on. Sehinom went into the ground, and came out under the log on the left side. He dug forward, as the fire moved, till he came near the end of the log. It was burned out now except a very short piece. He stopped under that.

Sutunut's people stood around watching for him.

"We should like to know where he is," said they. "The sweat-house is burned. He was not there or he would have run out." They pushed the cinders about, — found no trace of his bones. "He cannot be under this log," said one man; but he did not touch the burning log.

At last, about dark, when the log was burned almost to the very end, Sutunut and all his people went away.

Sehinom Chabatu heard everything they said. When they had gone and all was silent, he crept out from under the ground; he saw his friends lying dead, the houses destroyed, and the sweat-house burned down. He cried all night, — mourned for

his friends, mourned until daylight. At daylight
he walked around everywhere; looked at the ruins;
did not know what to do; walked around again and
again.

Just before sunrise he heard something and
stopped to listen. There was a sound like the cry
of a little dog. He looked, and saw at last a piece
of bark of the yellow pine. The noise came from
under that bark.

"What can be under this bark?" thought Sehinom, and turning it over he found two little boys
lying in each other's arms and crying. He stooped
down and took them up.

" Now, brother," said one of them, "we had luck.
We hid here and escaped."

They were Tsudi boys. Sehinom Chabatu took
the boys to care for them. He buried all the
people he could find, took the two little boys, and
went up Pui Mem to get kopus wood for arrows.
He found the wood, brought it home, and made
four hundred arrows. Then he made five bows of
yew wood.

The two boys grew very fast. Sehinom gave a
bow and forty arrows to each of them and said, —

" I wish you could do something for me, but you
are so small I don't like to send you."

"We can go wherever you send us," said the
elder boy.

"Well, my little brother," said Sehinom next
morning, "go and tell my two sisters, Kawas Loimis
in Waiti Nomken to come here. Tell them that I
am hungry, that I have nothing to eat. Say that

I am starving. Tell them to bring food to me. From my sisters go to my brother Kichuna; he lives at Kenwinis Pom. Go next to Wai Hau, at Hau Buli, then to Nomel Hiwili at Waiel Nomeltos. Go to Dokos Hilit; you will find his house by inquiring; from there to my father-in-law, Nom Sowiwi. Tell these people to come to me and bring all their forces."

Then, turning to the other brother, he said: "I will send you, my little brother, down south. I want you to go to Tidok Kiemila at Tidok Waisono. This old man and his people have plenty of feather dresses for war. Go to the Tede Wiu brothers; go to Hokohas Herit. Go eastward to Dokos Herit, at Dokos Hleï Puriton; go to Kaisus at Kaisansi Haraston, tell all to come to-morrow and bring their people."

The elder Tsudi brother came back in the evening. "Your sisters will come to-morrow morning," said he, "and the others will all come."

The younger brother came back a little later. "All the people will come to-morrow morning," said he: "all the Hokohas people with their elk-skins, all the Tidok people will come with their feather headdresses. When I went to the Tede Wiu brothers, they said: 'Sehinom Chabatu has great trouble.' I said: 'He has, indeed; my brother and I are all that are left.' 'He is our brother,' said they; 'we must help him.'"

Next morning the two Kawas sisters came, bringing many things. Each brought two elkskins and a great many arrows and otter-skins.

"Now, brother, eat and feed the two little boys," said they, taking out food.

People began to come. They came from every direction, from all sides. All that day they poured in; in the evening and night they kept coming. Sehinom Chabatu had to wait some days for all to come. The Kawas sisters had food for every one.

"We heard that you were killed," said the Tede Wiu brothers when they came. "We are glad to see you living."

"I am alone," said Sehinom. "I do not know what saved me. All my people were killed except these two little boys."

The Tede Wiu brothers were the first to come from the south. Next came the Tidok people. They came in crowds, in thousands, and every one had a feather net on his head. They began to come in the morning, and kept coming all day, all night, on the morrow, and second night, without stopping. They came without stopping for twelve days and nights, they came till there was no room for them anywhere around. More Tidoks remained at home than came, and more Tidoks came than all other people put together.

"You people," said Sehinom Chabatu, when all had come, "I did not cause this war and fighting. I did not begin. The war was made by the Tede Wiu brothers and Norbis."

"Now, my brothers," said Sehinom Chabatu to the Tede Wiu brothers, "people far off talk of me; but you caused the trouble. You began it, and you must do your best to help me. We must leave here to-morrow morning."

They started next morning early. Sehinom Chabatu gave orders to travel in parties. They moved toward the southeast. The last party of the first day left in the evening. When night came the van of the army camped and the rear marched all night.

When Sutunut's forces came northward from the edge of the sky in the south to attack Sehinom's people, they made a trail coming and going. Now, Sehinom's army followed this trail. They travelled the second day till they reached a camping-place of the returning southern army. There they spent the night. At noon of the third day they sent Kaisus and Bulibok ahead to look for the enemy. They went to the south. On the following morning they came back and said, —

"We found a cañon where they camped; you can camp there."

The army moved on. The two Kawas sisters had food to give the whole army; the two baskets were never empty, and all had enough.

They stayed three days in the cañon, and the Tidok people never stopped coming.

"We have far to go; you must hurry," said Sehinom next day; and the Tidok forces began to travel faster. Sehinom sent forward Hus as a scout. Before daybreak all rose and travelled till evening. Hus came back and said, —

"I have been very far down. I found another place where they camped. I went farther south

then, till I saw fire and smoke far away. We can
rest to-night in their camping-place."

"Sleep well, all you people," said Sehinom
Chabatu that night; "you must be fresh to-morrow morning."

Next morning Hus was sent forward again, and
the army started soon after. They travelled all
day. At sunset Hus came back and said, —

"I found the next camping-place; it is not far
from here. Then I went south a great way till I
came to a hill which runs east and west. I went to
the top of that hill and looked down. On a broad
flat I saw fires and a great many people. Their
camp is very wide from east to west, and runs south
as far as my eyes could see. Now, our friends, I
have seen the enemy; we must do the best we can."

When they reached the camping-place Sehinom
said: "We will rest here to-morrow, not travel
till the next day."

On the second morning they rose and started
early, went slowly, resting occasionally. About
sunset they came to the hill and camped on the
north side of it.

"I went to send some one to see how many
people there are in that camp," said Sehinom
Chabatu.

Bulibok went. On the end of the ridge was a
tree with one limb sticking out toward the east.
Bulibok went on that tree, sat on the limb, and
looked down. He saw the people moving around,
playing, and dancing. He could see a long distance. Pretty soon people below, who were look-

ing around everywhere, saw Bulibok, and one of them asked, —

"What is that sitting on the limb up there?"

"I don't know," answered another. "It looks like some person. Let us throw at it and see if it will move."

Notudui Ulumus, who always wore a sling around his head, took it off, put a stone in it, and said, —

"There must be some one there. I have never seen that thing on a limb before."

"Oh, that is nothing; that is always there," said others.

"I have never seen anything there before. I will sling a stone at it." Notudui hurled a stone, which just passed Bulibok's head; he did n't move. Notudui hurled another stone, almost grazed Bulibok's nose, but he never moved.

"Oh, that is a part of the limb," said some of the people: "it sticks up in that way."

"A man would move if a stone came so near him," said others.

"That is somebody; that is somebody watching us," cried a third party; and they disputed. The people watched for a while, but Bulibok sat there as motionless as the limb till, tired of watching, they went away, and forgot all about him. He slipped down from the tree then, went home, and said, —

"I sat on a tree, saw everything, and know now the best way to go. People saw me and hurled stones. They came near hitting me twice, but I did not stir, and they let me go."

"Now, my people," said Sehinom Chabatu, "this war was not made by me. I hate to take you to a place like that which is before us, but we must go there. I will go first; I will go alone and look at the place." He mounted the ridge, and from the top of it went underground till he came out in the chief house of the enemy. Then, thrusting his head up, he looked and saw a great many people. Soon some one saw him and said, —

"Why do you people not watch? Sehinom Chabatu may come. You say that he is dead — that you burned him to death in the sweat-house; but I don't believe that you killed him."

"Oh, he is dead long ago. We killed him; we burned him!"

Sehinom stuck out his head a second time. Again some one saw him and asked, —

"What is that over there? Maybe it is Sehinom Chabatu. I think he might come."

"Oh, he is dead long ago. Let's throw at that and see what it is."

Some one hurled a stone. It grazed Sehinom's nose and he dropped into the ground. "That is only a squirrel!" said a number of people, "Sehinom Chabatu is dead."

Sehinom went back to his army, and said to Nom Sowiwi, —

"I saw a great many people. They are the same who killed our friends. They will kill us unless we kill them. We will move to-morrow at day-break and fight. My brother, Tede Wiu, you must find Sutunut. When he came to my place he boasted greatly. He said that I could fight nobody. I want to see Sutunut. We must find him. Never mind others. Let us find Sutunut and Koip Herit, who boasted that they had killed so many of our people."

" I will go and look at that camp before dark," said Hau Herit.

He went, and just below the hilltop he found a piece of a hollow oak-tree as long as the height of a man ; he walked slowly in this dry trunk, his head just sticking above it, and of the same color. He reached the top of the ridge and went down the south side a short distance; there were no trees or brush there. As he stood looking around, his eyes above the stump, some people called out below, —

" What is that on the hill ? I have never seen that thing there before."

" I see nothing but a stump," answered others.

Hau was looking around everywhere, taking notice of everything.

" There is some one there," said another man.

" Oh, that 's a stump. I 've seen that there all the time."

" Well, let 's sling a stone at it."

Notudui took his sling and hurled a stone. Hau lowered his head a little. The stone hit the stump and made a loud noise.

" Oh, that 's nothing. Don't you hear the noise? That 's just a stump. We 'll throw again and be sure."

Hau was just putting his head out when he saw

another stone coming. The stone hit the stump, and made a great noise.

"There, do you think that is a person? Do you think the stone would make a noise like that if it hit some one?"

They threw no more stones. Hau waited till dark, when he went back and told Sehinom everything.

"Now, my brothers," said Sehinom Chabatu to the two Tsudi boys, "you must go to that camp. Go straight to the centre house, go into it together. Then let one go west and the other east. Look carefully, and when you see a bow, cut the string to it. Cut the strings in the first house before you part, and then cut alone. Go into each house and cut every bow-string. As you go around the houses inside, some one may see you and say, 'Look at those Tsudis,' but pay no heed, go on cutting."

The two Tsudi brothers went to the middle house together; then one went east, and the other west. They went through each house. In some they found a few bows, in others a great many. They cut till daylight was coming. They went home then, and said, —

"We cut bow-strings all night, and had to stop because daylight was coming, but we left only a few strings uncut. The people slept, except one man in the sweat-house. We don't think he ever sleeps. He talks always."

"I know him," said Sehinom. "He talks, but he is asleep while he talks [whistles]. Daylight is coming, we must go.   Do the best you can, do your best, all of you."

The army was so large, and there were so many Tidoks that they spread over the country like a flood; they rushed across the hill and ran down into the valley; when the people sleeping in the houses heard them coming, they sprang up and ran for their bows.

"Oh, my bow-string is broken!" cried one.

"Oh, my bow-string is broken!" cried another.

"Give me a bow! Give me a bow!" cried a third.

This was heard all over the camp; every one was crying: "My bow-string is broken! Give me a bow!"

Sehinom's army poured in on them like great waves of water. Sehinom rushed to the chief house, and shouted, —

"Where are you, Sutunut? I want to see you. You boasted so much in Dau Paki Olel, I want to see you. Where are you, Sutunut?"

Sutunut said nothing, kept still. He was in a house a short distance away, and some one else killed him.

The southern people could not fight well without bows and arrows; they did what they could to defend themselves, but at noon they were killed to the last person, not one escaped.

Sehinom Chabatu with his chief men and all their forces started for home, leaving Kot and Ho Herit behind, with some Tidoks to fire all the houses. Just as they had set fire to everything, a new force of southern people came up, surprised them, and killed a great many.

"Sehinom Chabatu has gone," said Ho Herit, when he saw them. "New forces are coming against us. Now, Tidok people, you must fight well."

The new forces chased Ho Herit and his men. The Tidoks fought bravely. Many were killed on both sides. Ho Herit himself was killed. Fresh people from the south were coming continually, while the Tidoks had no reinforcements. At last Kot Herit was killed, and most of the Tidoks who fought under him. Then the southern people turned and went home. The few Tidoks who escaped with their lives went north to their own place.

Sehinom Chabatu went back to Dau Paki Olel and lived there. He and those who came home with him did not know for a long time of the second battle and the death of Kot and Ho Herit.

This is the end of that war. All the people who returned with Sehinom Chabatu came home in safety. The first people fought no more after that, for soon Olelbis turned them into birds, beasts, and other things.

TULCHUHERRIS

TULCHUHERRIS

PERSONAGES

After each name is given that of the creature or thing into which the personage was changed subsequently.

Hawt, lamprey eel; **Kúlitek,** a white feather in the tail of **Komos Kulit,** the black vulture; **Nomhawena,** an earthworm; **Pom Pokaila,** earth old woman; **Sas,** sun; **Tichelis,** ground squirrel; **Tulchuherris,** etymologically, a person or thing that has been dug up; **Winishuyat,** foresight.

———————

IT was not in the east, nor the north, nor the south, but in the west, on a flat called Eli-Tsarauton (root flat), that a little old woman lived very long ago. No person lived on that flat but this old woman, whose name was Nomhawena Pokaila. She was called also Pom Pokaila.

This old woman had lived ten summers and ten winters on that flat, and one summer more; she dug roots there all this time, for roots were her food. The flat was broad, and she had dug, beginning at the edge and going round and round, till at last there was only a small piece left undug, and that was in the middle.

One morning, when she thrust her stick into the ground deeply, she heard a cry like that of a little child. She stopped and listened; heard the cry far down in the earth. She did n't know what to make of it, but thought: "Whatever this is I will dig it out."

She thrust her root stick down as far as she could at one side of the spot where the noise was, and worked hard, took much earth out; then she heard the cry a little forward, and dug forward.   She went next to the opposite side and dug all around the cry, dug till the middle of the afternoon, but found nothing.   Then she dug around again, thrust the stick deeper in the first spot, and said, "I must find that, I must have it."

She thrust the stick down deeper, — got nothing. She went on the other side, pushed the stick still deeper, and turned over the great lump of earth that was in the middle.   Under this she found a little boy.   The moment she saw him she heard a noise like thunder far off in the east, at Saskewil, the place where Sas lives.   When she raised him to the surface, she heard this noise a second time.

The baby's head, as she raised him to the surface, was to the east, his feet to the west; underground his head was to the south, and his feet to the north.

"Tsok tso, tsok tso!" (good baby, good baby), said the old woman, fondling him in her arms. She took the buckskin apron from her back, laid it on the ground, put the little boy on it, and wrapped him up carefully.   Then she fondled him again, saying, "Tsok tso, tsok tso!" and said, "I am old, I am your grandmother;" and she carried him to her house.   She took water and washed him, washed all his body.   Every morning she washed him.   She could not sleep at night, she was so anxious.   She watched him all the time.

All night, all day she watched, never put him on the ground, but washed him much, saying, —

"I wish you to grow quickly. You are the only person seen here. I wish you to walk soon."

In five weeks after she had found him he could walk a little and talk some. When he was able to talk well, the old woman said, —

" Now, my grandson, I will tell you a thing which you must remember. When you play around outside the house, never go to the east, never go toward Saskewil, where Sas lives. Play in the north or the south or the west, but never go east."

The boy grew fast and was able to play. As his grandmother was telling him always not to go east, he said to himself, —

"I wonder why my grandmother tells me not to go east. I'd like to know why."

One morning the boy went to play, went south from the house a short distance, and heard a voice, heard some one shouting, calling from some place, he did n't know where this voice was. He listened, and soon heard it a second time. It came from above, from the sky. He saw no one, but the voice said, —

" Little boy, your name is Tulchuherris. I know you, Tulchuherris. You are the first person in this place the greatest. You must do what you can to live. You must do your best to conquer. You are Tulchuherris."

The boy heard and understood. He went home, but said nothing to his grandmother, said nothing of that voice in the sky that had called him.

She told him again, as before, not to go east.
She told him this many times. Now he was almost
a young man, he had grown so fast. It was nearly
spring, and the old woman talked to him seriously.
When he had been with her all the winter, she said:
"My grandson, I suppose you wish to know
something. I am going to talk to you. You will
soon be full grown. I will let you know why
I have told you so often not to go east. You
wished to know why, now I will tell you.

"A long time ago all my people — my son, my
brother, my relatives — went away off to the east
and never came back again. I was left here alone.
There is a great house off in the east there, called
Saskewil. A big old man, Sas, with his wife and
two daughters, live in it. All my kin went to that
place and were killed there. When any one goes
into Saskewil, the old woman, Sas's wife, sits on the
east of the door, which is open to the south; her
daughters sit on the west side. The old woman
sits with her back toward the wall and her face to
the north. She never looks backward, but when
a visitor is inside a while and is sitting, she turns
slowly, puts her hands to each side of her eyes,
bringing her finger-tips to meet in the middle
of her forehead, and glares with big eyes at the
stranger. He looks at her then and drops dead.
There is a power in her eyes that kills him. Sas
has something in his nose. He takes this, rolls it
on his knee, and snaps it at people who go to his
house. Nobody sees him do this, but he kills
many people in that way.

"Now, my grandson, you know why I do not wish you to go east. I will tell you more. There was a man, the best of my people; he went to Saskewil, he went to the east and was killed there. I am sorry for him, I grieve for him yet. I am mourning now for him. He was your own brother, the one that I grieve most of all for. He was my grandson. His name was Kulitek Herit. You are large now, strong enough to hear this, and I tell you."

After the old woman had told him of the people who had died in going to Saskewil, Tulchuherris answered, —

"I am sorry for my brother. I am sorry that he was killed. Now, my grandmother, I must see what I can do."

He went out of the house then, went west and found a kind of white wood, brought it home and made an arrow, — a smooth, very small arrow; he painted this arrow red, blue, and black, painted it on the end and fastened feathers to it. Then he made a bow of wood which he found in the same place, far away west, and painted it nicely on the outer side.

Next morning before daylight, he went a short distance to the south from his grandmother's, took his bow and arrow, strung the bow and shot his arrow toward the east.

After the little arrow had left the bow it became a humming-bird as it went through the air. Before the bird reached Sas's house it turned to an arrow again.

A little way from Saskewil old Sas had his
sweat-house with only one door to it. That door
looked toward the south. The arrow dropped
east of the door and stuck fast in the ground
there. It dropped before daybreak, while Sas
was in the sweat-house. He heard something fall
outside the door, something that struck the ground
with weight like a great rock. He knew not
what to think. He had never heard such a noise
before.

When daylight came old Sas rose and went out
of the sweat-house. He had slept all the night
there. He looked around to see what had made
the great noise, and saw the little arrow. He
looked at the arrow, went up, grasped it, tried to
pull it out. He took a firm hold, tried hard,
twisted and pulled, but could not draw the arrow.
He rested and then did his best. He pulled,
braced himself. His hands slipped and he fell on
his back.

Sas had to leave the arrow where it was; he
could not draw it out. He went to his house,
where his wife and daughters were. The two girls
were very beautiful. Sas took his old wooden pipe,
filled it with tobacco, and began to smoke.

" My old woman," said he, " and my daughters,
I will tell you what I have seen just now. I have
seen a thing such as I have not seen for a long
time, a very long time. Long ago I used to see
things such as I have seen just now outside my
sweat-house. Something must be wrong. Some
one must be thinking of us, some one must be

thinking of our house. I believe that some day soon we shall see some person coming. I saw a little arrow, and tried to pull it out of the ground, but I was not able. I tried till I fell and hurt my back. Now, my daughters, you may go if you wish, and look at that arrow."

The girls went out, they looked at the arrow, and said, " Oh, that is a nice arrow;" and they tried to pull it out of the ground. It did not come, and they went back to their father's house.

" Now, my grandmother," said Tulchuherris in Eli Tsarauton, " I am going to leave you. I am going away. I am going to the east. I am going to Saskewil."

The old woman did not like to lose her grandson.

" Oh, my grandson," said she, " you will be killed. You will never come back to me."

" My grandmother, I am going," said Tulchuherris. " I am going, for I must go, and I will do the best I can."

He went west, and found flint, put pieces of it on each finger, made finger-nails of it, and made them very sharp. Then he went west a second time, got the marrow of Hunhunut (no one knows now what creature Hunhunut is), brought home the marrow, rubbed it between his hands, then rubbed himself with it, face, head, all his body except his legs.

A third time he went west, and took a little bush full of thorns, each about an inch and a half long, made leggings and a shirt of this thorn-bush. A fourth time he went west, and picked out in a gulch the firmest green water-stone. Of this green stone he made shoes. A fifth time he went west, and took a western panther as dog. A sixth time he went, and took a northern fox as dog. A seventh time he went west, got a sky spear pole, and a sky spear head, and a sky strap for the spear pole.

The old woman had a Winishuyat hidden away, and when she could not stop her grandson from going she gave him this Winishuyat, which he tied in under his hair on the top of his head. The hair was gathered over it and tied so that no one could untie it but Tulchuherris, and no one could see Winishuyat, who was like a little man, as big as a thumb. Winishuyat could talk to Tulchuherris and tell him everything, warn him of every danger. He always called him "my brother." When Tulchuherris was ready, he said, —

"My grandmother, I must go, and you will stay here while I am gone."

He stood up then to start, and his grandmother said, —

"My grandson, I cannot go out for wood, I am too old, I am too weak. I am not able to bring wood, and my fire will die."

Tulchuherris put down his quiver with his bow and went to the forest. He pulled up many of the biggest trees by the roots and bound them in a bundle. He brought the bundle to the house, put the trees on the fire, and said, —

"Now you have plenty of firewood, my grandmother, and I am going."

When he had gone a little way the old woman screamed: " My grandson, come back; the fire is dying!"

He put down his quiver and bow near his two dogs, went back, and saw that the fire was dying. The whole great bundle of trees which he had brought was burned out. Tulchuherris went then and pulled up by the roots great trees, larger than the first, and brought two bundles; put these on the fire — a great many trees. He was the strongest person in the world, and could do that.

" Now I am going!" said he. His two dogs stood waiting at the bow and the quiver. He had gone farther than the first time, he had gone about twice as far, when the old woman screamed, —

" My grandson, the fire is out!"

Tulchuherris put down his quiver and bow again, left the dogs with them, and hurried back. He found every tree burned and the fire going out. He stood there and thought and thought. At last he said, —

" I don't know what to do. I can't find wood enough, and I can't leave my grandmother without a fire."

Then Winishuyat said, —

" Tulchuherris, if you don't know how to keep a fire for your grandmother, I will tell you. Go out here anywhere. You will find wild sunflower roots, plenty of them. Put one handful of those roots on the fire, and it will not go out again."

Tulchuherris went and dug the roots; brought two handfuls; put them on the fire so that they would burn slowly, the ends touching the fire. Then he said, —

"I am going, grandmother. Take good care of yourself."

He went to where his quiver and bow and dogs were; then he looked back. His grandmother said nothing. She did not call to him this time. He went farther, looked back, listened, no call came. He went still farther, listened, all was silent; went farther yet, stopped, listened, heard nothing, made up his mind that all was right with his grandmother, and went on till he had gone a long distance, listened a fourth time, heard nothing. After this he went quickly till about midday, when he looked ahead and saw a great rock standing straight up in front of him, small at the top and very high. He looked and saw some one standing on the very summit. The rock was higher than a big pine-tree. A very old man was standing on the top of it.

Tulchuherris could go neither to the north nor the south, the rock was straight in his road. He looked everywhere for a passage, but could see none. He looked on the left side, all was dark; on the right, all was dark, — dark everywhere. There was light only in the road which went up the rock and over it.

The old man on the rock, when Tulchuherris came near, called out, —

"My grandson, come right up to me; there is no other road where people travel. When you are here, you will pass down on the other side easily."

"I will go to you," said Tulchuherris.

When he had said " I will go to you," Winishuyat, the little man under his hair, said, —
" My brother, be careful, he is going to kill you."
Tulchuherris stopped.
" Here," said Winishuyat, " is the place where
our people came in time past. Many were killed
here. They went to the old man; he threw them
down and killed them. If you go to that old man,
my brother, he will sway this big rock. In one
flash he will throw you into a dark place at the side
where you cannot see bottom. Run to the rock
quickly, kick it. If not, he will kill us. This old
man was sent here by Sas, he was sent here to
kill us."

Tulchuherris did not climb the rock, did not go
to the old man; but he rushed forward and gave
the rock one great kick with his shoe of green water-
stone. The rock fell, and the old man fell with it,
— fell into the dark place. The rock never sprang
back. It left a smooth road with a ridge on each
side of the place where it had been. Then the two
dogs ran forward, and Tulchuherris said to the old
man, —

" Hereafter you will not be what you have been;
hereafter you will be nothing but a ground squirrel.
You will live under rocks in the earth, and the
people to come will call you tichelis. You are not
like me; I am strong. You will be nothing hereafter but a poor little ground squirrel."

Tulchuherris followed the dogs then. He looked
back and listened; he could hear at a great distance,
he could hear all over the world. But he heard no

sound from his grandmother; so he went on till he came to a large and broad river. There he saw a man standing. Tulchuherris went nearer, looked up and down, but could see no place to cross the river. The man saw him and said, —

"Grandson, you cannot pass this big river; you must get some one to help you. I am the only one who ever crosses at this point. I can wade right through the water. I carry over all who come here. If you wish, I will take you to the other side; but you could never go alone; you could never cross yourself."

Tulchuherris did n't know what to do, and stood thinking.

"Go on, my brother," said Winishuyat. "Let him carry you, though this is one of the places where they killed many of our people who escaped the old man on the rock. But this man cannot kill us. Let him carry us."

"Very well!" said Tulchuherris to the old man. "Carry me over, take me across this river."

The old man came up and took him on his back. Tulchuherris had a pointed bone in his bosom where he could get at it quickly. He had brought this bone from Eli Tsarauton. The old man started into the river. At first it was not deep, but in the middle of the stream the water was up to his breast, and was growing deeper. Then it reached his neck, and was rising. The dogs made a leap from one side of the river to the other. The water was at the man's eyes now.

"Be careful, my brother," said Winishuyat, " be

careful. This man kills people in this way,— he drowns them, he will drown you right away if you let him."

Tulchuherris took out his sharp bone, stabbed the man's breast two or three times with it, wounded him, stopped him. Then he leaped from the man's head to the other bank, where his dogs were. Tulchuherris stood a moment looking at the wounded man. Then he said,—

" Hereafter you will not be what you have been. You will be nothing but an eel. You will be a person no longer. You will be only an eel, the people to come will call you hawt and will eat you."

Tulchuherris walked forward quickly after this. Sas's two daughters heard every step he took, as though he had been near, though he was far, very far away from them. They always heard men coming from the west, — always knew when they were coming.

Tulchuherris walked quickly till almost evening, when he came to a high ridge near Sas's house. Just as he reached the ridge he heard a sort of clinking noise on the other side. He stopped and looked, but saw no one. He was right at the spot where the noise was, but there was no one in sight. The ridge was like a straight wall reaching north and south farther than he could see, and high up out of sight, and down into the ground. No one could go through, or go around, or dig under that wall or climb over it. In the middle of the ridge was an opening in which stood a great sugar pine, and in the pine was a cleft large enough to let a person pass easily. When any one was passing, and half-way through the cleft, the pine closed and crushed him. The noise was made by a person hammering just beyond the wall. Tulchuherris looked through and saw an arm, and while he was looking his dogs sprang through the opening to the other side.

"What's this?" called the man, and he walked to the opening. "Ah, are you there? Is that you, my son-in-law?"

Tulchuherris said nothing, but looked and saw piles of bones inside.

"Come right in this way, come in, my son-in-law," said the old man. "Come in; you cannot pass at another place."

When the old man called out, "Come in, you cannot pass at another place," Tulchuherris said, "I must pass here, but I am afraid."

"This is the road that all people take, my son-in-law. Come straight through; have no fear, there is no danger."

The two dogs went up to the old man and smelled him. They growled, did not like him, nor did the old man like the dogs. This old man was Sas himself, he who lived in Saskewil.

"Now, my brother," said Winishuyat, "go ahead, go through as quickly as you can. If you are slow, he will catch us. This is a place where Sas has killed many of our people."

Tulchuherris took his bow and quiver in one hand, stood on one foot, braced himself sidewise, made a spring, and went through in a flash. That instant the tree closed with a great noise, became solid.

When Tulchuherris shot through, he went far off into the field, and Sas did n't see him, he went past so swiftly. Sas heard the tree close, and thought that Tulchuherris was caught in it. He looked at the tree and began to talk.

"Well, my son-in-law, you are caught, now you are nobody. I am Sas. You were weak, I am strong. You wore your grandmother's apron. You knew nothing; I know everything."

Tulchuherris had come up, and was standing behind while old Sas was talking. He listened, heard every word. After Sas had stopped talking, Tulchuherris asked, —

"My father-in-law, to whom are you talking? What are you saying?"

"Ha!" cried Sas, turning quickly. "Son-in-law, I was talking to myself. I was saying that I had done wrong to my son-in-law. I am old, my heart is weak, my head is half crazy. I am blind I did not know what I was doing. I was saying that I had done wrong. You are my son-in-law. I am old, I am weak, I am blind. My head is gray. I cannot do much now. You see my house over there; it is a poor house; it is poor because I am old. Go ahead; go in. I will follow as soon as I can."

Tulchuherris went ahead, and Sas followed slowly at a distance. The dogs had run on, and were at the house already. On one side of the door outside were ten grizzly bears, and ten on the other side. There were rattlesnakes in the door and around it. Before Tulchuherris came the panther dog had killed all the bears, and the fox dog all the snakes and things poisonous. When he came near the house, he stood a little way off and looked at his dogs. All around Sas's house he saw great piles of bones lying about everywhere, the bones of his kindred. He began to cry and lament for them.

When the dogs had cleared the way outside, they went into the house and killed all the grizzlies and rattlesnakes there; the house was full of them. Tulchuherris stood outside, crying over the bones of his people. When he had cried enough, he went in. Old Sas's wife was sitting on the east side of the door and his daughters on the west. When they saw Tulchuherris, the girls spread a mat, sat on it, and told him to sit down between them.

"Now, my brother," said Winishuyat, "be careful of that old woman; many of our people have been killed by her. If they were not killed outside, she turned and looked at them, and they fell dead when they saw her eyes."

While Tulchuherris was sitting with Sas's daughters, a large, long-legged, red-backed, very venomous spider came on him; then another and another. Many of these spiders crawled over him. He was wearing his thorn shirt, and they could not poison him; they got impaled on the thorns and died, every one.

Old Sas came at last, and when he walked into the house he took his pipe, filled it with tobacco, and drew a few whiffs of smoke. Then he said,—

"Take a smoke, my son-in-law; we cannot do without a pipe. It is best to smoke first and talk of affairs after that."

Tulchuherris took the pipe and pretended to smoke. He was not smoking; still smoke came, and the tobacco burned out. He gave the pipe back to Sas. Sas's tobacco was made of people's flesh and of their bones pounded fine.

After Tulchuherris had given back the pipe, he took his beautiful quiver, put in his hand, and took out his own pipe of green water-stone, a solid piece, not very big, but tremendously heavy. He took his own tobacco and put it into the pipe. His tobacco was the same kind of marrow that he had rubbed on his face, and something mixed with it (it is not known what that was). Tulchuherris lighted the pipe, smoked a little, and said, —

"Here, my father-in-law, take a smoke. I am only a young man. You are old, you are wise, you know everything. You say it is best for us to take a smoke. I am young, do not know much, but I think this pipe and tobacco are for talk. Smoke with me."

Sas took the pipe, but when Tulchuherris let go the old man could not hold it. It was slipping and falling. When he tried to catch it, it fell on his arm, threw him, and held him down.

Sas struggled to push the pipe off his arm, but had not strength enough. Tulchuherris looked for a moment, then reached out his hand, picked up the pipe, and asked, —

"Father-in-law, what is the matter? Take a good smoke. This is Tulchuherris's pipe."

Sas could not lift the pipe. Tulchuherris held it while the old man was smoking. When Sas drew in the smoke and swallowed it, it hurt him inside. The old man was choking. He fell on the ground, fell almost into the fire. His breath was taken from him. Tulchuherris put the pipe aside.

"Oh, help me up, help me, my son-in-law," called Sas.

Tulchuherris helped him to rise, and then sat with the girls again.

"My old father, Sas," said his elder daughter, "what is the matter? You have wanted this long time to see a man with strong arms. Why not talk now with this one? You have been waiting a long time for such a man."

While they were sitting there, Winishuyat said: "My brother, look out for the old woman. She is going to turn — be on your guard!"

Tulchuherris was ready. The old woman had not looked around since he came. She had been sitting motionless. Now she began to turn slowly, and Tulchuherris watched her. He sat with his right hand doubled up, and before she could look into his eyes he snapped two flint finger-nails at her, sent one nail into each of her eyes and put it out. She fell dead and rolled into the fire.

Night came now, and Tulchuherris lay down on the bed prepared by Sas's two daughters. They took their places, one on each side of him.

He never took out Winishuyat, he never let any

one know of him.   As Tulchuherris lay on his back, he saw something over his head, hanging from the roof of the house.   Two obsidian knives were hanging together by a very slender string of the inner bark of maple.   Tulchuherris fell asleep and slept until midnight.   He was roused then by Winishuyat, who said to him, —

"Oh, my brother, wake up.   The string holding the knives is ready to break.   Wake up, my brother, wake up!"

Tulchuherris woke up.

"Turn over! turn over!" said Winishuyat.

Tulchuherris turned in a flash.   That instant the knives fell, struck the ground just at his back, and were broken to pieces, both knives at once.

This was another way of killing people.   Strangers always slept soundly on that bed with Sas's daughters, were struck while asleep by two knives in the heart, and died the same moment.

Next morning after the knives fell, Sas rose and said, —

"Rise up, my son-in-law.   I have a small sweathouse out here.   I go there to sweat every morning, and then to the river to swim.   I swim in the river every morning.   We will sweat, and then swim."

Sas went ahead, he was first in the sweat-house. He made a very hot fire of the bones of people whom he had killed, — there were piles of those bones around everywhere.   Tulchuherris went out of Saskewil into the sweat-house.

"Now, my brother," said Winishuyat, when they were at one side in the sweat-house, "this is the place where Sas has killed many people who escaped in the house. He will smoke you to death if he can."

The sweat-house was built of bones, and was plastered outside with mucus from Sas's nose, so that no smoke could escape through the cracks. After Tulchuherris went in he saw how Sas made the fire. The old man never used wood, always bones. He piled on bones; fat and marrow came out of them, blazed up, made a great smoke, and the smell of the smoke was not pleasant. After sweating for a while Sas said, —

"I am old now and weak, nearly blind. I cannot stand much. My head aches. I must go out to rest. Stay here you and take a good sweat. When you have finished, come out."

Old Sas went out. The door was small, he could barely crawl through it. When outside, he lay across the door and stopped the passage with his body, so that no one could go out and no smoke could escape. After a time Tulchuherris said, —

"My father-in-law, I should like to go out. Go from the door, let me pass, I have sweated enough."

"Oh, I am old and weak," answered Sas. "I am lying here to rest. When I have rested some, my son-in-law, I will rise and let you out."

Tulchuherris was silent a little while longer. Then he groaned, "Oh, I'm nearly dead!"

"My brother," asked Winishuyat, "do you want to die? Do you want old Sas to kill you, to smoke you to death? You have no wish to die, I do not want to die. We are strong people, stronger than Sas. I will tell you how to go out. Take that Chirchihas bone which you have and make a hole in the north side of the sweat-house."

Tulchuherris made a hole in the wall of the sweat-house. He spat then and spoke to the spittle. "Make noise for an hour," said he, "and groan just as I do — 'enh, enh, enh!' Let Sas believe that I am here, that I am dying."

Tulchuherris slipped out through the hole, walked to the river, swam there, washed himself clean, went back to Saskewil, and sat down with his two wives, Sas's daughters. Sas heard the groaning of the spittle inside and said to himself, "Tulchuherris is dying."

After a long time the noise stopped, and Sas said, "Tulchuherris is dead." Then he went to the river, washed himself, and walked along slowly toward the house. When he came near, he was saying, —

"Tulchuherris, you are nobody. I have finished you now. I am wiser than you, stronger than you. You were brought up in your grandmother's apron."

Tulchuherris heard him. When Sas was outside the door, he stood a while and talked on, —

"You were dug out of the ground, Tulchuherris," said he. "You are nobody. I have beaten you. You'll never trouble me again."

He started to go into the house, looked around, and saw Tulchuherris sitting with his two daughters.

"Father-in-law, were you talking of me? What

were you saying?" asked Tulchuherris, when Sas had come in and sat down.

"Oh, my son-in-law, I cannot tell what I said, but I was thinking, 'Oh, I am so old, I know nothing. I am weak, I am blind. Sometimes I do not know what I am doing. I think that I have done wrong to my son-in-law, my poor son-in-law.'"

Soon after Sas went out, and at one side near the door he dug a grave for the old woman, his wife. When he had dug it, he buried her and with her all the bears and snakes, and said, "These are my children." He put them in the same grave, and cried, singing as he cried, —

> "Koki, koki, koki nom,
> Koki, koki, koki nom."
> (Creeping, creeping, creeping west,
> Creeping, creeping, creeping west.)

While he was burying his wife and the bears and the snakes, he had beaver teeth hanging on strings at the back of his head and on each side of his face. After he had cried awhile he danced and sang, and these teeth rattled as his head swayed from side to side. Then he went into the house, sat down, looked at Tulchuherris, and said, —

"Tulchuherris, you are my son-in-law; your wives, those two women, are my daughters. There are some things which they have wanted to play with this long time, and they have begged me to go for them, but I am old and blind; if I were to go I could not get what they ask for. My daughters want pets. My son-in-law, on a small tree, not far from this house, is a nest, and young woodpeckers chirp every day in it. Your wives want these red-headed woodpeckers, but I am blind and old; I cannot climb the tree, but you can get the woodpeckers. I will show the nest."

"Go ahead," said Tulchuherris, "show me the nest."

The tree was a mile away. Sas went to it and stopped. Tulchuherris stood near. Both looked up, and Sas asked, "Do you see the nest?"

The tree was very straight, and so high that they could hardly see the top of it; the trunk was as smooth as ice.

"My father-in-law," said Tulchuherris. "I do not think that I can go up there; I do not believe that I can climb the tree."

"You can climb it if I help you," said Sas, who took out a rope made of single hairs tied end to end, a great many of them tied together, hairs from the heads of his daughters. He threw the rope very high over a limb near the nest, and said: "Now, my son-in-law, I will hold the rope; you climb."

Tulchuherris began to climb the rope. He went up, up, up, till he reached the limb and stood on it. Sas was on the ground, holding the other end of the rope. When Tulchuherris let go his hold, Sas pulled the rope down, and left Tulchuherris on the limb very high in the air. Sas turned home. When a short distance he said, —

"Now, Tulchuherris, you are nobody. Your grandmother, Nomhawena, is old. She dug you out of the ground with a root stick. You grew up in her petticoat. You are not strong, you are not wise, you are only Tulchuherris. I am Sas."

When Tulchuherris looked down he was terrified, it was so far to the ground.

" My brother," said Winishuyat, "we shall get down. Lengthen the pointed bone which you have, and go higher."

Tulchuherris went to the nest, looked in, and saw a great many heads peeping out in every direction, — all heads of rattlesnakes. He looked awhile ; could not think what to do.

" Make the bone long," said Winishuyat. Tulchuherris stretched the bone. " Stick the bone into the head of each snake and gather them all on it."

Tulchuherris did this quickly; had them all; then he slipped them off and let them drop to the earth. After that he sat on the limb and thought : " What shall I do now ? "

" My brother," said Winishuyat, "what are you thinking of ? Why not try to do something ? Do you want to die ? If you cannot think of a way to escape, I will tell you a way."

" Tell me, my brother."

" Stretch your right hand toward the west. Something will come on it."

Tulchuherris stretched his hand toward the west, where his grandmother was, and immediately something came with a whirr and a flutter, and settled on his arm like a bird. It was a sky-strap, blue like the sky, narrow, and very strong. He fastened one end of it to the limb, knotting it in such a way that he could untie it with a jerk at the other end. He slipped down on it, and when on the ground jerked it loose. He strung the snakes on the long bone, they were all dead, and carried them to Sas's house. He laid them at the door, went in, sat down, and then said to the two women, —

"I have the woodpeckers if you wish to play with them. If you don't want them, you can send your father to look at them."

The girls told Sas. He went to the snakes and cried out: "Oh, my son-in-law, you are killing all my children." Sas buried them in the old woman's grave, and cried, and sang the same song over them as over his wife and the bears. Then he danced, wearing the beaver teeth.

Next morning old Sas rose first, and said: "My son-in-law, be up. My daughters always want me to fish and hunt; but I cannot fish now, I cannot hunt. I am old and weak. My feet are tender, I cannot walk; my head is dizzy. But you are young, my son-in-law. You can do many things. If you wish to hunt, I will show you where to find game in plenty. When I was young, I used to go to that place and kill game of every sort."

"I will go," said Tulchuherris.

When they were at the place, Tulchuherris saw only thick brush through which no man could pass. There was only one narrow opening, one little trail, and one tree at the end of it. "Stand against that tree," said Sas. "When deer come, they always run past that tree. I will drive deer in. You shoot."

Sas went north to drive deer in.

"Now, my brother," said Winishuyat, "be careful. You see the bones around here. They are people's bones. When Sas could not kill people elsewhere, he brought them to this place and killed them. He will drive ten grizzly bears up to kill us, and eat us. Tell your panther dog what to do."

"You, my dog," said Tulchuherris, "stand behind the tree till you see a grizzly bear spring at me. I will dodge. He will miss and turn again at me. Kill him when he turns."

Tulchuherris heard Sas driving bears in the distance. "Ha-ha, ho-ho! Ha-ha, ho-ho!" shouted Sas.

"Be ready; they are coming!" said Winishuyat.

Tulchuherris heard Sas coming. Then he saw a grizzly, and another, and another, till five were in sight. A little behind these were five others. When the first bear came near, he bounded at Tulchuherris, Tulchuherris dodged. The bear went past a good distance, and then turned to spring back. That moment the panther dog seized him by the throat and killed him. The second bear sprang at Tulchuherris. He dodged; the bear passed, and turned to come back. The panther dog seized and killed him right there. When he had chased the bears in, Sas turned home, saying as he went, —

"You are in a good place to-day, Tulchuherris. I have you now where my children will kill you. I know more than you; I am stronger than you. I am Sas."

After ten bears were killed and no more came,

Tulchuherris stood awhile, and taking the bears in one hand by the paws, he walked home with them; carried them as he would little birds. He put them at Sas's door, went in, sat down, and said to his wives, —

"I have something outside. You call them deer, I give them another name. But this is the only kind of deer that your father drove to me. You eat this kind of deer, I suppose. Go and see them, or tell your father to go."

Sas went out and saw the ten grizzly bears lying dead. "Oh, my son-in-law," cried he, "you are killing all my children!" Then, singing and crying, he buried the bears.

Next morning Sas rose early. "My son-in-law," said he, "there is something which I would like you to do to-day. My daughters have been asking me to do this for a long time; but I am too old. I will show you a brush house. I made it to kill birds of every kind and all kinds of game. It is near a spring at which birds meet to drink. Come; I will show you the house and the spring."

"My brother, be careful to-day," said Winishuyat, at starting. "Sas is taking us to Wintubos, where he has killed many people. There is no water near that place; no spring; but the house is full of snakes, poisonous things, and bears. Take both your dogs with you."

After Tulchuherris and Sas had gone a short distance, Sas stopped and said, —

"My son-in-law, you see that little house down there? Go into it and wait till you see some nice

birds or game coming, then kill them. I will go
back. I am old and cannot stand or sit here and
wait for you. I will go home and lie down till you
come."

Sas went home.

Tulchuherris went near the house, and stopped.
The two dogs sprang into the house at a leap, and
killed all the snakes and the bears in it. When the
dogs had come out, Tulchuherris went in to look
at the house and the spring. He saw piles of
bones everywhere. He cried when he looked at
them. There was no water in the spring. It was
mud, thick mud mixed with people's flesh. Tulchuherris looked toward the east, and far away he
saw an open plain. Soon he saw what seemed a
small speck at first. It was moving. As he
watched, it came nearer, and he saw it was a
person. Now far away he saw something else.
The first was a small man; the second still smaller.
Tulchuherris saw that they were running toward
him. They came near and stopped.

"Have no fear. Come up to me," said Tulchuherris.

The larger said : " O my brother, my brother, I
am thirsty."

" Oh, my brother," said the smaller one, " we
are very thirsty."

Their hair was clipped close to their heads.
Tulchuherris stepped back toward the north, struck
the ground with his heel, and clear, cold water
sprang up in a stream. He drank himself, and said,
" Come and drink."

The first of these strangers was Anakurita (orphan), the second Biahori (lone man); only these two were left of all people in those parts. Sas had killed all the rest. "The last of our relatives were killed at this spring," said they. "We alone are left. We are going home."

"If you come here again," said Tulchuherris, "do not go near the spring at the house. That is a bad place. Drink this good water which I have given you."

The two went away. Tulchuherris put the sharp end of his bone through the heads of the snakes which the dogs had killed, there were hundreds of them. The ten grizzly bears he carried home in one hand.

"I have something outside," said he to Sas's daughters. "You call them birds, I believe; they are all the birds that I found at the brush house. Tell your father to look at them."

Sas went out and began to cry. He enlarged his wife's grave and buried them. "These are my children," said he; and he sang and danced as before.

Sas rose early next morning. "My son-in-law," said he, "your wives ask me to get fish for them, but I am too old. When I was young I used to fish, but now I cannot see. You are young; I will show you a good place for trout. My old pole and spear points are there; you may use them."

They started, came to a river with a bridge over it formed of one hair. "My brother," said Winishuyat, "this is a place where Sas has killed many of our people."

"My son-in-law," said Sas, "cross this bridge and catch fish ; I will go home."

"Very well," answered Tulchuherris, who put his foot on the end of the bridge and crossed with one spring. On the other side he went to the fishing-hut, fixed so that a man could look up and down the river while fishing. Tulchuherris had his own spear-shaft, a sky-pole ; the string was a sky-strap. He had his own point, too.

He waited for fish, and at last saw something come slowly from the south. It stopped, and then looked at him. Tulchuherris saw a face and a head with long hair tied in a knot with a band of woodpeckers' scalps, a long band wound around many times. Tulchuherris wore just such a band, but the scalps were of mountain woodpeckers.

"Ah, my brother-in-law," called out the person in the water, "let us exchange headdresses."

"I am sorry for you, my brother-in-law," said Tulchuherris. "I hate to kill you, but I must, for my father-in-law sent me to kill you."

"Go ahead, go ahead," said Winishuyat. "Don't spare him. Sas says he is a fish. He is Sas's son, Supchit. You must catch him or suffer."

Supchit turned, as it were, to go back. Tulchuherris hurled the pole, speared him under the arm, and the point went through to his other side. Supchit rushed toward the east with great force. Tulchuherris held to the spear with one hand, grasped tule grass with the other, used all his strength. Then he let the spear go, and held the strap. Though strong, he could not stop Supchit.

He was drawn into the water to his waist, then to his breast, and at last to his chin.

"My brother," said Winishuyat, "do you wish to drown? Call your gopher — he had a gopher in his moccasin — "send him to fill up the escapes, to block all the doors to Supchit's houses."

Tulchuherris sent his gopher to fill every hole, all Supchit's doors. Sas was at home now. He heard the great struggle, and said, —

"Oh, Tulchuherris, my son will finish you. This is your last day."

The gopher stopped every opening, and Supchit went from place to place. Every door was closed. He had to stay. Tulchuherris came out of the water little by little, and pulled till he drew Supchit to the bank, where he died. He carried him home in one hand, as if he had been a small fish.

"My father-in-law," said Tulchuherris, "I saw no fish except one little trout. I speared and brought home that little trout."

Sas went out; the two sisters went. "That is our brother!" cried they. "That is my son," called out Sas, "the best son I had."

The old man buried Supchit with his head north, looking southward, and sang the same song that he had sung for his wife and the grizzlies. Sas and his daughters cut their hair in grief over Supchit.

"My son-in-law," said Sas, next morning early, "be up; I will show you a place where I used to play often when I was young. I am old now, and cannot play much, but I will show you the place, and I may play with you a little."

"I will go," said Tulchuherris; and they started.

"Now, my brother," said Winishuyat, "we are going to the place where Sas himself has always killed everyone who baffled him elsewhere. No man has ever escaped from the place to which Sas is now taking you. He will take you to a tree; he will ask you to climb it; he will bend it and let it spring back again; he will kill you if you are not careful."

They went to a very wide, level plain; in the middle of the plain stood a tremendous, big pine-tree, leaning to one side somewhat.

"My son-in-law," said Sas, "when I was young I used to play here. I cannot play much now, but I 'll show you how to play."

"My brother," said Winishuyat, "I will tell you what to do. Sas will try his best now to kill us. Do not kill him to-day; try him, lead him on, make him go higher and higher on the tree, and wait till to-morrow."

Sas climbed the tree some distance and said: "Now, my son-in-law, I am ready!"

Tulchuherris seized the top of the tree, pulled it toward him a little, and let it fly back. Sas kept his hold and slipped down.

"Now, my son-in-law, go up; go higher. I used to go very high when I was young like you." Tulchuherris went to where Sas had been.

"Go higher," said Sas.

"I wanted to stay where you were," answered Tulchuherris; "but I will go a little higher."

Sas took hold of the tree at the top, pulled it to

the earth, and let it go. It sprang back into the sky with a noise like thunder. Tulchuherris held on and slipped down unhurt.

"Well, father-in-law," said Tulchuherris, "try again."

"I cannot go high," said Sas; "but I will go a little higher than I did the first time. Don't give the tree a big pull." He went up.

"Go higher," said Tulchuherris.

"My son-in-law, I cannot go higher; I am old."

Tulchuherris teased him till he went a little higher; then he gave a harder pull than before. Sas held on without trouble and slipped to the ground.

"Now," said Sas, "I'll give you a swing." Tulchuherris went up.

"Go higher," said Sas. He went higher.

"Go higher; you are young," urged Sas.

"I don't like to go up," said Tulchuherris. But he went a little higher.

Old Sas gave a good pull, stronger than before. Tulchuherris held on and came to the ground safely. Going to one side, he said: "Whu, whu! let this day be made short!" So the day was made short; evening came soon.

"Well, father-in-law, you try now."

"Very well," said Sas, "give me a small pull; my arms tremble; I am old. I cannot hold on, I am so weak." Old Sas went up.

"Go higher," said Tulchuherris.

"I cannot; I'm old."

Tulchuherris pulled down the top of the tree,

but not so far. While he was pulling, Sas said :
" Oh, my son-in-law, don't let it go hard."

Tulchuherris gave a pull that would leave Sas on
the tree, and he came down unhurt.

" Now try once more," said Sas, " and we will go
home."

" Very well," answered Tulchuherris.

" Now, my brother," said Winishuyat, " this is
the last time to-day. He will try hard to kill you.
Jump off before he lets the tree go."

Tulchuherris went up two-thirds of the way.
Sas pulled the tree to the ground and thought that
he would kill Tulchuherris surely ; but just before
he let it go, Tulchuherris slipped off behind him
and rushed away. The tree flew up with the noise
of heavy thunder. Sas looked everywhere, but
could not see Tulchuherris.

" Now, Tulchuherris," said he, " I have finished
you at last. You are nobody, you are dead ; " and
he started to go home, talking to himself as he went.

" Father-in-law, what are you saying, to whom
are you talking? "

Sas turned around, amazed. "Oh, my son-in-law,
I am glad that you are here. We must go home.
We have no wood ; we must get wood."

Tulchuherris thought : " My father-in-law wants
to kill me. To-morrow I will do what I can to kill
him. When my grandmother spoke to me of Sas,
I knew nothing ; I paid no heed to her. When
she warned me, I did not listen, I did not believe ;
but I see now that she spoke truly when she told
me of Sas's house."

He rose in the night, turned toward Sas, and said :
" Whu ! whu ! I want you, Sas, to sleep soundly."
Then he reached his right hand toward the west,
toward his grandmother's, and a stick came on it.
He carved and painted the stick beautifully, red
and black, and made a fire-drill. Then he reached
his left hand toward the east, and wood for a mokos
(arrow-straightene:) came on it. He made the
mokos and asked the fox dog for a fox-skin. The
fox gave it. Of this he made a headband and
painted it red. All these things he put in his
quiver.

"We are ready," said Tulchuherris. " Now,
Daylight, I wish you to come right away, to come
quickly."

Daylight came. Sas rose, and they started soon
after for the tree.

" My son-in-law, I will go first," said Sas ; and
he climbed the tree.

" Go higher !" said Tulchuherris. " I will not
give a great pull, go up higher."

He went high, and Tulchuherris did not give a
hard pull. Sas came down safely.

Tulchuherris now went high, almost to the top.
Sas looked at him, saw that he was near the top, and
then drew the great pine almost to the earth, standing with his back to the top of the tree. Tulchuherris sprang off behind Sas and ran away into
the field. The tree sprang into the sky with a roar.

" You are killed now, my son-in-law," said Sas.
"You will not trouble me hereafter !" He talked
on to himself, and was glad.

"What are you saying, father-in-law?" asked Tulchuherris, coming up from behind.

Sas turned. "Oh, my son-in-law, I was afraid that I had hurt you. I was sorry."

"Now, my brother," said Winishuyat, "Sas will kill you unless you kill him. At midday he will kill you surely, unless you kill him. Are we not as strong as Sas?"

"Father-in-law, try again; then I will go to the very top and beat you," said Tulchuherris.

That morning Sas's elder daughter said to her sister, after Sas and Tulchuherris had gone,—

"My sister, our father Sas has tried all people, and has conquered all of them so far; but to-day he will not conquer, to-day he will die. I know this; do not look for him to-day, he will not come back; he will never come back to us."

Sas went up high. "I will kill him now," thought Tulchuherris, and he was sorry; still he cried: "Go a little higher; I went higher, I will go to the top next time. I will not hurt you, go a little higher."

Sas went higher and higher, till at last he said, "I cannot climb any more, I am at the top; don't give a big pull, my son-in-law."

Tulchuherris took hold of the tree with one hand, pulled it as far as it would bend, pulled it till it touched the earth, and then let it fly. When the tree rushed toward the sky, it made an awful noise, and soon after a crash was heard, a hundred times louder than any thunder. All living things heard it. The whole sky and earth shook. Olelbis, who lives in the highest place, heard it. All living things said, —

"Tulchuherris is killing his father-in-law. Tulchuherris has split Sas."

The awful noise was the splitting of Sas.

Tulchuherris stood waiting, waited three hours, perhaps, after the earth stopped trembling: then, far up in the sky he heard a voice, saying, —

"Oh, my son-in-law, I am split, I am dead. I thought that I was the strongest power living; but I am not. From this time on I shall say Tulchuherris is the greatest power in the world."

Tulchuherris could not see any one. He only heard a voice far up in the sky, saying, —

"My son-in-law, I will ask you for a few things. Will you give me your fox-skin headband?"

Tulchuherris put his hand into his fox-skin quiver, took out the band, and tossed it to him. It went straight up to Sas, and he caught it. "Now will you give me your mokos?" Tulchuherris took out the mokos and threw it. "Give me your fire-drill!" He threw that.

Another voice was heard now, not so loud: "I wish you would give me a headband of white quartz." This voice was the smaller part of Sas.

When Tulchuherris had given the headband, he said, —

"My father-in-law, you are split — you are two. The larger part of you will be Sas [the sun], the smaller part Chanahl [the moon, the white one]; and this division is what you have needed for a long time, but no one had the strength to divide you.

You are in a good state now.   You, Chanahl, will grow old quickly and die; then you will come to life and be young again.   You will be always like that in this world.   And, Sas, you will travel west all the time, travel every day without missing a day; you will travel day after day without resting.   You will see all things in the world as they live and die.   My father-in-law, take this, too, from me."

Tulchuherris threw up to Sas a quiver made of porcupine skin.

"I will take it," said Sas, "and I will carry it always."

Then Tulchuherris gave Chanahl the quartz headband and said, —

"Wear it around your head always so that when you travel in the night you will be seen by all people."

Sas put the fox-skin around his head, and fastened the mokos crosswise in front of his forehead.   The fire-drill he fastened in his hair behind, placing it upright.   At sunrise we see the hair of the fox-skin around Sas's head before we see Sas himself.

Next Tulchuherris threw up two red berries, saying, —

"Take these and make red cheeks on each side of your face, so that when you rise in the morning you will be bright, and make everything bright."

Tulchuherris went west and got some white roots from the mountain, threw them to Sas, and said, "Put these across your forehead."

Next he stretched his right hand westward, and two large shells, blue inside, came to his palm.   He threw these to Sas and said, —

" Put these on your forehead for a sign when you
come up in the morning.   There is a place in the
east which is all fire.   When you reach that place,
go in and warm yourself.   Go to Olelpanti now.
Olelbis, your father, lives there.   He will tell you
where to go."

Sas went to Olelpanti, where he found a wonderful and very big sweat-house.   It was toward morning, and Olelbis was lying down, covered with a
blanket.   While sleeping he heard a noise, and
when he woke he saw some one near him.   He
knew who it was.   Sas turned to him and said, —

" My father, I am split.   I thought myself the
strongest person in the world, but I was not.
Tulchuherris is the strongest."

" Well, my son Sas," asked Olelbis, " where do
you wish to be, and how do you wish to live?"

" I have come to ask you," replied Sas.

" Well," answered Olelbis, " you must travel all
the time, and it is better that you go from east to
west.   If you go north and travel southward, I don't
think that will be well.   If you go west and travel
eastward, I don't think that will be well, either.   If
you go south and travel northward, I don't think
that will be right.

" I think that best which Tulchuherris told you.
He told you to go east and travel to the west.   He
said that there is a hot place in the east, that you
must go into that place and get hot before you start
every morning.   I will show you the road from east
to west.   In a place right south of this is a very big
tree, a tobacco tree, just half-way between east and

west. When you come from the east, sit down in the shade of that tree, rest a few minutes, and go on. Never forget your porcupine quiver or other ornaments when you travel.

"While coming up from the east, you will see thick brush along the road on both sides. In that brush are the grizzly bears, your children. Be on your guard against them; they would kill you if they could. As you pass along, let your porcupine quiver touch the bushes; that will keep the bears away. When you go far west to the great water, jump into it; everybody will call that place Sasunhluaston. No one in the world will believe you except Sedit. You and Sedit want all things to die when they grow old. Go to the east; go into the hot place every morning. There is always a fire in it. Take a white oak staff, thrust the end of that staff into the fire till it is one glowing coal. When you travel westward carry this burning staff in your hand. In summer take a manzanita staff; put it in the fire, and burn the end. This staff will be red-hot all the day.

"Now you may go east and begin. You will travel all the time, day after day, without stopping. All living things will see you with your glowing staff. You will see everything in the world, but you will be always alone. No one can ever keep you company or travel with you. I am your father and you are my son, but I could not let you stay with me."

SEDIT AND THE TWO BROTHERS HUS

SEDIT AND THE TWO BROTHERS
HUS

PERSONAGES

After each name is given that of the beast, bird, or thing into which the personage was changed subsequently.

Dokos, flint; Hus, turkey buzzard; Klak, rattlesnake; Sedit, coyote; Wima, grizzly bear.

THERE were two brothers Hus in Olelpanti, and Olelbis had given them a place in his sweat-house. Now, when Olelbis had made up his mind to send all things down to the earth, the people in Olelpanti were talking and saying, —

"What shall we do now? How will it be in the world? Dokos Herit, Klak Loimis, and Wima Loimis have done wrong. They are angry and think bad things. They will make trouble."

" Come into the sweat-house, you my people," said Olelbis, "and talk. Say what you think is best to do."

All who were in Olelpanti at that time went into the sweat-house, where they talked five nights and five days. On the sixth morning Olelbis called the two Hus brothers and said, —

" I have a great work for you. Go down to Tsarauheril, where the first tree is. Right there a people will come up out of the earth, and they will come soon. A little above that place, you two brothers must go to work and make a stone road from the earth up here to Olelpanti. You will find stones and pile them firmly. Make the building very strong. The road itself will be like steps, one higher than another. When you have built half-way up to Olelpanti, you will make a place in which people may spend a night. Put good water there. When you have finished the whole road, people will come up out of the earth, and when they have come up they will go around on the earth everywhere, and live and grow old. When they are old, they can go to the beginning of the road made by you and climb the steps. When they are at the water, which is half-way, they will drink of it, rest one night, and next day travel on till they come here to Olelpanti.

" I will put two springs of water at this end, — one for them to bathe in, the other to drink. If an old man is coming up, he will drink of the water half-way, he will drink and feel better, and when he reaches this end and comes to the water here, he will bathe in one spring, drink from the other, and come out young, fresh, and strong. If an old woman comes, she will drink and bathe and come out a young girl. Then they will go down to the earth again young and healthy. When they grow old a second time, they will come up, drink, and bathe again, and be young a second time; and it will be this way forever. Nobody will die. No man will have a wife, no woman a husband ; all will be as brothers and sisters. When the trees grow large which are small now, there will be no limbs except at the top, and the acorns on those trees will have no shells. They will be ready to eat without husking or cracking, and it will be so on all trees, — no husks or shells on the acorns; nobody will need to climb; the nuts will fall ready to be eaten."

When Olelbis had finished talking, he sent away the two brothers. "Go now," said he, "and make that great road."

The two brothers started. They came down at Sonomyai, looked around, and said, —

"This must be the place of which Olelbis told us. This must be the place where we are to work: we will begin here."

"My brother," said the elder Hus, "I will bring stones to you; plenty of them; big stones. You will put them together, — lay them in order and make the walls."

They began to work. On the first day they piled the road up as high as a big house. Next day they piled all day; made the road as high as a tall tree. The third day it was very high; the fourth still higher. It was rising very fast. The brothers worked well, and had great power. The building was already the largest ever seen on this earth. On the fifth day the top could hardly be seen. On the sixth day it was touching the clouds.

A little before noon of the sixth day the two brothers saw something moving from the southwest. When it came near they saw a man with mempak around his neck. He wore an otter-skin headband, an otter-skin quiver, and a Sedit skin, which he wore like a coat. He had on buckskin leggings ornamented with kobalus, and his shirt was stuck full of kobalus, the sharp end of the shell out. He was dressed beautifully. When this man had come near, he watched the two brothers at work. They did not speak to him.

This was Sedit. At last he said, —

" My grandsons, stop work; rest awhile; come and tell me what you are doing. Come and sit awhile here with me, and we will talk. When an uncle or a grandfather comes, people always stop work and talk with their relative."

The brothers made no answer; kept on at their work; paid no heed to Sedit.

" Grandsons," said he again, " stop awhile; come and talk with me; tell me what you are doing. I want to learn, come and tell me what you know; rest awhile. I might tell you something better than what you know. Perhaps you think, grandsons, that I don't know anything. Come and sit down and I will tell you something wise. If you don't come, I will spoil your work. I will destroy what you are doing."

When the two brothers heard this, they were frightened; they thought that he might injure their work, and they came. When they reached the ground and walked up to Sedit, they asked, —

" Which way did you come, grandfather? Where do you live? "

" My grandsons," said Sedit, " I came from a place not very far from this. I was walking around to see if I could see something. I heard people talking last night about you. They said that you were making a road, and I thought that I would come here to look at your work, and talk to you."

"Very well," said the brothers. "This work which we are doing is not for us. It is for others. Perhaps you think this work is for us; it is not, it is done at command of another. This work is for Olelbis. Olelbis, sent us down here to make this great road."

"What!" cried Sedit, "are you working for Olelbis? Did he send you down here to do this? Did he tell you to make this road, and have you come here to make it for him, my grandsons? Do you believe what Olelbis says to you? Do you believe what he says to other people? Do you mind him and work for him? I don't believe in Olelbis. I don't believe what he says, I don't care for what he says."

"My grandfather," said the elder Hus, "hold on, stop talking. I don't like to hear you say such words, I don't like to hear you talk in that way. I am going to tell you why all this work is done, why this road is made. I have told you nothing."

Sedit sat down and said: "Well, tell me. I am glad to hear what you say. I am glad to hear why you are making this road."

The elder brother began: "Olelbis says that a new people will come on this earth soon, that they will live and go around, and after a while they will grow old. When very old, they will come to this road to go to Olelpanti and be young again. When half-way up, it will be evening. They will drink water from a spring and pass the night there. Next

day they will go on, and be at the end of the road
in the evening, — they will be in Olelpanti, where
Olelbis lives. They will find water there. They
will drink from one spring and bathe in the water
of another. When they come out, they will be
young. Next day they will come down half-way,
drink of the water, stay one night, then come to the
earth, and be young and fresh as they were at first.

"No man will have a wife, no woman a husband.
They will be to one another as brothers and sisters.
That is what Olelbis wishes, and because he wishes
it he has sent us to make this road. When the road
is built to Olelpanti, where Olelbis lives, these trees
around here, which are small now, will be large.
They will grow up and be very tall. They will
have no limbs except those near the top, where
branches will run out. On those branches acorns
will come, and the acorns will have no shells on
them. They will be all ready and fit to eat. The
people who are to come out of the earth will not be
able to climb these trees, and they will have no need
to climb, for the acorns will fall, and the people
will pick them up and have plenty of food without
work, without trouble."

Sedit listened and looked at the elder Hus
brother. Then he turned to the younger Hus
and said sneeringly, —

"Hu! Do you believe all that? Do you think
that every word is true which Olelbis says? Do
you think it is wise? Do you think it is good?
Now, my grandsons, you wait awhile, and I will tell
you something. You ought to know that an old

man like me has words to speak, — that he knows
something wise. I have something to tell you
which is better than all this. I will tell you what it
is. I will tell you now. Suppose an old man goes
up this road all alone, drinks from one spring,
bathes in the other, and comes down young. He
will be all alone just as he was when he went up."

Suppose an old woman and an old man go up,
go alone, one after the other, and come back alone,
young. They will be alone as before, and will grow
old a second time, and go up again and come back
young, but they will be alone, just the same as at first.
They will have nothing on earth to be glad about.
They will never have any friends, any children ; they
will never have any fun in the world ; they will never
have anything to do but to go up this road old and
come back down young again.

" Now, my grandsons, I will tell you something
better, and you will like what I tell you. I like it
because it is good. I am going to say something
wiser than anything Olelbis has told you yet. It
will be better, very much better if trees have limbs
to the ground, and if acorns have husks and shells on
them. When trees have limbs to the ground, a man
can climb them, take a long stick in his hand, and
knock acorns to the ground. Others will come
under the tree and gather them. When the acorns
fall, women will jump and say, ' Oh ! oh ! ' and laugh
and talk and be glad and feel well. I think that is
better. People can take the acorns home and put
them on the ground. Then they will say, ' Come, let
us husk these acorns.' Men and women will go

and sit down and husk the acorns. When they are
doing this, they will throw husks back and forth at
each other. They will have fun and laugh and be
pleased and feel well. I think that this is better ; I
know that you will like it.

"Besides, what are people to eat if nothing dies?
Deer will not die, fish will not die; the coming
people cannot kill them. What are they to eat?
They will have nothing to eat except acorns.

"I think it is better for women and men —
young men and young women — to marry, live
day and night with each other. When they get up in
the morning, the man will work for the woman, the
woman will work for the man, and they will help
each other. I think that the better way. If a man
has a wife, he will catch fish and kill deer, he will
bring them in, and give them to his wife to cook. She
will cook them, and both will eat. I think that is
the right way. If people live in this manner, and
a woman has a child, her neighbors will say, 'There
is a nice baby over there,' and they will go to see it,
and will say, 'What a nice baby that woman has!'
I think this is better than anything Olelbis told you.

"When that baby grows up and another baby
grows up, they will be a man and a woman, and the
two will get married and have children themselves,
and in that way there will be plenty of people always ;
new people, young people. When a man grows old,
he will die ; when a woman grows old, she will die.
When they die, others will go around and tell their
neighbors about it, and say, 'A woman died over
there,' or 'A man died over here. They will bury

him to-morrow.' Then all the people will make ready to help the relatives of the dead man ; they will cry, the dead man's relatives will cry and mourn. I think this is better. When a man dies, his nearest relatives will cut their hair very close, paint the face black ; and when people see one of them coming or going, they will say, ' His father is dead,' or ' His wife is dead,' or ' His mother is dead,' and they will talk about that man and his dead father, or dead mother, or dead wife, and say, ' Poor man, he has lost his father, or his mother, or his wife.' I think this is better.

" When an old woman dies, she will leave a daughter, and that daughter will have a daughter, or an old man dies, he will leave a son, and that son will have a son. As men and women grow old, they will die, and their places will be taken by young people. I think this is the right way. I think this is the best way. All living things should go this way, — all should grow old and then die. When the new people come on this earth, they ought to go this way. When those people come and live all around on this earth, they will die in many ways, — they will fight with each other and die ; when trees grow old, they will die and fall down ; everything will die in like manner.

" When a man dies, his friends will put mempak on him, like this which I have around my neck, and an otter-skin band around his head, and give him a quiver, dress him, and then put him in the ground. When a man goes to some place, a grizzly bear may catch and kill him, or a rattlesnake will bite and kill him, and when people fight they will use flint and kill one another.   People will get angry and fight.   When there is a gathering, somebody will come running in and say, ' People over there are fighting.'   Those inside will hurry to see, and will find a man killed, and say, ' A good man is killed ; ' then they will punish the others for killing him."

The two brothers sat there, made no answer.

" Well, my grandsons," continued Sedit, " I know that what I tell you is right.   What do you think ? "

The brothers said nothing at first.   They thought and thought.   After a while the elder looked at Sedit and said, —

" I think what you say is better.   I think that it is right.   I suppose it is true.   I believe that you are old enough and ought to know.   I think that you are right."

" Grandfather," said the younger brother, " would you like to die, too, the same as others, and be lying in the ground and not rise any more ; never go around with an otter-skin band on your head, and a beautiful quiver at your back, and fine things such as you are wearing to-day ?   You want others to die ; you want death in the world.   What would you say if you had to die yourself?   You want all the coming people to die, and all living things here-after to die and be gone from here.   Olelbis does not want any one to die, but you want all living things on this earth to die.   You want to spoil all the work which Olelbis sent us down here to do."

When the younger brother said this, the two stood up and walked off a little way, and Sedit said, —

"My grandsons, come back, come back. We have not finished talking yet. We must talk more. We will talk this all over again. Come back, my grandsons, come back."

But the two brothers did not turn back; they walked on, walked toward the east always — said nothing. After a time they turned and went to where their road was. They pulled out some great stones, and the whole road fell to the ground.

The two brothers flew up then, circling around for a while. They went higher and higher, till at last they disappeared and went to Olelpanti.

Sedit saw them fly up, watched them till they disappeared. He stood looking around for a long time. At last he said, —

"What am I to do now? I wish I had not said all that, I wish I had not said so much. I wish I had not said anything."

He stood around there and kept repeating: "What am I to do now? I am sorry. Why did I talk so much? Hus asked me if I wanted to die. He said that all on earth here will have to die now. That is what Hus said. I don't know what to do. What can I do?"

He looked around and found a plant with long, broad leaves, the wild sunflower. He found this plant in great plenty, and took many leaves from it. He pulled off all his fine clothes, threw them aside, then stuck the leaves into his body, all the way up and down his legs, body, and arms, and said, —

"Now I will go up to Olelpanti. I am not going to stay down here where people die. I am going up to the place where the Hus brothers went."

He made a tail of leaves; then he rose and flew around and around, rose pretty high; the leaves began to get dry and break one after another. After a while Sedit, whirling round and round, came down with great force, struck the ground, and was crushed to pieces.

The Hus brothers went up to Olelpanti. Olelbis said, —

" There are rocks at the south not far from the sweat-house; go there and stay."

Olelbis looked down, and saw Sedit trying to fly to Olelpanti; he saw him fall.

" It is his own fault," said Olelbis. " Sedit is the first to die, killed by his own words; hereafter all his people will fall around and die and be found dead at roadsides and places where people pass. The people to come will see them there."

The name of the place where the ruined road was is Sonomyai.

Our Wintu people say that ever since white men settled in the country they have been drawing away the stones which the Hus brothers piled up. They have taken them as far as fifteen miles to build chimneys.

HAWT

HAWT

PERSONAGES

ON the south side of Bohem Puyuk is a small mountain called Tede Puyuk. Near that small mountain lived Waida Dikit Kiemila. He lived all alone, without neighbors. There was no house near his. He lived long in that place, thinking what was best for him to do, thinking, thinking. After a great while he thought: "The best thing to do is to build a sweat-house."

He built a sweat-house about a mile west of the place where he was living. When he had finished, he took a kind of red earth and painted the eastern half of the house red on the outside. The western half he painted green with paint made from leaves of bushes. After he had painted the western half, all the different kinds of bushes whose leaves he had used for paint grew out of that side of the sweat-house.

The sweat-house was ready for use now, and Waida Dikit went to see a man, Tsaroki Sakahl, who lived farther south.

" My grandson," said Waida Dikit, " I wish you would come up and stay in my house. I have no one to keep me company. I wish you would come and live with me."

" I will go with you," said Tsaroki, and he went to live with the old man.

Waida Dikit had not told Tsaroki of the sweat-house, he took him to the old house. After two or three nights Waida Dikit said, —

" My grandson, what shall we do? What would you like to do? What will be best for us? We must talk about something. There should be something for us to talk about. We must have something to say."

" Well," said Tsaroki, " I think that you want what is best; you want to see somebody, to see something. I think that is what you want. I think I know what you want. The best way to get what you want is to build a sweat-house."

" That is wise talk, my grandson, I like to hear it. I have a sweat-house built — all finished."

" Where is it?" asked Tsaroki.

" I will show it to you soon," answered Waida Dikit.

Putting his hand behind him, he picked up a small basket, took out yellow paint with his thumb and forefinger, and drew a yellow streak from Tsaroki's head down his back. The young man had been all green ; now there was yellow on his back. Next Waida Dikit took a net woven of grass fibre, like a woman's hair net, and put it on Tsaroki's head. "You are ready now," said he. Then he led him out of the house and said, pointing to the west, —

"Look! There is our sweat-house. Now, my grandson, I am going to take you to that house. The east side is painted red. When we are there, don't go near the sweat-house on this eastern side ; pass by, but not too near, a little way off. When we go in I will take the eastern half and stay in it ; you will take the other half and stay on the western side, where there is green paint. That is where you are to lie, on the green side."

They started. The old man walked ahead. When they went in, Waida Dikit took the eastern half of the house and Tsaroki the western. The young man sat down, and then Waida Dikit took a pipe which was in the sweat-house.

"My grandson," said he, "you will find a pipe right there on your side of the house and a sack of tobacco. You may smoke if you wish."

Tsaroki took the pipe, looked at it, liked it well. This pipe was from Wai Hola Puyuk. When he drew in the smoke and puffed out the first whiff, the whole house was filled so that nothing was seen in it. Waida Dikit put his head outside the door. There was smoke outside everywhere. He could see nothing. Then he turned back and said, —

"My grandson, you are a good man. You are a

strong man. You smoke well. This will do for the first time. — If he does that again," thought the old man, " there will be nothing seen in this world; all will be covered with smoke; " and he said, " You are a strong man; that is enough for this time."

" I should like to know why he says, ' That is enough.' What does he want to do with me? " thought Tsaroki. " Maybe he is trying me in some way."

" My grandson," said the old man, after a while, " I should like to see somebody; I should like to see something, see people; I should like to have fun and see games of some sort."

" I should like to see them too," answered Tsaroki; " I should like to see them, my grandfather. You are older than I; if you tell me what to do, I will do it."

" My grandson, can you play on anything? "

" I should like to play if you would teach me," said Tsaroki.

The old man put his hand behind him into a basket of things, drew out a flute and gave it to Tsaroki, who took it quickly, he was so glad. He sat down, crossed his legs, and before he had blown into the flute, just as he touched his lips with it, beautiful sounds came out.

The young man was glad, wonderfully glad. The old man, who sat looking at him, asked, —

" How do you like the flute, my grandson? "

" I like it well," said Tsaroki.

" I am glad to hear you play, my grandson; I am glad when you do something good. When I was young, I used to say good things, I used to do good things. Now, my grandson, think what you would like best to do."

"I should like to hear something nice, to hear music, to hear beautiful sounds."

After he had taken the flute Tsaroki did not sleep; he played for three days and three nights without stopping; then he stopped and asked, —

"What is this flute? What is it made of? It sounds so sweetly."

"My grandson, I will tell you; that flute is of wood, — alder wood. That is an alder flute, but the wood is people's bones. There were people long ago, and that alder wood grew out of their bones. My grandson, would you like to have another young man with you, or do you wish to be alone? I think it would be better for you to have company."

"My grandfather, I should like to have another man with me; I could talk with him. I could live then more pleasantly."

"My grandson, to see another young man you must go to the west; you must go in the middle of the night, when it is very dark, so that no one may see you. My grandson, it is better for you to go to-night."

"Where? Which way do you want me to go, my grandfather?"

"Go west from here, far away; you will start when it is dark; you will get there in the dark. You will go to where the old woman Nomhawena Pokaila lives: she is your grandmother. When you

go to her house, ask her about your brother; she will
tell you where he is."

"My grandfather, I don't believe that I can find
her house. I don't know what kind of house it is."

"You cannot miss it, my grandson. The night
will be very dark; no one will be able to see anything, but you cannot miss the house. It is a little
house; no one can see it, but you cannot miss it.
You will go there very quickly, though 't is far from
here and the night is dark."

Then the old man showed him a small sand trail;
it was bright, just like a ray of light in the darkness,
though it was very narrow, as narrow as a hair, and
all around it was dark night. The old man had
made this trail purposely.

Tsaroki started, and could see the trail straight
ahead of him; he went over it as swiftly as an arrow
goes from a bow. He travelled right on, and at the
end of the trail, just on the trail itself, was a little bark
house. He went into this house, and saw an old
woman lying there with her back to the fire; she
was sleeping on the south side of it. He walked
in and stood at the north side. He sat down
then, and was sitting a while when the old woman
woke, turned her face to the fire, and saw some one
opposite. She rose, stirred the fire to make light,
looked at the young man, and said, —

"I see some person over there; who is it?"

"My grandmother, I am Tsaroki Sakahl. I have
come because my grandfather, Waida Dikit, sent me
to see you, so that you might tell me about my
brother. I should like to know where my brother

lives. I have come to see my brother and speak to him."

"Very well, my grandson, I will tell you. He lives right over here on the west."

As soon as she had finished speaking, Tsaroki stood up and went toward the west. He had not made many steps when he saw a large space, a broad space on which a great many people were sitting. The place was dark, but the people could see one another. Tsaroki saw all, and looked around carefully. He saw that all were at work except one man, who was sitting in the middle in a good place. He looked a long time, not knowing what to do, for Waida Dikit had said to him,—

"You must not let any one know but your brother why I sent you, and tell him not to tell others."

No one present saw Tsaroki, and he thought: "I don't know how I shall go to my brother without letting any one know." At last he made up his mind what to do. He went down under the ground where he had been sitting, and came up just in front of the great man, his brother.

The people were dressing skins, making arrow-points, and finishing arrows. All were at work but the man in the middle. Tsaroki came up in front of him and whispered,—

"My brother, I have come for you. My grandfather sent me to ask you to go to him and not to tell any one."

"That is well. I will go. Let us start."

That was all he said. This big man was Hawt.

Tsaroki had brought his flute, but he could not use it, for he had to keep his journey secret and not let himself be seen; he held the flute hidden under his arm.

"Let us go," said Hawt; "you go ahead."

Tsaroki went into the ground, came out where he had been sitting at first, and then went to the house of the old woman, his grandmother. Hawt stood up to make ready for the journey. The people kept on working. They were all of the Hawt people, and the big man was their chief.

Hawt dressed, and took his bow and arrows. When ready, he turned and said, —

"My people, I am going to leave you, to be gone two or three days, perhaps longer."

That was all he said; he did not say where he was going, nor why. He walked away and went to Nomhawena's house, where Tsaroki was waiting. The two brothers had been sitting just a little while when the old woman said to them, —

"Now, my grandsons, you must go; you must be at Waida Dikit's before daylight; you must travel while it is dark, we do not wish to let other people know of your journey. Go. I shall be in this house, but shall hear all that is happening at your place."

They left the old woman, and reached Waida Dikit's before daylight. The old man was up already, and standing by the fire in the middle of the sweat-house combing his red hair, which touched his feet. The moment he went into the house Tsaroki took his flute, lay on his back, and began to play. Hawt stood a while; did n't know where to sit. At last Waida Dikit said to him, —

"My grandson, I am living here in a small house. There is n't much room in it, but go north of the fire and sit there."

Just as Hawt was sitting down at the appointed side, daylight came. Tsaroki played two nights and two days. Hawt lay in his place and listened.

"My grandson," said Waida Dikit to Tsaroki, "I should like to hear you both play. You must give that flute to Hawt some of the time."

Tsaroki gave the flute to his brother, and from time to time they passed it from one to the other. Both played; both made beautiful music. They played day after day, night after night, ten days and ten nights.

"You play well now, both of you, my grandsons. Would you not like to hear other persons play?"

"Oh, we should like that very much; we should like to hear other persons play," said Tsaroki and Hawt.

"I used to hear a friend of mine long ago," said Waida Dikit, "and he played very well. Would you like to have him play with you?"

"Yes, yes; maybe he would teach us to play better."

"My friend is very old now," said Waida Dikit: "he is Kanhlalas Kiemila."

"I will go and bring him," said Tsaroki.

"Go, my grandson. I will show you a trail, but do not go near the east side of my sweat-house. It is not far. Kanhlalas lives northeast from here."

Tsaroki found Kanhlalas's sweat-house on the trail. He heard music inside, beautiful music. He stood awhile listening, then went in and saw an old man lying on his back playing. The old man stopped playing, but did not speak. Tsaroki touched him on the shoulder and said, —

"My grandfather, I have come for you. Waida Dikit, my grandfather, sent me to ask you to visit him."

"I will go," was all that the old man said. No questions were asked or answered. "I have come for you," "I will go;" no more. Those people of long ago talked in that way; they did n't talk much.

Tsaroki went home. Kanhlalas made ready to go, and went under the ground. Waida Dikit was lying in his house when on a sudden Kanhlalas rose at his feet. Waida Dikit sat up when he saw him, took a pipe, and told him to smoke. Kanhlalas smoked, and the two old men talked a good while. The young men played, first one, then the other. It was dark in the sweat-house, but after Kanhlalas came he shone and gave light like a torch in a dark house. You could see some, but not very much. Kanhlalas was a grandfather of Waida Werris.

"I sent for you," said Waida Dikit, "for I thought you might teach my grandsons to play better. They like to make music. They think of nothing else."

"I am old," said Kanhlalas. "I am not as I used to be. I cannot play much now. When I was a boy, when I was young, I could play. But I will play a little."

About dark he said a second time, "I will play a

little." So he lay on his back, took his own flute, which he had brought with him, and began. The two brothers lay and listened. Kanhlalas never took the flute out of his mouth from the dark of evening until daylight. Next day he played, and all night again. When morning came there was a light stripe down his breast, and when the sun rose his breast was white, for the breath was nearly out of his body. That morning old Waida Dikit said, —

"Now we will invite all people in the world who can play, to come here."

"If you invite all people in the world who can play," said Tsaroki, "this house will be too small for them."

"No," said the old man, "it will not be too small. You will find it large enough when they come."

Tsaroki was sent to the northwest to invite people. He went very fast. In a little while he was at a place just this side of where the sky touches the earth. He went to Nop Hlut. When near the sweat-house he heard stamping in a dance. He went in and saw a very big house full of people sitting around at the wall. Only one woman and a young girl were dancing in the middle of the house, Nop Pokte and Nop Loimis. The girl was very small, and had fawn's feet tied behind her head. These rattled so sharply that you could hear them when far away. As Tsaroki was coming in through the door on the south, he saw an old man lying on the north side. This was Nop Kiemila, the master of the house. Tsaroki went straight to him, put his hand on his shoulder, and said, —

"I have come for you."

"What kind of call do you make?" asked Nop.

"My grandfather is going to have a playing on flutes."

"I will go," said Nop.

"My grandfather is inviting people from all parts of the world. All will be invited who can play on the flute."

Waida Dikit himself went south to invite people living in the water, and sent Tsaroki to invite all the land people. They went far and near to invite all. After a time both grew wearied, and wanted to get some one to take invitations. They thought who would be best in heat and cold, light and darkness, and thought that Kinus would be; so they called him, and hired him to go.

Kinus went as far as he could go, went around the whole world to a distance a little this side of where the sky comes down. After a time he returned and said, —

"This world is wide and big. I called all the people as far as I went, but I was not able to go everywhere, — this world goes farther than I went. Whole days I could get no water, no food; but I invited all the people that I saw."

Now, while Kinus was speaking the invited people were listening; and there were many of them then at Waida Dikit's. Lutchi sat at one side and listened.

" There is," said Waida Dikit, "a man that we should like to see here. Waida Werris and also a man who lives far in the East, Patkilis; he lives behind the sky, beyond the place where the sky touches the earth, and Sedit lives with him. We want these three. Now Kinus cannot go to them, — nobody that we know is able to go to them. What shall we do?"

All talked about this. Lutchi sat back in silence, and listened to what they were saying.

" This sweat-house is too small," said Kanhlalas.

" You will see," answered Waida Dikit.

The sweat-house was spreading out, growing gradually, growing all the time as the people came. A great many came that afternoon. The house extended now as far as the eye could see. Whenever new people came, Waida Dikit would blow and say, " I wish this house to be larger!" And the house stretched, became wider and longer and higher. In the evening great crowds were there already.

Kinus and the rest talked all night and the next day. " Nobody can go to Waida Werris, Patkilis, and Sedit. That was what they said."

They asked all present, and each answered, "I cannot go to them." They talked and talked. At last one man said to another, "Let's ask that Lutchi Herit over there; maybe he can go." A third said, "Yes, let's ask him." And the three said to Waida Dikit, " Ask that little man; perhaps he can go." "He is small," said Waida Dikit, "but I will ask him." He went up to Lutchi, touched him on the shoulder, and asked, —

"My grandson, can you do something for me? You are small, but I am asking you."

Lutchi said nothing; just raised his brows, which meant "Yes." As soon as he did this, Waida Dikit put his hand under his arm and took out a kunluli (a delicate blue flower that grows near the water), and gave it to Lutchi. Lutchi took it in his open palm, looked at it, rubbed it between his two hands, spat on it, and made a paste which was a beautiful blue paint. Then he rubbed his face, arms, breast —he became blue all over (to this day Lutchi is blue, he was white before). He went out among the people then, and said,—

"People, look at me! What do I look like? Have n't I a nice color now?"

"You are beautiful," said the people. "You look well."

It was at the point of daybreak. They could see just a bit of light. When he was ready to start, Lutchi said,—

"I don't know how far it is, but if I go to those places I shall be back here at sunrise. If they are very far away, I shall be here when the sun is as high as the tree-tops."

"Do you think you will be back by sunrise?" asked Kinus. "Those places are very far away."

"I know they are far away," said Lutchi.

"I have been all over the world," added Kinus. "I was gone a long time, but those places are farther away than any spot where I have been."

"Ho! Now I am going!" said Lutchi; and he

darted straight up into the sky, next down, and up and down again. Then he called out, —

"How do you like that? Do you think I can go to those people? This is the way I travel."

He shot away east and returned. Then he went west and came back in a twinkle. Next he turned north and was gone. He had never travelled through the air before. Till that morning he had always walked on the ground, just as we do now. He went straight to Waida Werris's house and went in. It was dazzling there, and seemed to him just as bright as daylight seems to a man coming out of a dark place.

Lutchi saw some one inside, who was young and beautiful. He could not look at his face, it was so bright. There were two brothers in the house. The younger was Waiti, the elder Waida Werris. Waiti never left the house; never went abroad or wandered, stayed at home all the time.

"I have come," said Lutchi, "to invite you to meet people from all the world at a flute-playing in Waida Dikit's sweat-house."

"I will go," said Waida Werris. He knew all that was going on. He had seen it while travelling early, before daylight.

"I am going now," said Lutchi to Waida Werris. And as soon as he was outside he rushed off toward the west, came back, rose in the air, came down, and then shot away, like a lightning flash, eastward to find Patkilis and Sedit. Soon he was in the east, where the sky comes to the earth. He took a sky stick, which he had brought with him, pried up the sky, raised it a little, and then he went under to the other side. When the sky came down again behind him and struck the earth, it made an awful noise which was heard over the world. The whole world shook. All the people at Waida Dikit's heard the noise and wondered.

"What can that be?" asked they. "What awful noise is that?" Waida Dikit knew what the noise was, but he never told any one.

Lutchi went straight east from the other side of the sky, and never stopped till he found Patkilis and Sedit. They were in another world, another sky came down to their world, and they lived almost at the edge of that second sky. Lutchi went into their sweat-house. They were sitting just inside the door, one at one side, the other at the other; the door was on the east side. When Lutchi had sat a little while, Sedit rose and said, —

"My grandson, which way have you come?"

"I come here for you and Patkilis," answered Lutchi. "Waida Dikit sent me to invite you to a flute-playing at his sweat-house. Nobody else could come to you, so he asked me to come."

"We are glad," answered they. "We will go. You go ahead. But how shall we pass the sky?"

"I will wait at the edge for you," said Lutchi; and he went on.

When Sedit and Patkilis were ready, Sedit said, "I wish this road on which I must travel to be short, very short."

They started, and found the road so short that

Lutchi was waiting at the edge of the sky only a little while when they were with him. Lutchi pried up the sky a second time, and the three passed under to the western side. Again there was an awful noise, and the whole world trembled.

"Now I am going quickly; you can move as you like," said Lutchi. He went west like a flash, and just as the sun was peeping over the mountains he was back at Waida Dikit's.

"Have you heard what is going on in this world that makes such a noise?" asked Waida Dikit. "These people heard an awfully big noise."

"That was my travelling," said Lutchi. "Kinus, whom you sent first, could not go to those three people. I went. They are on the road, and will be here in a few days."

All the people heard this and were glad.

"Now we shall hear great music," said they.

While travelling along together, Patkilis spoke to Sedit and advised him. "When we are in Waida Dikit's house," said he, "don't talk much. Sit down like a wise man and look on; be silent; don't act like a little boy."

Sedit was talking all the time. He told Patkilis what he was going to do. He would do this and do that, he said.

Two days passed, and the two men had not come. On the third day, near the middle of the forenoon, people saw a beautiful little arrow come down just by the door of the sweat-house, — a bright arrow. When it struck the ground, it made a grating noise, and they said, —

"That is a nice arrow.   Who sent such an arrow?"   And all liked it.

There were crowds of people in the sweat-house. Some of them wanted the arrow.   "Let's pull it up!" said they, "and see who made it;" but Waida Dikit would not let them touch it.   "Let it stay where it is.   Do not touch it," said he, for he knew that it was Patkilis's arrow, and that it meant : "I am coming.   I shall be there soon."

While the people were talking about the arrow, two men swept in through the door.   No one saw their faces or their heads, just their legs and shadows.

"Give them room, let them in," said Waida Dikit.

"Where can they sit?" asked Tsaroki.

"Give each a place on the east side," said Waida Dikit.

The two, Patkilis and Sedit, went to the east side and sat down.   Nobody had seen Waida Werris come, but he was in the house.

When leaving home that morning, Waida Werris said to Waiti, his brother, —

"You will stay and keep house, as you do always. You will be here, but you will see me all the time, you will see me night and day.   Watch me; they will do other things there besides playing on flutes."

Patkilis and Sedit asked Waida Dikit if Waida Werris had come.

"I do not know where he is," replied the old man.   "No one has seen him."

"Oh, he will not come," said many people. "What kind of a person is Waida Werris?   He is nobody.   What do we want of him?"

Waida Werris was sitting there all the time listening. Waida Dikit knew well what kind of person he was, but said nothing. That night after all invited people had come, Waida Dikit said:

"Listen, all you people here present. I have called this gathering to find who is the best flute-player, who can make the best music in this world. Let us begin. Let each play alone."

Tsaroki began the trial. "I will begin," said he to his brother Hawt, "then let the others play. You can play when you like."

"I am satisfied," said Hawt. "I will play last."

"That is well," answered Tsaroki. "I will play first, all will follow, and you may play last."

Tsaroki began. He played a little while, not long; played well. Kanhlalas played next. All liked his music. Watwut Kiemila played third; played splendidly.

"Go ahead and play, all you people," said Waida Dikit.

Tsileu Herit played best up to his time, played till almost morning, till just before daylight. The inside of the sweat-house had become red, and some asked, —

"Why is it red everywhere inside the sweat-house?"

"We do not know," answered others; "something makes it red."

One man went up to Waida Dikit and asked, "Why is it red inside the sweat-house?"

"I will tell you. Do you see Tsileu Herit there? Well, he has been playing all night, the breath is gone out of him, he is all red, and the whole sweat-house is red from him."

About daylight Tsileu stopped, and then it grew as dark as in a house when a fire is put out in the night. Now Tsaik played all day, and at sundown the sweat-house was blue, for Tsaik had grown blue.

All played to see who could play best. Every kind of people played. When any one was out of breath, he stopped playing, and received a new color. When Murope lost breath, he was spotted. When Handokmit lost breath, he became striped. Patkilis played three nights and two days, and when he gave out after sundown, he was roan. Wai Hau played five nights, and at sunrise the fifth morning he was red. Kiriu Herit played five nights, and at the middle of the sixth night he was black, and his breath gone.

And so for many days and nights they played, one person after another, till one night all had finished except Hawt. Hawt was the last to play. All were asleep now. All had lost breath, and received new colors. Tsaroki went to his brother on the north side of the house, and said, —

" Begin, my brother; over near the fire there is a place for you; go under the ground, and when you come out, you will play."

Hawt went under the ground, and came out near the fireplace. He lay on his back and began to play. He had two rows of holes in his body, one on each side; he fingered these holes, drew in air through his nostrils, and sent it out through the holes in both sides. Hawt was playing on his own body. At first, all the people were asleep, except one person, Tsudi Herit. Tsudi heard Hawt, and he heard, as in a doze, wonderful sounds. He listened a long time, thinking it a dream. When Tsudi found that he was not sleeping, he shook the man next him, and said, —

"Wake up, wake up! Who is playing? All have played, but I have never heard music like this. Many have played here, but no one played in this way."

The person he roused was Hus. Hus said nothing, he was old and nearly bald, he took a pipe and began to smoke. Tsudi roused other people, one after another.

"Wake up, rise, sit up; listen to the music somebody is playing."

They woke, one after another. "Who is playing?" asked one. "Who is it?" asked another. "We have played many days and nights, but no one played like that. All have their own flutes. Who can this be?"

At last some one said: "I know who is playing. It is Hawt."

"How could Hawt play?" asked others. "Whose flute has Hawt? He has none of his own. Each of us brought a flute, but Hawt brought none. Whose flute has he now?"

Every one heard the wonderful music, and every one said, "We should like to see the man who plays in this way."

It was night, and dark in the sweat-house. All began to say how much they wanted light to see who was playing.   Waida Werris was lying back in the east half of the sweat-house, and heard every word.   He, too, wanted to look at the player.   He sat up, pulled one hair out of his beard, gave it to Tsudi, and said, —

"Go down near that man who is playing, and hold up this hair so that people may see him."

Tsudi took the hair and went along quietly.   No one heard him.   He held the hair over Hawt's head, and there was a light from it that filled the whole house.   It was as bright as day there.   All the people were seen sitting up, each hugging his flute.   No man would lend his flute to any one else in the world for any price.   All were looking toward the spot whence the music came.   In the light they saw a man lying on his back with his arms across his breast, but they could not see that he was doing anything.   He had no flute, he made no motion with his mouth, for he fingered his sides as he would a flute, and made the music by drawing in air through his nostrils, and sending it out through the holes in his sides.

Tsudi held up Waida Werris's single hair, and people watched Hawt to see how he made the beautiful music.   He was lying on his back making wonderful sounds.   He played the music of Tsaik's song, of Waida Werris's song, of Tsaroki's song. They could hear the music, but there was no motion of Hawt's mouth and they could not see his fingers play.   He gave the music of Patkilis's song and of Sedit's.   He gave the music of the songs of all people in the sweat-house.

"Hawt has beaten the world!" cried the assembly. "He can do more than we can; we yield, we are silent. Hawt is the best player in the world! No one can play as he plays!"

Hawt gave his own music next. No one knew that music but him, no one could play it but him. There was no other music so loud and strong, no other music so soft and low.

When the people had watched Hawt a long time and listened a long time, he stopped. All cried out then,—

"Hawt is the one great musician, the only great player on earth!"

Tsudi put down the hair and all were in the dark. He carried the hair back and gave it to Waida Werris.

People began to talk and ask one another: "Where did that light come from; whose is it?" One said Tsudi had it; another said, "No, he never had a light like that." "Who gave it to him?" asked a third. "Some one must have given it to Tsudi. Let us ask him about this."

Here and there people said: "Only Waida Werris could make such a light. What kind of person is Waida Werris? We should like to see Waida Werris."

"I have never seen Waida Werris, but I have heard people tell how nice looking he is, and that he can be seen from afar," said Patkilis. "If he were here he might make such a light, but he is not here, or we should all see him right away."

Waida Werris was lying near them, and heard all they said.

"Let us ask Waida Dikit," said Karkit Kiemila, a big man, lying on the west side, facing Waida Werris; and he began to talk to Waida Dikit.

"The people wish to see Waida Werris," said he. "You have invited all people in the world, and you have invited him. What will you do? Is he here? Will you let every one see him?"

"Oh, no," said one old man. "Waida Werris is bad. I don't want to see him." "We have heard that he is good," said others. "We want to see him." So they were divided.

Waida Werris smoked a while in silence. At last Waida Dikit bent toward Patkilis and Sedit and asked, —

"What do you think, shall I let people see Waida Werris or not?"

"They want to see him," answered the two. "You have invited them and invited him. If people wish to see Waida Werris, let them see him."

"Where shall I let them see him?"

"Let all the people go outside the sweat-house," said Patkilis, "and stand in two long rows, one on each side of the door, and let Waida Werris go out between them. If he goes out, every one can look at him; only a few would see him inside the house."

"Very well," answered Waida Dikit. "Now all you people go outside the house."

Tsaroki opened the door, and went out first. All

followed, each saying as he went, "It is dark: we shall not see Waida Werris."

"You can see him in the dark," said Waida Dikit. "Join hands, all of you, and go around to the north side of the sweat-house."

"Go you," said Waida Dikit to Tsudi, "and search inside. Tell me when all the people are out."

Tsudi searched everywhere. "All have gone out," said he.

Waida Dikit closed the door and said: "Some of you people are sleepy, but wake up, open your eyes, be ready to see — look north."

"What can we do here? Why did we come out in the dark?" asked a certain Chirchihas. "We can see nothing at this time of night;" and, turning to Lutchi, he asked: "Have you seen him, or his brother? What sort of a place do they live in?"

"I cannot tell you now; you will see him soon."

"Be ready, all of you," said Waida Dikit. "Look north."

All looked. There was a pointed mountain not far away, and straight out before them. They saw a small light rising till it reached the top of that mountain; there it settled, and soon it seemed near them, just a few steps from the faces of the people. That was Waida Werris. The place around was as if in daylight. All could see him; all looked at him.

"Now, you people, there is Waida Werris before you; do you see him?"

"We see him."

"Hereafter all people will see him there in the north, as you see him now," said Waida Dikit. "Come back to the sweat-house, all of you."

Tsaroki opened the door, and all went in. "We will talk," said the old man, "then eat, and after that separate."

Day had come — there was light in the sweat-house. They heard some one coming, and soon they saw an old woman in the door. This was Tunhlucha Pokaila. She would not go in, but stood a while holding in both hands two beautiful baskets of water. These she put down at the door, looked in, and went away. Waida Dikit took the baskets, put them on the ground north of the fire, and said, —

"Here is a little water, but come all and use it, —wash."

The old woman was Waida Dikit's sister; she lived north of her brother's, not far away. There was a rock at that place, with a spring in it. The rock was her house. Water rose in that rock to the surface and went into the earth again in another part of the same house. The old woman had two baskets; the smaller one held water for drinking, the larger one water for washing. Great crowds of people drank from the smaller basket and washed from the other; each used what he needed, the water never grew less; it remained the same always in quantity.

"Have all washed and drunk?" asked Waida Dikit.

"We have all washed and drunk."

The old man removed the baskets, and set out two others which the old woman had just brought, — one of cooked venison, and another a very small basket of acorn porridge. He put the baskets in the middle of the sweat-house and said, —

"Now, all people, I ask you to eat."

"I will try that food," said Karkit. He went and ate. Next Hus ate, then Yipokos. Now these three men ate deer meat since that time, and will always find meat by the smell, — this was the first time they ate venison. Tsihl and Wima, called also Bohemba, ate all they could from the little basket, yet the food was not less by one bit. Patit ate plenty. Hus ate, and so did Sedit. All ate as much as they could; still each basket was full. The food grew no less. Waida Dikit kept saying, —

"You people, here is food. I do not need it. Come and eat what there is."

He sent Tsudi around to ask each man if he had eaten. All said they had eaten till Tsudi went half around, when he found one man, Memtulit, who said that he had not eaten, but was willing to eat.

"I will eat if I see anything good," said he.

"Well, go and eat," said Tsudi.

"What kind of food have you?"

"Venison and acorn porridge."

"I do not eat that kind of food."

"Here is a man who has not eaten," said Tsudi; "he cannot eat that food."

Farther on was found Kiriu, who had not eaten,

and a third, a very young man, Tsararok. " I
should like to eat," said he, "but I am timid.
There are so many people here eating."

" What kind of food do you eat, Kiriu ? " asked
Tsudi.

" I cannot eat venison. I eat what lives in the
water." The other two men said the same.

Waida Dikit went to his old house, where he had
dried fish. He caught besides a net full of little
fish. He cooked both kinds and carried them to
the sweat-house, set them down in the middle, and
said, " Now come and eat."

Memtulit ate, so did Kiriu. Tsararok came after
a while. He began to eat the little fish, did n't see
the other kind; this is why Tsararok likes small
fish to this day.

The old man asked again, " Have all eaten? "

" We have," answered all.

There was as much food in the two baskets as at
first, and the old man put them outside the house.
Sedit saw this, and was angry. He said that people
should leave nothing.

" Don't talk so," said Patkilis. " What is done
is right."

" You are all free to stay longer," said Waida
Dikit, " but I suppose that you wish to go home,
I suppose you are in a hurry."

" Why should we go so soon? " asked Sedit.
" The people from the west might tell us what they
know ; we ought to tell them something."

" Keep quiet, Sedit," said Patkilis. " I told you
not to talk. There are many big men here, better

men than you, but they don't talk. Waida Dikit
says that we have stayed long enough ; that is what
he means ; you ought to know it. He spoke as he
did because he wished to say something nice to us
and be friends ; but you must keep still."

A man on the west side rose now and came
toward the middle of the house, near the fire, stood
there, looked about, and spat on the ground. All
the people saw him spit, and in an instant they saw
a small basket rise out of the spittle. Inside the
basket were acorns of mountain live oak. This man
was Patit. He went back to his place and lay down.
Waida Dikit set the basket in the middle of the
sweat-house, picked out an acorn, ate it, and said, —

"People, come and eat. My friend Patit has
made this for you, — this is his food."

They never had acorns of that kind till then.
Nop came first to the basket to eat, and to this
day he is fond of acorns. Then Tsihl and Wima
and Tichelis and Tsudi and Tsaik went to the basket
and ate, and all are fond of acorns now. No matter
how many they took from the basket, the acorns
were none the less.

Sedit sat back ill-natured ; he wanted them to
eat all the acorns. Waida Dikit put the basket
outside.

Tsihl rose now, went to the place where Patit had
spat, and put an empty basket on the ground. He
untied a wide strap, or braid of grass, which he wore
around his wrist, and held down his hand. Something flowed out of it, like water, till the basket was
filled. Then he tied up his wrist again. The basket

was full of seeds of sugar pine. Waida Dikit ate of them; then called all to eat. People came and ate all they wanted. The basket was as full as before. Sedit was very angry.

Hau came forward and put down a stone cup. He held his ear over it, scratched the ear, and out came a stream of manzanita berries. These were the first manzanita. No one had ever seen those berries in the world before. Waida Dikit ate a handful of the berries and sat down — said nothing. All the people hurried to eat, crowded around the cup, ate as long as they were able, but could not decrease the berries. Presently Waida Dikit began to itch. He did not know what troubled him. Soon spots came out all over his body — red, yellow, and black. This was because he had eaten the berries. His spirit was afraid of what he had eaten. His spirit did not wish that he should eat berries, they were not his kind of food; and that was why the spots came out on him. It was his spirit's fear that brought out the spots, and he has been spotted ever since. He ate not because he wished, but because he was master of the house. It was for him to taste everything, or people would think it bad food.

Now Wima came, put down a basket, and untied a white wristband which he wore, held his hand down, and wild plums dropped into the basket and filled it.

This time Waida Dikit sent Tichelis to taste the plums and set out the basket. People ate, but there were as many plums as before.

These different kinds of food were given to the world for the first time then, and this is why we have them now.

Tsaik came to the middle of the sweat-house. He tapped the ground with his nose, and out came a great pile of acorns.

Sedit had eaten as much as he could, and was angry because any was put away. He kept saying to Patkilis, " I don't like that."

" Sedit," answered Patkilis, " I have warned you against talking so much. Don't you know that after a while all the new kind of people, the people to come, will use food in this way, eat what they want, and put the rest away ? "

" You people have talked and been friendly," said Waida Dikit. " This is the food we need ; this will be our only food hereafter."

" Well," said Kanhlalas, standing up, " I think we have almost finished. If we stay here too long, some bad people may see us and talk about what we are doing."

Others said : " Yes, we have given all the food we have. If this gathering lasts longer, bad people may find us and make trouble."

" That is true," said the assembly ; " let us part."

" We will part," said Waida Dikit. " I am going to my old house and will stay there forever. If salmon come up the Wini Mem, they will come as far as my house and go back."

Next morning all set out for their homes. Tsihl changed his mind on the road, and went back to Tede Puyuk, where he found that all had gone except Sedit, Patkilis, Nop, and Hau.   These four were outside the sweat-house, and Tsihl said, —

"We have come back to look at this place again ; it pleases us."

They stayed awhile, travelled through the country, and when Olelbis sent people down here, coyotes, jack rabbits, deer, red-foxes, and black bear came to Tede Puyuk, and there were many of them ever after around that whole country.

NORWANCHAKUS AND KERIHA

NORWANCHAKUS AND KERIHA

PERSONAGES

After each name is given that of the creature or thing unto which the personage was changed subsequently.

Eltuluma, ——; **Hubit,** wasp; **Kériha,** ——; **Kuntihlé,** a small bird unknown; **Lasaswa,** large spider; **Nodal Mónoko,** ——; **Norwanchakus,** ——; **Norwinte,** ——; **Patkilis,** jack rabbit; **Pawnit,** kangaroo rat; **Pom Norwanen Pitchen,** daughter of the Southern Border, the same as **Norwan**; **Puriwa,** dark; **Supchit,** ——; **Sanihas,** daylight; **Tsaik,** blue jay; **Tsiwihl,** blue-breasted lizard; **Waida Werris,** polar star.

THE two brothers Norwanchakus and Keriha were on this earth before any place or thing had a name. When Olelbis took the sky pole and made a deep furrow from the foot of Bohem Puyuk to the lower valley, and a river came, the two brothers were at the end of the furrow and started toward the north. Norwanchakus was the elder; Keriha was very small.

When the brothers started, they could not see well. There was no sun then; there was only a kind of dim twilight. Waida Werris was in the sky, and saw the brothers. Fish had got into all rivers now from the southern pond, where Kuntihle Herit had caught the first fish.

"There are fish in the river," said Keriha; "let us catch some. Let us take a net up the river and come down with it."

"We have no net, and there is no light; we cannot see anything," said the elder brother.

"Go, my brother," said Keriha, "to where the sky comes down on the northwest; go out under it. You will find there the plant kúruti; bring it."

"I cannot go there," said Norwanchakus; "you go, my brother."

Keriha went through the air quickly; brought the plant — brought all there was.

"We must have more," said Norwanchakus.

"Well, go and get it," answered Keriha. "It grows beyond the sky in the southwest."

"I cannot go there; go you," said the elder brother.

Keriha went beyond the sky on the southeast; found plenty of kúruti. The elder brother made strings of the fibre.

"I am in a hurry to fish," said Keriha. "You are slow, my brother."

"Go straight east beyond the sky," said the other, "and get ash wood while I am making a net."

Keriha brought the ash. Norwanchakus had the net made, and now he fixed the ash stick.

"My brother," said Keriha, "we cannot see anything. How can we fish? There are people around us in the world, perhaps, but we have no good light to find them."

There was a kind of dim light all the time. The two brothers started, came north as far as Nomlopi, opposite Pas Puisono, and sat down.

Keriha heard voices in the north and asked, "Do you hear shouting?"

"No; I hear nothing," answered Norwanchakus.

"Let us go toward the shouting," said Keriha.

They went to a place about six miles beyond the river, where they found a sweat-house.

"These are the first people we have seen," said Keriha. "We shall call this place Tsarau Heril." They stood near the door of the sweat-house.

"Oh, my brother," said a big man who saw them and came to the door.

"Yes," said Keriha, "you are our brother, you are Norwinte."

Another came and said, "Oh, my brother!"

"You are our brother, too," said Keriha; "you are Eltuluma."

"It is dark. We do not know what to do," said Norwinte.

"And we do not know," answered Keriha.

"Not far from here are more people," said Norwinte. "Let us send to them to come here. Perhaps we may learn what to do."

Norwinte sent a messenger to the north. He brought a new person soon, a good-looking man; and when this stranger had talked a while he said, "There is a person in the southeast who can help us."

"Will you bring him here?" asked Norwinte.

"I cannot go there," said the stranger.

"You go, Keriha," said Norwanchakus. "No one can go there but you."

Keriha went, and was not long gone. He brought back Patkilis.

"My brother Patkilis, do you know of any more people anywhere?"

"I know of no more people.   I have seen none;
but in the far east I hear shouting, with dancing and
singing."

"Well, my brother, I wish you would go and see
what kind of people are making that noise there."

"I will go," said Patkilis.   "I don't think it is
very far from here to where they are."

Patkilis was gone a long time.   When he came
back, he said: "I saw many people, but they did
not see me.   There is a hill beyond the sky in the
east.   On the northern slope of it are houses.   On
the southern slope there are houses, also.   A river
flows from this hill westward.   South of the hill
every one is dancing.   I went into the houses on
the north side.   All were empty except one.   In
the middle house of the village I found a blind boy.
I looked around and saw much in the house.   'Why
have you so many things here?' asked I of the boy.
'What are they good for?   I live on the other side.
We haven't such things in our houses.'   He said
nothing.   I talked a long time to him, asked many
questions, but got no answer.   All he said was,
'My people have gone to dance.'   There were
piles of acorns inside and outside, great baskets of
them put around everywhere.   I sat down.   'What
is this?' asked I.   'What is that?   What is in
those baskets there?'   'Oh, something,' said the
blind boy; and that was all the answer he made.
There were many bags, all full of something.   I
saw two small bags hanging in the house, and they
were very full.   'What is in those small bags that
are so full?' asked I.   'Can you tell me, little

boy?' 'Why do you want to know everything?'
asked the blind boy. I asked about those two bags
in different ways, but he would n't tell me for a long
time. I teased him and teased him to tell. 'You
want to know everything,' said he, at last; 'I will
tell you. In one is Puriwa.' 'Well, what is in the
other bag? Tell me. You have told about one,
now tell about the other.' He thought a while
and asked, 'Why do you want to know so much?
Sanihas is in the other bag.' He would tell no
more, and I came away."

When Patkilis had told all this, Keriha said, after
thinking a while: "This is the best news that we
have heard in this world yet; some one of us ought
to go there. We must bring those two bags here.
If we open one, the world will be dark; if we
open the other, there will be daylight. Those
acorns, too, are good. You must send some one
for those two bags."

"There is a man up north here, Pawnit. He
could go; send for him," said Patkilis.

They sent for him, and he came. They told him
what they wanted.

"I can go for those things," said he, "but I don't
like to go alone. My brothers, you bring a man
here who lives up north, Tsaik. He is blind of
one eye."

When Tsaik came and heard about the acorns,
he said: "I should like to have them; they are
good. If I go, I will take the acorns, and you can
bring the two bags," said he to Pawnit.

"When you come to that hill in the east," said

Patkilis to Pawnit, "you will see many houses on the north side of it, and many on the south, where people are dancing; but go to the north, and right in the middle of the village you will see a big house, with the door toward the south. When you go in, don't let the blind boy know that there are two of you. Let one talk to him while the other takes the bags. The one talking will make him believe that he came from the south side of the hill, where people are dancing. When you are going in through the door, you will see the two bags right opposite, both smooth and very full. Get those bags, so that we can see what kind of place this is. We want plenty of light. We want darkness, too, so that there may not be too much light."

Pawnit and Tsaik started off on their journey. How long the journey lasted no one knows. They went beyond the sky and reached the eastern hill, they saw the villages south and north of it, and heard a great noise of dancing at the south. They went to the northern village, found the big house in the middle of it, and stopped before the door.

"Go in," said Tsaik. "I will stay outside. I have a strap. I am going to carry away the acorn baskets. You go in. I will stay here and tie them together."

Pawnit went in and sat down on the west side. The blind boy was lying on the east side.

"Well, blind boy," said Pawnit, "I am cold. I have been dancing. I have come here to warm myself."

"I should like to know why you people come

here while there is dancing at the other side," said the blind boy.

Pawnit made no answer, but went out to see what Tsaik was doing. "Where are you, Tsaik?" asked he.

"I am here making ready to carry acorns," answered Tsaik.

Just then they saw some one near them. "Who is this?" asked Pawnit.

"I am here," said Patkilis. "Come, Pawnit, you and I will go in and get the two bags. You, Tsaik, take the acorns."

Tsaik put a big load on his back and started on, while the others were in the house. Patkilis took daylight, and Pawnit took darkness. As soon as they were outside the house, the blind boy stood up and screamed, —

"Who was that? Some one has stolen something!"

He felt for the bags, then ran out and screamed, —

"Some one has stolen Puriwa and Sanihas! Some one has stolen Puriwa and Sanihas! Some one has stolen Puriwa and Sanihas!"

The people who were dancing heard him and said, "Some one is screaming!" Then they heard plainly, —

"Some one has stolen Puriwa and Sanihas! They have run west with them!"

When they heard this, the dancers stopped dancing and ran west. Soon they saw the three men racing off with the bags.

They saw Tsaik far ahead with a pack of acorns

on his back. They could see him a long way, for the pack was a big one. Pawnit and Patkilis carried their bags in their hands. The people ran fast and shouted to each other, —

"Catch them! Catch them! Do your best! Head them off! Surround them!"

They could not overtake Tsaik. He went through under the sky before they could come up.

When Pawnit and Patkilis were rising from under the edge of the sky, those behind were ready to seize Pawnit and would have caught him, but he tore open the mouth of his bag, and that instant thick darkness spread everywhere. No one could see; all were as if blind in one moment.

The eastern people had to stop. They could follow no farther. Patkilis knew the country west of the sky, and he and Pawnit stumbled on, came along slowly in the dark, and groped westward a good while. At last Patkilis opened his bag, and that moment daylight went out of it. They could see a great distance; they were very glad now, travelled quickly, and were soon at Norwinte's.

Keriha and Norwanchakus lived for a time with Norwinte (it is unknown how long), and then took their net and went up the river to fish downward. They went up Bohema Mem and Pui Mem as far as Panti Tsarau.

"Let us fish down from this, my brother," said Keriha. "I will hold the end of the net stick that goes out in the river, so that I may take the fish quickly when they are caught. You can go along the bank."

They fished down to Nomlupi, and Keriha
named all the places as he and his brother came
down. He gave them the names which they have
now, the names by which we Wintus call them.
The first place below Panti Tsarau was Lorus Pom
and Keriha left no place unnamed between Panti
Tsarau and Nomlupi. They stopped at Nomlupi,
built a brush house there, and lived some time
in it.

One day the two brothers went to Norwanbuli
to the great sweat-house where the woman Pom
Norwanen Pitchen or Norwan lived.

"My brother, you must not make this woman
angry," said Norwanchakus, when they were near
Norwanbuli. "This is a very powerful woman;
she has a great deal of food, a great deal to eat,
but you must not take anything; eat nothing
except what she gives; don't talk much; do just
what I tell you."

"I will do what you tell me," said Keriha.

They went in at the south side of Norwanbuli,
and stopped east of the door. Norwanchakus sat
down, and held Keriha between his knees. The
woman put her hand behind her, took acorn bread,
held it toward the brothers, and said, —

"Take this, you two men, eat it, and then go
away."

"This woman has a great deal to eat," said
Keriha. "Let's stay here a while with her. Let's
not go away, my brother."

"Be still," whispered Norwanchakus. "Don't
talk."

"My brother, I 'm hungry. Tell her to give us more bread. This is n't enough."

Norwanchakus barely tasted the bread, but Keriha ate with great relish. "Now, my brother," said Norwanchakus, "we must go. I will carry you." He put his brother on his back, drew Keriha's arms around his own neck closely, and started. When they were almost out of the house, Keriha began to struggle and kick.

"Let me go, my brother," said he, "let me go!"

Norwanchakus held him firmly. Keriha pulled and pulled till he got his right arm free. At the door was a large basket of acorns. He seized a handful of those and kept them. Norwanchakus went out, and when a short distance from the house he felt the ground swaying, rising, and falling. He stopped and saw the earth open around him and sink slowly. Then he made one great spring and came down on Bohem Buli. He was barely on that mountain when it began to crack, and he was sinking again. He made a second leap, and came down far away southwest.

Keriha dropped the acorns, and the earth stopped opening that moment. The brothers stayed some time in the southwest, then went to Tsik Tepji. This was a strong eddy of the river in which it was easy to catch salmon. They made a brush hut at the river bank, and a house not far from the river, on a hill. Norwanchakus caught a great many salmon, and Keriha ate and ate; he ate all the time and never grew larger. Norwanchakus scarcely ate anything. One morning Keriha was in the house

while his brother was fishing. A stranger came, a
very small man, no larger than a boy five years
old. Keriha looked at him, then jumped up and
ran to his brother.

"Oh, my brother," said he, "some one has come
to our house." Norwanchakus said nothing.
"There is some one at our house," repeated Keriha.

"Did he say anything?" asked Norwanchakus.

"No."

"Did you talk to him?"

"No."

"Why not?"

"I don't like him, he is so little."

"Never mind, go back and give him something
to eat; call him uncle."

Keriha went back and stared at the stranger.
After a while the little man looked up and asked, —

"Why do you look at me so? I left a small bag
of roots north of the house. Would you bring it
here? The roots are very good to eat."

Keriha went. The bag was small. There were
roots in one corner of it, not many. He snatched
at the bag, but could not lift it; he tried with both
hands, could n't stir it; tried every way, could n't
move it; scratched his arms and legs in trying, left
the bag, and went back without it.

"I cannot lift that bag," said he to the little man.
"How did you bring it, you are so small?"

The stranger, who was Nodal Monoko, went out,
brought the bag to the house in one hand, and put
it down outside. Norwanchakus knew who the
stranger was, and he brought up a great sturgeon.

Keriha cooked the fish, put it down before their guest, and said, " Eat this."

The little man said nothing, waited till the fish was cool, then raising it to his mouth in one hand, he swallowed all at a mouthful.

Keriha cooked for the little man all the forenoon, while Norwanchakus was fishing. About midday their wood was nearly all burned.

" My uncle," said Keriha, "we are going to cook a great deal of fish. Would you help me and bring wood ? "

The little man said nothing.

" My uncle, will you bring wood for me ? " asked Keriha.

The stranger sat a while, then went out to a mountain, took the largest dry trees, pulled them up by the roots with one hand, put a great many in a pile, and tore up two young green trees; with these he bound the dry ones, and took them on his shoulder to Keriha.

Now Keriha saw what kind of person the little man was. He cooked salmon and sturgeon till midnight without stopping, and still the little man was hungry. Keriha cooked fish the whole night, and Nodal Monoko ate till daylight.

Norwanchakus came up from the river next morning and said to the little man, who looked as if he had eaten nothing, —

" My uncle, you wish to go home, I suppose. If you want fish, fill your bag; it will hold a couple of good ones. The fish did not come up last night very well, but I can give you enough to fill your bag."

So saying, Norwanchakus went back to the fish-
ing-place. Nodal Monoko went out and emptied
his bag. When the roots were thrown out, there
was a pile of them many times higher and bigger
than the house. It covered all the open space,
while some roots rolled down the hillside and fell
into the river.

Nodal Monoko's bag would hold mountains.
He could put the whole world into it. Nodal took
his bag to the river, where Norwanchakus had been
fishing all night, and saw salmon in piles there.

"Take all the salmon you can," said Norwanchakus.

The stranger put two hundred salmon in one
corner of his bag, two hundred more in the other,
two hundred in the middle — all large fish — and
the bottom of the bag was hardly covered. He
twisted the top of the bag then, and tied it. Nodal
Monoko had a beaver-skin quiver. In this he was
carrying five great baskets of acorns, each basket
holding three bushels, and these acorns filled only
the very tip of the beaver tail.

He went down to the river to swim across.

"He cannot cross the river with that bag and
quiver," said Keriha.

At the edge of the water Nodal Monoko took
the bag and quiver in one hand, and swam across
with the other.

The two brothers stayed fishing at Tsik Tepji
till a day when Keriha said, "Let us go up the
river, my brother." They went to Bohem Tehil
and stopped at a large tree. Keriha hung a salmon

on a limb of it. " I will watch this fish," said he " I 'll see if Hubit comes here to eat it."

He watched that day from dawn till dark; no one came. He watched five days more; no one. Five other days, and five days more, and then five days, — twenty-one in all; he saw no one.

Next morning he was waiting, when all at once he heard a noise, and looking he saw Hubit come from the west and go to the salmon. Norwanchakus sat some distance away, watching Keriha.

" Oh, my brother," cried Keriha, " Hubit has come. He is at the salmon. What shall I do? I want to know where Hubit lives, I want to see his house. I must follow him."

" My brother," answered Norwanchakus, "you say that you know more than I. You think that you know everything. You must know what to do with Hubit."

" Oh, my brother," said Keriha, " do not tease me. Tell me quickly what I am to do with Hubit."

" Go straight south to a level place, get a pawit, and bring it. I will watch Hubit while you are gone."

Keriha brought some pawit quickly. " Now what shall I do? "

" Stick one tuft in the salmon's tail, and fasten it well," said Norwanchakus. " Let Hubit carry off the fish. You can see the tuft far away, and follow."

Keriha fastened the tuft to the salmon, gave the fish to Hubit, and watched. Hubit would n't bite, would n't taste. Keriha tried all day to make him taste the salmon, tried a second day, tried five days. Hubit would n't even bite it. On the sixth day Keriha said, —

"Hubit, why are you here? I thought you came to eat salmon, but now you will not taste it."

Keriha talked five days more to Hubit, ten days in all. "Hubit, I wish you would eat some fish and take home the rest." Hubit made no answer.

Five days more Keriha teased him, and then five days longer, twenty days in all.

"Hubit," said Keriha on the twenty-first day, "tell me what you are going to do; I'd like to know;" and he pushed him. Not a word from Hubit. "Are you asleep or dead?" asked Keriha. "Hubit, you make me so angry that I want to kill you."

All these days Keriha had watched Hubit from daylight till dark, giving him no chance to steal the fish, and Hubit wanted salmon so much that he would not go without it. Norwanchakus sat watching Keriha.

"My brother," said Keriha, "I cannot make that Hubit take the salmon; what shall I do? Tell me."

Norwanchakus said nothing.

"I am getting angry. If you cannot tell me what to do, I will kill Hubit to-morrow."

"Why kill Hubit? You have teased him a long time; tease him a little longer. How will you find Hubit's house, if you kill him?"

"Hubit, will you bite this salmon?" asked

Keriha, next morning. "I have bothered long enough. Will you bite to-day?" He put the salmon to Hubit's mouth. Hubit bit a little. Keriha lifted the salmon with Hubit on it, and threw it in the air to make Hubit fly. All came down like a stone. Keriha threw it a second time. It fell again. He tried all day.

"I don't know what kind of man that Hubit is; he won't eat, he won't talk, won't go home, won't do anything," said Keriha.

Next morning he said to Hubit: "Hubit, what kind of person are you? I wish you would go home."

But Hubit would n't go without the salmon, and would n't take it for fear that Keriha would follow him. Keriha threw him up again with the salmon. Again he fell with the salmon, and he teased Hubit for five days more. On the sixth morning Hubit began to eat.

"Ah, you are eating!" said Keriha; "will you go to-day?"

He threw the salmon; it fell again. Five days more he tried. Hubit would eat, but would n't fly. Now he had tried twenty days more. On the twentieth evening he said to Norwanchakus, "I will kill Hubit to-morrow."

"Oh, you are not angry," said Norwanchakus. "Play with him a little longer. You want to know everything, to see everything, to have everything. You ought to find out what he means; he has some reason for doing as he does."

Next morning Keriha went to Hubit. "Will

you tell me what you are going to do? Unless you tell me I will kill you. When I throw you up, I will kill you unless you fly."

He threw up the salmon. Hubit moved his wings and flew along a little above the ground, then settled down.

"Oh, he is going now, he is going! I'm so glad," cried Keriha; and he threw the salmon a second time.

Hubit opened his wings and flew around Keriha, flew around the tree.

"Go, go!" cried Keriha, clapping his hands.

Hubit shot away toward the north, near the ground, and Keriha ran with all speed, but Hubit went far ahead; then he flew a little toward the west, turned, and darted off directly northward.

Keriha did not lose sight of him, but rose in the air and flew north, going parallel with Hubit and going faster. He was at the sky first. A moment later Hubit came.

"I am here before you!" cried out Keriha. "You cannot go out here!"

Hubit flew around a while and shot back to Bohem Tehil. Keriha was just behind him.

"Hubit, you are so slow," called out Keriha. "I want to go fast, I like to see you go fast."

Hubit flew around the tree a little, then darted to the south. Keriha went a little to one side, was at the south before him, clapping his hands.

"No escape on this side, Hubit; I am here before you."

Hubit turned to Bohem Tehil. From the tree

he rushed east to where the sky comes down. Keriha was there before him. He rushed to the west, to where the sky comes down. Keriha was there before his face, barring the way. Hubit had been at all four points, — no escape at any of them; still he would n't drop the salmon. He turned a fifth time to Bohem Tehil with Keriha behind him. He flew around the tree a few times, then rose straight in the air, carrying the salmon. He rose quickly, went very high. Keriha stood looking at Hubit, watched him growing smaller and smaller. Keriha shaded his eyes.

Hubit was nearly out of sight. Keriha could barely see him with the salmon and the tuft, a little spot in the sky. He looked very hard, strained his eyes till blood was running down both his cheeks; still he kept looking.

Hubit thought he was out of sight now, and soon Keriha saw him turn to the west and come down. When he was above Bohem Buli, he dropped straight to it on the north side and went in.

" I 'm glad, I 'm glad. Oh, I 'm so glad!" cried out Keriha, clapping his hands. " I know now where Hubit's house is. Get ready quickly, my brother, we will go and see Hubit. Oh, you are so slow, my brother, I can't wait for you. Come when you can; I 'll go on alone."

Keriha hurried to Bohem Buli. Norwanchakus followed, and saw Keriha doing strange things; did n't know what he was doing; wondered at him. He was dodging from side to side, lying down and springing up again. Norwanchakus went toward him.

"What are you doing?" cried he. "What is the matter!"

"Don't come so near," called Keriha. "Stop, stop!"

When Hubit dropped down to his house in Bohem Buli, he began that minute to make it bigger. He was hurling out immense rocks, and Keriha was dodging them. They came quickly one after another (there are many of those rocks now all around Bohem Buli, at Puitiel Ton, at Waikidi Pom, and on the west beyond Tayam Norel). After the rocks Hubit hurled out great showers of earth; then he stopped.

"How shall I get at that Hubit?" asked Keriha of his brother.

"Go south to a level valley where sakkus grows. Get the tops of that plant."

Keriha brought plenty of sakkus tops quickly.

"Go now to Halat Pom, in the east, and bring the longest vines possible."

Keriha brought ten very long vines and made a rope of them, and tied it around a great bundle of sakkus tops, to which he set fire, and then lowered the bundle. He stopped the door with grass and sticks. Soon there was a great rumbling, struggling, and roaring in Hubit's house. After a while it stopped and all was still.

"Now, my brother," said Keriha, "Hubit is dead, and I am going to have his honeycombs."

He took a large sharp stone, drew a great circle around the entrance to Hubit's house, and said: "You, Hubit's honeycomb, be as large as this circle is. Now, my brother," said he, "you can go to Bohem Tehil. I will come soon."

Norwanchakus went home. Keriha began to dig, found many combs, dug till night, stayed all night in Hubit's house — stayed there digging honey and eating, for twenty-five days.

Norwanchakus waited at home for his brother, waited that evening till midnight, waited till morning, saw no sign of Keriha. He waited the next day; then two, three, five days; then twenty days more.

" Well," said Norwanchakus, " I can do nothing. Perhaps he is dead, perhaps he is working yet."

On the twenty-sixth night after Hubit's death, some one came into the house. Norwanchakus looked up. It was Keriha.

After that the two brothers went to Puri Buli. At the foot of the mountain they saw some one half sitting, half lying, and looking at them. When they came nearer, it went into an opening.

" My brother," said Keriha, " I want that."

" Nothing can pass you," said the elder brother. " You want everything. You would better let this go."

Keriha paid no heed to Norwanchakus: he split the earth with his little finger and killed the stranger, a Supchit. He skinned the body and said, " I think that this skin will be warm; I will sleep on it."

" My brother," said Norwanchakus, "you are the only person who has ever killed a Supchit — you may be sorry."

Next morning a terrible snow came. It snowed five days and nights; everything was buried under

snow. Keriha and Norwanchakus lay twenty-one
days under the snow without food. On the twenty-
first night, the Supchit woman whom Keriha had
killed came and stole him away.

Next morning Norwanchakus looked outside.
Keriha was gone; the snow was gone. He looked
for tracks, looked all day, found no tracks. He
searched five days, ten, twenty days — searched all
the mountains, went down the rivers, up the rivers,
north, south, east, west. He searched one year,
found neither track nor trail; searched ten years,
then ten years more; inquired of every one in all
the world — no one knew of Keriha.

At last he went back to the house where Keriha
had been lost to see if there was track or trail there.
Behind Keriha's sleeping-place he saw a large stone.
He raised it, found an opening and a passage sloping northward, saw tracks made when the Supchit
woman took Keriha away. He went into the passage, followed the trail till he came to the top of
Bohem Puyuk. He came out on the top, went in
again and followed a trail going south; followed it,
winding west and east, till he came out at Waikidi
Pom. There he saw tracks on the ground, lost
them, found them again, found them going under
the ground, travelled under the ground, came out,
lost and found tracks till he lost them for good.

He inquired in the west for five years without
finding trail or tidings of Keriha. At last he said, —

"I have asked every one in this world, except
my two cousins Lasaswa at Lasan Holok."

He turned east, then, and went to Lasan Holok,

near Pas Puisono, where he found a big house with a door on the south side.   One old man was sitting on the east, and another on the west side of the door. The house was full of people.   The two old men were rubbing their thighs and rolling something. All the people inside were doing the same, all were making ropes.

Five years before these old men had heard that Norwanchakus had lost his brother.   All people had been telling one another that Norwanchakus was looking for Keriha.   As soon as the old men heard of this, they began to make ropes.

Norwanchakus stood in the door, and raised one foot to walk in.

"Don't step this way; step east," said the old man on the west.

"Don't step this way; step west," said the old man on the east.

"I 'll go straight ahead," thought Norwanchakus.

"Don't come this way!   Don't come this way!" cried all those in front.

One small boy was sitting behind all the others. As shreds of fibre dropped from the hands of those in front, he picked them up and twisted them into a rope.

"I suppose you have been travelling a long time, my grandson," said the old man on the west side of the door.

"I have travelled a very long time, and have come at last to talk with you.   I have asked all who live on this earth about my brother, and no one can tell me where Keriha is."

"We heard about your brother five years ago," said the old men, "and we told our sons to make ropes because you had lost Keriha."

"How much rope have you made?"

"We can tell to-morrow."

Next morning they cleared a broad space in front of the house. While they were doing this, Norwanchakus said to the rope-makers, —

"I wish you would send for Tsiwihl, an old man near by here."

They brought him quickly. After Tsiwihl came, Norwanchakus said, —

"I want some of you young men to try to go up and ask Sas if he knows where my brother is. I think Sas must know."

"I will try first," said the old man at the western side of the door; "I think that I have the longest rope."

"I will give you something for Sas," said Norwanchakus. "Here is an arrow-straightener, a headband of silver gray-fox skin, and a fire-drill. If you go to the top of the sky, you will see a road from east to west. Sit at the south side of it under a tobacco tree which is there. Soon Sas will come from the east, going west. He will stop at the tree. Give him the three things."

The old man brought out a great coil of rope to unwind and go up with it.

"Who is to stand and watch?" asked the other old man.

"Tsiwihl," said Norwanchakus.

Tsiwihl put oak leaves near the coil, lay on them,

and looked up. Old Lasasswa took one end of his rope, pulled it, and started. The rope was unwinding, and he was going up. Tsiwihl kept his eyes on Lasaswa. After a while he said, " Lasaswa is half-way up." A little later he said, " He is more than half-way up ! "

" But the rope is gone," said Norwanchakus.

" Lasaswa is coming down," said Tsiwihl.

The old man came to the ground. " My rope is too short. Some one else must try now," said he.

" I will try," said the other old man. This one had more rope. Five men had to help him roll it out of the house, there was so much. He took the presents for Sas and began to go up.

Tsiwihl watched closely. The rope was unwinding and Lasaswa was going up. " He is half-way up ! " said Tsiwihl; " he is near where the first man was." Tsiwihl moved his head a little, but never lost sight of Lasaswa. " He is as high as the other was ; he is higher ; he is going still higher ! "

" But the rope has given out," said Norwanchakus.

" He is coming down ! " cried Tsiwihl.

All were looking at the sky except the small boy, who was inside making rope as before.

" We are old," said the second Lasaswa; " our ropes are too short. You young men must try to-morrow."

Each old man had nine sons. Each person was one day making the trial — all were twenty days trying — no one had a rope long enough. " What shall we do now?" asked the old men on the twenty-first day.

"There is a boy in the house making rope yet; let him try," said Norwanchakus.

"Oh, he is only playing. He has n't much rope; he just makes ropes of the shreds that others throw away," said one of the old men.

"Go in and ask him," said the second old man.

Norwanchakus went in and said, "You are a small boy, but will you try your rope for me?" and he took hold of the boy's hand. He kept his rope in a little basket. When Norwanchakus took his hand, he seized the basket with the other hand and carried it out.

"Why do they bring out that little boy?" cried the young men. "He has n't any rope. We had long ropes, and all were too short; his rope is only to play with."

"My cousin," said Norwanchakus, "you are small, but I think you know something. Here are three presents. When you reach the sky, give them to Sas." Then he told him what to do.

When Norwanchakus had finished, the boy bowed his head and said "Yes" to him. "You men have long ropes, but they were too short. My rope may not reach the sky, but I will try;" and he started.

Tsiwihl's breast and stomach were as blue now as the sky, and blood was trickling from his eyes, he had looked so long and so hard. After the boy was some distance up, those below could not see him, and they said to Tsiwihl, "Tell us, tell us often what he is doing."

After a while Tsiwihl said: "He is almost as

high as the others were.   He is as high; he is as
high as the highest was."

They looked at his rope.   There seemed to be
more than when he started.   It seemed to grow all
the time.

"He is higher than any — he is going and going."

"Do not lose sight of him," said Norwanchakus.
Tsiwihl's eyes were full of blood.

"How much rope is there?" asked Norwanchakus.

"Oh, there is plenty of rope," cried the others.

"He is going and going," said Tsiwihl.

"How far up is he?   Can you see him?"

"He is high, very high, almost as high as I can
see — he is nearly at the sky."

"He will go to it, he will go to it!" cried some.

"He is at the sky," said Tsiwihl.   "He is there,
he is there!   He has his hand on it — he is on the
top of it — he is there!"

There was plenty of rope on the ground yet.

"Well," said one of the old men, "he is on the
sky.   He never talked much, that little boy, or
seemed to know much, but he has gone to a place
where we could not go."

The sun was almost half-way up in the sky.
Tsiwihl lay watching, watching, looking hard.   Sas
had passed the middle of the sky when Tsiwihl said:
"I see the boy.   He is coming down, he is
coming nearer and nearer."

Soon all could see him.   At last he was standing
on the ground.

"Now, my cousin," said Norwanchakus, "tell

me. Let me know what you saw and what you heard. What do you think of that country up there?"

"I went to the top," said the boy. "The country up there is good. I saw a road from east to west. I went east a little, and at the south of the road saw a tobacco tree. I sat under the tree and looked east. Far off I saw an old man coming with a pack on his back. I sat watching him. At last he came to where I was and passed without looking at me, went forward a little, stopped, put down his pack on the south side of the road, and then came toward me. I was sitting with my face to the north. He sat down at my left side, looked at me, looked at the headband, the fire-drill, and the straightener, and laughed. 'What are you doing here?' asked he. 'From what place are you? How did you come up to this land, where no one ever travels but me, where I have never seen any one? You are small. How could you come here?' 'I am here,' answered I, 'because Norwanchakus sent me. He sent me because he has lost his brother, Keriha. He has looked for him all over the world, has asked every one, and no one knows about Keriha. He sent me here to ask you about Keriha. He said that you must know, for you look over the whole world, see all people, see everything.' I put the three things down before him and said, 'Norwanchakus told me to give you these things for your trouble in telling about Keriha.' Sas smiled again, took up the headband, the fire-drill and straightener, held them in his hand, and said : 'These are good

— I know all that is passing in the world. I know where Keriha is. I have seen him every day since he went from his brother — I know where he is now. The Supchit woman took him one night, took him under the ground, came out on the top of Bohem Puyuk, went down again, came out, travelled by crooked roads westward, crossed the bridge made of one hair, went under the sky to the other side, to the middle house in a large village. She put Keriha in a little room in that house; he has been there ever since, he is there now. He is very weak and will die to-morrow unless some one saves him. Tell Norwanchakus to start to-night and be there in the morning if he wants to save Keriha.' "

" Then Sas put his hand in his bosom and took out a kolchi bisi [sky cap], gave it to me, and said, ' Take this to Norwanchakus, and tell him to give it to Tsiwihl for his trouble.' Sas gave me also a piece of the sky. ' This is for Tsiwihl, too,' said he; ' let him wear it on his breast for a blue facing.' "

Norwanchakus gave these to Tsiwihl, and then made him a blanket of oak leaves. He wears all these things to this day.

" My cousin, are you sure that Sas said this ? " asked Norwanchakus.

" I am sure. Sas told me all this."

" Wait now, my cousin." Norwanchakus went northeast, stretched his hand out; an armful of kúruti (silkweed which grows at the end of the world) came on it. " Now, my cousin," said he,

" I will pay you well for your trouble. All your life you can make as much rope as you like of this kúruti, and you can go up on it anywhere, — north, south, east, or west."

Norwanchakus started at midnight, and went westward quickly. He knew the way well. He crossed ridges and valleys, passed places where he had found tracks of Keriha and lost them, went to the bridge of one hair, sprang from the bank to the middle of the bridge. The bridge swayed and swayed. Underneath was a wide, rushing river, but Norwanchakus did not fall. With one spring more he touched the other bank, ran swiftly till he reached the big village beyond the sky. He saw the chief house, ran in through its door at the east, went to the little room, and found Keriha with his head on the palm of the Supchit woman's hand. He caught his brother and rushed out, shot past all the people, and stopped only when he was far outside the village.

"Now, my brother," said he, "you told me always that you knew something great, that you wanted to do something great, that you wanted to be something great. What have you been doing here thirty years? I have looked for you everywhere. You never let me know where you were."

"Oh, my brother," said Keriha, "I am so drowsy, I was sleeping, I did n't know where I was."

Norwanchakus crossed the river at a bound, without touching the bridge of one hair. He went on then, never stopped till he reached Keri Buli.

Next morning at daybreak Keriha heard a voice from above. The voice said, —

"Leave that place, Norwanchakus and Keriha. The world will change soon. You two must come here. Leave that place down there quickly."

"Now, my brother," said Keriha, "you are so slow, I don't know where you wish to go, or what you want to do."

"My brother," said Norwanchakus, "I will do the best I can, and do you do the best you can. We have finished our work here. People to come will know the names that you gave to rivers, mountains, rocks, and hills. Hereafter they will call these places by the names we gave them."

While in this world Keriha wore a duck-skin, and when they were ready to go he threw off this skin on the other side of Bohema Mem, and from it have come all the ducks on the rivers of this country.

Norwanchakus had always carried his ash stick from the fish-net. When he was going, he thrust it into the ground at Tsarau Heril. "I will leave this here," said he, "and people to come will make pipes of it." There is plenty of ash to this day in Tsarau Heril.

At the other side of the sky the brothers parted. Norwanchakus went up on high, and stayed there. Keriha went far away to the east, and is living there now.

KELE AND SEDIT

KELE AND SEDIT

PERSONAGES

After each name is given that of the creature or thing into which the personage was changed subsequently.

Hinwu, big owl; Kele, mountain wolf; Kleréu Lulimet, wild lily; Pili Lúlimet, reed grass blossom; Pokok, ground owl; Pom Piweki, crooked land; Satok Pokaila, ——; Sas, the sun; Tsurat, red-headed woodpecker; Tunhlucha, frog.

IN Puidal Winnem lived Kele. Olelbis built a great sweat-house there, and told him to stay in it. Kele was old and lived all alone in that place; lived there a long time, thinking, making up his mind what to do, — he was lonely and thirsty. "Why did Olelbis put me here?" thought he.

Once he rose about daybreak, hurried out, went westward, went to a creek. A great clump of mountain maples stood near the bank. Kele saw a straight stick among all the others. He cut the stick, drew it out, and took off a short piece. On the way home he split the stick, smoothed it, and fixed it as he walked. He put the two sticks overhead in the sweat-house, went out a second time, found a white oak sapling, firm and strong, cut a piece two feet long from it, put it at the hearth. The next day he lay with his back to the fire, lay there all night without sleeping. Just before daybreak he heard steps, and was struck on the back.

A minute later he was struck again in the same place. The old man rose then and made a good fire of manzanita wood.

It was daylight, and Kele said: "My children, come to the fire, warm yourselves, sweat, and then swim in the creek."

Two girls came to the fire, warmed themselves standing, and soon they were sweating from heat.

"My daughters," said Kele, "there is a creek near here. Go and swim in it."

These girls were from the stick that Kele had split in two parts and put in the house wall. The girls bathed in the creek, came back, and were good-looking. When they came in, Kele brought venison for his two daughters to eat.

"My daughters," said the old man, "I will tell you something. You must go to work, do good things. There are roots in the woods all around us, roots fit for food. You need to walk. Go out and get roots." They went out to dig wild lily roots. After that they went every morning.

Soon they began to say: "We should like to have other food; we should like to have game to eat. We saw mountain quail to-day; we saw deer." At last they talked this way every night. Kele listened, thinking what to do. These girls had a nice bed made of skins, and they talked every night to each other; but one night they went to bed early and fell asleep right away. Kele had wished them to sleep; that is why they fell asleep quickly. He hurried down to some mountain-ash trees, went to the middle of them, and cut off five sticks. He whittled these, made them smooth, cut each in two. He had ten smooth sticks then. Next he cut five other sticks. These he left rough ; cut them also in two ; had ten of them. Kele placed the twenty sticks overhead in the house on the north side, and lay with his back to the fire. The fire was a good one, a hot manzanita fire. His club of green oak was there at the fireplace.

Kele lay without sleeping and waited. He was awake and was thinking. The two girls were sound asleep all the time. Just before daybreak he heard a sound as if some barefooted person had sprung from above to the floor. Next moment some one took the club and struck him. Another came down in the same way and struck him. Ten times he was struck with the club.

The ten smooth sticks had turned into people. Each man gave him a blow, went to the wall of the house, and sat there. Kele did not rise yet. He heard some one barefoot jump down and seize the club. This one hit Kele once. A second one sprang down and hit him twice, a third three times, a fourth four times, and so on to the tenth, who struck him ten times. There were twenty in all ; ten from the smooth and ten from the rough sticks.

The first ten sticks he had whittled smooth, and they made ten good sons, but from the ten un-trimmed sticks came ten rough, uproarious sons. Kele hadn't smoothed them, and they struck him many times. When the tenth rough son struck him the last blow, Kele stood up and made a big fire; he could barely move, he had been so beaten with the club. He lay down then and said, —

"Now, my boys, come here; warm yourselves, dance and sweat, then go to the creek to swim, and come here again." He sang then, and made his sons dance. The boys danced, and hurried to the creek to swim, shouting as they went. They came back to the sweat-house good-looking persons.

The two girls rose now. They knew already what their father had done.

"Go, my daughters, and cook for your brothers," said Kele.

The two sisters made the food ready and placed it before their brothers.

"Now, my sons, eat what we have," said Kele. "You will go out after that, you will hunt, and bring game."

The first ten, the smooth men, had good sense; the second ten were inferior; the ninth and tenth of the second ten were very bad. The first ten took each only one mouthful; of the second ten, the first took one mouthful, the second two, the third three, and so on to the tenth, who took ten mouthfuls. After that they sat back and made ready to go out.

"What are we to do?" asked the first ten. "We have nothing to hunt with."

Kele brought out bows and quivers with arrows, and gave them to each; gave five ropes to them also, ropes of grass fibre. "You are armed now," said Kele; and he showed them where to set snares for deer.

They went far down to the foot of the mountain

and set snares. The ten smooth brothers stood on the mountain top; the second ten, who were rough, drove the deer. "You must shout so that we can hear you all the time," said the smooth brothers. Toward evening the smooth brothers saw deer in the snares. The smooth ten took the bodies, the best of the game; the rough ten the legs, ears, horns, all the poor parts. The smooth ten took the best meat to the house; the rough ten made a great uproar — they had little sense. The two sisters cooked roots and venison for all.

Next morning Kele made a big fire of manzanita wood. "Be up, my boys," called he. "Go and swim." That day the twenty stayed at home, and the sisters went for roots.

They lived this way a long time, the brothers hunting, the sisters digging roots and cooking, till at last the sisters wished to see other persons besides their brothers. One day when they went for roots they sat down on the mountain slope. "What are we to do?" said one sister; "we wish to see people, we see no one now but our brothers and father."

That evening, when all had lain down, the elder sister went to Kele and sat near him. "My father," said she, "I wish to know my name."

"Your name is Klereu Lulimet," said Kele; "your sister's name is Pili Lulimet."

She told her sister what their names were. Both liked the names, and were glad to have them. Every day the men sweated and swam, killed deer and snared them. The sisters dug lily roots and cooked them.

One time instead of digging roots they went high on the mountain side and sat there, sat looking westward. They could see very far, and things seemed right there before them, though away off near the edge of the great western water.

This was the first time that the sisters had a chance to see far. Till that day they had only a mountain slope or a forest opening in front of them ; now they had the whole country to look at. Just after midday they saw a man going northward, going slowly.

"What a nice man that is! Look at him," said one sister to the other.

He stopped all at once, seemed to sit down and disappear through the earth. That day they saw him no more.

"Oh, we should like to see that man," said the sisters, "and talk to him." They watched, talked, and forgot to dig roots. At last, a short time before sunset, they said, "Let us go for roots!" They ran down the mountain, dug a basketful quickly, and hurried home.

"Oh, father, will you teach us how to sing?" said the younger sister to Kele that evening. "We tried all day to sing. I tried to teach my sister, she tried to teach me. We could do nothing."

"You can sing this way," said Kele, and he began, —

"O wi, no á, O wi, no í,
O wi, no á, O wi, no í."

"That is good," said she, going away. She said nothing to her sister and lay down.

Soon after the twenty brothers came. Ten of them made a great noise. The house just trembled and shook from the uproar. The second ten had smeared themselves with deer blood, hung deer entrails around their necks. They looked wild and ferocious. When inside, they were quiet; in going out and coming in they always rushed and shouted.

Next morning Kele kept the twenty brothers in the sweat-house. " Rest a day," said he.

The sisters went to the mountain top and looked westward. Soon they saw some one go toward the north, as on the first day.

" Did our father tell you how to sing ? " asked the elder sister.

" He did, but I have forgotten."

She tried to remember the song, and soon after it came to her, —

" O wi, no á, O wi, no í,
O wi, no á, O wi, no í."

" This is the way our father sang," said she. " You try it, sister."

The elder began ; soon both sang together.

" Oh, we have a nice song now," said they.

Their song went straight to where the man was, a long distance. This man was Sedit. He was getting red earth for acorn bread. Water soaked through red earth was used to moisten acorn meal. Sedit was covered with shells. He was very splendid to look at. As he dug the earth, it seemed to him that he heard something. He stopped, listened, listened with all his ears. The sisters stopped singing, and he dug again ; again he heard the singing and stopped.   When he stopped, the sisters ceased to sing; when he dug, they began again. Thus it continued the whole afternoon.   They kept Sedit all day there doing little, almost nothing.

Sometime before sunset the sisters dug their roots and went home.   Sedit went home too.   He lived at the house of Satok Pokaila.

"What were you doing?   I waited all day, forenoon and afternoon, for you.   It is too late to make bread now," said Satok.

This old woman lived alone till Sedit in his wanderings came to her and worked, brought wood, and dug red earth for her.

"I got a headache," said he, "and had to lie down all day nearly."

"I am sorry," said the old woman; and she gave him food, but he did not want any.   Next day Sedit went for red earth.   He did not eat much that morning.   He had not slept all the night.   He was thinking of that song on the mountain.

That day the sisters went to the mountain top, looked westward.   Soon Sedit came to the same place and worked, put two or three handfuls in his basket, heard singing, heard it plainly, stopped, strained his eyes to see who was singing, saw no one.   Again he dug, again they sang; again he stopped work, again they ceased singing; again he worked, again they sang.   Sedit thinks now how to follow the singers, tries to whistle their music — cannot catch it — looks around, sees no one.   "Well, I must sing," says he.   He sings, and this time he catches the music.

The sisters sang now in response to him. They moved on, as he thought, and he followed. But they were not moving, they stayed in one place. They simply made their singing seem farther each time.

Sedit followed till they stopped at last, would not sing any longer. He could not tell what to do. " It is better for me to go back to my basket," said he at last. He went back, put his basket on the bank east of the pit, and said : " Now, my basket, I will leave you a while, I am going away. I place you east of the pit. Rootstick, I place you east of the basket. If Satok Pokaila asks where I am, you will move east, basket, and you will fall east, rootstick. She will know which way I went."

He went eastward, went a short distance, forgot the song, stopped, thought what to do. The song then came back to him. The sisters began to sing again. Sedit followed their song.

Satok Pokaila waited for red earth, waited till midday, then thought, " I 'll go and see if Sedit has a headache." She found the basket partly filled with red earth, and the stick standing east of it. She looked in the pit where Sedit had dug, and thought, " He must be here somewhere." She searched, but could not find him.

" Where is Sedit? " asked she of the basket. " Where did he go? — Where is Sedit? " asked she of the rootstick.

The basket moved eastward till it reached the stick, the stick fell toward the east. Old Satok knew now what had happened. She took the basket and digging-stick home with her, put them up safely.

Sedit followed the sisters, sang himself, and listened to their song. The song went southward, went away from the mountain. He followed till he reached Tayam Norel. Sedit sat down. People asked where he came from, where he was going. He would not tell, would not talk, did not care for people's words. He thought of nothing, heard nothing but the song of Kele's daughters.

He sat only a little while, and went away singing and listening to the song of the sisters. Now it went eastward. He followed it to a mountain, where he saw an old man setting a trap. This was old Pokok.

"Uncle, where are you going in such a great hurry?" asked Pokok.

"I am going east," replied Sedit. "You will not see me pass this way again."

He hurried down the mountain, crossed a creek, and went straight up another mountain; was just at the top, when he saw a very big man coming toward him on the right hand as Sedit was going east. Sedit stopped, looked, was afraid somewhat. The two stared at each other. The stranger was very tall and very thick. Sedit was frightened. The big man never stopped, went straight ahead westward. Sedit looked at him a long time, did n't move, watched him going down the mountain. After he had gone Sedit stood a long time, and then sat down.

"Why did he not speak to me?" thought Sedit.

" He is the first person I have met who would n't speak to me. Who is he? I should like to know."

Sedit sat and thought all that day about the big man. He heard the song always, at times very near him, but he thought so much about the big man that he did n't follow it. He wondered if the big man would come again, and said to himself, " I will wait and see."

About night Sedit thought, " If he comes and will not speak to me, I 'll kill him." All night he waited. He rose very early, had not slept any. About sunrise he saw a man coming from afar, from the east, moving westward. Sedit watched, had his bow and arrows ready. It was he who would not speak the day before. Sedit shot him in the breast, shot again. The big man paid no heed, passed right along. Sedit shot twenty arrows. The stranger looked all the time at Sedit, said nothing. Sedit shot twenty arrows more — spent all his arrows.

After he had shot away the forty arrows, and the man had passed right close to him, Sedit sat down and thought, " Who is this that I cannot kill him? " He thought a long time, and then knew that he must be Sas Kiemila.

It was old Sas. Sas had been fooling Sedit, just as Kele's daughters had fooled him.

Sedit heard the song again, and followed it. He went to the Bohema Mem at Sawal Pom, went up Norken Mem till he came to Hin Pom where he heard a great noise. Many people were dancing there.

"Oh, there is Sedit coming," said they. "Where is he going so fast?"

"Uncle, where are you going in such a great hurry?" asked one of the men. "What news have you? Tell us what you have seen on your journey."

"I am travelling this country to look at it. I saw no one, can give you no tidings of any one. I shall not pass this way again."

The man who spoke and the dancers were Hinwa people. Sedit rushed on, came to a flat, saw a spring, and many persons drinking water.

"My grandsons, what are you doing, why do you drink so much water? Water is bad for young people" (these people were birds of all sorts). Sedit called the place Chilchil balus (bird drinking). He went on without stopping or talking, — had no time for either. He listened, heard the singing near a hill, ran there; heard talking of many people, the Tsurats arguing about acorns.

Sedit passed these people, crossed the Norken Mem, ran along the trail, came to an old man lying across it at the foot of a mountain. Sedit, going fast, thought to jump over the old man, but he moved, and Sedit stopped. "Grandson, what are you doing?" asked Sedit. This was Pom Piweki. "I cannot tell what to do," said Pom. "I am old, I cannot travel; so I lay down here."

"I will go on," said Sedit, "and come back this way, I think." He heard the song nearer now; followed it, followed till sunset, when it ceased. He stayed all night in that place.

Next morning, some time after sunrise, the song began again. Sedit answered, and followed it. Then it ceased; he stopped again; then the song began a second time; he followed; the song ceased. The song circled around the mountain, going a little higher gradually; sometimes it was near, sometimes it seemed far away, but he never came up to it.

After wandering ten days, perhaps, he reached the top of the mountain by going round and round the side of it. The singing was in the mountain now all the time. He was on the highest part of Kele's sweat-house. Kele, his twenty sons, and two daughters were inside, and the girls and old man knew that some one was walking on the roof of their sweat-house. Kele's sons went out each morning, and so did his daughters. Although they were many, Sedit never saw one of them, — they fooled him. At last, when Sedit was on the mountain, Kele shouted, —

"If any one is on my house, let him go down to the western door of it."

Sedit heard, and went back the way by which he came. He went to Pom Piweki and asked: "Do you know where the door to this sweat-house is?"

Pom Piweki made no answer. He stood up and pulled open a door; it seemed as though he had been lying across the entrance. When he opened the door, Sedit saw far into the house.

"Sedit, if you are here to go in, this is the way for you," said Pom Piweki. "You will see an old man lying on the east side, go to him and talk; this is his sweat-house."

Sedit went in and sat down near Kele, said nothing.   Kele rose up and gave Sedit food, talked to him, told him what kind of person he, Kele, was, and about his children, and said: "Sedit, if you have come here to stay, you must do what I tell you; you must be careful.   I have rough sons; if they know that you are here, they will make trouble. I will hide you.   They will make a noise, but you will not suffer if you keep quiet; if you move, they will find you, and abuse you, surely."

Kele put Sedit in a basket in the ground, hid him there, leaving a small hole to look through. "You may look out, but do not move," said Kele.

As soon as Sedit was hidden the girls came in with roots, and sat down at their sleeping-place. Sedit was near them.   He thrust out his hand and pinched the younger sister.   She said nothing.

"Sister, have you seen any one?" asked she, after a time; "some one pinched me."

"'Sh!" said the elder, "be quiet and say nothing; don't let our father hear."

The elder went to cook, and Kele's twenty sons came hammering and tramping.

The first ten, the smooth ones, came, as always, quietly; the second ten came with a rush and an uproar.   Sedit peeped out at them.

The younger sister pushed him back.   "Be still," said she.

Sedit tried to rise; she kept him down.

The first man of the second ten cried, "Pshu! I smell Sedit."

The second said, "Pshu! I smell Sedit; throw him out!"

"Be quiet, boys; don't talk so," said Kele. "Sedit is your uncle."

"Phew! I smell Sedit," cried all the second ten.

Kele could hardly keep his sons from taking Sedit. After they had eaten they grew more excited. "Where is Sedit?" cried they. "Let us find Sedit!"

At last they found Sedit, dragged him out, played ball with him, threw him around the whole night from one side of the great house to the other. Kele could do nothing, could not stop them. He went and lay down. About sunrise Sedit screamed. He was almost dead. Kele's ten rough sons were covered with deer blood and shouted all night. The smooth ten sat still, could do nothing against the rough ten.

About sunrise Sedit could hardly breathe. He had a root under his left arm, and as he was hurled across the house it fell into the fire and made a great smoke. The odor was very pleasant. Kele's sons liked it. They threw Sedit back to where they found him, left him, and began to breathe in the smoke.

"My sons," said Kele, "I told you last night not to hurt or harm Sedit; let him alone. That root which he dropped will be good for you, and hereafter you will like it. Future people when going to hunt will take this root, tsarauhosi, hold it out, and say, 'Kele, give us deer.' They will give you the root, and you will give them deer. When they go hunting and have bad luck, they will make a fire, burn this root, hold it out while it smokes, and say, ' Kele, will you put deer where we can see and kill them ? ' " (Wintu hunters carry this root and burn it if they have bad luck in finding deer. Kele likes the odor and sends them deer). Kele rubbed Sedit with deer marrow, put him on the west side of the sweat-house, and said, " This is your place; you will stay here."

The boys went to hunt, the girls to dig roots as before.

" How did you get those sons, brother ? " asked Sedit once.

" You have no need to know; I will not tell you," replied Kele.

" How did you build this house ? Two old men should not live in one house. If I had a house, your sons could visit me when they wished, see their uncle's house, and stay all night, perhaps."

" I don't think you could have sons, Sedit, or keep a house. I don't believe you have strength for it; these things are hard to do," said Kele.

But Sedit talked on about sons and a sweat-house. Kele asked Sedit to sing for his sons while they danced and sweated. He sang twice and sang fairly. " I could sing well if I had a house and sons of my own," remarked Sedit.

" I will build a sweat-house for him," thought Kele, at last. " He may go through as I have. I don't think he will, but I can let him try."

The next night Kele made all sleep soundly. He went north a short distance and wished for a sweat-house. A mountain stood in front of him next moment. Kele went home before daylight and lay down. That day Sedit talked on as before.

"Come," said Kele; and he took him to the new mountain. "You can live here if you like. This is your house." Kele left him then.

Sedit made a fire, found a pipe and tobacco, smoked, stayed many days and nights by himself there. "I should like to know how Kele got his sons," thought he one night. "I must ask him."

"I come to tell you," said Sedit one morning, "that I am lonesome. I want to know how you got your sons and daughters."

Kele made no answer for a long time. At last he told him how he got his daughters.

Sedit went home, did exactly as Kele had done, then lay down without sleeping. Toward morning he heard some one jump to the floor; next he got a blow on the back, then a second. The two persons went away and sat down. Sedit rose, made a big fire, and began singing for a sweat-dance. Two girls stood near the fire, sweated, then went to the creek, swam, and went home. They had very long hair and were nice looking. Sedit gave them wooden combs and mink-skins for their hair, gave them food and nice baskets painted red, told each to dig roots and cook them.

Sedit lived a while with his daughters, till he thought once, "I want to have sons." He went to Kele, and Kele told how he had got sons, told carefully.

Sedit cut the sticks, did everything as Kele said,

and lay by the fire, but he could not keep from looking up; the moment he looked all the sticks fell to the ground. Sedit put them in place again, lay by the fire, looked up. The sticks fell a second time; he put them up again, lay down, looked a third time. The sticks fell a third time. He was putting the sticks up till daylight, when he had to stop. Sedit went to Kele that day. "My sticks were falling all night," said he.

Kele knew what had happened already. "Why not do as I told you? I told you not to look up."

"I will not look any more," said Sedit.

Next night he put up sticks again and waited, took the blows till the last one of the second ten was giving him ten blows, then he sprang up and screamed. All the twenty sons dropped down and were sticks again. It was just daylight. Sedit gathered the sticks into a basket, and looked to see if the girls were awake. They were sticks as well as the others.

Sedit felt very sorry, could not tell what to do. He put the two sticks with the other twenty, took one at a time, held it up, and said, "This was my son, this was my daughter." He was sorry and wondered if he could make others. He went to Kele and said, —

"My brother, I could not stand it."

"What did I tell you?"

"Can I not make more?"

"Perhaps you cannot endure it." Kele did not want him to try.

"I am sorry for my girls," said Sedit, "I want them back; I was fond of them."

"You may try for sons, but those girls will not come back."

Sedit tried a third time. The beating was so hard that he almost screamed; but he held out this time, and had twenty sons. Sedit's house was full of sons, but he had no daughters; the sticks would not turn to girls again, though he did with them as he had the first time.

Sedit sent his sons to hunt. "Go wherever you like," said he. "On the west side is a ridge; go on that ridge, keep in one line, and when you turn some one may see you and think, 'What a crowd of nice boys!'"

Kele's boys were hunting that day, and saw Sedit's sons in a long line. "Look at that row of men on the ridge," said they. "Those are our cousins," said one of the smooth ten; "those are Sedit's sons."

Sedit's sons went to a flat, danced and played all the day, took yellow clay, made paste of it, painted themselves yellow — that is why coyotes are yellow to this day; the paint would not wash off. All went home in a line. Sedit had supper for them.

"Why do you come without deer?" asked Sedit.

"We danced on the flat and painted."

Sedit said nothing. All ate; then Sedit thought, "I wish you boys to sleep." All fell asleep. Sedit went to Kele, woke him up, and said, —

"My sons went to hunt, but came home without deer. What shall I do with them?"

" Let them hunt birds. Let them hunt gophers and grasshoppers in the meadows. Gophers are as good as deer."

" All right," said Sedit; and he went home and slept.

They brought grasshoppers and gophers from the hunt next day, and Sedit was satisfied.

" Let them live on that kind of food," thought he.

They told of their hunting that day. "We wanted water," said one of them, " and met an old woman. ' We are dry and cannot find water,' said we to her. ' I will give you water,' said the old woman; ' come with me.' We followed her a while. I was afraid and said to my brothers, ' Do not drink the water she gives.' One of my brothers shouted at the old woman and frightened her. She fell back and turned into a swamp with a spring in the middle of it. We did n't go near the spring, but were nearly lost in the swamp."

" That is a wicked old woman," said Sedit. " That is Tunhlucha Pokaila. She drowns people often. I met her once and she came near drowning me. Don't you go near her again. Hunt gophers and grasshoppers elsewhere."

" Now, my sons," said Sedit, some days later, " go and scatter around through this country. Whenever you want to see me come here to my sweat-house."

Sedit's sons scattered north, south, east, and west. They were at every ridge and point, in every valley and meadow, at every spring and river.

Kele's sons stayed at their great mountain sweat-house, doing the same things, living in the same way. The two sisters never married, and all Kele's people are in that mountain now. When they go out they look like wolves; but when inside, when at home in the mountain, they are people.

KOL TIBICHI

KOL TIBICHI.

KOL TIBICHI was born at Norpat Kodiheril on Wini Mem, just before daylight. When a small boy, he used to go out by himself. If he went to play with other boys sometimes, he would not stay with them. He went out of sight, disappeared, and was lost. Then his father or mother or others would find him in this place or that unexpectedly. Sometimes they found him at home, sometimes at a distance, far away in some gulch or on some mountain. It happened that his mother would look at his bed in the night-time and see him there sleeping. She would look again and find that he was gone. She would look a third time, and find him just as at first. In the day he would be seen in one place and be gone the next moment.

Once he was playing with children; they turned aside to see something, then looked at him. He was gone. After a while they saw him in the water under the salmon-house. Another time he disappeared.

"Where has he gone?" asked one boy.

"I cannot tell," answered another.

Soon they heard singing.

One asked, "Do you hear that?"

'Yes," said the other; "where is it?"

They listened and looked. Soon they saw Kol Tibichi sitting near the north bank of the river, under water.

"We must run and tell his father and mother."

Two of the boys ran to tell his father and mother. "We lost your son," said they. "He went away from us. We looked for him a long time and could not find him. Now we have found him; we have seen him sitting under water; we don't know what he is doing."

His mother hurried out; ran to the river.

"We think he must be dead," said people who had gathered there. "We think that some yapaitu [spirit] has killed him."

They soon saw that he was alive; he was moving. "Come, my son," called his mother, stretching her hands to him, — "come, my son; come out, come to me." But he stayed there, sitting under water.

A quarter of an hour later they saw that the boy had gone from the river. The people heard singing in some place between them and the village. They looked up and saw that the boy was half-way home and going from the river.

"That is your son," called they to the woman.

"Oh, no," said the woman; but she ran up and found that it was her son.

Another time the boy goes south with some children. These lose him, just as the others had. In half an hour they hear singing.

"Where is he?" ask some.

"On this side," says one.

" On that," says another.

South of the river is a great sugar-pine on a steep bank. They look, and high on a limb pointing northward they see him hanging, head downward, singing.

They run to his mother. " We see your son hanging by his feet from a tree."

The woman hurries to the river, runs in among the rocks and rubbish around the tree, reaches toward the boy, throws herself on the rocks, crying, " Oh, my child, you 'll be killed ! "

In a moment he is gone; there is no sign of him on the tree. Soon a shouting is heard at the house : " My wife, come up; don't cry, our son is here ! "

She crawls out of the rocks and dirt, runs home, finds the boy safe with his father.

The people began now to talk of the wonderful boy. Soon every one was talking of him. There were many people in the place. Norpat Kodiheril was a very big village.

" Some yapaitu is going to take that boy's life," said they; " some yapaitu will kill him."

One morning the boy went down on the north side of the river with children, but apart from them, behind, by himself. He looked up, saw a great bird in the air flying above him. " Oh, if I had those wing feathers ! " thought the boy. Then he blew upward and wished (olpuhlcha). That moment the great bird Komos Kulit fell down before him. Just after the bird fell he heard a voice in the sky, a voice high, very high up, crying, —

" Now, you little man, you must call yourself

Kol Tibichi. You are to be the greatest Hlahi [doctor] on Wini Mem."

"Look at that boy!" cried the other boys. "See! he has something."

They were afraid when they saw the great bird, and the boy stretching the wings and handling the wonderful Komos Kulit. Some of them ran to his mother and said to her, —

"Your son has a very big bird. It fell down from the sky to him. We are afraid of that bird. We could not lift such a big bird."

Old people ran down; saw the boy handling Komos Kulit. "How did you get that bird?" asked they. "Did he fall to you?"

"Yes. I saw the shadow of a big bird on the ground. I looked up. It fell, and was here."

The old people talked, — talked much, talked a long time. There were many of them.

"We do not know what to do; we do not know what to think. We do not know why that bird fell," said some. "We ought not to talk about the bird, but we ought to think about this boy, find out what he is doing."

"Oh," said others, "he made that bird fall by blowing at it. That boy will be a great Hlahi."

The boy killed the bird with a yapaitu dokos (spirit flint); he wanted its wings.

The father and mother of the boy said: "Two wise men should pull out the longest wing feathers for the boy. He wants them; he wants them to keep."

"Let that be done," said the people; and they

found two men to pull out the two longest wing feathers. The boy went to one side while they were pulling them, pretended not to see or care what they were doing; but the two men knew that he knew why he did so. When the two men had pulled out the feathers, the boy said to his father, —

"I like those feathers; save them for me; I want them."

His father took the feathers home and saved them.

Another time this boy was walking up Wini Mem — some time before he had been at a Hlahi dance, and had seen there beautiful collars of flicker-tail feathers, and remembered them. He walked forward and said to himself, —

"I wonder where that man found those feathers. I would like to have feathers like them."

"Pluck a bunch of grass with your mouth," said the yapaitu, "drop it into your hand, and look at it."

He did so, and flicker feathers were in his hands. He counted them, and found five hundred. "These are nice feathers; I will keep them," said the boy.

"Kol Tibichi is your name," said the yapaitu. "You will be the greatest Hlahi on Wini Mem, but you must obey us. You must listen to our words, you must do what we tell you."

Kol Tibichi took the flicker feathers and walked westward, walked across a wide gulch till he came to a black-oak tree above Norpat Kodiheril.

"I like that oak-tree," said Kol Tibichi. "I think that is a good place for my mother to get acorns." He blew then, and said: "You must be very big, wide, and high, give many acorns every fall. I will call your place Olpuhlchiton" (blowing upward place, *i. e.* wishing place).

He went home then, and gave the flicker-tail feathers to his mother. "Now, my mother," said he, "I wish you to keep these feathers for me."

"Where did you find them, my son?" asked she. "You are always doing something. You did not find these yourself; the yapaitu got them. I will keep them. I am sorry for you, but I cannot stop what you are doing. You cannot stop it yourself. But I will keep these feathers for you; I will keep them safely."

All the people talked much of Kol Tibichi now.

Once there was a doctor's dance, and the boy remained at home till one night when the yapaitu came to him and he began to hlaha. His father and mother did not know what the trouble was.

"Bring him here," said the oldest doctor.

"He is a Hlahi," said the doctors, when they saw him. "Sak hikai [the rainbow] is his yapaitu. You must give him to us till the yapaitu leaves him. While the yapaitu is with him, let him stay inside."

They were five or six days making Hlahis (doctors). The boy stayed in the sweat-house six days, never eating, never drinking; some others ate and drank, but Kol Tibichi neither ate nor drank.

"Something must be done to make that yapaitu leave him. You must put a band around Kol Tibichi's head," said the chief, 'and the yapaitu will leave him."

They got a white wolf-tail headband. The yapaitu did not go. "This is not the right kind of a headband," said the doctor, after a while. They tried fox, wildcat, coyote, a white-deer band, without effect.

"We don't know what he wants," said some Hlahis.

Next they tried otter, fisher, coon, badger, black bear, grizzly bear, silver-gray fox, mink, beaver, rabbit, red-headed woodpecker.

"What does he want?" asked some.

"Now," said the old doctor, "you ought to know that this boy should have food and drink, and he cannot have them till the yapaitu goes. You should know that the headband that his yapaitu wants is a tsahai loiyas" (woman's front apron made of maple bark, painted red).

They brought this apron, made the headband, and tied it on his head.

"This is the one," said the yapaitu.

Kol Tibichi began to sing; the Hlahi danced a few minutes. The boy blew then, and the yapaitu left him. Kol Tibichi ate venison first and drank water, then took other kinds of food. From that time on Kol Tibichi was a Hlahi.

Soon after the great Hlahi dance, perhaps two weeks, Notisa, chief of Norpat Kodiheril, fell sick; he began to have a bad feeling at midday, and in the evening all his friends thought he would die. In the early night people in Norpat Kodi saw a light going to Kol Tibichi's house.

"People are coming; there must be some one

18

sick in the village," said the boy's father and mother. " People are coming.   See, there is a big light moving this way."

Two men came to the door.   " Come in," said Kol Tibichi's father.   " We thought some one was sick when we saw your light coming."

" We are here because Notisa is sick," said the men.   " He got sick at noon."

The two men spread out a marten skin and said : " We brought this to show it to you and your son. We have heard that he is a powerful Hlahi.   The chief gave us this skin to show you.   We are afraid that Notisa will die.   We want your son to go with us to see him."

They gave the skin to Kol Tibichi.   It was the best skin in the chief's house.

" We will go," said Kol Tibichi's father.   " I do not say that my son is a Hlahi, but he can do something."

They waked the boy, made him ready to go. " Come," said his mother; and she carried him to the chief's house.

" My mother, put me down," said Kol Tibichi, when they had come near the house.

" I do not like to put you down," said the mother.

" Put me down, put me down a moment," said the boy.

His mother put him down.   Then he saw some one looking around Notisa's house, pushing about, looking, watching in the dark, lurking around, holding arrows.   This was a yapaitu, ready to shoot Notisa and kill him.

Kol Tibichi called his own yapaitu, who went to the one who was watching and said : "What are you doing here? What do you want at this house?"

"I am doing nothing," answered the yapaitu.

"You are waiting to do something. You want to do harm."

"Oh, no; I am only looking around here, just trying to find the door. I wanted to see some one."

"You are ready to shoot a yapaitu dokos. You want to kill Notisa. You are watching around here to kill him."

"Oh, no, I am not. I am just looking around, not doing anything."

"You are ready to kill Notisa, the chief. You are waiting to kill him," said Kol Tibichi's yapaitu, who just took hold of the strange yapaitu, twisted him, killed him right there, and buried him.

Kol Tibichi's mother took her son into the chief's house. The boy knew what had been done. His yapaitu told him what he had done, and came in with him. The boy sat down near Notisa.

People thought the chief ready to die, thought that he might die any moment. "Let the boy put his hand on the sick man," said they.

"Put your hand on the chief," said the father. "You must do what you can. You must try, do your best to cure him."

Kol Tibichi spat on his hands, passed them over Notisa's breast and face. "I am sleepy, my mother, oh, I am so sleepy," said the boy, when he had passed his hands over the chief.

" He cannot do more to-night," said the father.
" We will go home."

Next morning people in the sweat-house heard a man talking outside. He came in and said, " I am well ! " This was Notisa.

" We are glad," said the people. " Kol Tibichi has saved you."

The boy grew up and became a great Hlahi. When twenty years old, he was the greatest Hlahi on Wini Mem.

One year there was a Hlahi dance in El Hakam. Kol Tibichi was a man. He was thirty years old then. He went to the dance. Tulitot was the great Hlahi in that place, and he thought himself better than Kol Tibichi. While dancing, Tuletot took a snake from his mouth, a large rattlesnake, and held it in both hands as he danced. The snake was his own child. Kol Tibichi looked, and thought he could do better; and, dancing forward, he blew, as Hlahis do, and threw out long burning flames on both sides of his mouth. All present were afraid, and with Tulitot ran back before him in fear.

When the dance was over, Kol Tibichi went to Norpat Kodi and lived on, a great Hlahi: lived till he was a hundred years of age and more. He could not walk any longer. He knew that he could not live. " I cannot live any more," said he. " My yapaitu tells me this, — I cannot walk. I cannot do anything. My yapaitu tells me that I must leave Norpat Kodiheril. [He was not sick, but decrepit.] My yapaitu is going to take me and leave my bones in this place with you. When I go from my body, do not bury it. Leave it on the ground out there. Let it lie one night. Next morning you will see a large rock in place of it. When people are sick, let them come and take a piece of the rock, or some earth, or some moss from it; that will cure them."

"We will not do that," said Notisa, a son of the first chief; "we bury every body, and we will bury yours like all others."

"Do not bury my bones," said Kol Tibichi.

"We should not like to see your bones all the time. We have no wish to see a rock in place of them."

"Well, take my body to the black-oak tree, put it eight or ten feet from the ground, leave it there one night; next morning you will see water in a hollow of the oak. Any man may come and get that water, rub it on his body, and drink some. It will cure him."

"No," said the chief, "we don't want to see the tree there every day. We do not wish to look at it all the time."

"Dig a deep grave, then," said Kol Tibichi; "put my body in with nothing around it. When you come to mourn, do not stand east of the grave-mound. On the morning after my burial you will see a rainbow coming out of the grave."

Kol Tibichi died. They did everything just as he told them. All saw the rainbow and said, "We ought to have left his body above ground, and to have done all that he asked of us at first. The yapaitu is mourning for him."

The rainbow stood there two days and two nights at the grave, then moved two feet eastward. Next morning it was four feet away, then eight, going farther day by day till it was at the salmon-house where Kol Tibichi used to go when a boy. It stood there by the salmon-house five days. Next it was on the north bank of the river, then on the hillside beyond, then on the hilltop, then on the mountain-slope, then on the mountain-top. Next all the people in Norpat Kodiheril heard a noise and knocking in the grave-mound one night, and early next morning they saw an immense bird rising out of Kol Tibichi's grave. First the head came, and then the body. At sunrise it came out altogether, and flew to the sugar-pine from which Kol Tibichi had hung head downward in childhood. It perched on the tree, stayed five minutes, and then flew away, flew to the mountain, to the rainbow, went into the rainbow. The bird and rainbow went away, disappeared together. The bird was Komus Kulit. The rainbow was Kol Tibichi's yapaitu.

THE WINNING OF HALAI AUNA
AT THE HOUSE OF TUINA

THE WINNING OF HALAI AUNA AT THE HOUSE OF TUINA

This myth and all that follow it belong to the Yanas, a nation of Indians described in the notes. The nine preceding myths are of the Wintus, neighbors of the Yanas.

The languages of these two nations are radically different.

PERSONAGES

After each name is given that of the creature or thing into which the personage was changed subsequently.

Chuhna, spider; Halai Auna, morning star; Igupa Topa, ——; Ochúl Márimi, mountain lion; Pul Miauna, colored bow, the rainbow; Pun Miaupa, son of rainbow; Tuina, the sun; Utjamhji, mock sun; Wakara, the moon; Wediko, meteor; Marimi means woman.

OLD Pul Miauna had a son, Pun Miaupa, a wife, and two daughters.

Pun Miaupa had a quarrel with his father and made up his mind to leave him. "I am going away," said he to his father and mother one day. "I am tired of living here."

The mother began to cry.

"Which way are you going?" asked the father.

Pun Miaupa gave no answer; would n't tell his father where he was going. The father stood up and walked out of the house. The mother stopped crying and said, —

"I want you to go straight to my brother, your uncle Igupa Topa. Tell him where you are going. Do not go without seeing him."

Pun Miaupa left his mother, went to his uncle's, stood on the roof of the sweat-house. The old man was very busy throwing out grass that day. A great many people had gambled at his house a day earlier; they had left much grass in it.

"Uncle, are you alive?" asked Pun Miaupa.

The old uncle looked up and saw his nephew, who said, —

"Uncle, I am full grown. I am going on a very long journey, I am going far away. My mother told me to come here and see you."

"Where are you going, my nephew?"

"To the north."

"I thought so," said the old man, who knew that his nephew would go to get Wakara's youngest daughter.

Wakara took all his daughter's suitors to Tuina's sweat-house, and they were killed there. Igupa Topa knew this and said, "Wait a little, nephew, I will go with you."

"Uncle," said Pun Miaupa, "you are too old. I don't want you to go; the journey would kill you. I want to travel very fast on this journey."

"I will go at my own pace, I will go as I like," said the uncle.

"Well, come with me if you can go fast."

Igupa Topa dressed, took a staff, and looked very old. "Go on, I am ready," said he.

Pun Miaupa started. He turned around to look at his uncle, and saw the old man; saw him fall while coming out of the sweat-house. Pun Miaupa stopped, held down his head, and thought, "He will not go, even as far as Wajami."

The uncle rose and followed on.

"You are too old, uncle ; you cannot walk well. Stay at home ; that is better for you."

"Go ahead," said the old man ; "walk fast. I will come as I can."

Pun Miaupa went on ; his uncle followed. Igupa Topa stumbled every few steps, fell, hurt himself, tore his skin. Pun Miaupa looked back very often. The uncle was always tumbling. "He must be bruised and broken from these falls," thought the nephew.

Pun Miaupa was on a hill beyond Chichipana. He sat down and smoked. His uncle came up while he was sitting there.

"Let me smoke ; then I want to see you jump to that mountain over there," said the old man, pointing to it.

"I shall leave you behind if I do that."

"Leave me to myself," said the old man.

Pun Miaupa put on deerskin leggings and a beaded shirt, — a splendid dress. He went then with one spring to the top of the opposite mountain and looked back to see his uncle ; but old Igupa Topa had jumped too. He was just passing Pun Miaupa and went far beyond him.

"I thought you were too old to jump," said Pun Miaupa, coming up to him.

They jumped again, jumped to a second mountain, and the uncle was ahead the second time. After that they walked on. The old man fell very often, but Pun Miaupa did not pity him any longer; he laughed when his uncle fell.   They travelled a good while, travelled fast, and when both reached Wajami Mountain, they sat down to rest there.

"I want Wakara to send out his youngest daughter for wood," said Pun Miaupa in his mind; and the next minute Wakara, who was far away in his own sweat-house, told his youngest daughter to take a basket and go for wood.   This daughter was Halai Auna.

At that moment, too, Wakara's wife, Ochul Marimi, said to the girl: "Why do you lie asleep all the time and not help me?   I want you to get me leaves for acorn bread."

Halai Auna took the basket and went upon the mountain side to find wood and leaves.   Pun Miaupa saw the girl filling her basket.

"That is Wakara's daughter," said he to his uncle.

"Stop!   Be careful!" said Igupa Topa.

The uncle put himself into his nephew's heart now to strengthen him.   There was only one person to be seen.   Igupa Topa went into his nephew, went in because he knew that Tuina killed all men who tried to get Halai Auna, and he wished to save his sister's son, Pun Miaupa.

When the girl had her basket full and turned to place it on her back, she saw Pun Miaupa behind her; she could not move, she was so frightened.

"Why are you afraid?   Am I so ugly?" asked Pun Miaupa.

He pleased her ; but she said not a word, just ran, hurried home with the basket, and threw it down at the door.

"What is your trouble ? " asked the mother. "You don't like to work, I think."

"What is the matter? " asked Wakara. "You are frightened."

"I saw a man on the mountain, a man with woodpecker scalps on his head."

"The southern people wear woodpecker scalps," said Wakara; "that must be one of the southern people."

Pun Miaupa sprang through the air, came down in front of Wakara's sweat-house, went in and sat near Halai Auna on a bear-skin. Nice food was brought for all, and when they had finished eating, Wakara said, —

"Now, my daughters, and you, my wife, Ochul Marima, make ready ; let us go. I wish to see my brother, Tuina, and hear what he says of Halai Auna's new husband."

They dressed, put on beads, and put red paint on their faces. Halai Auna said nothing. She sat with her head down; she was sorry; she liked Pun Miaupa, she felt sure that they would kill him.

When all were ready, Wakara took his wife's hand and danced around the fire with her. He had two unmarried daughters besides Halai Auna; one of these took her father's hand, the other took Halai Auna's, and all danced around the fire and circled about Pun Miaupa. They put him in the middle and danced in a circle ; they began to sing,

and rose in the air then and danced right up out of
the sweat-house, went through the smoke-hole and
moved westward, singing as they went, —

"I-nó, i-nó, i-nó, no-má
I-nó, i-nó, i-nó, no-má."

They moved faster as they went, and danced all
the time.   It was dark when they danced up through
the roof of the sweat-house ; no one saw them,
though there were many people round about.   Old
Wakara's sons-in-law lived in that place ; all the
stars were his daughters, and his daughters were
married, except Halai Auna and the two who danced
around the fire.   Wakara went without being seen.
He would let no one have Halai Auna unless one
whom Tuina could not kill.

Now, a little before daylight they reached Tuina's
house.   Wakara stood on the roof of the sweat-
house and called, " My brother, I want you to
spring out of bed."

Tuina was asleep in the sweat-house.   He had
three daughters and no son.   The daughters were
called Wediko, and his wife was Utjamhji.   Wakara
went down into the sweat-house and sat at the side
of Tuina.   Tuina took a bear-skin and put it down
at his other hand, and told Halai Auna and her
husband to sit on it.   Tuina took up a big sack
of tobacco and a large pipe cut out of maple wood.
The tobacco was made of his own hair, rolled and
cut fine.   He put this in the pipe and gave it to
Pun Miaupa.   Wakara and Tuina watched now,
and looked at him.   The young man smoked all
the tobacco and gave back the pipe.

Tuina filled the pipe now with a different, a stronger tobacco. He used to rub his skin often, and what he rubbed off he dried and made fine. This was his tobacco of the second kind. He had a sackful of this stored away, and he filled his pipe now with it.

Pun Miaupa smoked, seemed to swallow the smoke. It was not he who was smoking, though, but the uncle in his heart. He emptied the pipe and returned it. Tuina took now tobacco of a third kind, — his own flesh dried and rubbed fine. He filled the pipe, gave it to Pun Miaupa, and waited to see him fall dead at the second if not at the first whiff.

The country outside the sweat-house was full of dead people, all killed by Tuina's tobacco. Some of the bodies were fresh, others decayed ; some were sound skeletons, others a few old bones.

Pun Miaupa smoked out this pipe, gave it back empty. Tuina handed him a fourth pipe. The tobacco was made of his own brains, dried and rubbed fine. Pun Miaupa smoked this and gave the empty pipe back to Tuina.

Tuina now tried the fifth pipe. He filled it with marrow from his own bones, gave it to Halai Auna's husband. Wakara and Tuina watched now, waiting to see him fall. Pun Miaupa swallowed all and gave the pipe back.

Tuina had no other kind of tobacco and could do no more. He dropped his head. " I don't know what kind of person this is," thought he. All at once he remembered old Igupa Topa, and thought:

"This may be a young one of that kind. I can do nothing with him, he has beaten me."

Halai Auna was very glad to have such a husband. This was the first man of all who had come to see her who had not been killed by Tuina. She laughed all this time in her mind.

Pun Miaupa went out, killed five deer, and brought them in. The women cooked a great deal that day. Wakara and Tuina sat in the house, talked and ate Pun Miaupa's fresh venison. The next night all slept. Igupa Topa went out of Pun Miaupa's heart, went about midnight, and sat north of the pillar in the side of the house, sat without saying a word. He had a white feather in his head, and looked very angry and greatly dissatisfied.

Early next morning Tuina and Wakara were up and saw the old man sitting there with that big feather in his head, and they looked at him.

"Oh," said Tuina, "I know now why Halai Auna's husband can smoke my tobacco. I know that old Igupa Topa this long time. I know what that old fellow can do."

They put plenty of food before Igupa Topa, but he would eat none of it. Pun Miaupa killed five deer that morning and brought them in. The two old men were glad to see such nice venison, and see so much of it. Igupa Topa sat by himself, and ate nothing.

"Uncle, why do you not eat?" asked Pun Miaupa.

He made no answer, but watched till all were

asleep; then he stood up and ate, ate the whole
night through, ate all the acorn bread, all the roots,
ate all that there was in the house, except venison.
That was not his kind of food; he would not touch
it. He sat down on the north side of the central
pillar when he had finished eating.

"You must work hard to cook food enough,"
said Tuina next morning to the women. "Some
one in this house must be very hungry."

The women worked hard all that day; in the
evening the house was full of good food again.
Pun Miaupa's uncle would not eat a morsel placed
before him, but when night came he ate everything
there was except venison.

"There must be some one in this house who is
very hungry," said Tuina, when he rose the next
morning. "Make ready more food to-day, work
hard, my daughters."

"We will not work to-day; that nasty old fellow eats everything in the night time. We will not
carry wood and water all day and have nothing to
eat the next morning."

"I don't like him, either," said Tuina; "he will
go very soon, I hope."

Igupa Topa heard these words and remembered
them. Tuina's wife and Wakara's wife, both old
women, had to work that day without assistance.
In the middle of the forenoon a great cloud rose in
the south. Pun Miaupa's uncle raised it. "Let
rain come, thick heavy rain," said he in his mind.
"I want darkness, I want a big storm and cold
rain."

The cloud was black; it covered all the sky; every one came in, and soon the rain began. It rained in streams, in rivers; it filled the valleys, filled all places. The water reached Tuina's sweat-house, rushed in, and filled the whole place; all had to stand in water; and the rain was very cold.

Old Tuina and Wakara were shivering; their teeth knocked together; their wives and daughters were crying. Igupa Topa had taken his nephew and Halai Auna up to his place on the north side, near the roof of his sweat-house, where they were dry.

The sweat-house was nearly full of water. All were crying now. Some time before daylight one of Tuina's daughters was drowned, and then the other two, and Wakara's two daughters. About dawn Tuina and Wakara with their two wives were drowned. All were dead in the sweat-house except Igupa Topa, his nephew, and Halai Auna. At daylight the rain stopped, the water began to go down, and all the bodies floated out through the doorway. The place was dry. Pun Miaupa made a fire. Halai Auna came to the fire and began to cry for her father, her mother and sisters.

"You must not cry," said Pun Miaupa; "my uncle did this. He will bring all to life again quickly."

But Halai Auna was afraid, and she cried for some time.

Just after midday Igupa Topa went outside, saw the dead bodies, and said: "Why sleep all day?

It is time to be up, you two old men and you five young girls!"

Tuina and Wakara sprang up, went to the creek, and swam. "No one but Igupa Topa could have done this to us," said they.

All the women rose up as if they had been only sleeping.

"My brother, I shall go home to-morrow," said Wakara. "It is time for me."

Very early next morning Wakara and his wife began to dance, then the two daughters, then Halai Auna and her husband. They danced out by the smoke-hole, rose through the air, sang, and danced themselves home.

Wakara had been five days away, and all his daughters' husbands were saying: "Where is our father-in-law? He may have been killed." All were very glad when they saw old Wakara in the sweat-house next morning.

Before leaving Tuina's sweat-house Igupa Topa had gone into his nephew's heart again. When Wakara came home, he took his new son-in-law to try a sport which he had. The old man had made a great pole out of deer sinews. This pole was fixed in the ground and was taller than the highest tree. Wakara played in this way: A man climbed the pole, a second bent it down and brought the top as near the foot as possible. He let the top go then, and it shot into the air. If the man on the pole held firmly, he was safe; if he lost his grip he was hurled up high, then fell and was killed.

"Come, my son-in-law," said Wakara one day, "I will show you the place where I play sometimes pleasantly."

They went to the place. The old man climbed first, grasped the pole near the top. Pun Miaupa pulled it down; his uncle was in his heart, and he was very strong. He brought the top toward the ground, did not draw very hard, and let the pole fly back again. It sprang into the air. Wakara was not hurled away; he held firmly. Pun Miaupa brought down the pole a second time, he brought it down rather softly, and let it go. Wakara held his place yet. He tried a third time. Wakara was unshaken.

"That will do for me," said Wakara. "Go up now; it is your time."

Pun Miaupa went on the pole and held with his uncle's power. It was not he who held the pole, but Igupa Topa. "I will end you this time," thought Wakara. He bent the pole close to the ground and let go. Wakara looked sharply to see his son-in-law shoot through the air, — looked a good while, did not see him. "My son-in-law has gone very high," thought he. He looked a while yet in the sky; at last he looked at the pole, and there was his son-in-law.

He bent the pole a second time, bent it lower than before; then let it fly. This time Wakara looked at the pole, and Pun Miaupa was on the top of it.

Wakara was angry. He bent the pole to the ground, bent angrily, and let it go. "He will fly away this time, surely," thought he, and looked to the sky to see Pun Miaupa, did not see him ; looked at the pole, he was on it. " What kind of person is my son-in-law ? " thought Wakara.

It was Wakara's turn now to go on the pole, and he climbed it. Pun Miaupa gave his father-in-law a harder pull this time, but he held his place. The second time Pun Miaupa spoke to Wakara in his own mind : " You don't like me, I don't like you ; you want to kill me. I will send you high now."

He bent the pole, brought the top almost to the foot of it, and let it fly. He looked to the top, Wakara was gone. He had been hurled up to the sky, and he stayed there.

Pun Miaupa laughed. " Now, my father-in-law," said he, " you will never come down here to live again ; you will stay where you are now forever, you will become small and die, then you will come to life and grow large. You will be that way always, growing old and becoming young again."

Pun Miaupa went home alone.

Wakara's daughters waited for their father, and when he did n't come back they began to cry. At last, when it was dark and they saw their father far up in the sky, they cried very bitterly.

Next morning Pun Miaupa took Halai Auna, his wife, and his uncle, and went to his father's house.

Chuhna, the greatest spinner in the world, lived among Wakara's daughters. All day those women cried and lamented.

"What shall we do?" said they; "we want to go and live near our father. Who can take us up to him?"

"I will take you up to him," said Chuhna, the spinner, who had a great rope fastened to the sky.

Chuhna made an immense basket, put in all the daughters with their husbands, and drew them up till they reached the sky; and Wakara's daughters, the stars, are there on the sky yet.

THE HAKAS AND THE TENNAS

THE HAKAS AND THE TENNAS

PERSONAGES

After each name is given that of the creature or thing into which the personage was changed subsequently.

Darí Jowá, eagle; Haka, flint; Hakayámchiwi, the whole Haka people; Ilhataina, lightning; Tenna, grizzly bear; Tsawandi Kamshu, red flint clover; Tsawandi Kamshupa, young red flint clover; Tsuwalkai, a reddish flint. Marimi means woman.

AT first about two hundred people lived with the old woman, Tsuwalkai Marimi, in one great house; they were all descended from her. They were the Hakayamchiwi, — all the Haka people.

Now, there was a deadly quarrel between the Hakas and the Tennas, who lived near them, and it began in this way: The Tennas invited the Hakas to a hunt in the mountains; ten of each people were to make a party of twenty. One Tenna went early the first morning to make a fire at some distance from the sweat-house, at a meeting-place for the hunters of both sides. Ten Hakas went out early, were first at the fire; but the Tennas came, and then the twenty stood around to warm themselves, — the Tennas on the north and the Hakas on the south side of the fire.

The Hakas had flint arrow-heads, good ones; the Tennas had arrow-heads of pine bark. While they were warming themselves, a Tenna said to a Haka, " Let me see your arrow-point."

" Here it is," said the Haka ; " look at it."

" He, he, he ! " laughed the Tenna ; " that point is no good ! " He held it out, looked at it, and laughed again. " If I put it down my throat, it won't hurt me."

" Let me see your arrow-point," said the Haka.

" Here it is," said the Tenna.

The Haka looked at the pointed pine bark, laughed, and said : " That is no arrow-head ; that is nothing but pine bark. If I stab myself behind with your arrow-head, it won't hurt me. I shall not die."

" Let me see you stab yourself," said the Tenna.

" Look at me. I 'll stab myself behind with it."

The Haka stabbed himself, and the Tenna's arrow-head broke ; it did not hurt him a bit. " You see," said he, " I am not dying."

" Let me see your arrow-head," said the Tenna.

He gave the arrow-point, and the Tenna stabbed himself in the same way that the Haka had. The arrow-head was very sharp and went into him, cut him, — cut his intestines. He fell over and lay on the ground, lay there groaning.

" You see that my arrow-head is good ; it will kill any one," said the Haka.

Right away the Tenna was dying ; very soon he was dead. When the Tennas saw that their brother was dead, they rushed at the ten Hakas and killed them hand to hand before they could use arrows, before they could save themselves.

The Tennas went home, but the Hakas did not go home that evening.

Next morning early one of the Tennas came to the house of the Hakas, and called out, —

"Come to the fire, cousins; come to the fire. We will meet you there. Oh, cousins, it is time to go hunting; be up. Your brothers who went yesterday are going again to-day."

"We will go," said the Hakas, who did not know that their brothers were killed.

The Tennas had a fire in the same place as the first day, and were there waiting. After a time the ten Hakas came and stood at the fire in the same way as their brothers had stood a day earlier. They did not quarrel now, but went to the woods soon. The Tennas had everything ready for hunting; other Tennas were hidden in the woods, and ten more Hakas were killed by them that day.

On the third morning a Tenna came to the Hakas and called, —

"Cousins, it is time to be up, time to hunt. Your brothers of yesterday and the day before are all waiting."

"We will go, we will go," said the Hakas.

The fire was ready; the Tennas were there. They came earlier, and acted just as they had acted the second day. Ten more Hakas were killed by them that day.

The Hakas would not go on the fourth day. The Tennas began now to kill Hakas whenever they found them out hunting, or fishing, whenever they saw them in the woods anywhere. When the

Haka women went to dig roots, or find worms, or gather acorns, the Tennas killed them wherever they caught them. When the children went out to play or went to get water, they killed them. The Tennas killed on till only one old woman, Tsuwalkai Marimi, and her grandson, Tsawandi Kamshu, were left of all the Hakas.

One evening Tsawandi Kamshu hung his bow (an old bow bound around closely with deer sinew) over his bed on the south side of the sweat-house. With this bow he hung an otter-skin quiver full of arrows.

" My grandmother," said he in the night, " I may not come back to-morrow. If anything happens, the bow and the quiver and all that are with them will fall on the bed. You will know then that some one has killed me. But a child will rise from the spittle which I have left near the head of the bed ; a little boy will come up from the ground."

Tsuwalkai Marimi listened, said nothing, made no answer. Tsawandi Kamshu went out the next morning at daybreak, stayed out all that day. At dusk the bow fell with the quiver.

The old woman began to cry. She cried bitterly. " All our people are dead," said she. " All our people are gone, and I am alone."

She went around crying ; went along the four sides of the house ; went to where the bows, arrows, and otter-skin quivers were hanging ; cried all that night, cried all the next day.

The Tennas watched for the old woman, watched closely. They wanted to kill her, but they could

not break into the house, and she would not go out
to them.   They wanted to kill her and put an end
to the last of the Hakas.

While Tsuwalkai was crying the second night, the
Tennas were near the house listening and watching.

" The old woman is laughing," said they.   " She
is having some feast; that is why she is laughing.
She must be glad, that old woman."

Tsuwalkai heard these words of her enemies.
" Oh, Tennas, do not talk that way," said she.
" Something may happen yet that will hurt you.
Some one may come who will make your hearts
sore.   You may drop tears yet, you may be sorry."

The old woman cried the third night and third
day.   The fourth night she dropped no tears, but
she could not sleep.   In the middle of the fourth
night she heard crying on the ground near Tsawandi
Kamshu's sleeping-place.   A little baby was crying, rolling, struggling, wailing.   The old woman
listened, she heard " U ná, u ná."   She was frightened at first.

" I must be dreaming of a baby, I must be dreaming," said she.   " Oh, my people are making me
dream.   I hear a noise like the crying of a baby in
my sweat-house.   Oh, it is no baby; I am only
dreaming."

The baby cried on, kept crying.   The old woman
went to the spot where the crying was, looked, found
a baby covered with dirt, mud, and ashes.   She had
not carried the ashes out since her grandson had
gone; she could not carry them.   The Tennas were
watching outside for her, watching to kill the old

woman. The baby rolled around in the dirt and the ashes.

"I don't think any one brought that baby into this house," said the old woman to herself. "Tsawandi Kamshu said that a baby would come from the ground, would rise from his spittle. Maybe this is his spirit that has come back and is a baby again. I will call this baby Tsawandi Kamshupa."

She took up the baby, a little boy, washed him, washed him all night, the little child was so dirty. She washed him in cold water, and he grew while she washed. She washed him till morning, but gave him no food.

The Tennas heard now the noise of two people inside. Tsuwalkai Marimi felt glad, she had the company of this little boy. All day and two nights she washed the child. He ate nothing.

"I want you to live and grow large, little boy," said the old woman. "I want you to grow quickly; you will be a great help to me."

The little boy did not know what was said yet. She washed the child, talked three days and three nights to him. The little boy could creep around the house now, could creep through every part of it. She washed him in the night, in the day; washed him often. He grew very fast. In ten days he was a man full grown. He could talk now as well as any one, and one day he asked the old woman, —

"What house is this? What people live here?"

She told him the whole story of her people; told how all had been killed by the Tennas in the woods, in the fields, on the water.

"I am sorry to hear what you tell," said he.

He asked now for a bow. She gave him a fresh one. He broke it.

"I want one to kill birds outside with it."

"You must not go out," said the old woman; "bad people are near us."

"I only want to kill birds. Whose arms are these?" asked he, pointing to knives, bows, and arrows on the walls.

"Oh, it makes me sorry to tell you, it makes me sorry to talk of them. These are the arms of many men. The Tennas killed all of them."

She went to the west side of the house and gave him bows. He broke one after another. He broke every bow on the walls except one. When he came to his own bow, his old bow, he laughed. He took it himself without asking. He tried and could not break it; tried again, laughed, and was glad.

"Tsuwalkai, whose bow is this?" asked he.

"That was the bow of a good man."

"He was a good man, I think," said Tsawandi Kamshupa; "why did he die? There was a good man in this house; he had that bow; he was a great fighter."

Tsawandi Kamshupa tried again to break the bow with his feet and hands, but he could not.

"There was a good man in this house," said the old woman, "the best man of all the Haka people. That was his bow."

"I wished to go hunting to-day, but I will go very early to-morrow. I will go before daylight," said Tsawandi Kamshupa. " I am going to look around. I am going a short distance to hunt. I will come back ; have no fear."

The old woman was afraid. She had lost the owner of the bow, the best of her grandsons.

" I will only go down south a little way," said he.

Early next morning he took a deerskin, wrapped it around his body, tied a belt around his waist, and took his arrows. There was dew on the grass yet. He looked down the mountain-side, saw many people near a big fire, and said, —

" I know who those people are; they are Teptewi " (Tenna women).

There were fifty of them. They had come to that swampy mountain-side early in the morning. They had come before daybreak to dig worms and gather clover. Each had a stick to dig worms with.

The young man stood watching these women, and said to himself : " What shall I do ? These Tennas have killed all my people except my old grandmother. They tried to kill her. They will kill her and me if they can. What shall I do ? There are a great many women there. I will kill a lone one to begin with, then hide my bow and quiver and go to those farther down."

He went along the slope somewhat, came to one Tenna woman, and killed her. The others did not see him, did not know that he was on the mountain, thought that all the Hakas were dead.

He opened the Tenna's throat, took her heart, put it inside his blanket, and left the body dead on the ground. The other Tenna women were working not far from a fire. These women had taken their teeth out and hung them on a tree near the fire. Whenever they were angry the women put these teeth in their mouths to bite with.

Tsawandi went along the mountain-side carefully. "I will go to that fire," thought he. Then he sprang up and stood near the fire, warmed his hands. The women did not see him yet. One looked up at the fire, but saw no one. "Hei!" cried he, "you women are out very early. Come here and warm yourselves. Cook worms for me; I am hungry, I want worms."

The women gave no answer, said nothing. They were afraid; they could not bite, for their teeth were out. "If I had my teeth, I would kill that man," thought each woman.

Tsawandi kept his eye on the teeth, which were at one end of the fire; he would let no woman come near them. "Come up! come up!" called he. At last they came up and sat near the fire, but could not get their teeth. "I did not know that women go out in the morning so early," said he. "I saw a deer some distance back here and killed it. I was in a great hurry. I took only a small piece of meat."

He took out the heart, cut it into pieces, roasted them by the fire; then he gave some to each woman. The women were hungry, and were glad to get meat.

"Have you no bread?" asked Tsawandi.

"We have no bread," said the women.

"Well, I have acorn bread." He had no bread, but he put his hand in his bosom and thought, "I want bread of red flint meal." This bread came to his bosom, and he gave each woman a piece of it. "My grandmother makes good bread," said he. "I carry it with me always to show people and let them have some to eat. Every one likes my grandmother's bread."

The bread tasted well; all ate. He watched their teeth closely. Very soon a woman fell dead; then all fell quickly and died. He cut their hearts out — fifty hearts — and carried them under his deerskin. He went farther south now; ran quickly. He saw fifty more women working near a fire; went near the fire, sprang up to it, and cried, —

"Hu, hu! women, you are out early; why so early? It is cold; come warm your hands. Give me something to eat; give me worms and clover; give me something to eat, and I will give you something; I will give bread, I will give venison."

These women had come out to dig roots; their teeth were hanging on a tree near the fire. The Tenna women never kept their teeth in their mouths while they were working. "I wish my teeth were in my mouth," thought each woman, "I would kill that man."

All these fifty women came up to the fire, ate acorn bread as the others had eaten, and died.

From this fire Tsawandi Kamshupa went to another, and that morning he killed all the Tenna women who were out; not one was left alive, except a few who had remained at home in the sweat-house.

He went farther south now; went to their sweat-house. It was still early morning. All the Tenna men were at home. "How shall I kill them?" thought Tsawandi. "I will go into the house and say that I am sent by my brother to invite them to a feast and a hunt. They 'll believe that."

He looked down from the top of the house. There were many Tennas there. All the Tenna men were in the sweat-house. Tsawandi Kamshupa went in boldly; sat near the fire, warming his hands. The Tennas whispered to each other, "That 's my blood, sister; that 's my blood, brother!" meaning, "he 's my share; I 'll eat him."

"Oh, you Tenna people, what are you talking of? I am your neighbor. I do not live very far from you, I am no stranger. I have come down here early this morning to invite you to a feast, to a hunt. Tsawandi Kamshu sent me down here to ask you; he would like to see you at his sweat-house."

"This one here looks like Tsawandi Kamshu himself," whispered some.

"Oh, no," whispered others. "Tsawandi Kamshu is dead this good while. We killed him."

"What are you telling each other?" interrupted Tsawandi Kamshupa. "I am not Tsawandi Kamshu. He does not look like me. He is my brother. He sent me to ask you to hunt. I killed some deer on the way here, but could bring only their hearts. Here are the hearts."

He cut the hearts into pieces, gave them all to the Tennas. They roasted the hearts and ate them. He gave flint bread to them, as he had to the women on the mountain slope. All ate the bread, praised it, asked for more, ate it very eagerly. They began soon to fall on every side. Four Tennas only would not eat the flint bread. They closed the ground door, fastened it outside, went to the top of the sweat-house, and watched. Soon every Tenna in the sweat-house was dead.

Tsawandi Kamshupa looked up and saw the four Tennas there looking down at him. Their four heads were close together, and they looked very angry.

"Why are you four looking down here so? What are you watching for, what are you trying to do up there? The people down here have all gone to sleep, and can't talk with me. I want you men to talk a while. Come down, you, and talk with me; then I'll go home."

The four Tennas said nothing.

"You want to catch me; I know that. I will show you how I can jump."

They said nothing, watched sharply, sitting opposite each other with their long teeth sticking out. When he saw that they would not leave the opening, he said again, "I will show you how I can jump."

He bent to one side a little, shot up like an arrow, darted out between the four. The next thing the Tennas saw was Tsawandi Kamshupa in the field beyond the house.

When he had passed through the opening, the Tennas closed their jaws with a snap, and almost bit each other's noses off. Their bite was too late.

Tsawandi Kamshupa now sent three arrows from his old bow. They went through the hearts of three Tennas; they dropped dead where they stood. The fourth ran away, ran with all his strength, was never seen in that place again. He ran northwest, and from that Tenna come all that are in the world in our time.

Tsuwalkai Marimi could go out now and dig roots. She was free to go anywhere. While digging one day she saw the strong stalk of shitpayu sticking out of the ground. She dug around it and below the roots, found a little baby. The stem was growing out of the child's navel. She took the baby, twisted the stalk off, and bound up the child. She had nothing to wrap around the little one; so she took her skirt made of buckskin, the only clothing she wore, and wrapped it around the baby. Holding it close to her breast, she fondled the child and said, —

" Grow, little boy, grow quickly; you will be company yet for your grandmother."

She brought the boy home, washed him, washed him many times, put him in a wildcat skin. When Tsawandi Kamshupa came and saw Tsuwalkai with the baby, he wondered and cried, —

" Oh, grandmother, where did you find the little boy? "

She told how she had found him in the field, dug him out of the ground, and brought him home. That same day Dari Jowa, Tsawandi Kamshupa's great friend, came, and, seeing the little boy, laughed loudly.

" Oh, my aunt," said he, "that is not your baby. Where did you find that little boy?"

She told him the same story that she had told her grandson.

The baby grew quickly, grew large in a little while.

" Oh, my aunt," said Dari Jowa, " give this boy to me. I want to hear him talk. I want him for myself. I will take good care of him. I want to hear him talk, I want to hear him shout. He will be a great shouter. Oh, my aunt, give this little boy to me."

The old woman agreed at last. Dari Jowa took the boy and called him Ilhataina. One day Dari Jowa brought Ilhataina to the sweat-house and said, " Talk now."

Ilhataina began to talk, and the sweat-house trembled. He shouted; the whole earth shook. He was thundering.

ILHATAINA

ILHATAINA

PERSONAGES

After each name is given that of the creature or thing into which the personage was changed subsequently.

Ahalamila, gray wolf; **Demauna,** pine marten; **Gowila,** lizard; **Ilhataina,** lightning; **Jul Kurula,** woodgrub; **Jupka,** butterfly of the wild silkworm; **Tsoré Jowá,** a kind of eagle.

NEAR Jigulmatu lived Tsore Jowa, a very old woman. Once in the spring she went west to dig roots, and found a great clump of them. "I 'll come to-morrow and dig these," thought she, and went home.

Next morning she went to get the roots. She dug around the whole clump, but could not pull it up. She dug deeper, pulled and tugged; at last the roots came, and on them a little boy with eyes staring out of his head. She pushed the eyes back, cured him, put him in a rabbit-skin blanket which she wore, and went home. She washed the boy all day, and did not sleep at night. She washed him all the time. When five days old, he had grown a good deal. On the sixth day he crept; on the ninth he walked. When fifteen days old, he was a strong but very small boy.

"I want a bow and arrows," said he.

"You must not go out," said the old woman, "you must not leave my sight."

He teased till at last she gave him a bow and said, "You must stay on the housetop, and not go away."

While he was on the house a bird flew up, perched on a tree-top, and asked, " Why does n't your mother nurse you?"

The bird repeated this and flew away. The boy cried; came down and told his grandmother.

" Where are our people? Tell me," said he.

" Our people were many," said she, " but Gowila killed them all. We have no people now."

" Who is Gowila?"

" Oh, he is strong and terrible; you must not see Gowila."

The boy walked around the house then, looked at the walls, and asked, " May I have that bow hanging there?"

" You may if you like," said she, " but you are too weak to use it. You are very small, a little fellow."

He started at the east side of the sweat-house and went northward, tried the first bow, broke it; went on, took another, broke that. Then he went around the whole house, breaking every bow that he came to, till on the south side he reached the last bow. It was made of deer sinew. He bent that, tried his best, tried again and again, could not break it. " What kind of a bow is this?" thought he. " It is the ugliest, the oldest, but I cannot break it." He took the bow and a big stone to crush it. The bow flew out of his hand, and the stone fell.

" How did the man die who used this bow ? "
asked the boy.

" Gowila killed him, and those who had the
other bows," answered the old woman.

" I will go for wood now and sweat."

" Do not go far," said Tsore Jowa.

The boy ran off to the east, seized a big pine-
tree, tore it up with one pull, and took it home
in one hand. He made a big fire and put stones
on it.

" Bring water, my grandmother," said he ; " then
I will tell you what to do." The old woman filled
a great basket with water. The stones were dropped
in when red-hot, and the water boiled quickly.

" Grandmother, put me into the boiling water."

The old woman was frightened, but did what he
told her.

" Cover me closely," said the boy.

She covered him with another tight basket. He
lay in the water till the cover flew from the basket,
and he was thrown through the opening in the top
of the sweat-house and dropped on the roof outside.
He ran down, swam in the river close by, and then
went back and talked with the old woman.

" You will be very strong," said she. " You will
be called Ilhataina."

He ran east a second time ; brought sugar-pines.
He did not sleep, he sang without stopping. Rocks
were made hot as before, and dropped into a bigger
basket. The old woman put in Ilhataina, and covered him with four closely woven baskets. He was
in the boiling water till the four covers burst off,

and he flew up through the opening in the top of the sweat-house. He ran down again to the river, and while swimming talked to himself, saying, —

"I will meet Gowila to-day, I will meet Gowila to-day."

At sunrise he went home. "Grandmother, I am going out a short way," said he, taking down his old bow and one arrow.

"Oh, grandson, you must not go far; you must not leave my sight," said the old woman.

He counted twenty otter-skin quivers filled with arrows, and said, "I will take these."

She cooked roots for his breakfast, and brought a small basket full for him to take with him. He went west to a grove of trees, made a fire there, and caused salmon to hang all around on the tree branches. Crowds of men and women were heard talking and laughing near by. He made it so. There were no people in the place. He made the noise to entice Gowila.

He began to dig roots then. He dug without raising his head, dug and worked on, singing songs as he worked. Soon a big ugly old man from the north came. This was Gowila. He had a great dog, and a deer head was hanging at his back, with long horns on each side of it.

"You sing a nice song," said he.

Ilhataina never looked up.

"Come to the fire," said Gowila.

The boy said nothing; dug all the time.

"Come to the fire; I am hungry," said Gowila.

After a time Ilhataina went to the fire.

"You sing well," said Gowila. "Where did you come from?"

"From Jigulmatu. People sing well at Jigulmatu, and they dance well."

Gowila sat down near the fire. "Put roots in my mouth. Put in more," said he, when the boy gave him some.

The boy fed Gowila until he had eaten all the roots in the basket.

"How many people are digging roots around here?" asked he.

"I do not know; a great many," said Ilhataina.

A loud noise of people was heard a short distance away, — a noise of men and women laughing and talking. Gowila saw blankets and baskets near the fire. Ilhataina made the appearance of them. There was nothing there but the twenty otter-skin quivers and the ugly old bow and one arrow in his hand.

"Give me your bow," said Gowila; "let me look at it."

He asked again and again till the boy gave the bow. Gowila threw it into the fire.

"Why do that?" asked Ilhataina, snatching his bow from the fire. "Let me see your bow."

Gowila handed the bow to him. Ilhataina broke it with his left hand, and then sprang toward the east. Gowila was very angry, and said "Teh!" to his dog. The dog rushed at the boy. Ilhataina shot and hit the dog. He shot all the arrows but one from ten quivers. Every arrow hit but did no harm to the dog. Just then one of the seven stars (the Pleiades) called to Ilhataina, —

" Shoot him in the little toe and he will die."

The boy hit the dog's little toe. He fell dead.

Ilhataina ran to the fire where Gowila was standing. " You cannot kill me," said he to Gowila ; " you are big and strong, but you cannot hurt me."

" I will kill you," said Gowila ; and he sent an arrow at him. It missed.

Ilhataina shot his arrow and it struck. Every arrow that he sent went into Gowila, but no arrow struck Ilhataina. All the arrows but one were gone from the second ten quivers. That moment one of the seven stars called to Ilhataina, —

" Shoot at his little toe. If you hit him there, he will die."

Ilhataina struck Gowila's little toe, and he dropped dead.

Ilhataina skinned Gowila, stripped him from head to foot, put the skin on himself, and became just like his enemy. Next he struck the dog with a red rose switch, and the dog jumped up alive and glad to see his master. Ilhataina hung the deer head behind his shoulders, took his quivers, and went home. Gowila's dog followed him. When near the house, he made heavy steps, and the old woman looked out.

" Oh, Gowila is coming ! Gowila is coming ! " cried she, terribly frightened.

" Grandmother, don't be afraid ; it is I. Gowila is dead. I have killed him. I am wearing his skin. I am as big and as ugly as he was. I will go to his

house to-night, I think. I have brought his liver
and lights with me."

" Go, grandson, go. I fear nobody now."

Ilhataina went away, saying, " I will be here about
sunrise to-morrow."

He went north to Gowila's sweat-house, went a
long way, went quickly, walked up to the house,
was just like Gowila. A great many people lived
in that house. All kinds of snake people were there,
— rattlesnakes, bull-snakes, water-snakes, striped
snakes, all kinds of snakes.

He hung Gowila's liver and lights outside, went
in, and sat down between Gowila's two wives. The
dog lay down in his own place. The wives were
Pupila women, two sisters.

" Bring in the meat which I hung up outside and
cook it," said Ilhataina to the elder wife.

He cut the liver and lights into small bits, and
the two women boiled them. There was a great
steam and a strong smell from these pieces. All in
the house were blind except the two wives, and only
one of the blind people spoke, Gowila's younger
brother. " I smell Gowila's flesh," said he.

" How could you smell Gowila's flesh when I am
Gowila ? "

Ilhataina was very angry, and dashed live coals
through the house. All were terrified. All ate of
the meat except Gowila's younger brother. He
was very wise and would n't touch it.

Ilhataina went out and found a great many legs
around the house. Gowila had eaten the bodies of
thousands of people and thrown the legs away.

Ilhataina gathered these into one place and went back to the house.

"Blind people," said he, "I wish you would sing, and you, my wives, dance for me. I 'll go to sleep then."

"We will sing," said they, "and dance."

The blind people sang, and the two women danced. Soon the men and the two women stopped. Ilhataina made them all drowsy, and they fell asleep. Then he went out, fastened the door, and said, —

"I want the walls of this house to be covered with pitch."

The whole house was covered with pitch, and then he set fire to it. Soon he heard terrible screaming inside and crowds running around in the sweat-house. None could get out, and all were burned to death quickly.

Ilhataina tied the legs together with a long grape-vine and carried them home. He was there about daylight. He placed them all in the river and went to the sweat-house.

"Hide me, and then lie on your face with your arms under your head," said he to his grandmother.

The old woman put him in one basket and covered him with another, then lay herself as he had directed.

In the middle of the forenoon there was a great noise of people rising out of the river. They came in through the top of the sweat-house. When all were inside, the old woman stood up. All her people were alive there before her, — Demauna, Jupka, and others; all had come back.

"Who brought us to life again?" asked Demauna. "Show me the person."

The old woman took Ilhataina out of the basket and carried him to them. Demauna caught him in his arms. " Well done, my brother!" said he. All the rest called him brother.

" Let me have him," said Ahalamila.

" No," answered Demauna; " I will keep him myself."

They asked the old woman where she had found Ilhataina. She would not tell.

" Will you sweat? " asked Ilhataina.

" Yes," said all the people.

" I will bring wood," said he.

When he ran out, the sweat-house danced in its place. All thought he was too small to carry wood, but when he snatched a tall fir the earth trembled. When he touched a big sugar-pine, he crushed it. He brought great trees in a moment, and when he put them down the place shivered. All were in terror.

When Ilhataina talked the whole world was afraid, and when he moved the ground which he walked on was quivering.

All sweated, swam in the river, and went back to the old woman's. Ilhataina walked across the house, and his heart shook as if it would jump from his body.

" I am not going to stay here," said he.

When Demauna heard this, he cried, and the old woman cried.

" My brother," said Demauna, " I should like to know where you are going. I wish you would stay with us."

Ilhataina made no answer.

" My brother," said Jupka, "if you will not stay here, I wish you would go to the sky. Now," said Jupka, "will you take beads as a gift from me?"

" No."

" Shells?"

" No."

" Wolf robes?"

" No."

" Wildcat robes?"

" No."

" Foxskin robes?"

" No."

Jupka wore an old ragged rabbit-skin robe. He had worn it a long time. "I think you like this," said he.

" Yes," answered Iihataina, "that's what I want." He took the old robe and tied it with weeds around his waist. "Now I am ready to leave you. Come out and see me go."

There was a black cloud in the sky. Ilhataina had brought it there. "I will go up to that place," said he. "Whenever rain comes in future, it will be water falling from my rabbit robe."

All hurried out. Jupka's son, Jul Kurula, who was wrapped in a black bearskin, came down into the sweat-house and cried; he did n't wish to lose Ilhataina.

" Now, my friends," said Ilhataina, "I leave you; hereafter when you see me travel I shall go like this;" and he went with a flash to the black cloud.

He was taken into it, and now he stays there.

HITCHINNA

HITCHINNA

PERSONAGES

After each name is given that of the creature or thing into which the personage was changed subsequently.

Hitchinna, wildcat; Hitchin Marimi, wildcat woman, his wife; Hitchinpa, young wildcat; Metsi, coyote; Putokya, skull people, or head people.

HITCHINNA had a wife and a son a few days old. Hitchinpa, the little son, was sleeping, and Hitchin Marimi, the wife, was taking care of her child. Hitchinna had dreamed the night before, and his dream was a bad one.

"I had a dream last night," said he to his wife, "a very bad dream."

"What did you dream?" asked she.

"I dreamed that I climbed a big pine-tree; the tree was full of cones. I was throwing them down, had thrown down a great many, when at last I threw down my right arm. I dreamed then that I threw down my left arm."

He told her no more. That morning early, before he had talked of his dream, the woman said, —

"I should like to have pine-nuts; I want to eat pine-nuts; I am hungry for pine-nuts."

He went out to find the nuts, and she went with him, taking the baby. They came to a large pine-tree, and he climbed it. Hitchin Marimi put the baby aside on the ground, and made a fire at some distance to roast the pine-cones.

Hitchinna threw down cones; she roasted them to get out the nuts. He threw down a great many cones. She roasted these cones and pounded the nuts out.

After a while Hitchinna's right arm fell off; he threw that to the ground, then he threw down his left arm. His left leg came off; he threw it down. Next his right leg dropped off, and he threw that to the ground.

The woman was roasting and pounding the pine-cones; she did not look around for a good while. At last she went to the tree, found blood on it, and looking up, saw that her husband was throwing himself down, that there was not much left of his body.

Hitchin Marimi was scared half to death; she ran away home. She was so terrified that she left the little child behind, forgot all about it. When she reached home, she called the people together and said, —

" My husband went up into a pine-tree; he threw down a great many pine-cones. Then he began to throw himself down; first he threw one arm, then the other. We must hurry and hide somewhere; he will be bad very soon; he will kill us all if he finds us."

The people asked, " Where can we go to hide from him, — north, south, east, or west? "

" I know a good place," said one man, "and it is not too far from here, — Wamarawi."

" Well, we must go to that place, and go very

quickly," said Hitchinna's wife; and all the people agreed with her.

The people ran to Wamarawi, which is a round mountain; they ran the whole way and went into a cave in the mountain. When all were inside, they closed the entrance very firmly, shut it up tight. Nothing could get in through that door.

After his wife had run home, Hitchinna threw down his ribs one by one, and kept asking his wife if she was there. He got no answer. She was gone and he did not know it. He threw down first all the ribs of his right side, then all of his left side. Every time he threw a rib he called, "Uh! Uh!" to his wife.

At last there was nothing left of him on the tree but his head, and that came down soon after. His eyes were very big now, sticking out, staring with a wild and mad look. The head lay under the tree a while. Hitchinna had become another kind of people. He had become a Putokya. He was one of the skull people, a very bad terrible people. Each one of them is nothing but a skull.

Putokya is new now. He has a new mind, new wishes. He is under the tree, and lies there a little while. He cannot walk any more. He can only roll on the ground like a ball. After resting and thinking a while, he starts to find his wife; rolls till he comes to the fire. There is no woman there. He looks around, cannot find her, looks again, and sees the baby. He rolls to the baby, catches it in his mouth, eats up the baby in one moment. The head talks then, and says, —

"I dreamed last night that I ate up my own son."

He is dreadful now. He scatters the pine-cones, quenches the fire, rages, roars awfully, a real Putokya. He rolls, bounds, knocks against a tree, cuts it down, breaks it to pieces, scatters it.

Next he starts for the village, springing and bounding along like a football, making a terrible wind as he goes, reaches the house, looks through it. All are gone from the house and from the village. All have run off to Wamarawi.

First he knocks against his own house, breaks it, smashes it to pieces, and then he breaks all the other houses in the same way, one after another. He scatters and smashes up everything, wrecks the whole village, just as if a strong whirlwind had gone through it. The people are all in Wamarawi, in the stone cave in the mountain, a very great crowd of them.

Putokya looks around, finds tracks, follows the people southward, goes with a terrible roar, raising a storm as he moves. He breaks everything he strikes, except rocks. From these he bounds off like a football.

He follows the people of the village, follows on their tracks, stops before Wamarawi, rolls up to the entrance, listens quietly, hears a sound inside like the buzzing of bees. Putokya is glad. He stops a while and thinks what to do. "You cannot go from me now," says he.

All the people were inside except Metsi; he had gone north somewhere.

" I will break in the cave," said Putokya.

He began at the west side, went back a whole mile, bounded, rushed, hurled himself at the mountain, whistled through the air with a noise like the loudest wind, struck the mountain, made a great hole in it, but could not go through to the cave. Putokya felt sure that he could break through. He went back a whole mile again from the north side, bounded, rushed forward, made a tremendous hole in the north side; but he could not go through, and the rock closed again.

The people inside are glad now; they are laughing, they think themselves safe, — jeer at Putokya. Putokya hears them. He is angrier than ever, he is raging. "I will try the east side," said he; "that is better."

He went back as before, bounded forward, made a deep hole in the east, but it closed again, and he left it. He tried the south. It was just like the other sides. Putokya stops a while, is afraid that he cannot get in, that he cannot get at the people.

"The Yana are not very wise," said he. "I should like to know who told them what to do. They did not know themselves. Who told them to go to Wamarawi?"

He tried to go to the top of the mountain and make a hole there. He could not roll up in any way. He fell back each time that he tried. He could travel on level ground only, he could only rise by bounding.

"I cannot go up there, I am not able," said he.

He lay down close to the entrance of the cave and thought a while. He made up his mind to bound like a ball, to spring from point to point, higher and higher, on neighboring mountains, till he got very high, and then come down on the top of Wamarawi. He did this, went far up on the top of other and higher mountains till at last he was very high; then with a great bound he came down on the top of Wamarawi, came down with a terrible crash. He made an awfully big hole in it, bigger than all the four holes he had made in the sides put together; and this hole did not close, but it did not reach the cave.

After that blow he came again to level ground. He lay there and said to himself: " I have tried five times to get at those people. I will try once more. I may get at them this time. "

He went high up in the sky, higher than before. He was angrier and madder than ever, and he came down with a louder crash; the whole mountain shook and trembled. No one inside the cave was laughing now; all the people were terrified.

Putokya went almost through to the cave. The rock above the people was very thin after this blow, and the hole did not close again.

" I will not try any more," said Putokya; " I cannot get at the people." He was discouraged, and left Wamarawi.

All the people within were in terror. " If he tries once more, we are lost," said they. " He will burst through and eat us, eat every one of us."

The great hole remained on that mountain top,

and people say that there is a lake up there now
with goldfish in it.

Putokya started north, went toward Pulshu Aina,
his own village. As he went toward home, he made
a great roaring and wind, cut down trees and brush,
people, beasts, everything that he met; he left a
clean road behind. He swept through Pulshu Aina,
and went farther north, went almost to Jigulmatu.

Metsi was coming down to the south, along the
same trail; he was very well dressed. Metsi always
dressed well. He wore a splendid elkskin belt and
a hair net; he was fine-looking.

Metsi was right in the middle of the trail. He
had learned that Putokya was out killing people in
the south; he heard the roar a great way off, and
said to himself, —

" I hear Putokya; he is killing all the people."

Metsi thought over what he was to do. " I will
meet him. I will say to this Putokya, ' You are
smart, you are good, but you are sick. I will cure
you.' "

Metsi took off all his fine clothes in a hurry and
hid them, made himself naked. " I must be quick,"
said he ; " the noise and wind are coming nearer and
nearer. I wish a rusty old basket to be here before me." The basket was there. He wished for
an old strap to carry it. The old strap was there
with the basket.

Metsi made buckskin rings around his arms and
legs, turned himself into an old, very old woman,
all bent and wrinkled, with a buckskin petticoat.
He put the rusty basket on his back.

Putokya was hurrying on ; the roar grew louder and nearer. Metsi knew that Putokya was very dangerous, and that he must be careful. He took white clay, painted his face, made a regular old woman of himself. Putokya came near. Metsi was ready, the basket on his back and a stick in his hand. He was walking along slowly, a very old woman and decrepit. The old woman began to cry, " En, en, en !"

Putokya stopped on the road, made no noise, listened to the old woman.

" He has stopped; he is listening to me," said Metsi; and he cried more, cried in a louder voice and more pitifully.

Putokya was quiet. Metsi walked right up to him, looked at him, and said, " I came near stepping on you." Metsi was crying more quietly now.

" Are you a dead person ? " asked Metsi.

Putokya was silent

" I heard you from where I was," said Metsi; " when you had a bad dream, I heard you in the south, heard you everywhere, heard you when you turned to be a Putokya, one of the head people, and wanted to kill everybody. You used to be good, you used to be wise, but now you are sick; you will die, and be among people no longer unless you are cured. That is why I started to come south ; I started south to find you, to see you. It is a good thing that you came up here; now I see you. I am your relative, your cousin. I want you to be healthy, to be as you were before; to have your arms and legs again, to feel well. I want to cure you."

Metsi was sobbing all this time. He pretended to be awfully sorry; he was n't, for Metsi was n't sorry for any one, did n't care for any one on earth; he only wanted to put Putokya out of the way, to kill him. Metsi was a great cheat.

"A good while ago," said Metsi, "I met a man like you. He had had a dream, and he was nothing but a head, just like you. I travelled then as I am travelling to-day, and met this man just as I meet you now on this road. If you believe what I tell you, all right; if you don't believe, it's all the same to me. I will tell you what I did for that man, how I cured him. Do you want me to tell you what I did for him?"

Putokya was looking all the time with great wildcat eyes at the old woman. Now he spoke, saying: "Talk more, tell me all, old woman. I want to hear what you have to say."

"Well, I made a man of that head," said the old woman. "I cured that Putokya; I made him over. I made him new, and he walked around as well as before; I gave him legs and arms; all the bad went out of him; I made him clean and sound and good again."

"How did you do that, old woman?" asked Putokya. "How can you make a man over again? I want to see that."

"I will tell you how I do it. I will fix you; I will fix you right here on this road, just as I fixed that other man. I made a hole in the ground; a long hole, a pretty big one. I lined it with rocks; I made a little fire of manzanita wood, and when it was nice and warm in the hole, I put plenty of pitch in, and put the man on top of the pitch. It was good and soft for him, and nice and pleasant on the pitch. I put a flat rock over the hole. He stayed there a while and was cured."

Putokya believed all this; had full faith in Metsi, and said, —

"Very well, you fix me as you fixed that other man; make me new again, just as I used to be."

Metsi added: "I put pitch very thick, one foot all around, and put him in the warm hole; covered him up. Pretty soon he began to stretch and grow; grew till he was as good as ever. That is how I cured that man."

"That is good," said Putokya. "Fix me in that way; fix me just as you fixed him."

"I will," said Metsi. "I will fix you just as I fixed that man, and you will come out just as he did; you will be in the right way and have no more trouble; you will never be sick again."

Metsi did everything as he had said; made a long deep hole, put in fire and a great deal of pitch, a foot thick of it.

He placed Putokya on the pitch; put a wide flat stone over him, put on others; put the stones on very quickly, till there was a great pile of them.

The pitch began to burn well, to grow hot, to seethe, to boil, to blaze, to burn Putokya.

He struggled to bound out of the pitch; the

stones kept him down, the pitch stuck to him. He
died a dreadful death.

If Putokya had got out of the hole, there would
have been hard times in this world for Metsi.

When Putokya was dead under the pile of rocks,
Metsi threw away his old things, his basket and
buckskin petticoat, put on his nice clothes, and went
along on his journey.

Metsi was a great cheat. He could change himself always, and he fooled people whenever he had a
chance; but he did a good thing that time, when he
burned up Putokya.

TIRUKALA

TIRUKALA

PERSONAGES

After each name is given that of the creature or thing into which the personage was changed subsequently.

Chíchepa, spotted chicken-hawk; Chikpina, weasel; Hapawila, water snake; Jewinna, chicken-hawk; Jewinpa, young chicken-hawk; Kedila, soaproot plant; Matsklila, turkey buzzard; Pakálai Jáwichi, water lizard; Tirúkala, lamprey eel; Wirula, red fox. Weanmauna means the hidden one.

TIRUKALA lived near Jamahdi, on the Juka Mapti Mountain, and he was thinking, thinking for a long time, how to change this world, how to make it better.

" I have to fix this country. I will fix it now," said Tirukala. " I will make it better to live in."

When he had said this he went off walking and began to sing. All the mountains stood too near together at that time, and Tirukala pushed the mountains apart from one another, made room between them. He put creeks everywhere, and big and little rivers. He made springs in different places and swamps. He put salmon and other fish into rivers and creeks, plenty of them everywhere.

Tirukala had two persons to help him, Pakalai Jawichi and Hapawila. The three lived together, working and making the world better to live in.

Tirukala never ate anything; never took food of any kind. He worked always, and sang while at work. Hapawila made salmon traps and caught many salmon. Just like Tirukala, he sang all the time. After a while two young girls heard this singing. They were the two daughters of Kedila. They went out to get wood one day and heard the singing.

They filled their baskets and went home, put the wood down, then went out and listened to the singing. They thought it was very sweet and beautiful.

"Let us go nearer to the singing," said the younger sister.

They went a little way from the house, sat down, and listened. Again they stood up and went on. Two or three times they did this, going farther and farther. Soon they came in sight of a salmon trap and went up to it.

"I see no one here," said each of the sisters. "Who can be singing?"

They looked on all sides of the trap and saw no one. They looked up and down the river. There was no one in sight. They sat down near the trap, watched and listened. At last the younger girl saw who was singing. She saw Hapawila in the river, where he was singing.

When he saw the girls sitting and listening, Hapawila came out to them.

"Which way are you going?" asked he.

"We heard singing, and came out to listen. That is why we are here," answered the elder.

"Let us go home," said the younger.

"Take some of my salmon to your father," said Hapawila; and he gave them two very nice salmon.

They took the salmon home to their father.

"Where did you get these salmon?" asked Kedila.

"A man who sings and has salmon-traps sent them to you."

That evening Hapawila went to old Kedila's house. The girls saw him coming and were frightened. They liked his singing, but they did not like his appearance. They ran away, found a great tree, climbed it, and thought to spend the night there. But Hapawila tracked them, came to the foot of the tree, looked up, and saw the two sisters near the top. He walked around, and looked at the tree.

"Let him come up," said the elder sister, "let him talk a while : we may like him better if he talks to us."

"No," said the younger sister, "I don't like him ; I don't want to talk with him."

He tried to climb the tree, but could not. The trunk was smooth, and the tree had no branches except at the top. Now the elder sister fixed the tree so that he could climb to them ; she wished for branches on the trunk — they were there at once, and Hapawila climbed up to Kedila's two daughters.

The younger sister was angry at this; hurried down the tree, ran home, and told her father that her sister and Hapawila were talking to each other in the tree-top.

Old Kedila said nothing, and went to bed. A few minutes later the elder sister was at home. She, too, ran from Hapawila when she saw him the third time.

Early next morning Kedila was very angry. He caught his elder daughter, thrust her into the fire, burned her, and threw her out of doors. The younger sister took up her sister's body, and cried bitterly. After a while she carried it to a spring, crying as she carried it. She washed her sister's body in the water. It lay one night in the spring. At daylight next morning the elder sister came out of the water alive, with all her burns cured and not a sore left on her.

"Where can we go now? Our father is angry; he will kill us if we go home," said the younger sister.

Both started west, singing as they travelled.

"I wish that I had a basket with every kind of nice food in it," said the younger sister toward evening. Soon a basket was right there. It dropped down in front of her. She looked. There were pine nuts in the basket, different roots, and nice food to eat.

Now, Jewinna lived in the west. He had a very large sweat-house and many people. His youngest and only living son he kept wrapped up and hidden away in a bearskin.

At sunset the two girls came to Jewinna's house, and put down their basket of roots near the doorway. Jewinna's wife went out and brought in the two girls. Jewinna himself spread out a bearskin and told the girls to sit on it. He said to his son, who was wrapped up and hidden away, —

"Come out and sit down with these two young girls who have come to us."

The youth looked through a small hole in his bearskin; saw the two women, but said nothing; did n't come out. When night fell, the two girls went to sleep. Next morning they rose, washed, dressed, and combed nicely. Then they went eastward, went toward their father's house.

Jewinna's son, Jewinpa, came out soon after, swam, dressed, ate, and followed the two girls. They went very fast, went without stopping; but Jewinpa caught up and went with them to their father's house.

Kedila was pleased with Jewinpa, and treated both his own daughters well. He spoke to them as if nothing had happened.

Old Jewinna in the west called all his people and said: " I want you, my people, to sweat and swim, then come here and listen to me."

After they had done this, Jewinna said: " I am sorry that my son has gone. I must follow him to-morrow. I don't know why he went. I do not wish him to go far from this place. Be ready, all of you, and we will go to-morrow."

Jewinna rose before daylight, called all his people, and said: " I cannot eat. I am sorry that my son has gone."

All took plenty of arrows and beads and otter-skins and red-headed wookpecker scalps, and started to follow the young man. As he started, Jewinna sang, —

"I-no-hó, i-no-hó no-há, i-no-hó ! "

A great many followed and repeated, —

"I-no-hó, i-no-hó no-há, i-no-hó ! "

They went on all day, went quickly, and at sunset they were on a smooth plain, not far from Kedila's place. Kedila had a large, rich sweat-house, and it was full of people. The old chief had a great many sons-in-law, and a great many people to serve him.

Jewinna and his men reached the place some time before nightfall, and Kedila went to the top of his sweat-house and said to the strangers, —

" I want you all to come in and enjoy yourselves. Perhaps my house is small; we will make it bigger."

He blew toward all the four sides then, and said, " Be bigger, my sweat-house, be bigger! "

The sweat-house stretched out and was very large. There was room for every one, and all came in.

" Bring food, my sons-in-law, for Jewinna and his people," said Kedila.

They brought in all kinds of good food, and fed every one gladly.

" Bring your beads, otter-skins, and red-headed woodpecker scalps, and put them down here at this side of the sweat-house," said Jewinna to his people.

All were brought in and given to Kedila. He took these rich things gladly, and put them away.

Kedila put down on his part wolf-skins with deer-skins and gave them to Jewinna.

" Let ten of you go out and hunt squirrels," said Jewinna to his people next morning; " let others fix heads on their arrows."

One of the ten saw a squirrel on a tree; he took a club, climbed after the squirrel, and killed it; he saw another and another; the tree was filled with squirrels. A second man saw squirrels in a second tree, and then a third and a fourth in other trees. Right away the ten were killing squirrels on ten trees, and soon they had ten piles of squirrels, each pile as large as one man could carry.

The two chiefs were delighted when they saw the ten loads of game, and there was a great feast of squirrel flesh that day at Kedila's.

Both sides sat down then to gamble, played with sticks, gambled all day, played till sunset. They bet all kinds of skins. Jewinna's men won a great many things, and won more than the presents.

Next morning Kedila's sons-in-law wanted to win back the beautiful skins and other things which they had played away, but before noon they had lost everything. When all was gone, Kedila's men were angry.

"You don't play fairly," said they to Jewinna's men; "you shall not have these things."

"We have won everything fairly," said Jewinna's men, "and we will take these things home with us."

They began to fight at once. Kedila's sons-in-law attacked Jewinna's men as soon as they were outside the sweat-house.

"We are here to fight if there is need," said Jewinna; "go ahead, my men, you are likely to die, every one of you."

Jewinna's men fought, going westward, fought carrying with them what they had won. Jewinna fought bravely, and sang as he fought. Kedila's people followed.

They fought till near sunset. All were killed now but eight men, four on each side, — Jewinna, his half-brother, and two more western people. Kedila and three others of the eastern people were alive yet.

These eight closed once more in fight; both chiefs fell with Jewinna's half-brother and Kedila's youngest son-in-law. Matsklila was so sorry for this last one that he threw away bow and arrows and fell to the ground crying bitterly. Seeing this, Chikpina picked up a rock and beat Matsklila's brains out. Wirula on Kedila's side killed Chikpina, and there were only two left, — Chichepa, the last of Jewinna's men, and Wirula, the last on Kedila's side.

" Now," said Wirula, " we have fought enough. You are alone. Go home and tell the women that your people are all killed. I am alone. I will go home and say that all our people are dead."

Jewinna had taken his son with him when he left Kedila's house, and he, too, had been killed in the struggle.

Now Wirula and Chichepa started off in opposite directions; went a little way; lay down and rolled along the ground, crying and lamenting. Wirula sprang up and said, —

" I will kill that Chichepa. I will kill him surely, and there will not be one left of our enemies."

Wirula turned and followed Chichepa slowly; drew his bow and sent an arrow after him. But Chichepa dodged; the arrow missed. Then Wirula ran away.

" I will kill that Wirula now," said Chichepa.

He turned and followed carefully, cautiously;

came up with him, and struck him fairly on the skull. Wirula dropped dead.

Chichepa turned homeward now, crying all the time. When he was near home, the women saw him stagger, then saw him fall. When he reached the top of the sweat-house, he fell in, rolled along the floor, and cried. He ate nothing that night; he was too sorry for his people. He slept a while and then woke up crying.

Early next morning he took ten otter-skins; went back to the dead people, pulled one hair from the head of each one of them, and filled the ten otter-skins with the hairs. He had the work done before sunset.

" Build a good fire," said he to the women when he reached home that night. " Give me four big water-baskets." They gave the baskets. He filled these with water, and put hot rocks in them. Then he emptied the ten otter-skins into the water.

" Stay all night in your houses. Let no one put a head out. I will stay in the sweat-house," said he.

The four baskets boiled hard. Just at daylight the largest basket fell over; then the second, the third, and the fourth fell. After that there were voices all around the sweat-house, hundreds upon hundreds of them.

" We are cold; open the door," cried the voices.

When full daylight had come, Chichepa opened the door, and all hurried in. Jewinna came first, and with him his son. All followed them, dressed as they had been when they went to Kedila's; all alive and well, strong and healthy. Jewinna laughed. He was glad.

On the way home Kedila's two daughters had two sons, the sons of Jewinpa. The boys were born the next day after Jewinpa had looked on their mothers. They had come from the eyes of their father. He had just looked through his fingers at Kedila's two daughters.

After Jewinna's son had been killed and then brought to life by Chichepa, he went east to Kedila's great sweat-house, stayed five days and nights there, then took his two wives and two sons and went back to his father's.

Kedila's youngest son, born when his father was old, came to life. He had sat always at the central pillar, at the edge of the ashes, and had always kept moving his arms, but he had never danced on that or on any floor. He had burned his face because he had sat so near the fire, and had sweated often from being so near it.

Every one laughed at him; jeered at that " Burnt Face," who sat night and day in the ashes. He spat always in one place. Kedila's eldest son had said many times, —

" If we are killed, we shall come back to life again."

" I don't think that you will," said Burnt Face; " but when I am killed I shall live again through my own power."

Burnt Face went out to fight, and was killed with the others. Now a little baby came right up out of the spittle of Burnt Face, a boy. The women took him and washed him. In one hour he had grown a good deal, in two hours still more. On the following day he had full growth.

Then this young man who had risen from the spittle went out of the house. He followed the course of the struggle, found all Kedila's people dead, struck each with his foot, turned him over. All came to life and rose up, as well as ever.

When Jewinna came for his wives, their brothers and brothers-in-law gave the women presents; but when his two wives and two sons went home with him and old Jewinna saw them coming, he took two bearskins quickly, and when they were on top of the sweat-house, he caught the young boys, put them into the bearskins, rolled them up, and put them away to be Weanmauna.

SUKONIA'S WIVES AND THE ICHPUL SISTERS

SUKONIA'S WIVES AND THE ICHPUL SISTERS

PERSONAGES

After each name is given that of the creature or thing into which the personage was changed subsequently.

Chikpitpa, young weasel; Jahtaneno, a kind of shell creature; Metsi, coyote; Ichpul, frog; Sukónia, a name of pine martin, whose ordinary name is Demauna; Tsoré Jowá, a kind of eagle.

OLD Jahtaneno had a great many daughters, and all but two of these were married.

At that time Sukonia was a great chief in this country about us. He had a large sweat-house, and many people to serve him.

One day Jahtaneno called his daughters and said : " My girls, I want you to go to Sukonia's house. I have heard that he is very rich ; go and see him. He has no wife yet ; he may marry you. Rise early in the morning, bathe, comb your hair, go and see the chief Sukonia."

The two sisters made no answer, said nothing, obeyed their father. They rose early next morning, bathed, combed their hair, painted their faces red (young people painted red always). Their mother gave each girl a nice basket; she hung beads on their necks, and put food in their baskets.

" If any man meets you on the road," said Jahtaneno, at parting, " do not look at him. A man richly dressed and wearing many beads will come toward you, will speak to you ; do not look at that man ; he is no one but Metsi."

The two girls began to sing when they started, and their song was : —

> " Au ni á, au ni á, mo a wé, he ló,
> Au ni á, au ni á, mo a wé, he ló."

They went northeast, the way which the old man had told them to go. He warned them further, saying, —

" There is a house this side of Sukonia's, and not very far from it ; two women live in that house, two old maids. Be sure not to stop at that house. Do not go near these women ; pass their place quickly, do not stop before it, do not talk to the women. They are bad, evil women. If you go into their house, you will never come out of it; if you go, you will be killed there."

Jahtaneno's daughters started, walked away quickly, singing as they went, —

> " Au ni á, au ni á, mo a wé, he ló,
> Au ni á, au ni á, mo a wé, he ló."

Metsi heard the song; he listened and said to himself: " That is a good song, that is nice singing; I like to hear that song. I think those two girls are going to the chief. I think they are going to visit Sukonia Mujaupa. Now, otter-skins be here before me, and beads in plenty, and beautiful shells."

He wished for all other things that he liked. Metsi dressed himself richly and waited.

Jahtaneno's daughters walked and walked on without stopping, met no one on the way till they came to where Metsi was waiting. The younger sister was walking ahead; she saw Metsi at one side of the trail, but would not look at him a second time. The elder sister looked a second and a third time.

"I think that is Sukonia Mujaupa," said she.

"Your father would not say so," answered the younger sister; "that is Metsi."

But the elder sister liked the stranger's appearance; she looked at him many times.

"I think this is Sukonia," said she.

"Come on with me," said the younger sister. "Have you lost your eyes? That is Metsi."

The younger girl was ahead now some distance; the elder stopped to look at the stranger more closely.

"Which way are you going?" asked Metsi.

"Our father sent us to Sukonia the chief."

"Oh, I am chief," said Metsi; "you are to come with me. I will start for home very soon."

"My sister is ahead, she is waiting. I must hurry and tell her first. I will come back to you then."

She caught up with her sister and said: "I will go with this man; this is Sukonia, the chief. He said he was chief."

"You must have lost your mind," answered the younger sister; "that is Metsi. He is no chief, he is not Sukonia."

The elder sister went with the younger, but she

wanted to go back to Metsi, she wished to go with him ; she liked his dress, his words pleased her, she believed him. Both went on, though the elder went against her will.

"You will see two black bearskins hanging over the sweat-house door," said the father, when his daughters were starting. "Stop there ; that is Sukonia's house, that is the house to which you are going."

Toward sunset they came near the place where the Ichpuls lived.

"Let us stop here," said the elder sister, "and get something to eat. I am hungry."

"Our father told us to pass this house ; he told us not to stop near it, not to go to it, not to look at it," said the younger sister ; and she went on without looking, she went straight ahead.

The elder sister followed her, but followed unwillingly. At last both came near Sukonia's, and saw the two bearskins hanging out over the sweat-house.

Chikpitpa, Sukonia's little brother, was on the roof, and Tsore Jowa, his sister, was at work making a house for herself a little way off at one side. Chikpitpa ran into the house, calling loudly, —

"Two girls are coming ! Two girls are coming with baskets !"

The old man, Sukonia's father, brought bearskins for the young women to sit on, and waited. The sisters came in and took the places shown them. Chikpitpa was in a corner when the sisters sat down. He ran to one and then to the other, looked at them, sat on their laps. He was very glad that the sisters had come; he liked to be with them and talk to them.

Old Sukonia went out and called to Tsore Jowa, " Come, my daughter; bring food to our guests, to the young women who have come to us."

She brought deer's marrow; she brought other kinds of food, too. The sisters had put down their baskets outside, near the door. On the way they had said to the baskets, " Let the food in you be nice; " and when leaving them at the door, they said, " Be large and be full."

The two small baskets stood outside now, very large and full of every good food. Sukonia came home with his men about sunset. Chikpitpa sprang up to the roof of the house, and called to his brother, —

" Two guests have come to our house. Two women are sitting inside. They are sitting in your place."

The men came in, and Sukonia sat down with the sisters. They pleased him; he liked their looks.

" Have you brought food to our guests? " asked Sukonia.

" I brought some," said Tsore Jowa.

" Oh, give more. Bring plenty of everything! "

The two baskets which Jahtaneno's daughters had brought were carried into the house. The sisters invited all present to try their food. All the men ate food from the baskets and praised it. Sukonia, the chief, was pleased more and more with the sisters that evening, and married them.

After all the people had eaten next morning, Sukonia went to hunt. He took many men with him.

That day Sukonia's sisters showed his wives every place in the house and outside it, — showed them where venison, roots, and acorns were kept; showed them where the water was. The spring was in the house in one corner, carefully covered.

After some days Sukonia said to his wives: " I want you to tell me what your father said when you were leaving him. When does he want you to go back? When does he wish you to visit him? "

" He did not tell us when to go to him. He did not tell us to go back at all, he only told us to come here; but we want to see him. We want to tell him how we live here."

" Well," said Sukonia, " go to-morrow; go to see your father. What does he eat? What does he like? "

" He eats salmon; he likes nice beads, furs, and shells."

" I will send him some of my meat, I will send him venison. I will send him beads and furs."

" May I go with my sisters-in-law? " asked Chikpitpa.

" No, I want you here," said Sukonia. " I want you here, my little brother."

The two women rose early next morning, and Tsore Jowa helped them to make ready. Sukonia gave them fat venison, and every kind of bright beads and rich presents for their father.

They started; went as far as the Ichpul house,

where the two frog sisters lived. The two old maids were in the road and spoke to Sukonia's wives. They were very kind and pleasant.

"Put down your baskets and sit a while with us to talk," said they.

The Jahtaneno sisters were fr'ghtened. They did not wish to stop. They feared the Ichpul women, did not like to make them angry by refusing. They were afraid to sit down, afraid to refuse.

"Oh, how your hair looks! let me see your head," said one Ichpul woman to the elder sister.

"Oh, how your hair looks!" said the other to the younger sister; "let me look at your head."

"Put your head on my lap," said each Ichpul sister to each of Sukonia's wives.

Each was afraid, but still put her head on the old maid's lap. The Ichpul sisters killed Sukonia's wives, flayed their bodies, and put their skins on themselves.

About sunset next day the two frog women went to Sukonia's house; went in and sat where Jahtaneno's daughters had always sat; took the place of Sukonia's wives; looked just like them because they had their skins on.

About dusk Sukonia came home from the hunt. Chikpitpa, who ran ahead, rushed into the sweathouse to see if his sisters-in-law had come back from their father's. He saw the two women, looked at them; they seemed like his sisters-in-law, but when he came near he cried out at once, —

"Phu! they smell like frogs! The Ichpul sisters are here: these are the frog old maids!"

He cried and ran out to meet his brother.

"Brother," said he, "the Ichpul women are in our house. They killed my sisters-in-law to-day. I know they did." And he kept crying, "They killed my sisters-in-law, they killed my poor sisters-in-law!" and he cried without stopping, cried bitterly.

The two old maids wearing the skins of Sukonia's wives were making acorn porridge. When it was almost ready, Sukonia looked at the two women. They seemed like his wives, and he was in doubt, till all at once he thought: "I will ask them to bring water from the spring. If they know where the water is, they are my wives; if not, they are false."

"Bring me water, my wife," said he to one of the women.

She stood up, took a water basket, turned toward the door, and said to Chikpitpa, "Come out with me for water, my little brother-in-law."

"Wait," said Sukonia. "You need not go now."

She came back to the fire and sat down with her sister. Sukonia knew now that those were strange women.

"Whip me," said Chikpitpa to his brother, "I will cry, roll around and kick. I will kick those nasty frogs! I will kill them."

When the acorn porridge was boiling hard, Sukonia struck Chikpitpa with a switch and scolded him: "Why are you crying? I can do nothing, you cry so."

The boy rolled on the floor, cried more than ever, kicked, rolled around, kicked as hard as he could, rolled toward the fire and kicked, kicked one woman into the boiling porridge, kicked the other one into the burning fire, and in this way he killed the false sisters.

Chikpitpa was glad; he laughed. Sukonia threw the two women out doors, and mourned all that night for his wives. Next morning early he rose and said, "Stay home to-day, all of you."

"Where are you going?" asked Chikpitpa.

"Stay here, my little brother," said Sukonia. "I am going somewhere."

Sukonia followed the trail of his wives, reached the place where the Ichpul sisters had stopped them, and found their dead bodies. He took out his bow-string of deer sinew, struck the two women, called them, raised them to life.

"How were you killed?" asked Sukonia; "how did it happen? Did you go to the Ichpul house?"

"We did not go to that house; those two women were out on the road and they stopped us. They asked us to sit down and talk with them. We were afraid to sit, afraid to refuse. We sat down, and they killed us."

Sukonia took his wives home. When they were in sight of the house, Chikpitpa was on the roof watching.

"Oh, those are your sisters-in-law," said he to Tsore Jowa; and he ran out to meet them.

"Go, now, to your father," said Sukonia, next morning. "Carry presents and venison to him, and be here at sunset."

The two sisters rose early, took two baskets, and

started. At noon they were at their father's house. Old Jahtaneno was glad when he looked at his daughters and saw the nice presents.

" Our husband told us to go home to-day, and we cannot stay long with you."

They took back many presents from their father, and were home at sunset. They met no trouble on the way. The Ichpul sisters were dead, and Metsi did not meet them a second time.

THE FINDING OF FIRE

THE FINDING OF FIRE

After each name is given that of the creature or thing into which the personage was changed subsequently.

Ahalamila, gray wolf; Au Mujaupa, master of fire; Chil Daiauna, big hail; Chil Wareko, big rain; Juhauju, west wind; Júkami, north wind; Jukilauyu, east wind; Juwaju, south wind; Gagi, crow; Metsi, coyote; Patcha, snow; Sabil Keyu, small hail; Shushu Marimi, dog woman; Siwegi, a small bird, unknown.

———

IN the beginning Au Mujaupa had fire very far down south on the other side of a big river. The people in this country had no real fire; they had a kind of fire, but it was n't good. It just warmed a little; it would n't cook like the fire which we have now. People killed deer and fished, but they had to eat fish and venison raw.

In the west people had fire, but it would n't cook. In the north there were many people, and in the east; but they had no fire that would cook.

"There must be fire in some place," said the people at Pawi; "how can we find it?"

"I will go out to-night to look," said Ahalamila.

That night he went to look for fire. He went to the top of Wahkanopa, looked east and west, saw no fire in either place. Next he looked north; no fire in the north. He looked south; saw no fire anywhere.

Ahalamila came home and talked to the chief and people. " I saw no fire," said he ; " I could not see any, but I will go to a better place the next time and take some one with me.   I will go to-morrow night to the top of Wahkalu.   Who here has a good head, who a sharp eye to see fire?   I want to look for fire to-morrow night from the top of Wahkalu ; from that place I will look all around the whole world to find fire."

" We have a man here," said the chief, " who can see through a tree, who can see down through the earth to bed rock, who can see through a mountain. You can take him to-morrow night with you.   He is Siwegi."

Ahalamila went to Siwegi.   " Will you go to-morrow night to look for fire ? " asked he.

" I will go if the way is not too long."

" Oh," said Ahalamila, " it will not be long.   I will shorten it."

Siwegi agreed to go ; and when the time came, they started.   Ahalamila doubled up the trail and made it short ; in an hour they were on the top of Wahkalu, both ready now to look for fire.   The night is very dark ; they can see the smallest fire easily.

They look to the east, look with great care, look a good while, see no fire ; they look to the north in the same way, see no fire ; they look to the west, no fire there.   Now Ahalamila looks south, looks a long time, and sees nothing : he looks half an hour to the south, sees a little glimmer like a light very far away.

"Siwegi," said he, "I see a small light down south; it seems like fire far away. I think it is fire."

"Look again," said Siwegi, "look sharply." "Maybe it is fire."

"I have looked enough, I think it is fire," said Ahalamila; "but I want you to see it, I want you to look now."

Siwegi looked a little while. "Yes, that is fire," said he.

"Well," said Ahalamila, "we see fire, we know that it is far off in the south."

Ahalamila made the road short, and they were back at Pawi in an hour. "We have found fire," said Ahalamila to the chief and the people. "We know where fire is, we can have fire now."

"We must have that fire," said the people.

"There is no way to get the fire but to go for it," said Ahalamila.

"Well," said the chief, "since Ahalamila saw the fire he will go for it; but the road is long. Who will go and help him? Who will go for fire with Ahalamila?"

About fifty men offered to go, and they started next morning. The journey was long and very hard. Soon two or three men were tired and went home; not long after more were tired, and when they had gone far down to a great river, just north of where the fire was, of the fifty who started only three were left, — Ahalamila, Metsi, and old Shushu Marima.

Just south of the great river Au Mujaupa had a very big village, and in the village a large sweat-house. In that house he kept the fire, and had a great crowd of people living in the country outside who served him, and kept every one in the world from stealing his fire. These people were Patcha, Chil Wareko, Chil Daiauna, Sabil Keyu, Juhauju, Juwaju, Jukami, Jukilauju.

The three, Ahalamila, Metsi, and old Shushu Marimi, were at the northern end of the bridge, and sat there watching till all at the sweat-house was quiet. The bridge was very narrow and slippery; so Ahalamila put pitch on his feet and hands, and on Metsi's and Shushu's feet and hands. All three crossed without slipping, and found every one asleep in the sweat-house.

The old chief, Au Mujaupa, had covered the fire well with ashes. All was silent within and without. Ahalamila, Metsi, and Shushu crept onto the sweat-house quietly, and looked in. All were asleep.

" I will go down first," said Metsi.

" No, I will go first," said Ahalamila. " I will get the fire and reach it to you; you take it and run very fast."

Ahalamila slipped down. Metsi and Shushu remained on the roof. Ahalamila opened the fire carefully, took out a good piece and handed it to the old woman. She put it in her ear. He handed her another; she put it in her other ear, slipped down from the top of the sweat-house, ran across the bridge, and hurried away.

Ahalamila gave Metsi two pieces. He put them in his two ears and started. Ahalamila filled his own ears and followed.

The three had run over two mountains when Au Mujaupa woke up and saw that the ashes had been opened, and that fire had been taken, that a coal had fallen near the central pillar. He sprang up, went to the top of the sweat-house, shouted, called to all his people, —

" Fire has been stolen ! Fire has been stolen ! Go, you, and follow ! "

Now Patcha, Chil Wareko, Chil Daiauna, Sabil Keyu, and all the wind people rose up and followed, raced and stormed in every direction. So much rain came that the whole country was covered with water.

Now Juwaju was ahead of all Au Mujaupa's people chasing the three robbers. Chil Wareko came too, and fell upon the three furiously ; he drenched and chilled them. Next came Jukami and Patcha, who nearly froze them.

Metsi was almost dead ; the fire went out in both his ears. Ahalamila lost his fire, too. Chil Wareko, Juwaju, and Patcha quenched it, and then he let it fall.

Old Shushu was behind a good way, but she ran all the time. She kept her hand on one ear as she ran. She lost the fire out of her other ear, and when the piece fell out it broke in two and fell apart. Chil Wareko picked up the fire and took it back ; he found six pieces, thought that he had all. He and the others stopped following.

Ahalamila and Metsi ran ahead, left old Shushu to get on the best she could, and reached home first. They were wet, very cold, and tired.

" Where is your fire ? " asked the chief.

"I have none; Chil Wareko took my fire," said Ahalamila.

"Where is your fire?" asked the chief.

"Chil Wareko took it," said Metsi.

The chief was very sorry, and all the people were sorry. The old woman did not come, and the people said, "She must be frozen dead."

At sundown old Shushu came back; she came very slowly, was terribly tired, but courageous. She reached the sweat-house, came in, said nothing, lay down wet and cold.

"Where is the fire?" asked she; "did not Ahalamila and Metsi bring fire? They are young and strong, and had plenty of fire."

After a while she stood up, drew some wood-dust together, then sat down, opened her ear and held it over the dust; a big piece of fire came out. Wood was brought quickly, and soon the whole sweat-house was warm. The people who were cold before were warm now and glad.

"Bring meat and we will try how it tastes when 't is roasted," said the chief.

He cut some venison and roasted it. One and another tasted the meat. "It is very good," said they; a third one said, "I 'll try it," and Gagi took a taste. "Oh, it is sweet, very good," said Gagi.

Each one roasted meat and ate heartily. Next day all went to hunt, and had a great feast in the evening. A chief from another place came to the feast and got fire, took it home with him. Soon all people had fire; every one had fire in all parts of the country.

HAKA KAINA

HAKA KAINA

PERSONAGES

AFTER their transformation the personages in "Haka Kaina" were mainly birds. I have not been able to identify the majority of them, and would refer to the notes to this myth. Hwipajusi, the father of the three girls, is a whistling swan; we find among the characters Gowila, a lizard, Malwila, meadow-lark, and Maibyu, wood dove. The only way to identify such characters surely is to hire men to shoot them in the woods and mountains. This I have done as often as possible, but in the present case the specimens were lost before I could fix their identity. All the information at my disposal now will be found in the notes.

HAKA KAINA was the greatest chief in this country; his very large and beautiful sweat-house was Wahkalu.

One time Haka Kaina stole the three daughters of Hwipajusi, a chief who lived down in the far south, beyond the valley of the Daha. When Haka Kaina had brought the three girls home, he said, —

"I must find a good man, a careful man, now, to guard these three girls, a man who never sleeps in the night-time. Hwipajusi will send people here to steal them back; we must be ready for his men."

At last the chief chose Hohwitina because he whistled all night. Every one thought that he never slept, for he whistled all the time, whistled without stopping from evening till daylight. Hohwitina watched the three girls a good many nights;

he never looked after them during daylight, for he rested at that time. They were brought to him at dusk every evening to the central pillar of the sweat-house. The arms of each girl were tied together; one girl was tied to Hohwitina's left arm, the second to his right arm, and the third behind to his waist.

After a time old Hwipajusi sent ten of the best southern men to bring back his three daughters; the names of these men were Pusi Tena, Wija Lala, Chami Nuri, Malwila, Gowila, Grana Rana, Dekkech, Pushi Chowa, Manu Rana, Taki Lapiki. These men were called Yolaina, — that is, the bravest, men who feared nothing.

These men painted their arms and faces black before starting, took good bows and arrows, and went to Wahkalu.

Hwipajusi had kept his three daughters always hidden away in his sweat-house, rolled up in otter-skin carefully; but Haka Kaina, the chief of Wah-kalu, had stolen in while all were sleeping and carried away the three maidens.

Hwipajusi's ten men came near Wahkalu one evening between dusk and darkness, and were right there near the sweat-house. Haka Kaina, the chief, saw them coming, and prepared all his forces to fight.

"These are people," said he, " sent by Hwipajusi, very brave and strong men. You must not let them come near the three girls; you must not let them go from here; you must not let them take the girls nor go away themselves; you must kill these ten enemies."

One of the Haka Kaina's men had a great hammer. He put a block of flint at the point which the ten men attacked when they came near; he struck the flint with his hammer; small sharp bits flew off from it like rain, fell on the attackers, and cut them terribly. The ten men had no fear of flint nor of other things. They rushed on until five were killed; the five others were not frightened and they went forward. The man with the hammer struck away on the flint block till five more were killed.

Now Hwipajusi's ten brave men who feared nothing were dead.

Hwipajusi waited for his men to come back, looked for them, hoped to see them bring his daughters, but the men could not come; they were dead. They had promised their chief to bring the girls surely, but they could not bring them; the ten were dead at Wahkalu.

Hwipajusi sent ten other men, men who were very wise and cunning. These ten were Itchi Watibila, Chini Pachuna, Maibyu, Tsigaga, Maltama, Howichi Laina, Aichuch Hisipa, Tsawila, Haiyude Maupa, Tarku Wana. These ten men came near the sweat-house, sat down, and hid there in the evening.

"I will go up first on the sweat-house," said Maibyu; "you are too heavy, your tread is heavy. If you go, they will hear you, they will wake up; we shall be killed, like the ten who came before us."

"I know the man who watches the girls," said Maibyu; "he whistles all night, but he sleeps; no one in the sweat-house sleeps more soundly than he does. Now, when he is asleep, I will go down and take the girls from him."

" I will go myself," said Itchi Watibila.

Haka Kaina's people danced that evening, and played till late at night. Hwipajusi's ten men crept near and watched the people dancing, but no one saw them. Haka Kaina sat inside the sweat-house, smoking and talking, talking loud; the ten heard his voice. At last, when it was late, all the men went into the sweat-house and other houses, and in time they were asleep everywhere. All were silent except Hohwitina, who sat watching the girls at the central pillar; and he whistled all the time.

The ten went around the sweat-house; saw that all were sleeping. They heard no noise but the whistling of Hohwitina.

" I know that he is asleep now," said Itchi Watibila.

Four men went to the top of the sweat-house. The watcher was whistling not so loudly, but whistling. Itchi Watibila gave his arrows to Chini Pachuna, and Chini Pachuna gave them to Maibyu, for he had to lift up the girls.

" That man sleeps, I know," said Itchi Watibila; and he went down slowly along the pillar, reached the bottom, and sat a while to listen. He looked closely at Hohwitina, and saw that he was whistling with his eyes shut. Itchi Watibila laughed to himself. He saw that one girl was tied to each of Hohwitina's arms and one to his waist from behind. The girls were awake, all three of them.

Itchi Watibila untied the right-hand girl carefully; raised her to Chini Pachuna, who gave her to Maibyu at the top of the sweat-house. Hohwitina whistled on, and Itchi Watibila took the left-hand girl, raised her to the other man; at last he took the third, the youngest daughter of Wipajusi, made no noise, raised her to the others, then climbed up himself, rested a moment on the top of the sweat-house, looked down. Hohwitina was whistling away and asleep all the time. The ten slipped down without noise and started home; hurried off toward the south with Hwipajusi's three daughters.

Old Haka Kaina rose up at daylight, walked around the sweat-house, went to the central pillar to look at Hohwitina and the three girls he was guarding. He saw Hohwitina, heard how he was whistling, saw nobody near him, — no girls tied to his arms or his waist.

"He has let the girls go," thought Haka Kaina. "You whistle all night, but don't watch," said Haka Kaina, pushing him. He woke him.

Hohwitina looked at his right arm, no girl; looked at his left, the second was gone; felt at his back, there was no one there.

"Where are the girls?" asked Haka Kaina.

"I cannot tell," said Hohwitina.

Haka Kaina looked around and saw tracks in the ashes.

"You said that you never sleep at night; now look at those tracks; those are somebody's tracks, somebody came here last night. What were you doing? Were you awake? were you sleeping? Did you let the girls go because you were willing, or did somebody take them while you were sleeping?"

Hohwitina said nothing, held down his head. Haka Kaina went out, and saw tracks on the sweat-house, then he saw tracks below at some distance away from the sweat-house.

"People came from the south and took the three girls," said he; "of course they were sent by Hwipajusi."

Haka Kaina talked all the next night to his people, told how sorry he was that the girls had been taken, and to two men he said, "You must go and bring back the girls to us."

The two were Bohkwi and Simu Nupchowa; they could run fast, and were very wise persons.

Now, on the top of his sweat-house, at the central pillar, Hwipajusi had posted Matsklila as a sentry, and he watched carefully to see who would come. Hwipajusi knew that Haka Kaina would try to get the girls back again. Matsklila had a knife in his nose and one in each arm.

Bohkwi and Simu Nupchowa set out to bring the girls back from the south. Just at sunset one evening they came near the village; they saw crowds of people everywhere, young men and women at play in the great village.

Old Hwipajusi sat talking; and a great many people, old and young, men and women, sat around him and listened. Haka Kaina's two men went near the sweat-house.

"I am going in," said Bohkwi.

"No, I am going," said Simu Nupchowa. "You

cannot run fast. You stand near, and when I come out you run ahead, and I can carry the three girls easily. I will catch up with you."

The people sat there near the sweat-house and listened to the chief as he talked. "Be on the watch; they will come to-night, they will come, I am sure," said Hwipajusi.

After a time all separated, went to their houses, and lay down to sleep. At midnight, when all was silent, Haka Kaina's two men crept up and climbed the sweat-house to look in at the top. Matsklila was at his post behind the central pillar, standing still. Haka Kaina's men did not see him.

"I will look in," said Bohkwi.

"So will I," said Simu Nupchowa.

They stretched their heads and looked. They leaned over the opening, stretched their necks far. That moment Matsklila moved quickly, and both their heads dropped off, rolled down, and fell to the earth outside the sweat-house.

When Hwipajusi rose up in the morning, he went outside and saw two heads lying near the sweat-house.

"Wake up, jump up, my sons," cried he, calling to the people; "enemies were here last night."

All hurried out and saw two bodies and two heads. One asked, "Who is this lying dead?" A second asked, "Who is the other man?"

"I know them both," said Hwipajusi. "One is Bohkwi, the other Simu Nupchowa, two great men in Haka Kaina's forces."

The two lay there behind the sweat-house all the

day. That evening Hwipajusi summoned in his people, and talked to them. " Fix your arrows well, look at your bows, and have all your arms ready. Haka Kaina will send men here against us; he wants to steal my daughters again, or take them away in spite of me."

They waited at Wahkalu for Bohkwi and Simu Nupchowa. When the two men did not come, old Haka Kaina said, " I think those two men are dead."

He called all his people together and said : " We must go down and make war on Hwipajusi; there is no other way. He stole those three girls from me. Those three girls are mine. I must have them back again."

All dressed next morning, put on their feathers, blackened their faces.

" Now, my men," said Haka Kaina; " arm, stand out on a broad place, let me see you, then stand in a circle round the sweat-house. I want to see how you look when all together."

They went out and stood together on a broad place. Haka Kaina was a long time going among them. After that all came back and stood in a circle around the whole sweat-house. All shouted and sprang about a good while; then they went back, took off their big elkskin armor.

" You look well," said Haka Kaina. " You are ready for war, and we will start to-morrow early."

Next morning the women painted their faces, put on feathers and beads, danced behind the men, sang, and said good words to them at parting. As the men marched along southward, there were so many that the dust which rose from them went up to the sun. They went forward singing. Haka Kaina himself sang as he led this great army. When near Hwipajusi's country, Haka Kaina sent Pokil Kama, Gaman Atpa, Pahninopa, and Tsanu Noipa to examine everything and bring back news.

These four men saw many villages belonging to different people, and visited four of them. They went to the villages of Pareko, Chapilkeya, Chil Wareko, and Chil Dayauna. They saw a great many people at these four villages; each chief had an immense sweat-house, and Chil Dayauna's people had elkskin armor to fight in.

The four men went back about dusk and had not seen all that there was to see. They said to Haka Kaina, "We saw a great many people; you must be careful; our people must fight well."

Haka Kaina's men sharpened their arrow-points.

Two Tsoplaina boys went with Haka Kaina. The chief was very fond of these boys, and they liked him. They heard what the four scouts had said, and at dusk these two boys went to Wipajusi's and saw the three girls playing around the fire.

"Look, look at the mouse," said one of the girls.

"That is a mouse coming after you," said Hwipajusi, laughing.

"Where are the two brothers?" asked Haka Kaina, when he missed the Tsoplaina boys. No one had sent these young men to Hwipajusi's.

Now, the Tsoplaina brothers worked hard, worked all nignt. They went through more than half the houses, and destroyed a great many bow-strings. At daylight they went back and told Haka Kaina what they had done.

Hwipajusi's people saw Haka Kaina's great army coming; they ran for their bows, but many were destroyed. Those who had bows left fought well. But Haka Kaina's men had arms of flint and arms of all kinds, and they beat down everything before them. At midday Hwipajusi's people were destroyed and he himself was killed.

Haka Kaina took the three girls and set out for Wahkalu again, taking everything that Hwipajusi and his people had. Now there were two brothers, Mini Auna, who lived with their sisters at Wamarawi, near a trail which Haka Kaina had not used before, but he started home on it this time.

When Haka Kaina's forces came in sight of Wamarawi, the two sisters were out husking acorns. They were frightened and ran home. One of them ran to her brothers and cried, —

"Come, brothers, hurry out and look. A great many people are coming. I do not know where they come from nor where they are going. Perhaps they will kill us."

Each of Haka Kaina's men had a great pack on his back holding all that he could carry. They were taking home everything from Hwipajusi's village.

The two Mini Auna brothers ran quickly to their sweat-house; each of them caught up a great piece of fire. The two sisters ran into the sweat-house and hid there. The two brothers went to the top of the sweat-house, and when Haka Kaina's great army was near enough, they hurled fire around it, north, south, east, and west. All were surrounded. They looked to every side, tried to get out, but there was no escape anywhere. The great fire closed in around them, and every man perished. All were burned to death. Hwipajusi's three daughters died with the others. As soon as all were dead, the fire went out and disappeared; the two brothers went back into their sweat-house.

When the Mini Aunas were going to hurl the fire, Haka Kaina sent two swift runners to Wahkalu to let his women know that all were coming with great plunder, and bringing Hwipajusi's daughters. Sooner than these men were out of sight the fire was around the whole army, which perished before the eyes of the two swift runners.

When the swift runners reached Wahkalu, all the women were dancing; they thought that their husbands were fighting yet against Hwipajusi. When the swift runners were coming near, the women stopped dancing, and when both came up and said that Haka Kaina and his army were dead at Wamarawi, burned by the Mini Aunas, the women raised a cry of sorrow such as no one had ever heard in Wahkalu before. Soon some women said, —

" We must go down to Wamarawi, we must go a good many of us, and beg the two brothers to bring our men to life again."

They took beautiful presents, shells and otter-skins, put them on their backs, and started; went without waiting, travelled all night, travelled quickly.

They were at Wamarawi next morning. They went to the two brothers, gave them presents, begged them to bring their husbands to life again.

The brothers were willing at last to do this.

There was a great spring near their sweat-house, a spring as large as a lake of good size, and the brothers told the women from Wahkalu and their own two sisters to carry the bones to that water.

The Wahkalu women and the two sisters took baskets, carried bones all that day, and put them in the spring. At sunset the field was clear and all the bones were in the water.

"Now," said the brothers to the women from Wahkalu, "you must camp far away from the spring, and not go near it till broad daylight to-morrow; and our sisters you must not rise up to-night to go out of the sweat-house."

The two brothers closed the top of the sweat-house and did not sleep themselves.

About daylight they heard talking at the spring, then more talking, and later a great sound of voices. At broad daylight all had come out of the spring, and all the place around was full of people, crowds of people everywhere.

The two brothers looked from the top of the sweat-house, saw all Haka Kaina's army standing there strong and well. Each man had his pack with its treasures, the plunder brought from Wipajusi's village; each had on his war-dress and feathers. Wipajusi's three daughters were there, too, as well as ever.

Haka Kaina went to the house of the Mini Aunas

and talked to the brothers. He gave them otter-skins, beads, elkskins. He was grateful and very kind; called them cousins. After that he went home with his army and women. All those left at Wahkalu came out to meet the men, went far, danced, danced because all had come to life again and because the three girls were brought back.

The men put away their bows, arrows, and elk-skins; all washed the paint from their faces.

"Now give us plenty to eat," said Haka Kaina.

They went into the sweat-house; all ate and talked till midnight. At midnight each went to his own place and rested.

TITINDI MAUPA AND PAIOWA

TITINDI MAUPA AND PAIOWA, THE YOUNGEST DAUGHTER OF WAKARA

PERSONAGES

After each name is given that of the creature or thing into which the personage was changed subsequently.

Hemauna Márimi, ——; Hitchinna, wildcat; Lawalila, chicken hawk; Paiowa, new moon's youngest daughter; Titildi Marimi, black bear woman; Titindi Maupa, her brother; Topuna, mountain lion; Tuina, the sun; Wakara, new moon.

TITINDI MAUPA lived at a place called Kurulsa Mauna, where he had two sisters. Three miles west of that place lived young Topuna with his father, who had a great sweat-house at Motiri Mauna.

Titindi Maupa wished his elder sister to marry Topuna, his great friend, who was a good hunter and killed many deer. One day Titindi Maupa told his two sisters to make ready much food, — roots, acorns, and pine nuts.

The women made these things ready and put them into a round basket. He put the basket on his back, took two otter-skins as presents, and went to Motiri Mauna.

Old Topuna was sitting at home. His son had gone off before daylight to hunt deer in the mountains. Titindi Maupa saw a great deal of venison and deer fat hanging around in all parts of the sweat-house.

He looked in from the top of the sweat-house, and saw the old man cutting meat, breaking bones, and taking marrow out of them. He went in. Topuna stood up to meet him, made a fire, cooked meat, put it in a basket, and set it down before Titindi Maupa. He gave him also fat and dried venison.

"I have food on the top of the sweat-house," said Titindi Maupa. "I left my basket there."

Topuna went and brought it, put it down, then ate of it himself. The visitor ate much, and the two sat long together talking and eating; sat till midday, when young Topuna came home. He had killed five deer and was glad.

"You came to see us," said he, sitting down near the visitor.

"Yes," answered Titindi Maupa, "and you will come soon, I hope, to my house. You will come to-night, perhaps?"

Topuna gave Titindi Maupa nice venison and deer fat, — a great deal of it. "Be light and small till he takes you home," said Topuna to the meat; "then be as big as you now are or bigger."

He gave the visitor a beautiful buckskin dress, and Titindi Maupa went home.

The pack was light till he set it down at home. Then it grew as big as a small house. His elder sister would not eat Topuna's venison; she did not like her brother's friend; she loved young Hitchinna, and would not look at the other man.

Topuna put on three pairs of moccasins, three pairs of thick buckskin leggings trimmed with beads; put on three buckskin blankets, and at dark he went out of the door to go to Kurulsa Mauna.

"My son," said old Topuna, when his son was going, "you will come back sorry; you will be angry in the morning; I know that woman well."

All were asleep at Titindi Maupa's when Topuna came; but Titildi Marimi had wished the whole house outside to be covered with sharp rocks and thorny brush, for she knew that Topuna was coming.

When he reached the place, he could not go in; he could not find the door, even; everything was hidden with sharp rocks and thorns. He was outside all night, and never stopped trying to find the way in; he wore out his three pair of moccasins, tore his three pair of leggings and three blankets; bits of them were scattered all around the sweat-house. At last he was naked and nearly frozen.

Topuna went home before daylight, very angry. Titildi Marimi had heard him, but said not a word. He lay down in his father's sweat-house and stayed there all day.

When daylight came, Titildi Marimi rose up and went out of the sweat-house; the rocks and brush were all gone at her wish; nothing there now but the nice beads that had fallen from Topuna. She went to the spring; washed there, combed and dressed her hair, painted her face red, put on a nice woven cap, took a little basket with a sharp stick, and went out on the mountain; went far; dug sweet roots by the creeks on the mountain flats.

Titindi Maupa was angry at his sister all day; he stayed in bed until evening. Titildi Marimi dug roots, dug a great many, singing all the time while she worked.   Hitchinna heard the singing from his place and came to her.   She liked him.   She went to meet him ; was pleased to see him ; they sat down together, talked, and were glad.   They parted for that day ; he hunted deer, she filled her basket with roots and went home about sundown.

Titindi Maupa was in bed yet.   He did not raise his eyes when she came ; did not look at his sister.

Next morning she rose early ; rose at daylight. She had promised Hitchinna to meet him a second time.   She washed, combed her hair, painted her face, took a basket with a root stick, and started.

She had not gone far when her brother sprang up, hurried to the river, swam in it ; went back to the sweat-house, striking his hair as he went with a stick to make it dry quickly.   Then he ate, and said to his younger sister, —

" I am going away ; I must leave you ; you will cry, I think, because I am going."

He put on rich clothes, then tied a string of nice beads to a staff, and fastened the staff in one corner of the house corners.

" If I die," said he, " those beads will fall to the ground ; do not touch them while they are hanging, and say to our sister not to touch them.   When she comes, do not say that I have gone ; if she knows herself, you must not show her the way that I have taken."

Then he turned to each thing in the house and said, " You, my poking-stick, must not tell my sister how I have gone, nor you, my baskets, nor you, my fire, nor you, my basket of water, nor my roots ; not one of you must tell her." And he told everything except the acorn flour; he forgot to tell the acorn flour.

" Now I go," said he; and pushing up the central post of the house, he went in to the ground, and the post settled back after him. He went under ground until he reached a spring of water. From the spring he turned back and went west, then back; went north, then back; went south, then back to the spring. Next he went in circles around his house to mislead his sister, so that she might not track him. At last he went west two or three miles; then he rose to the top of the ground, and went off on a trail.

When she went to the mountain flat on the second morning, Titildi Marimi stood a while thinking. She knew that her brother was out of bed, that he was very angry. " My brother will go away to-day," thought she. " I must be home again soon."

She threw down her stick and basket quickly and hurried home. She saw that her brother was not in the house, that her sister was crying.

"Where is my brother," asked she; " tell me, my sister."

The sister would not speak, gave no answer; held down her head and cried bitterly.

" Tell me quickly. The sun is high. If I cannot come up with him, he will die; if I do not find him, his enemies will kill him." The sister did not answer.

"Tell me, you rock, which way my brother went; tell me quickly. Tell me, you poking-stick; tell me, baskets." Nothing gave answer. "Post, tell me, tell quickly; it is too late almost, he will escape me." She asked everything and got no answer, till at last she said, "Acorn flour, will you tell me?"

"Your brother is gone," said the acorn flour. "He is angry because you injured Topuna, his friend; he is very angry, and does not wish you to follow him."

"Which way did he go?"

"Under the post."

"That is well."

She was glad then. She made ready quickly; put on nice, new things, took her best bow and a big otter-skin quiver filled with arrows, put on leggings like a man.

"My sister, be well, take good care of yourself," said she. "I don't want my brother to die. He thinks that the journey is pleasant, that the journey is easy. I will go, too; I will help him."

She pushed up the post and followed her brother; went to the spring, came back, followed him everywhere; came out at last on the trail and tracked him, followed him, toiled along over Backbone Mountain. She followed hard and fast, gained on him, kept gaining; still she was afraid that she could not come up with her brother. She turned then to Sun and called out, —

"O Sun, I wish you to be slow. Go very slowly to-day, O Sun. Let the day be long. Give me time to come up with my brother."

The Sun went more slowly, gave her time, and she hurried on.

Titindi Maupa all this while was hurrying, going on quickly; and he sang as he went. His song was of Paiowa, Wakara's youngest daughter, a maiden far off in the west.

Wakara had a great many daughters. All the stars in the sky were his children, and all his daughters were married but this one, the youngest, the one whom Titindi Maupa was going to marry if her father would give her.

He went along the Daha, went as the stream flows, swam across and sat down to smoke. When he had emptied his pipe, he went up on the mountain ridge west of the river, reached the top, and walked some distance down on the western slope, sat again and smoked a second time. Now Titildi Marimi, his sister, had crossed the river and was following. She came to where her brother had sat to smoke the first time.

" I will come up with you soon," said she. " You cannot go from me now; " and she followed on, followed quickly.

The brother, when he smoked the second time, sat at a little spring on the western slope of the mountain ridge; the sister reached the ridge from the top; she saw her brother a little below her. He heard some one behind, looked up, and saw Titildi Marimi. He held his head down, he said nothing.

" I shall be with you soon," cried the sister. " We can go on together. You have come a long way to find a good smoking-place."

He said nothing, looked at the ground, waited for his sister. Soon she was there with him.

"My brother, I am tired," said she, "give me tobacco; I wish to smoke."

He gave her tobacco; she smoked.

"My brother," said Titildi Marimi, "I want you to shoot at that quartz rock over there on the mountain side."

He raised his bow with an arrow and took good aim.

"Now hit that rock," said she.

He sent one arrow, after it a second, and then a third. They hit the rock, but bounded back from it.

"You might go a long way to hurt an enemy with arrows of that sort!" laughed the sister. "Do you think those good arrows, my brother? You will see enemies enough in two days; you will see enemies in the house of Wakara."

She drew out her own bow then, took an arrow from her otter-skin quiver, and said, "Look now at me, my brother!"

She shot at the rock; hit it. Her arrow shivered the rock to pieces.

"This is what my arrows do!" said Titildi Marimi.

Titindi Maupa hung his head; said not a word, but rose and went down the mountain side till he came to a creek; then he crossed another mountain, going westward all the time till he was in sight of Wakaruwa, the place to which he was going; then he sat down a third time and smoked.

" O smoke," said he, " I wish you to make friends to-night and to-morrow for me."

He looked down into the valley, where he heard much noise; he saw many people playing games and shooting.

Just before this Wakara had called his youngest daughter, Paiowa, and said, " I want you to gather oak leaves for the acorn bread, and red earth to mix in it."

She went with a basket on her back, went up to the mountain side, gathered red earth to mix with the acorn flour and make the bread light. The leaves were to be put on the top of the dough and cover the bread while baking. Titindi Maupa put his sister with her quiver in an otter-skin and carried her. She had made herself small, and seemed just like an otter; he hid her on his shoulder in this form.

Paiowa, Wakara's youngest daughter, had put red earth in her basket and filled it with leaves. She turned around now to stoop and raise it, but could not, it was too heavy.

Titindi Maupa had slipped up and was holding the basket. She turned to see what the trouble was, and saw him right there almost touching her.

" Oh ! " cried she, frightened and dropping her head ; she was shamefaced before the stranger.

" Why are you afraid ? " asked Titindi Maupa. " Is it because I am ugly ?

She raised the basket to her back, and rushed away. When she reached Wakaruwa, she threw down the basket outside, and ran into the house past her mother.

" Why are you so frightened ? What is the matter? " asked her mother.

Not a word did she answer.

Old Wakara was sitting inside. " Why are you
frightened, my daughter?" asked he. " Has anything happened, has any one hurt you?"

" I saw a man over there on the mountain."

" What kind of man was he ? " asked Wakara.

"He has an otter on his back and wears buckskin; his hands are both red with deer blood."

Titindi Maupa had a large piece of fat venison in
his otter-skin quiver.

" He is a good hunter, I think," said Wakara ;
and he took down an otter-skin, put it on the north
side of the house, and said to his daughter, " Sit
there and let this man come to you."

It was night soon. All the people came into the
house, sat down, and ate supper. Titindi Maupa
stopped outside for a while, and found a place where
Wakara stored acorns. " I will leave you here for
this night," said he to his sister. " To-morrow I
will come to get you."

Titindi Maupa left his sister in the acorn crib,
sank in the ground then, and came up inside
the sweat-house right at the side of Paiowa. Old
Wakara laughed when he saw him sitting near his
daughter. He was glad.

" Give the stranger food," said he.

Paiowa brought food and gave it to the stranger.

Titindi Maupa ate some and said, " Look in my
otter-skin, I have some venison."

She put her hand in, found a good piece, a nice

saddle of venison. She could not draw the piece out, it was so heavy. She went then to her father and said, " I must have a big basket."

She took a large tray basket over to her place. Titindi Maupa drew out the venison and put it on the tray, saying, —

" Now, be no smaller, my venison, stay as you are, no matter how much they take from you."

Two girls carried the basket and put it down before Wakara and Hemauna Marimi, his wife. The two old people ate. After them all in the house ate, and the saddle of venison was as large as at first. When all in the house had eaten, old Wakara went out on the housetop and shouted, —

" My sons, I call you all to come in for a short while."

Now, all the stars in the sky were Wakara's children ; they were his sons and daughters. The greatest, a son, came in first. When near the house, he had caught the odor of venison. Behind him came a great many people. All the stars were in Wakara's sweat-house ; the whole place was filled with them. When they looked and saw Titindi Maupa sitting with their sister, they laughed. They were glad. Some sat down ; others cut off the venison and roasted it. All ate what they wanted.

Now, old Wakara himself cut off venison, and gave a large share to each son to carry home for his wife and children. All went away laughing.

Titindi Maupa rose before dawn the next morning, took a deer head, and went hunting to a mountain. He put on the head. Deer came and stood before him, ten, then ten more, and soon there were a hundred. He killed the hundred deer. Taking the smallest, he opened it, made the others very little, and put them into the small one, which he carried in one hand.

All were sleeping in the sweat-house when Titindi Maupa came. He threw down the small deer, and the ninety-nine others were as big as at first; they burst out of the small one, made a great noise, and filled all the space before the sweat-house. Wakara's wife had got up to make acorn bread. She tried to go out, but could not, there were so many deer lying around everywhere. She hurried back and called her husband.

" There is something outside," said she; " I do not know what it is. Get up and look, get up quickly ! "

Wakara went out and saw piles of deer; he ran back, took his knife and sharpened it. Then going to the top of the house, he called to the whole village, " Come here ; come, all of you ! "

All the people of the village came soon, and there were so many that the venison was dressed quickly. They cooked and ate in company. Others came from beyond the river south of them, and ate all the venison they wanted. Many sat down under oak-trees and gambled ; some shot arrows at marks, and others raced.

All day they amused themselves ; all day they feasted, and went home at sunset very glad and praising Titindi Maupa.

West of Wakaruwa, was a large village and many

people, all Wakara's sons-in-law, all married to his
daughters; and the chief was Lawalila.

"I wonder what my father-in-law is doing," said
each of these people; "he has very loud talk in his
sweat-house. There has never been such talk there
before."

Lawalila called his two sons and said: "Go and
see what your grandfather is doing. Your youngest
aunt has a husband; perhaps that is why there is
such loud talk at the sweat-house."

The two boys stole up to the house carefully, and
peeped into it. The younger saw Paiowa, his aunt,
in one corner, and Titindi Maupa sitting near her.
Wakara saw the boy peeping in, and hurled a stick
at him. The two boys ran home.

"My aunt has a husband," said the younger boy.

"She has not," said the elder.

"I saw him," said the younger.

"You did not," said the elder.

Lawalila stopped the boys; he was satisfied. He
went out, and calling to all said, "Paiowa, the youngest daughter of Wakara, is married!"

All were very angry now, all were enraged, for
there were many in that village who wanted Paiowa.

Next morning Lawalila roused the village early,
and said: "I want you, my people, to play to-day.
You must play your best; you must beat Titindi
Maupa, Wakara's new son-in-law."

After they had eaten he called all his people
together and said, "We will go over to my father-
in-law's, to Wakara's, and shoot at a mark there
with arrows."

They went to Wakara's and asked : " Where is Titindi Maupa ? We wish to try him ; we want to shoot arrows at a mark against him."

Titindi Maupa came out and shot. He won the first shot, the second ; he won all the time, won everything that Lawalila's people wagered.

Just at noon Lawalila lost his temper, got angry, sprang up, tried to seize and take back all the things that his people had lost. Titindi Maupa would not let him do that ; he stood in his way, would not let him take anything.

Lawalila struck Wakara's new son-in-law. Titindi Maupa threw down his opponent. Lawalila jumped up, ran toward his people, drew his bow, and tried to send an arrow through Titindi Maupa. A great fight now followed.

Wakara's sons came and took Titindi Maupa's part. Lawalila's people hurried to his side. Titindi Maupa's young wife ran out to help her brothers and her husband.

They fought very hard on both sides. In the middle of the afternoon all were killed on La- walila's side except himself. New forces came to Lawalila. Titindi Maupa was so tired that he could not stand. At this moment his sister came. She picked up Titindi Maupa, put him on her back, and gave him her bow and arrows. He shot from her shoulder, and used her strong arrows. Every man that they touched fell that moment. Every one from the west was killed, Lawalila with the others.

Titindi Maupa rested, and went to the sweat-house. His sister went with him. The dead of both sides lay all night where they fell.

Before daybreak Titindi Maupa rose, took his fire-drill, went out, and turning the faces of all his brothers-in-law to the earth, struck them with the fire-drill. All came to life and went back to Wakaruwa.

Lawalila's people lay on the field all night, the next day, and the night following. Titindi Maupa did not like to see all those dead people lying there ; so he went before daybreak of the second day and struck each with his fire-drill. All came to life, rose up, were glad, and went home. Next morning they came to Wakaruwa, and had games again, with good feasting and pleasure. They did not get angry a second time.

Titindi Maupa brought in deer every morning. His brothers-in-law came and ate with him ; they were friendly and happy. Titindi Maupa stayed twenty days at Wakaruwa. He killed deer for all of them. On the twenty-first morning Wakara said to his daughter, —

" I think your husband would like to go home now."

Next morning Titindi Maupa set out for home with his wife and sister ; they went in one day to Kurulsa Mauna.

Three nights later Topuna came to visit them ; he came again to see Titildi Marimi. She let him come now. She was afraid that her brother might leave her a second time.

So at last Topuna got the wife he wanted, and they all lived together at Kurulsa Mauna.

THE TWO SISTERS, HAKA LASI AND TSORE JOWA

THE TWO SISTERS, HAKA LASI AND TSORE JOWA

PERSONAGES

After each name is given that of the creature or thing into which the personage was changed subsequently.

Chuhna, spider; Haka hasi, loon; Hitchinna, wildcat; Jamuka, acorn worm; Juka, silkworm; Metsi, coyote; Tsanunewa, fisher (a bird); Tsore Jowa, eagle.

AT some distance east of Jigul matu lived old Juka. He had a great many sons and two daughters — a big house full of children.

Juka's two daughters were Tsore Jowa, the elder, and Haka Lasi, the younger. After a time Haka Lasi fell in love with her brother Hitchinna. One day she fell asleep and dreamed that he had married her.

Metsi lived, too, in Juka's house. He was no relative; he just lived as a guest there.

One day all the men were out hunting. It was then that Haka Lasi saw Hitchinna in a dream. She began to sing about him, and she sang: " I dream of Hitchinna; I dream that he is my husband. I dream of Hitchinna; I dream that he is my husband."

All the men came back from the hunt at night. At daylight next morning they went to swim, and Tsore Jowa made ready food for them. Haka Lasi took a very nice staff in her hand, and went on top of the sweat-house. She looked in and sang, —

" Where is my husband ? Send him up here to me. I will take him away. We must go on a journey. Where is my husband ? Send him up here to me."

All knew that she had no husband.

" You have no husband," said they.

Hitchina was lying in one corner wrapped up in the skin of a wildcat.

" You have no husband in this house ; all here are your brothers," said Juka.

" I have a husband, and I want him to come here to me," answered Haka Lasi.

" Well," said the eldest son, " I will go up to her. Let us hear what she will say." He went up.

" You are not my husband," said Haka Lasi. " Do not come near me."

She drove that one down, and called again : " Where is my husband ? Send him up to me."

" Go you," said Juka to the second son.

" I don't want you," said Haka Lasi to the second son.

She refused one after another, and drove them away until none was left but Hitchinna. Juka went then to Hitchinna and said, —

" My son, get up and go to her; it looks as though you were the one she wants."

" He is the one," said Haka Lasi; " he is my husband. I want him to go away with me."

Hitchinna said not a word, but rose, washed, dressed himself nicely, and went to the woman.

"The sun is high now," said Haka Lasi; "we must go quickly."

She was glad when taking away the one she wanted. They travelled along, and she sang of Hitchinna as they travelled, sang of him all the time. They went a long distance, and at night she fixed a bed and they lay down on it.

Young Hitchinna could not sleep, he was frightened. When Haka Lasi was asleep, he rose very quickly, took a piece of soft rotten wood, put it on her arm where she had held his head, covered it, and then ran away quickly, hurried back toward Juka's sweat-house with all his might. About daylight he was at the sweat-house.

Now Chuhna, Juka's sister, lived with him. She was the greatest person in the world to spin threads and twist ropes. She had a willow basket as big as a house, and a rope which reached up to the sky and was fastened there.

"My nephew," said she to Hitchinna, "I will save you and save all from your terrible sister. She will be here very soon; she may come any moment. She will kill all in this house; she will kill every one if she finds us here. Let all go into my basket. I will take you up to the sky. She cannot find us there; she cannot follow us to that place."

"I will lie lowest," said Metsi. "I am a good man, I will go in first, I will go in before others; I will be at the bottom of the basket."

Metsi went in first; every one in the sweat-house followed him. Then Chuhna ran up, rose on her rope, and pulled the basket after her.

The sweat-house was empty; no one stayed behind. Chuhna kept rising and rising, going higher and higher.

When Haka Lasi woke up and saw that she had a block of rotten wood on her arm instead of Hitchinna, she said, —

"You won't get away from me, I will catch you wherever you are."

She rushed back to the sweat-house. It was empty; no one there. She ran around in every direction looking for tracks, to find which way they had gone. She found nothing on the ground; then she looked into the sky, and far up, very high, close to the sun, she saw the basket rising, going up steadily.

Haka Lasi was raging; she was so awfully angry that she set fire to the house. It burned quickly, was soon a heap of coals.

The basket was almost at the sky when Metsi said to himself, "I wonder how far up we are; I want to see." And he made a little hole in the bottom of the basket to peep through and look down.

That instant the basket burst open; all came out, poured down, a great stream of people, and all fell straight into the fire of the sweat-house.

Now, Tsore Jowa was outside on top of the basket. She caught at the sun, held to it, and saved herself.

Hitchinna went down with the rest, fell into the burning coals, and was burned like his brothers.

Haka Lasi was glad that they had not escaped her; she took a stick, fixed a net on it, and watched.

All were in the fire now and were burning. After a while one body burst, and the heart flew out of it. Haka Lasi caught this heart in her net. Soon a second and a third body burst, and two more hearts flew out. She caught those as well as the first one. She caught all the hearts except two, — Juka's own heart and his eldest son's heart.

Juka's heart flew high, went away far in the sky, and came down on the island of a river near Klamath Lake. It turned into Juka himself there. He sank in the ground to his chin; only his head was sticking out.

The heart of the eldest son flew off to the foot of Wahkalu and turned to be himself again. He fell so deep into the earth that only his face was sticking out on the surface.

Now Haka Lasi put all the hearts which she had caught on a string, hung them around her neck, and went to a lake east of Jigulmatu. She wanted to live at the bottom of the lake, but could not find a place deep enough. So she went northwest of Klamath Lake to Crater Lake, where she could live in deep water.

Two Tsanunewa brothers lived near the lake with their old grandmother. One morning early these brothers were out catching ducks, and just at daybreak they heard some one call.

" Who is that ? " asked the elder brother.

" I don't know," answered the younger.

Soon they saw Haka Lasi spring up on the water and call. She had a large string of hearts around her neck. Then she sank again in the water.

Again she came up at some distance and called a second time.

Now Tsore Jowa came down from the sun and went to the old sweat-house, where she found nothing but a heap of bones and ashes. Putting pitch on her head and on her arms, and strips of deerskin around her neck with pitch on them, she cried and went around mourning. After a time she began to look for her sister. She went everywhere; went to Klamath Lake.

For some time the two Tsanunewa brothers had heard a voice singing, —

"Li-wa-éh, li-wa-há,
Li-wa-éh, li-wa-há."

This was old Juka. He was lying in the ground where he had fallen, and was crying.

Tsore Jowa searched, inquired, asked every one about Haka Lasi, and told what she had done, — that she had killed her own brothers and father.

Tsore Jowa came at last to the house of the two Tsanunewa brothers one day about sunset, and spoke to their grandmother. " My sister, Haka Lasi, has killed all my brothers and my father," said she; and she told the whole story.

The old woman cried when she heard what Tsore Jowa told her. The two brothers were away hunting; they came home about dark with a large string of ducks. " This woman," said the grandmother, "is looking for her sister, who has killed all her people."

The two brothers cried when the story was told to them. When they had finished crying, they said to the old woman, "Cook ducks and let this woman have plenty to eat."

When all had eaten, the two brothers said to Tsore Jowa: "Tell us what kind of a person your sister is. Which way did she go?"

"I don't know which way she went," said Tsore Jowa.

"Three days ago," said the elder brother, "just as daylight was coming, we saw a woman jump up in the lake where we were fishing. She seemed to have large beads around her neck. That woman may be your sister."

"Catch that woman for me. I will give you otter-skins and beads. I will give bearskins. If you wish, I will stay with you here, if you catch her."

"We want no beads nor otter-skins nor bearskins," said the brothers.

"What do you want?"

"We want red deer-bones and green deer-bones; small, sharp ones to stab fish with."

",You shall have all you want of both kinds," said Tsore Jowa.

Next morning she set out with a sack, went away to high mountains, gathered deer-bones, red and green leg-bones, and put them in her sack. At sunset she went back to the house, with the sack full.

The two brothers were glad, now. The elder took red, and the younger green bones. (The fat on the leg-bones of deer turns some red and others green.)

"You must catch her bad sister for Tsore Jowa," said the old woman to her grandsons.

All that night the brothers sat sharpening the bones and then fastening them to the spear-shafts. They did not stop for a moment. " Let us go now; it is near daylight," said the elder brother.

They started. When they reached the lake, they went out on the water. Every morning at daybreak Haka Lasi sprang up to the surface and called from the lake. The elder brother took a stem of tule grass, opened it, placed it on the water, made himself small, and sat down in the middle of it. The younger brother fixed himself in another stem of tule in the same way. The two tule stems floated away on the water, till they came near the place where the brothers had seen Haka Lasi spring up the first time.

" Let me shoot before you," said the elder brother.

" Oh, you cannot shoot; you will miss her," said the younger. " Let me shoot first. You will miss; you will not hit her heart."

" I will hit," said the elder.

They watched and watched. Each had his bow drawn ready to shoot. Daylight came now. Haka Lasi rose quickly, came to the top of the water, and held out her arms before calling.

The younger brother sent the first arrow, struck her in the neck; the elder shot, struck her right under the arm. Haka Lasi dropped back and sank in the water.

The brothers watched and watched. After a time

they saw two arrows floating, and were afraid they had lost her. She had pulled them out of her body, and they rose to the surface. After a while the body rose. Haka Lasi was dead.

The brothers saw that she had a great many hearts on a string around her neck. They drew her to the shore then, and carried her home. They left the body hidden outside the house, and went in.

"We did not see her," said the elder Tsanunewa to his grandmother.

All sat down to eat fish, and when they were through eating, the elder said to Tsore Jowa, "Come out and see what we caught this morning."

She ran out with them, and saw her dead sister with a string of hearts on her neck. Tsore Jowa took off her buckskin skirt, wrapped up the body, and put it in the house. She counted the hearts.

"My eldest brother's heart is not here, and my father's is not here," said she.

"Every morning we hear some one crying, far away toward the north; that may be one of them," said the two Tsanunewas.

Tsore Jowa started out to find this one, if she could, who was calling. She left the body and hearts at the old grandmother's house, and hurried off toward the north. She heard the cry soon and knew it. "That is my father," said she.

Tsore Jowa came near the place from which the cry rose; saw no one. Still she heard the cry. At last she saw a face; it was the face of Juka, her father.

Tsore Jowa took a sharp stick and dug. She dug

down to Juka's waist; tried to pull him up, but could not stir him. She dug again, dug a good while; pulled and pulled, until at last she drew him out.

Juka was very poor, all bones, no flesh at all on him. Tsore Jowa put down a deerskin, wrapped her father in it, and carried him to the old woman's house; then she put him with Haka Lasi's body, and carried them home to the old burned sweat-house east of Jigulmatu.

She was crying yet, since one brother was missing. She put down the basket in which she had carried them, hid it away, covered it carefully.

At the foot of Wahkalu lived a certain Jamuka, an old man who had a wife and two daughters.

" Bring in some wood," said the old man one day to his daughters.

The two girls took their baskets and went to bring wood. Soon they heard some one singing, —

" I-nó i-nó, I-no mi-ná
I-nó, i-nó I-no mi-ná."

" Listen," said the younger sister; " some one is singing."

They listened, heard the singing; it seemed right at the foot of Wahkalu. They went toward the place from which the sound came.

" That is a nice song," said the younger sister. " I should like to see the one who sings so."

They went near, saw no one yet. " Let us take the wood home," said the elder sister, " then come back here; our father may be angry if we stay away longer."

They took the wood home, put it down, and said nothing. Both went back to the place where the singing was and listened. At last the younger sister came to the right place, and said, " I think this is he who is singing."

There was a head sticking out of the ground, and the face was covered with water. The man had cried so much that he looked dirty and ugly.

The sisters took sharp sticks, and dug all around the head, dug deeply. They could not pull out the person; they had only dug to his waist when night came and they must go.

" Why did you stay out so late ? " asked their father.

" We heard some one singing, and wanted to know who it was, but were not able. We will go back in the morning and search again."

" That is well," said Jamuka. He had heard how Juka's sons had been killed. " Perhaps one of those people is alive yet," said he ; " you must look for him."

They went early next morning to dig, and drew the man out. They took off their buckskin skirts then, and wrapped him up carefully. He was nothing but bones, no flesh at all on his body. The younger sister ran home to get wildcat skins to wrap around him.

" We have found a man, but he is all bones," said she to her father.

" Take good care of the stranger, feed and nurse him well," said Jamuka ; " he may be Juka himself, and he is a good man."

They wrapped the man in wildcat skins. A great stream of water was running from his eyes, and deer came down the hill to drink of that water.

The girls lay on each side of the man, and gave him food ; stayed all night with him. Next morning they went home for more food.

" Feed him, give him plenty," said Jamuka; " he may get health and strength yet."

The sisters went back and stayed a second night. The man began to look better, but he cried all the time, and many deer came to drink the water that flowed from his eyes. The girls went home the second morning. " The man looks better," said they to their father.

" I have heard," said old Jamuka, " that Juka's sons were killed. This must be one of them."

They went back right away, and stayed another day and night with the stranger. The man looked as though he might get his health again. He began to talk. " Has your father a bow and arrows ? " asked he of the sisters.

" He has ; he has many."

" Bring me a bow and arrows ; many deer come near me to drink, I may shoot one."

They took the man's words to their father. Jamuka gave them a bow and some arrows, and they went back to the sick man.

" You may go home to-night," said he. " I wish to be alone."

The girls left him. At sundown a great buck came and drank of the tears, he killed him ; later another came, he killed that one ; at midnight a third

came, he killed the third; now he had three. At
daylight a fourth buck was killed; he had four
now. " That is enough," thought he.

When the girls came and saw four great bucks
lying dead near the stranger, they were frightened;
they ran home and told their father. Old Jamuka
was glad when they told him. He sharpened his
knife, hurried out to the woods and looked at the
stranger. " That is Juka's son," said he; " take
good care of him, daughters."

Jamuka dressed the deer, carried them home, and
cut up the venison for drying. Next evening Juka's
son sent the girls home a second time, and killed
five great deer that night. Next morning the girls
came to see him, and ran home in wonder.

Their father was very glad. He dressed the five
deer as he had the four, and cut up the venison.

Tsore Jowa was hunting everywhere all this time
to find her brother. She had left the hearts, her
sister's body, and her father hidden away carefully;
had done nothing yet to save them.

The night after Juka's son killed the five deer
the two girls took him home to their father. He was
well now and beautiful, in good health and strong.
He cried no more after that. A salt spring was
formed in the place where he had fallen and shed
so many tears. The spring is in that place till this
day, and deer go in herds to drink from it. People
watch near the spring and kill them, as Juka's son
did. Tsore Jowa went to every house inquiring
about her brother. At last she came to Jamuka's
house, and there she found him. She was glad

now and satisfied. She left her brother with his two wives and hurried home.

Tsore Jowa made in one night a great sweat-house, prepared a big basket, and filled it with water. When the second night came, she dropped hot stones into the water; put all the hearts into the basket. Opening her sister's body, she took out her heart and put it in with the others. At this time the water in the basket was boiling. She covered the basket and placed it on top of the sweat-house. Then she went in, lay down and slept.

The water was seething all night. At daybreak the basket turned over, and there was a crowding and hurrying of people around the sweat-house. They began to talk briskly.

" We are cold, we are cold ! " said they. " Let us in ! "

Soon broad daylight came. Tsore Jowa opened the door, and all crowded into the sweat-house. Tsore Jowa said not a word yet. All the brothers came; behind them Haka Lasi. She looked well, she was good. Her heart was clean; there was nothing bad now in it.

" Where is our eldest brother ? " asked all.

" He is well; I have found him. He has two wives," said Tsore Jowa.

Juka was in good health and strong. She had washed him and given him good food.

All were happy, and they went hunting.

" I think your husband would like to go home," said Jamuka one day to his daughters.

Juka's son and his two wives set out to visit his

father; Juka saw his son coming; took a big blanket quickly, caught him, placed him in it, and put him right away.

Now the wives of Juka's son came in and sat down in the house. Two other brothers took them for wives. They stayed a long time, never saw their first husband again. Old Juka kept him secreted, made him a Weänmauna, a hidden one.

After a time the two women wished to go home to visit Jamuka. They took beads and blankets, nice things of all kinds, and went to their father at the foot of Wahkalu.

"We have never seen our husband," said they, "since we went to his father's. We have new husbands now."

"I think that is well enough," said Jamuka. "His father has put him away. His brothers are as good for you as he was."

The sisters agreed with their father, and went back and lived at Juka's house after that.

THE DREAM OF JUIWAIYU AND HIS JOURNEY TO DAMHAUJA'S COUNTRY

THE DREAM OF JUIWAIYU AND HIS JOURNEY TO DAMHAUJA'S COUNTRY

PERSONAGES

After each name is given that of the creature or thing into which the personage was changed subsequently.

Damhauja, the moon just before renewal; **Darijua**, gray squirrel; **Halaia**, morning star; **Jupka**, butterfly of the wild silk worm; **Juiwaiyu**, acorn of the Eastern black oak; **Kechowala**, blue jay; **Mahari**, Eastern black oak; **Pahnino**, a kind of ocean-shell : **Periwiriwaiyu**, another kind of Eastern black oak.

JUIWAIYU lived far away in the east, in the southern part of it. His father, Periwiriwaiyu, was old. His mother, Maharia, was old, too; but both were very beautiful.

Juiwaiyu hunted, fished; was happy till one night he dreamed of two girls who lived beyond Wahkalu, lived north of that mountain.

"I dreamed of two sisters," said he to his father and mother next morning, "I saw two women last night. They are both very beautiful. I must find them; I will bring them home if I can."

"You must not go," said his father and mother. "If you go, you will never come back to this country. We shall not see you again if you leave us. We know that those people will kill you. We shall never see you again if you go from here." Then they cried bitterly, both of them.

But his father and mother could not stop Juiwaiyu; he would go. When he was ready to start, his mother said, —

"Your uncle lives at Shultsmauna, near Kamshumatu. Stop there. You must see your uncle, you must talk with him. His name is Jupka. He is very wise; he will help you. There will be thunder and a sprinkle of rain here when you touch your uncle's house. I shall know then that you have got that far in safety."

Juiwaiyu began to sing. He started, and rose through the air. He went very high, and cried — cried and sang as he travelled. Though he had made up his mind to go, he feared that his mother's words might come true, that the people beyond Wahkalu might kill him. He looked far ahead, and saw smoke near the edge of the sky. "That may be smoke from my uncle's house," thought Juiwaiyu.

He moved toward the smoke; went on till he was straight above his uncle's house. He went down to the roof then, and peeped in through the smoke-hole. The old man, who was lying with his back to the fire, saw him look in. Jupka stood up, looked again, grabbed his spear.

"Is that the way you look into my house? What do you want here?" cried Jupka, aiming his spear at the stranger.

"It is I, uncle, — I, Juiwaiyu."

"Why did you not call me uncle when you looked first? Why did you not say who you were when you came? I might have killed you; I came

very near killing you with my spear.   Come down,
come down; let me see you, my nephew."

"I will," said Juiwaiyu; "I have travelled far
to-day, I am tired."

He went down on the central pole.

"Uncle, I have come to talk with you, to let
you know where I am going."

"You would better eat first," said Jupka; and
he took Juiwaiyu in his arms, smoothed his hair,
and was glad to look at him.

"You are tired, my nephew; you are hungry;
you must eat."

"I am not hungry; I have no time to wait; I
am in a great hurry."

"Where are you going, my nephew?" asked
Jupka.

"I had a dream last night, my uncle; I dreamed
of two sisters, daughters of Damhauja."

"You would better stay at home.   My nephew,
stay at home; you would better not go for those
sisters.   Forget them; don't think of those girls,"
said Jupka.   "If you go, you will never come
back.   The place where they live is a bad one;
every stranger gets killed who goes there.   I have
seen many men on the way to Damhauja's; many
a man has passed here to look for those sisters, but
never have I seen any come back with or without a
woman.   I have been in that country myself, I
know it well.   I had to fight for my life there, and
came near being killed.   I am many times stronger
than you, know people better than you do, and I
would not go to that country."

"No matter what kind of country that is, no matter what kind of people live in it, I must find those two sisters. I have dreamt of them. There is no use in trying to hold me back. I must go; I cannot stop, I cannot help myself."

"Well," said Jupka, "if you must go, I will go with you; you would be lost without me. I must save you, my nephew. I will make myself small; you can put me on your head, you can tie me up in your hair easily."

The old man made himself small, and Juiwaiyu put him on the top of his head, bound him firmly in his hair, bound him so that no one could see him. Then he went up on the sweat-house and turned toward the sun.

"Sun, O Sun, I wish you to be slow," said he. "I must go very far; I wish the day to last long."

"I will tell you now of the road," said Jupka. "When you come near a small mountain east of Wahkalu, there will be three roads there before you; one on the right hand very narrow. You can hardly see that road, it is so little beaten, but you must find it, for you cannot go by another. There is a middle road, smooth and wide; you will see fresh clover scattered on the road, just as if women had carried some over and dropped a little here and there. If you go over that road, you will be killed by lice and wind. On the left hand is a road; if you take that, you will lose yourself and never reach any place."

"I will sing now," said Juiwaiya, "and my song will be heard everywhere, north, south, east, and west."

He began, and rose in the air as he sang; he rose, and as he moved forward, the whole world heard him; every one looked up to see who was singing, but no one saw anything.

"That sounds like the song of Juiwaiyu," said some of the people. "I think that is the voice of Periwiriwaiyu's son," said others; "I think that is he, for that's how he sings when he travels."

They tried to see who was singing, but saw no one. The song seemed just above them, but it was high up, very high in the air.

"Hurry, my nephew, hurry," said Jupka; "I don't like to camp on the journey, I want to be at that place before sunset."

Juiwaiyu sang faster now; he could not move without singing. He moved swiftly, and soon they were east of Wahkalu.

"Look down carefully," said Jupka; "if you see clover scattered on a road, you must not go over it. Go over that road on the right, do not look at the other."

Damhauja had sent people to scatter clover on the middle road and entice men, make them think that the road to his sweat-house.

"The middle road lies straight toward the mountain," said Jupka; "all people die who try to pass over it. A great many lie dead on that road now, my nephew; do not go near it."

Juiwaiyu kept on; soon they heard laughter ahead on the small mountain, loud laughter.

"You are on the wrong road," said Jupka. "Turn back, my nephew; if not, you will die surely. That was the laughter of people sent by Damhauja to kill all who go over the middle road."

Juiwaiyu kept on; he would not listen to his uncle. Soon a great wind came, bringing clouds of lice with it; the air was filled with them. They fell on Juiwaiyu, and ate the flesh off his body. The wind drove him far back on his journey, and blew the beads from his neck. The people of the mountain did this, — people put there and kept by Damhauja.

Juiwaiyu was angry. He rushed forward a second time.

"I will pass, I will go through this time," said he.

"I told you of this trouble," said Jupka, "I warned you. I said that this was an evil road over which no one can pass. Stop, or you will be dead before night comes. Stop! Let me down; I will save you."

Juiwaiyu came to the ground, and took out his uncle.

"I will save you," said Jupka; "I will give you back flesh and strength."

The old man took his pipe and drew smoke through it. The wind went away; the lice disappeared, not one was left anywhere. Jupka took up a rose-twig. With this he whipped Juiwaiyu, and he was as sound and strong as ever. He had all his flesh back in a moment.

The people of the mountain saw this. "We cannot kill him," said they; "he has too much power for us."

" You must turn back and start where the roads part," said Jupka. " On the right is a small narrow trail ; you can barely see it, but you must find this trail. You cannot go to Damhauja's house by an-- other way."

Juiwaiyu went back to where the paths parted.

" You are looking for the way," said Jupka. " If you see a narrow little trail, that is it."

He found that trail at last. " That is the right way," said the uncle.

It was so narrow that Juiwaiyu was barely able to see it. He went forward easily; went fast, like a man who is running down hill. They came to the small mountain, and when Juiwaiyu was above it, he heard laughing at a distant village. " That must be the place to which we are going," said he.

" My nephew, look out now, be careful. When you go into Damhauja's sweat-house and sit with his daughters, he will give you a pipe filled with crushed bones of people instead of tobacco. If you breathe smoke from that pipe, you will die the next moment. With this smoke he has killed those who escaped lice and wind from the mountain."

Juiwaiyu rested a while, and thought of the beads he had lost. " I wish my beads would return to me," said he. That moment the beads were on his neck. They were as beautiful as ever.

" My beads, you must not go again from me. You must stay with me, and you must be in plenty. Pahnino Marimi, I wish you to send your daughters for leaves, wood, and water. Be kind when I come to you. Do not kill me. Let us go on," said he to his uncle.

They went forward, and soon they saw two girls, one holding the other by the hand. These girls were coming toward the mountain, swaying their hands and singing. Juiwaiyu came to the ground, hid behind a tree, and said, " Let there be wood here in plenty, wood for these women." The wood was right there in one moment.

The two girls set down their baskets and filled them. " I wish that man would come," said one sister to the other, " the man we dreamed of last night."

They put down their hands to take the baskets. Juiwaiyu caught their hands. They looked around, saw him, and were frightened.

" Why are you frightened? I dreamed of you last night, you dreamed of me. Go home, go ahead, hurry forward, I will follow; I will be at your father's house soon."

They put the baskets on their backs, ran quickly, reached home soon, threw down the baskets outside the doorway, and rushed into the sweat-house.

" What are you scared at, my daughters? You saw some young man in the woods, I think," said Pahnino, their mother, who was making acorn bread outside the doorway. " I think that some brother-in-law was watching you near the mountain."

" You have never seen the man we met," said the sisters.

Pahnino went to look; she looked carefully, but saw no man coming toward her from any side.

The two sisters spread a black bearskin and sat on
it, sat near each other and waited. The old man
went out to look, put his hand over his eyes to see
a new son-in-law, but could see no one. Juiwaiyu
was on the house now; he went down through the
central pillar, passed through the ground, and came
up between Damhauja's two daughters. Pahnino
Marimi walked in at that moment to scold her
daughters. She looked, and saw Juiwaiyu between
them.

"Some one is sitting with our daughters," said
she to the old man.

Damhauja went for his pipe, put in crushed bones
of Mapchemaina, and handed the pipe to his
daughters.

"Give this to my son-in-law," said he.

They did not like to take the pipe, but they
could not refuse their father, they could not help
themselves. They were crying.

"You must not smoke this," whispered they;
"we will give you another kind." They took the
tobacco out and put in some of the common sort.
The old man did not watch sharply at first; he was
thinking only to see Juiwaiyu drop dead. The
girls handed back the empty pipe to their father.

Jupka, who was sitting on his nephew's head,
laughed in his own mind.

"I don't know what sort of man this is," thought
Damhauja; "I have never seen such a person. I
think he must have come to fight with me; I will
try him once more."

He filled the pipe a second time, and gave it to

his daughters. They handed it to Juiwaiyu. This time they could not change the tobacco. Damhauja was watching too carefully. Jupka smoked this pipe. No smoke could hurt him. Damhauja, who hoped to see Juiwaiyu fall dead, became frightened when he saw him as well as ever.

"What am I to do?" thought he. "I give this tobacco to every man who comes for my daughters, and every man who smokes dies right away. I am afraid of my new son-in-law. I will not fight with this man. Let my other sons-in-law try him. My daughters, I want you to give nice food to your husband; give him good things to eat, take the best care of him, treat him well. My boys, I want you to bring plenty of nice food to my son-in-law."

" I will give venison now to these sisters," thought Jupka; and he took out a small piece of fat venison as large as a walnut. This he gave to Juiwaiyu, and told him to ask for a large basket. They brought it.

"You, venison, keep this size," said Juiwaiyu; " be no smaller, you must not be gone;" and then he cut slices.

Damhauja carried off three great baskets of meat, then went out on the house-top and called all his sons.

"Come for venison, my sons," said he. " There is plenty for all of you."

Damhauja had a great many sons-in-law on the west beyond a river. All his daughters were married except two. These sons-in-law heard him call and wondered. "What has happened?" asked they of one another. "We've never heard the old man talk that way before. He must have found a new son-in-law; he must have found a husband for Halaia and Pahnino Marimi."

All Damhauja's sons came into the sweat-house.

Kechowala, a son-in-law and chief on the west side, sent his two sons, Kechowala and Darijua, to see what was happening at the sweat-house,

When the boys came and looked in, the elder saw a man, he thought, but did not know him. Damhauja's sons were dancing a fire-dance. The two brothers looked around carefully, but the younger did not see the strange man. They ran down from the sweat-house, and on the way home began to quarrel.

"I think our grandfather has a new son-in-law; I saw him," said Kechowala, the elder.

"You did not," said the younger.

"Why do you try to hide him, why do you deny? I saw him surely."

"When we get home, you will say that you saw a stranger in the sweat-house; but if you do, you will lie."

"We shall see great trouble, I think," said the elder; "there will be fighting now our grandfather has a new son-in-law, there will be great fighting."

The two boys ran very fast, disputing as they went. They got to the river, swam across, ran home.

"There is a strange man over there; grandfather has a new son-in-law," said Kechowala.

"Don't believe what he says," cried Darijua to his father; "I could not see any man."

"Why do you want to hide him, why do you deny? You must have seen him plainly."

"I did not see him, and you did not. I saw all who were there, but I saw no stranger."

"I saw him sitting between the two girls," said Kechowala.

"He is there," said the father. "I will see that man to-morrow."

"My son-in-law," said Damhauja, "you must be careful to-morrow. I have a great many daughters besides your two wives; their husbands will try to kill you." Then Damhauja said to his sons: "We will go to sleep and rise early; take good care of your brother-in-law to-morrow."

All went to rest; Juiwaiyu and his wives as well as others.

When all were asleep, Juiwaiyu took Jupka out of his hair and rose up. "I wish for daylight quickly," said he.

Thunder roared then, and some rain came; Juiwaiyu wished to let his mother know that he was well. He went out, took one step and went from the sweat-house to the other side of the nearest mountain, with the second step he went to the top of a mountain beyond.

Jupka was angry because Damhauja had tried to kill Juiwaiyu with the poisonous pipe. Now he took vengeance. He put the two sisters on a high place in the sweat-house, made a great storm of wind and rain. Soon the whole place was filled with water. It rolled and swept through the sweat-house, drowned Damhauja and his wife; washed their bodies out through the door away.

Juiwaiyu on the mountain took his yaiyauna flute and began to play. All the world heard him, all people went to hill-tops and mountain-tops, all stretched their heads up and listened, all said, " That must be Juiwaiyu; no one plays in that way but Juiwaiyu." Deer began to come from the east along the same way over which Juiwaiyu had come, and all stood before him.

" Let one stand in front of me and look this way," said Juiwaiyu, " let all the others stand behind that first one."

They stood in the line, a fawn in the first place. He shot them all with one arrow, hundreds of them. The arrow entered the mouth of the front deer and went out near the tail of the last. Then Juiwaiyu took the little fawn and opened it, made the deer very small, put them all inside the fawn's body, took that home in one hand, threw the fawn down on the sweat-house. The deer inside the fawn became as big as ever, rolled down, filled the whole place around the sweat-house.

Juiwaiyu now saw Damhauja and Pahnino Marimi lying cold and dead. He ran then to Jupka in the sweat-house. " Bring them to life, my uncle; bring them to life again ! "

Jupka whipped both with a rose-twig and brought them to life. Damhauja shook himself and said, " I slept too hard."

" You would not have waked up at all but for

my nephew. You wanted to kill him. I punished you."

Damhauja knew Jupka now. "Oh, why did you not let me know that you were here? I would not have tried to hurt Juiwaiyu."

The old man saw so many deer around the sweat-house that he did n't know what to think. At last he went up on the sweat-house. "Come, my sons, come," cried he; "there is venison here for all of you."

All the sons came. Each had one deer, and there were many others to spare.

All the sons-in-law in the west were angry that Damhauja's sons had so much venison.

"We will go over and see this man," said Kechowala, the chief. "We will have some fun to-day with him."

When Damhauja's eldest son was bringing venison to his father, he saw Kechowala. "He is coming," said the son.

Kechowala had an angry face; he walked fast. When he reached the sweat-house, all were eating venison. He went to the top of the sweat-house, took his arrow from under his arm, and said, "Wake up, be ready; we must play to-day."

Then he looked in and saw Juiwaiyu sitting between the two sisters. "I know now who that man is; he is from the east. Feed him well, dress him well, father-in-law; we must have fun before he goes from here. He must show what he can do before he leaves us."

The old man went out and scolded Kechowala:

"You talk loud, you want fat venison; that's what you have come for, that's why you are at this sweat-house."

Jupka heard all that Kechowala said.

"I will go home now," said Kechowala, "and be here after breakfast."

"My son-in-law will be killed to-day," said Pah-nino Marimi; "what can we do? They are going to kill our son-in-law who brings so much venison. Stay in the house, do not go out," said Pahnino.

"Do not go out," said the brothers; "we will meet those people."

All looked, and saw a great crowd coming from the west. The brothers-in-law were coming, and when near they shouted to Damhauja's sons. The two sisters tried to stop Juiwaiyu.

"Let me go, wives," said he, "let me go. If I stay here, they will call me a coward; I will let no one give me that name."

"I want to see that new man who is here," cried Kechowala, "I want to talk with him."

"I will go out," said Juiwaiyu, to his wives. "My father and mother told me of this place. I know what it is."

"Come out!" called Kechowala at the door, "come out; don't be afraid of us, don't be a coward."

"I will come when I am ready, I will meet you."

Kechowala went to his people. "He will be here soon," said he.

All laughed; all were glad. "If he comes," thought they, "we will kill him."

Juiwaiyu went out and stood on the house-top, looked around, looked at his enemies, went down slowly, went as if he did not like to meet them.

"Why are you afraid?" asked Kechowala. "Do you think that we will hurt you?"

He went to them, he sat on a stone. He had but one arrow, and that without a point. This was a staff which his uncle had given him. The playground was beyond a hill at some distance from the sweat-house. "Stand up and play," said the sons-in-law; and they pushed Juiwaiyu to throw him, but he did not fall. All went to the playground. Juiwaiyu caught the bones on his club at the middle point, then hurled them; ran and caught them the second time, ran again, put the bones beyond the barrier. He did the same a second time, and won the first game. He won two games; no one else could win.

"Well," said the western brothers-in-law, "we have never seen any one play bone like him. We will try him in some other way."

Next they gave him a start in racing. The race was to a mountain opposite. Juiwaiyu was to get there first if he was able. They thought to strike him from behind, kill him easily, but they could not come near him. He was at the mountain before they had run half the distance. In the afternoon they played bone a second time. They thought to kill him surely in this way. Between the middle of the playground and Juiwaiyu's barrier they put a great poison spider right on the path where Juiwaiyu was to run, Jupka knew their plan, and pointed out the spider to his nephew. Juiwaiyu jumped on the spider, crushed it right away before it could turn to poison him; then he took the bones beyond the barrier.

He went back to the middle of the playground. Kechowala's men said nothing, made no mention of the spider. Juiwaiyu took the bones beyond the barrier that time, and won the second inning. This made the first game of the afternoon. While they were making ready for the second game, Kechowala had flint knives and spear-points put on the path so that Juiwaiyu should fall and kill himself.

They commenced the second game. Juiwaiyu took the bones from all and ran ahead, ran quickly. When near the knives and spear-points, Jupka told him where they were; he came down between some, sprang over others, took the bones beyond the barrier, came back as if nothing had been put upon his path; went a second time and won the second game.

He had beaten all who had played against him. They were very angry. "We must kill him surely in another way," said Kechowala.

The playground was far from the sweat-house, and when Juiwaiyu had won the second game he turned to go back to the sweat-house. Kechowala sent a rattlesnake to meet him at one place and a grizzly bear at another. Juiwaiyu jumped on the snake, and crushed his head. When he came to the bear, he struck him one blow with his foot and killed him. He skinned both, took the skins, and hung them up before the sweat-house.

When Kechowala's men saw the skins, they were angry, terribly excited; they stopped before the sweat-house, jumped, and shouted, —

"We want to look at Juiwaiyu. Let Juiwaiyu come out here; we want to see him."

Juiwaiyu went out. All the brothers-in-law from the west crowded up toward him, all wanted then to kill him. He had no arms but the staff given by Jupka. All he needed was to point that at any one and say, "I wish you dead;" that moment the person fell dead. No one could come near Juiwaiyu when running or hit him, and before they stopped threatening he killed half of Damhauja's sons-in-law. The others ran home then, killed their own wives and those of the dead men. "We will have nothing," said they, "that comes from Damhauja's." They killed all the children, too; none escaped but Darijua, who ran over to the sweat-house and told of the killing.

That night Jupka made a great storm, and drowned every western man left alive by Juiwaiyu. Next morning early he went over, struck the dead women and children with his rose-twig, brought all except the men to life again, and took them to Damhauja's.

Juiwaiyu had brought as many deer that morning as he had the first one. Damhauja made his house stretch out and grow to give room enough for all the children. They cooked venison and feasted, feasted all that day at the sweat-house.

Next morning Juiwaiyu went home with his two wives and his uncle.

THE FLIGHT OF TSANUNEWA
AND DEFEAT OF HEHKU

THE FLIGHT OF TSANUNEWA AND DEFEAT OF HEHKU

PERSONAGES

After each name is given that of the creature or thing into which the personage was changed subsequently.

Ahalamila, gray wolf; Bohkuina, silver-gray fox; Chichi, fish hawk; Demauna, pine marten; Gagi, crow; Haka Kaina, flint; Hehku, horned serpent; Jihkulú, big owl; Jupka, butterfly of the wild silkworm; Kaítsiki, ground squirrel; Kechowala, bluejay; Malewula, wolf; Malwila, meadow lark; Manjauchu, gopher; Mapchemaina, the first people now turned into birds, beasts, and other things; Matauwila, beaver; Matdasi, spring salmon; Míniau Marimi, fire-drill woman; Tillipka, crane; Periwiri Yupa, acorn of the black oak; Petaina, skunk; Topuna, mountain lion; Tsanunewa, elk; Tsuwalkai, red flint; Pútokya, skull people, *i. e.* people who could turn themselves into a head.

A LONG time ago, when Jupka and Bohkuina were sitting in the sweat-house Jigulmatu, Jupka called to him people of the Mapchemaina; he called Demauna, Wirula, Matauwila, Topuna, Ahalamila, Manjauchu, Kechowala, Malwila, Gagi, and many others. He did not make them; he just called, and they came from different parts of the earth to him. He gave them their names and said, —

" Hereafter all who live in the world will call you as I do now."

One side of Jigulmatu was filled with these people called up by Jupka.

" This is Jigulmatu, my small sweat-house," said Jupka, " but I am going to make my Igunna " (great house); and later he made Wahkalu (Mount Shasta), made it to be his great house, but he lived at Jigulmatu till he made the Yana, and went to Jigulmatu often afterward.

At this time Tsuwalkai Marimi, an old woman, had reared a small boy. His name was Tsanunewa. She called the boy grandson, and he called her his grandmother. He was an orphan. All his kindred were dead; all had been killed one after another, and he was alone when the old woman found the boy and reared him.

"I want to go west and catch mice," said Tsanunewa one day to her.

"I don't want you to go away from the house. I don't want you to trap mice; you might go astray; you might get killed," said the old woman.

Tsanunewa began to cry. He cried and teased till at last she said: "Go, if you wish, but be careful; you may get hurt. The traps may fall on you; something may kill you."

The old woman made acorn bread for him, and showed him how to set rock traps and other traps, and how to bait them with acorns.

"Stay around the house," said she. "You must not go near that rocky mountain off there. That is a bad place, a very bad place; it is dangerous. You must not go to it."

The boy started, went some distance from the house, then stood still and looked at the rocky mountain.

"I will go to that place," thought he; "I will go where my grandmother told me not to go. Why

is she afraid? Why did she tell me not to go there?
I will run and see."

He hurried off to the mountain, went up on the
rocks, looked around all the time; he remembered
his grandmother's words, and said to himself, —

"I should like to know who is here; I should like
to know what frightens my grandmother."

He went around the mountain, saw no one,
set all his traps, big traps and little ones; he
stayed there till near sunset. After that he ran
home.

"I am afraid to eat to-night," said he. "If I eat,
perhaps the mice will not like the acorns in my
traps."

"You must not eat," said his grandmother; "I
do not wish you to eat anything. You must not
touch salmon this evening. You may eat a little
just at midnight. Now go and play around the
house; all the mice will see you; they are out playing and will go to your traps."

Hehku Marimi lived at that mountain. She
killed all the people who went there to trap. It was
she who had killed Tsanunewa's kindred.

Next morning at daybreak Tsanunewa went to
see his traps. He looked at the first, second, third,
fourth; he had not caught anything. The traps
were empty, just as he had left them. He found
nothing till he reached the last one; he saw that
there was something in that trap. He stood and
looked at it; saw Hehku Marimi; she was there in
the last trap. She had made herself small and gone
in. She looked ugly, and Tsanunewa was frightened.

He ran home as fast as he could; he was pale, and trembling.

"Why are you frightened?" asked his grand-mother. "What have you caught?"

"I have caught something. I don't know what it is. I am terribly afraid of it."

"I told you yesterday not to go to that mountain. I knew that trouble would come if you went there. I will go myself and see what you have caught."

Tsuwalkai Marimi was ready to run to the mountain and look at the trap. She wanted to know what was in it.

"You, my grandson, stay here at home," said she; "perhaps the thing that you have caught is not dead yet. I will look at it."

The old woman started, but as she was going out she said: "Maybe Hehku is in your trap. If she is, she will get out, run here and kill us both perhaps; kill you, surely, if she finds you. Save yourself, my grandson. If you see her coming, run west, run very hard, run till you come to a great river. On the other side of it is Mipka's house; shout to him, call him uncle, tell him to take you over; say that you are running for your life, that he must save you."

While the old woman was talking, she looked and saw Hehku far off at the mountain.

"My grandson," cried she, "Hehku is coming! She will kill you. Run! I will stay here and stop her a while."

Tsanunewa looked and saw Hehku. Then he

ran west; ran till he reached the great river. He stopped at the edge of it and shouted.

Hehku had made herself small the night before, and gone into Tsanunewa's trap purposely. The boy thought that she was angry because he had trapped her. She wanted him to think so. She went into the trap to have an excuse to kill him as she had killed all his kindred. When Tsanunewa ran home to his grandmother, frightened because he had seen Hehku, Hehku went out of the trap, crushed red rottenstone, painted her face, made it blood color. She had a big cap made of skulls, skulls of people she had killed. She put the cap on her head then, and started. She started, ran quickly, singing as she went, —

"I am following Tsanunewa; I am on his track.
I am following Tsanunewa; I am on his track."

She sang till she came to the door. There she stopped, said " Whu !" and drew a long breath.

" Tell me, old woman," cried she, " tell me where Tsanunewa is; I have come to this house on his track."

" I have not seen that boy," said Tsuwalkai Marimi. " I do not know where he is. I am alone, all my people are dead; you killed them."

" I will not hurt you," said Hehku; " I will not touch you, but tell me where the boy is; tell me which way he went. He went west, I think. I will follow till I catch him."

She started and ran very fast; raised a great wind as she went. She ran with her hands clasped behind her, and sang, —

"I am following Tsanunewa; I am on his track.
I am following Tsanunewa; I am on his track."

The boy ran swiftly, ran with all his strength; was at the great river first. Mipka was at the other side.

"Save me, my uncle!" cried Tsanunewa; "put your leg over the water, put it over quickly. Hehku is hunting me. I am running for my life. Save me, my uncle, save me!"

Mipka came out, saw the boy on the opposite bank, stretched his leg over the water; the boy ran across on it. Hehku came to the river just after Tsanunewa had run into the house, and Mipka had drawn his leg back again. Inside was a large log with a small hole in the heart of it. Tsanunewa crept into that hole and hid quickly.

"Hehku will not find me here," thought he. But Hehku saw him from the other bank, knew where he was hidden.

The old man hurried after Tsanunewa. Hehku reached the river when Mipka stepped across the door.

"Old man," cried she, "put your leg over the water. Let me cross. Put your leg over the water!"

Mipka stood inside the door; seemed not to hear.

"Put your leg over the water!" cried Hehku.

"Creep out and run west for your life," said Mipka to Tsanunewa. "Run; I will stop Hehku; I will keep her here for a while. Run to Matauwila's; he may be able to save you."

Tsanunewa crept out through the western end of the sweat-house and ran.

"Old man, put your leg over the river. Let me cross on it!" cried Hehku. She was very angry now, but Mipka refused for a long time.

At last he stretched his leg from inside the door to the opposite bank of the river. He did this hoping that Hehku would run in on his leg, be speared in the doorway and die there. Mipka had long and very sharp spears fixed in above the doorway to kill people whom he hated.

But Hehku jumped off his leg at the river side. She would not go in at the door; she climbed to the roof of the sweat-house.

"Old man, give me Tsanunewa. I saw him run into your house. Old man, give me Tsanunewa or tell me where he is."

"I cannot tell where he is. He is not in my house," said Mipka.

"Tell me, old man, where that boy is, or I will kill you. I do not want to go into your house, but if I go in I will kill you. Only tell me where Tsanunewa is. If you hide that boy I will kill you."

"If you think Tsanunewa is here, come down, come in, look through my house," said Mipka.

Sharp spears were pointing upward toward this door in the roof of the sweat-house. Hehku was very angry; she slipped down in a hurry. The spear-points went into her body and killed her. She fell dead on the floor of the sweat-house. She lay a while dead there; then came to life and stood up again. She caught Mipka right away, and they fought, fought a long time, fought till she swallowed him down at one mouthful.

While Hehku and Mipka were fighting a long battle in the sweat-house, Tsanunewa had run far away toward the west. He was now in sight of Matauwila's sweat-house. When he was near enough to call, he shouted, —

" Grandfather, I am running for my life ; save me ! "

Matauwila ran out and helped the boy into the sweat-house.

" Grandfather, I want you to set traps in this house, set traps all around in it. Hehku is hunting me ; she will kill me if she catches me."

Matauwila made four rows of double traps in the house.

" I will catch Hehku," said Matauwila, " but you would better run west; run till you come to the house of the Chichi brothers."

The boy ran away to the west. He was hardly out of sight when Hehku came. She made a great wind as she ran to the house.

" Old man," cried she, "where is Tsanunewa ? Tell me where that boy is. I have tracked him to your house. Tell me where he is, or I will kill you."

" Come in," said Matauwila; " but you will not find the boy here. Come in. Sit down in my house, look all over it. Come in, but you 'll not find the boy. Come in."

The central pillar of Matauwila's house was large

and very smooth. Hehku could not hold to it, but fell down and dropped into the first trap. She broke right through that, and went through the three other lines of double traps.

When Hehku burst through the traps, her body was flashing red fire from every part of it, she was so angry. This fire from her body killed Matauwila.

Hehku ran after the boy again; ran with her hands clasped behind her. She ran that way always, and sang as she ran, —

"I am following Tsanunewa ; I am on his track.
I am following Tsanunewa ; I am on his track."

The boy rushed to the house of the Chichi. There were two brothers of them.

The Chichis had two smooth rocks which looked like ice, but were more slippery than any ice (rock crystals). One of these was at the eastern door, the other at the opening on the roof.

"Grandfathers, save me!" cried Tsanunewa, running up to the door of the house. "Grandfathers, save me!" cried he, running in.

Hehku was close behind now; she had almost caught him. When she reached the door, she stepped on the crystal rock, slipped, and fell. One Chichi closed the door in her face then. She sprang up, climbed the side of the house, went to the door in the roof, stepped on the second crystal in front of that door, slipped, and fell headlong; fell into the sweat-house. She sprang up, caught one Chichi, fought with him. His brother helped that one. The two fought a long time against

Hehku till she caught each by the arm, held them both with one hand, and pounded them with the crystal from the lower door which she held in her other hand. At last she said, " Whu ! " and swallowed both at one mouthful. While she was fighting with the Chichi brothers, Tsanunewa ran on, ran to the west. Hehku was tired now.

" I cannot run farther," said she. She went to the housetop and cried, " I wish this house to stretch out after that boy and catch him."

She sat on the housetop, and the house stretched out westward stretched more quickly than any one could run, and carried her after Tsanunewa. The boy had run very far ; he was near Jupka's house now.

" Uncle ! " cried he, " I want to come in quickly. I am almost dead. Hehku is chasing me. Hide me, my uncle, hide me. Save me, my uncle, save me, or Hehku will kill me."

" Why are you frightened ? " asked Jupka. " I should like to see the person who is chasing you. I should like to see any one dare to hurt you. Come in, my nephew, come in."

" Carry me, uncle. I am too tired to walk alone. Carry me. Hehku is hunting me ; she has almost caught up with me."

Jupka took the boy, carried him in. The sweat-house was full of Mapchemaina people, all those people called in by Jupka.

Hehku jumped off the house of the Chichi brothers, which had brought her almost to Jigul-matu. She was rested.

"Go back now to your own place," said she to the house; and it shrank back to its own place.

"Tell me, old man," said she to Jupka, "tell me where Tsanunewa is. I saw him go into your sweat-house. I want him."

"Come in," said Jupka. "Come if you like. Why are you hunting that boy? What do you want of him?"

"Do not speak in that way to me," said Hehku. "Tell where the boy is."

"Come in, I will give you a husband," said Jupka. "I will give you a husband; let the boy go. Take Demauna."

Hehku shook her head.

"Well, I will give you Wirula for husband; let the boy go."

Hehku shook her head a second time.

He offered every one in the house except himself. She refused one, then another and another; refused all.

"Tell me where that boy is," said she. "I want him; I want no one else. I want nothing more from you. Just tell me where that boy is. I want none of your people; the only one I want is Tsanunewa."

Jupka had put the boy under his own hair, under the hair at the back of his head, and kept him hidden there.

"I must know what you are going to do with that boy," said Jupka to Hehku Marimi. "I am not willing to give him to you; he is too small to be your husband. I want to keep him here in my sweat-house."

After that he went aside and said to Tsanunewa, "If you like this woman, I will let you go with her; if you do not wish to go, I will keep you."

"I will not go with her; she would kill me on the road. She wants to kill me; that's why she is hunting me, that's why she came here."

"Bring out that boy!" cried Hehku; "I want to see him. I want to go home; I want to take him home with me."

"This is a bad woman. I have heard much of her. Give her the boy, put him down; let us see what she will do with him," said each of those present.

But Jupka kept Tsanunewa hidden, would not give him up.

"I know that woman," repeated each of the Mapchemaina: "she is bad. When she is angry, fire flashes from her body. She kills every one. You would better let the boy go and save us."

"Spread robes out," said Jupka. "Let her come in here; let her sit down. We will hear what she says."

Jupka rubbed the boy's face and body, made him smooth, and from being small he was large, full-grown, and very beautiful. Jupka seated him on the robe. Every one could see him.

Hehku came in and sat on the robe. When she took her place, fire flashed from her through the whole sweat-house. She took off her cap made of skulls and put it at her side.

The people looked down. All were afraid except Jupka. They thought she would kill them right there in a moment. When Jupka saw the fire, he took tobacco from a small pouch which he kept in his ear, and while lying stretched out he began to smoke without putting fire on his pipe. The tobacco burned when he drew his breath through it. The smoke rose and then settled down. It grew dark in the sweat-house, and the fire from Hehku's body died away. She stopped her mouth and nose so as not to breathe Jupka's smoke.

"Go to sleep," said Jupka to Hehku Marimi.

She would not obey. She kept her mouth and nose closed, sat awake and would not sleep.

"Lie down; let us talk," said Tsanunewa. He thought, "If she lies down the smoke will kill her."

"I will not lie down," said Hehku.

"Why not? Lie down. We will talk together."

"I never sleep," said Hehku. "I am Mapchemaina. I never sleep at night, I never sleep in the day. I do as my father does; he hunts at night and hunts during daylight."

Jupka filled his pipe again with another tobacco which he kept in his ear, and again he puffed smoke which was very strong, the strongest smoke of all. "This will do," said he, "this will make her sleep, I think."

The smoke rose first, then came down and settled like a thick cloud right on Hehku's head.

"Why this woman tries to trick me?" thought Jupka; "I know more than she does."

When this strong smoke settled down, Hehku

began to nod; her head went first to one side, then
to the other; soon it turned backward little by little.
Jupka took a large roll of gray wolfskins, slipped it
behind her, and she dropped on it sound asleep;
lay as though lifeless.

["We have never seen this tobacco here," said
the narrator of the story. "It was turned to rock
long ago; this was done far in the East, way off
where the sun rises. The rock is there now, and it
is called Talpapa — white tobacco rock. This is
Mapchemaina tobacco." The first tobacco Jupka
used was moiyu, the Yana tobacco that we have in
our time.]

"If Hehku dreams, she will beat me when she
wakes, if she is wise; but I will not let her dream,"
said Jupka. He blew his breath on her face; she
could not dream after that.

Hehku used to dream bad things which came to
pass later on. She used to dream of killing people,
but after Jupka blew his breath on her face she
could not dream in his sweat-house. Next day,
when she woke, she was very angry at Jupka. She
stood up, walked out of the sweat-house, went to
the east; went quickly, went to that same rocky
mountain where Tsanunewa had set his mouse-
traps.

"Make a good fire and sweat," said Jupka to the
Mapchemaina.

All sweated and bathed in the river, and that day
Hehku became a Putokya, a skull person. She stayed
one night at the rocky mountain; dreamed of gambling with Jupka and all the people at Jigulmatu.

Hehku had a sister, Miniau Marimi. She took this sister as a companion. Both started, went together, and never stopped till they reached Oaimatu, a great hollow mountain northeast of Jigulmatu. Hehku brought a pipe with her, and made tobacco of dried brains. " My smoke will be stronger than Jupka's," thought Hehku. She spent one night in the hollow mountain, and dreamed again of gambling in Jupka's sweat-house. She rose early, and was in Jigulmatu at daylight. She stood with Miniau Marimi on the roof of the sweat-house, and sang to herself, —

"I shall win, I shall win, I shall win surely."

" Jupka, I wish to go into your sweat-house," said she. " When I go in, you will like me, you will like to see me. I am nice to look at."

She changed; made herself very beautiful then. No one could know her; no one could know that that woman was the Hehku who had hunted Tsanunewa.

At sunrise all the people in Jupka's sweat-house heard steps above, heard walking on the sweat-house. The two women were there. Hehku came to the roof-door and said, —

" Jupka, put away your things; clear your house. I want to come down and gamble with you. I dreamed last night that I played with you."

Jupka was lying with his head to the north. He made no answer. Hehku went down.

" Sit on the west side," said Jupka to the two sisters; and he told Malewula to spread out two robes, one of cinnamon, the other of black bearskin.

All the people held down their heads. None looked at the women except Malewula.

" I should be glad to give these women something to eat," said Malewula, " but I don't know what they like ; let us offer them venison."

He roasted venison, put it before them in a basket ; they would n't eat it, would n't taste or touch it. Then he brought dried salmon in small pieces ; the women turned away their faces. Next he put salmon flour and mountain-pine nuts before them ; they would n't eat, turned aside their faces.

" Take this food away," said Hehku ; " we don't wish to eat. I came here to see people, I came here to gamble."

The Mapchemaina said nothing for a long time. At last Kaitsiki spoke up.

" I do not know how to gamble, I cannot play," said he.

" I do not like to hear you talk so. I know you," said Hehku. " I know that you gamble a great deal. I know that you began to gamble long ago."

Kaitsiki made no answer. He went to get gambling-sticks (counters). He brought grass and fixed everything for the play. They sat down, Hehku on the west, Kaitsiki on the east.

" What will you play for, what will you bet ? " asked the woman.

Kaitsiki took his shell necklace, hung it up, and said, " I will begin with this."

Hehku handled the Jupaiauna ; it was hers, and made of a finger-bone. Kaitsiki guessed " north " the first time, and lost; after that he guessed north once and south once, lost both times; after that he lost his ten sticks.

"Take the necklace and hang it on our side," said Hehku to Miniau.

When Hehku put her hands out, she held them together in front before opening them, and sang "Wahau Putokya jinda Marimi" (You will not win against Putokya Marimi); and the bone went to the side opposite the one guessed. The singing made it go. When Kaitsiki guessed "north," if the bone was in Hehku's right hand, the south side, it stayed there; if it was in her left hand, the north side, it went to her right. In this way no one could ever win against Hehku.

"Play again," said Hehku.

Kaitsiki bet and lost. He lost one thing after another till he bet his last, a belt of red-headed woodpecker scalps. It was very beautiful. Hehku was glad.

"This is the bet," said she, "that Perriwiri Yupa always makes. He bets a girdle like this when I play with him."

"I will guess south all the time now," said Kaitsiki. He lost five times, then changed his mind, guessed north.

All the Mapchemainas looked on, watched the play, but said nothing. They knew what was coming; knew that Kaitsiki would lose. He guessed north five times; lost his girdle.

"I have nothing more to bet; you have won all I had," said Kaitsiki.

" Bet yourself," said Hehku. " I will bet all I have won from you."

Kaitsiki bet himself. He guessed south first, and lost.

" Oh, if I had only bet north!" said he. Next time he bet north, and lost.

" Oh, if I had said south!"

He went on in this way till he lost his ten counters and himself.

Hehku threw the finger-bone on the ground; the earth shook; there was a noise like thunder. The bone flew up, struck Kaitsiki, killed him. Miniau Marimi threw him out through the roof to the north of the sweat-house.

" I will play now," said Ahalamila, sitting down in the place left by Kaitsiki. He guessed, lost, guessed on and played till he lost everything; bet himself, lost, was killed and thrown north of the sweat-house. Petaina played next, lost everything, was killed and thrown out. All in the sweat-house except Jupka played and lost, one after another, first all they had and then themselves. After Petaina came Matdasi, Tsurewa, Jihkulu, and then Tsanunewa, who remained at Jigulmatu.

Hehku danced with delight when Tsanunewa lost. She threw him out of the sweat-house herself, then played with others till none were left except Jupka.

Jupka rose up then and said: "Now we will try. I will guess once; that will finish the play and settle all."

" I am willing," said Hehku.

Jupka brought a blue stone and sat on it. He

had a walking-stick made of the heart of sugar-pine; this he put at his side.

Hehku arranged the bone, put it in her left hand, and Jupka said " lililim " (let it be north) but said the word in such a way that another would think he said "ililim," and Hehku thought so, too; the bone remained in her left hand. She brought both hands from behind her back, opened them, and was going to throw the bone to kill Jupka.

" Stop! What did I say? " asked Jupka.

" Ililim."

" No, I said ' lililim ; ' look north and see."

Hehku looked north and saw Wahkalu (Mount Shasta), Jupka's Igunna, his great new house which he made by saying " lililim." Wahkalu was white, shining. Hehku had never seen anything so beautiful, so great. She had never seen it before, neither had any one else.

The bone was there in her open left hand on the north side, she could not deny. She could not change her play, she could not help herself. Jupka seized the bone, threw it to the floor. The earth trembled; there was a roar like thunder; the bone bounded up and killed Hehku. Jupka threw her out of the sweat-house.

"You must play too," said Jupka to Miniau Marimi.

He put the bone behind his back; she guessed, lost her life, and was thrown out of the sweat-house.

Jupka walked away southward, went to the creek, washed and swam. When he came out of the water, he grew very beautiful and large. He took then the stem of a wild rose-bush and went home; he went to the north side of the sweat-house. There he found the bodies of the Mapchemainas who had played with Hehku and lost. He gave each a blow of the rose-bush, and all came to life; all went to the sweat-house, not one was missing.

At dawn the dead Hehku began to move and sing. At clear daylight she stood up, struck Miniau with her right foot. That moment she rose up alive. The two women started for the rocky mountain. Hehku was raging. She was terribly angry because Jupka had beaten her.

"I had all," said she, "but Jupka fooled me; now I have nothing."

She grew so angry that she turned into a great head and bounded off to the east. She went a whole mile every jump she made. She screamed with rage and shouted as she went, and her sister Miniau (the fire-drill) kept pace with her.

Haka Kaina heard the noise and said, "I wonder what troubles Putokya to-day."

THE FIRST BATTLE IN THE WORLD AND THE MAKING OF THE YANA

THE FIRST BATTLE IN THE WORLD AND THE MAKING OF THE YANA

PERSONAGES

After each name is given that of the creature or thing into which the personage was changed subsequently.

Ahalamila, gray wolf; Bohkuina, silver-gray fox; Chichepa, spotted hawk; Chuhna, spider; Hehku, horned serpent; Hitchinna, wildcat; Howichinaipa, a small bird; Hurskiyupa, orphan; Jewina, reddish chicken hawk; Jihkulu, large owl; Jupka, butterfly of wild silkworm; Kaitsiki, ground squirrel; Kaltsauna, swift (kind of lizard); Kechowala, bluejay; Lawalila, large hawk; Maibyu, dove; Malewula, wolf; Mapchemaina, first people; Pakalai Jawichi, water lizard; Petaina, skunk; Popila, duck; Topuna, mountain lion; Tsanunewa, a little bird; Tuina, the sun; Wihlaina, chipmunk.

AFTER Hehku had risen from the dead and gone home, Jupka said to all the Mapchemaina : "Sweat now and swim. You will go to hunt to-morrow early."

The Mapchemaina went to hunt on the following day, but could not kill deer. They had no good arrow-points. The points which they had were made of common stone. When they went back to Jigulmatu in the evening without venison, Jupka said, —

"There is an old man in the south who kills a great many deer; his name is Kaltsauna. I must bring him up here to show you how he kills them. I will send some one south for him. Maibyu, you go for that old man; you travel very quickly."

"I don't know where his house is; I cannot find him," said Maibyu. "You would better send some one else."

"Lawalila, you go," said Jupka.

Lawalila dressed himself nicely; took his bow, quiver, and arrows, and went. He went as quickly as though it were only one long step to Kaltsauna's house. Kaltsauna was sitting inside the door with his legs crossed. He was making flint arrow-points.

Lawalila stepped in at once and surprised old Kaltsauna. He had a flint knife at his side, and made a thrust at Lawalila as if to kill him.

"Stop. It is I, uncle; you must not kill me."

"Why do you call me uncle?" asked Kaltsauna, hiding his arrow-points quickly.

"I have come for you, uncle. The chief sent me here. Jupka invites you to come to Jigulmatu. He wants you to come to his house. He wants to see you. We cannot kill deer with stone arrow-points. We have no other kind. The chief knows that you kill deer all the time. He wants you to come to his place and show his people how you kill deer."

Kaltsauna rubbed his hands, rubbed them clean, rubbed all the flint dust from them, and rolled up his flints in a skin very carefully. Next he mixed flint dust, rubbed it on his face, made paint, covered his face with it, and thrust a piece of sharp flint through the septum of his nose. He looked very threatening and strong when he was dressed and armed for the road.

" I am ready; you go ahead; I will come later,"
said he to Lawalila.

Kaltsauna's quiver was a grizzly bearskin; his
bows and arrows were made of black oak. He put
his flints under his left arm, took his bow and arrows
in his right hand.

" Go on; go ahead. I will come later; I will
come by myself. Go now and tell the chief to make
a great fire of manzanita wood."

Lawalila went ahead, and gave Kaltsauna's message to Jupka. The chief had the fire made, — a
great fire of manzanita wood. " He is coming, he
is coming," said the people, when they saw Kaltsauna in the distance. When he was near, they
did n't try to look at him, they hung their heads.

" Make way for me, make way! I 'll strike
unless you give me room!" said Kaltsauna, as he
came near the crowd of people.

" The old man always talks like that," said
Jupka; " he is very strong. That 's why he is so
bold; that 's why he talks so."

" Spread out a skin," said Kaltsauna to Jupka.

The skin was spread, and Kaltsauna emptied his
robe full of arrow-points on it. He sat down then
and said, —

" I will divide these and put them in different
places."

He gathered each kind of flint into a heap by itself, then pushed it, and said while he pushed,
" You go to this place or to that place."

White flint he pushed and said, " Go you, to
Hakamatu."

The white flint went away; disappeared from the robe; went to Hakamatu, and there is plenty of white flint in that place to-day.

Blue flint he sent east to the edge of our Yana country. Yellow flint he fixed at Iwiljami. To the west he sent flint with fine black, blue, and white stripes; he sent it to Hakachimatu. Green flint he put in Jigulmatu and said, —

"You will find these flints always in the places where I put them to-day, and people who come after you will find them there. There will be flint in those places forever, as long as people want it."

Besides flint Kaltsauna gave each of the Mapchemaina a wedge made of deer-horn, and a piece of stone; showed them how to dress the flint and make arrow-points. The first arrow-points on earth were those which Kaltsauna made.

Next morning, after he had given the flint and shown the Mapchemaina how to make arrow-points, Kaltsauna went home. On the second day Jupka called all the Mapchemaina together and said, —

"Get your arrow-points ready; sweat to-night; swim early in the morning, and go out on a great hunt to-morrow."

They did all that Jupka commanded, and went on the following morning toward Jidjilpa. They went west along Jidjilpa, went on both sides of it; went west toward Tahaujwakaina, which is in the cañon beyond Hakamatu. They went to the rock and went beyond it.

Some distance west of the rock a grizzly bear ran

out of a clump of live-oak brush. Among the people hunting was Chichepa, and the bear rushed at him. Chichepa had dreamed the night before that this rock in the cañon had jumped up from the ground and frightened him. When he came near the live-oak brush, the bear growled and sprang out.

Chichepa ran back, ran till he came to Tahaujwakaina, the bear close after him. The bear was so angry that he tore up big oak-trees as he ran. There was a hole in the top of the rock. Chichepa sprang into it. The bear stood on his hind legs. He could barely look over the top of the rock. He looked and saw nothing, dropped down, ran all around the rock, looked everywhere, saw no sign of Chichepa. Then he turned back and went into the thick clumps of brush from which he had started.

The people went west a while, then toward the south, and began to find deer. Bohkuina killed the first deer, Howichinaipa the second, Kechowala the third, Jihkulu the fourth, Petaina the fifth, and so on till twenty had deer. The party divided then into two. Those who had deer turned home toward Jigulmatu, and went in the order in which they had killed them, Bohkuina first, the others following each in his turn.

The second party hunted toward the east and then toward Jigulmatu. After a while they came to Ketmatu, where Malewula killed a deer, and Topuna killed one, and Tsanunewa killed a terribly ugly big deer which seemed as though all its flesh and body were swollen. Hitchinna, Kaitsiki, Wihlaina, and others killed deer; each person killed one deer.

The whole party turned toward Jigulmatu then, and there was great gladness in Jupka's sweat-house. The women prepared acorns and mice to eat.

Jupka himself never went hunting; he stayed at Jigulmatu always, just lay in the house there, told all what they were to do, and showed them how to do what was needed. When they came in from hunting, all put their venison in front of the chief, put down before him all the deer they had killed. Jupka took his flint knife then, and cut the meat into pieces. He roasted ribs of it, roasted all they brought in. When it was cooked, the Mapchemaina sat down and ate the meat together. Jupka placed out before them three very large baskets of mice in three different places, and in front of each basket were people to deal the mice out to each person who wished some. When they had eaten, Jupka stood up and talked to all present.

" I wish you all to come into the sweat-house to-night," said he; " I wish to tell you where you are to hunt to-morrow."

They went into the sweat-house that evening, sat down and smoked, and while they were smoking Jupka rose up and spoke to them. Jupka himself never ate anything of any kind; he smoked tobacco, smoked all the time; that was the only thing that he ever took into his body. When he spoke, he said, —

" I think it is better to hunt in the north to-morrow."

" We do not like to go north when we hunt," said some of the people.

"Well, let another tell where to go.   To-night I will have Howichinaipa sing and dance for deer."

Then Jupka thought a while and said: "No, I will get Ahalamila; he is a good person to dream and sing about deer and to dance.   I will tell Ahalamila to sing and dance to-night.   He will tell where you ought to go, he will say which road to take.   I want you all to lie down and sleep to-night, old men and young, and all the women; let all sleep till morning, sleep till I call you to the hunt."

When the time came that evening, Ahalamila made a fire and took his pipe.   He blew smoke around in every direction.   He put down his pipe then and took fir-leaves; these he threw on the fire, and while they were burning he sang, —

> "Wilichuláina kúlmachi, Wílichuláina kúlmachi
> (A quartz rock, a white rock, a quartz rock, a white rock)."

and he put a beautiful white quartz rock on the ground; at each side of it he thrust into the earth a small twig of fir and one of blue beech; he put these on the east, west, north, and south sides of the quartz.

Ahalamila kept looking at the twigs, which rose quickly, grew up, and became little trees.   He walked around them and sang; sang and pinched off a leaf or a bud from one limb or another as he walked.   Soon the stone began to move of itself, and it swelled and changed shape, till at last it turned into a white fawn. Just at daybreak the fawn began to walk around among the trees and sniff as though it smelt something.

Ahalamila picked up the little fawn; blew smoke

from his mouth; blew it around on all sides; then he put the fawn down again and it turned back into quartz.

It was daylight then, and Ahalamila stopped singing. "I have finished now," said he. "It will be better for us to hunt on the south side."

"I want you, my people," called Jupka, "to rise up, start out and hunt. Howichinaipa will go ahead and make a fire."

Howichinaipa went ahead: went south for some distance; the Mapchemaina followed soon after; went to the place where Howichinaipa had made the fire. When they came up, there was a good large fire at a place called Wewauna, half a mile from Hakamatu.

"Come to the fire, wait a while before we start, talk and get ready to hunt," said Howichinaipa.

Ten men went on farther south to find deer, while the others waited at the fire. Those ten men went south quickly; then five turned east, and five turned west to meet again at Wewauna. They came back about the same time, but not one of them saw deer or game of any kind. Every one wondered that there was no game in any place. Ahalamila and Howichinaipa began to dispute and then to quarrel because the ten men could find no deer.

Howichinaipa was angry; he was offended because Jupka had named him first, then changed his mind and called Ahalamila to sing for deer. He was angry, too, and jealous because he wanted one of Ahalamila's wives who was his own wife's sister. Howichinaipa's wife was a Chuhna, and Ahalamila's wife was her only sister.   Howichinaipa wanted to have the two sisters as his wives; he wanted both of them.   For these two reasons the Mapchemaina could find no deer that day.   Howichinaipa had power over the deer, and had sent them all under ground.   The ten men had looked in a great many places; they had run south, east, west, and could find no deer.   Then the whole party turned to the southeast; they went to Chupirkoto.   Some said, "What is the use in going farther?   We can find no deer to-day.   Ahalamila told us that we should find deer.   Where are they?   We cannot see them."

"I do not know," said Ahalamila, "why we find no deer.   I sang and danced last night.   I dreamed that I saw deer, that I saw them south of Jigulmatu."

"You will not see deer or any other game to-day," said Howichinaipa; "you cannot find deer, no matter how much you sing and dance.   You are not able to find deer, but you have a nice wife.   She is very pretty."

"The deer were coming," said Ahalamila, "but you stopped them, you drove them away;" and he sprang at Howichinaipa to strike him.   Howichinaipa dodged and went down through the ground.

All the people took sides and began to fight; some were for Ahalamila, others were on Howichinaipa's side.   Howichinaipa sprang out from under the ground, stood before Ahalamila; shot at him.   Ahalamila dodged and shot too; Howichinaipa dodged very quickly.

They fought on in this way, fought hard, moved toward Jigulmatu, fighting all the time.   At last

Ahalamila was struck and fell dead; Topuna was killed too, and Hitchinna. A great many tried to kill Howichinaipa; but he dodged all the time, dodged so well, so quickly that not one of all his enemies could hit him. Jihkulu helped Howichinaipa; never stopped fighting for a moment.

They fought all the way to Hwitalmauna just south of Jigulmatu; the battle there was very hard, and people fell on both sides. There are many rocks at Hwitalmauna now, and these rocks are the Mapchemaina killed in that first battle.

Ahalamila's friends fought hard against Jihkulu and spent many arrows, but could not hit him, for he had a robe of rabbit skin around his body.

"We must hit that Jihkulu, we must kill him," said Ahalamila's friends.

"You need not talk like that,"said Jihkulu; "you cannot kill me. I am the best fighter in all this world. I have been in every part of it; no one has ever hit me, no one has ever hurt me."

Jihkulu shot at Jewina, but missed. "You can't hit me!" cried Jewina. Jihkulu shot off Jewina's coyote skin, and then he killed him. Jewina had dreamed a long time before that if he wore coyote skin in battle he would not be killed, and that was why he wore it; but when Jihkulu shot off the skin, he killed him easily.

Now Jupka was lying in the sweat-house on Jigulmatu, and he heard the noise and shouting at Hwitalmauna. "They are fighting; I must stop the battle!" cried he. So he ran south — rushed into the middle of the fight.

"I want both sides to stop!" shouted Jupka.

The battle was at an end right there; all followed Jupka to Jigulmatu. That evening he said, "You will hunt in the north to-morrow." All were in the sweat-house then and were listening. Jupka spoke to them some time, and then they all talked at once; it seemed as though the house would burst when they were talking.

Next day they found deer in the north, and found them in plenty. Each had one to bring back to the sweat-house. When they were coming home through thick brushwood, Popila wished to please Ahalamila's friends, and made himself a bear to kill Howichinaipa, who fought the day before with Ahalamila and killed him.

The bear came out and threw his arms around a clump of brush in which Howichinaipa was. Howichinaipa slipped out in time and ran. The bear rushed after him, hunted him, and almost caught him at a rock near Hakamatu. Howichinaipa sprang on to the rock and said, —

"I am nearly dead; I wish this rock to open; I am too tired to run; I can go no farther."

The rock opened, and Howichinaipa dropped in. The bear rushed up, stuck his head and fore paws after Howichinaipa; but the rock closed, and the bear was caught and killed.

Howichinaipa came out and stood beside the bear. "I am tired," said he. "I was almost dead. You tried your best to kill me, but I am hard to kill." Then he took his flint knife, cut around the bear's neck and behind his two fore paws, and skinned him, put the skin on his shoulder, and started for Jigulmatu. He came behind the others, reached home at dusk. He hung the skin near the door, and said, —

"We shall hear what Ahalamila's friends will say to-morrow morning."

Popila's mother heard what her son had done, and when she saw the bearskin she cried and rolled upon the ground. Next day the old woman was sweeping; she swept out a little red-eared boy, a Pakalai Jawichi, and as she swept, he squealed. Popila Marimi took him up, took a deerskin, and made a blanket of it, and put the little fellow in this deerskin. She boiled water then with hot rocks and washed him, and every time she washed she sprinkled flint dust on the little boy to make him strong. He could creep around next morning; but she said:

"Stay in one place; you must not move. There may be poison in some place; if you touch it, it will kill you. Stay right where I put you."

The second day the boy could talk. "You cry all the time, grandmother; why do you cry?" asked he.

"Do not ask that question, grandson; it makes me grieve to hear you. All my people were dead except my son; now he is killed and I have no one."

The fifth day the boy was walking around the house outside.

"Grandmother," said he, "make a great fire."

She made a fire in the sweat-house. The boy stood near the central pillar and sang, "Hála watá, hála watá."

He fell asleep while sweating; slept till morning. Next day when he woke he said to his grandmother, " What am I to do with my hands ? "

The old woman gave him a flint knife and said, " I have had this a long time; take it now and fix your hands with it."

His fingers were joined together as far as the first joint, and she showed him how to separate them from each other. He cut the little finger first, then the third, the second, and the first. The thumb he called big finger; and when the five fingers were separated and free of each other, she told him to call the thumb the big finger, and call it one, the next two, the next three, the next four, and the little finger five.

This was the first time that counting was ever done in the world. And when Jupka made the Yana, he gave them hands like Pakalai Jawichi's.

When his left hand was finished, Pakalai Jawichi said, " I don't know how to cut with my left hand."

The old woman helped him to free the fingers of the right hand. When all his fingers were free, the boy was able to shoot, and he wanted a bow and arrows.

The old woman brought all the bows of her dead kindred; he broke all but one, which had a string made from the shoulder sinews of a deer. He took that and went out. This day Howichinaipa hid himself in a cedar-tree : he was watching a bird.. Pakalai Jawichi knew that he was there, and called with the voice of the bird that Howichinaipa was watching.

Howichinaipa came down on the tree lower and lower, looking to see where the call came from.

Pakalai Jawichi was hidden in a tree opposite, where Howichinaipa could not see him; he kept calling, and Howichinaipa kept coming down. Pakalai Jawichi had a good sight of him.

"If I hit him in the body," thought he, "the arrow will not hurt him; I must hit him in the outside toe."

He did that, and Howichinaipa fell to the ground wounded. Pakalai Jawichi pinned him to the earth with one arrow, then with another; pinned his two sides to the ground with two rows of arrows. Pakalai Jawichi ran home.

"Oh, grandmother!" cried he.

"What is the matter?" asked the old woman; "you came near falling into the fire."

"There is some one out here; I want you to see him."

The old woman took her cane and followed Pakalai Jawichi.

"Do you see that person lying there?"

The old woman looked, and saw the person who had killed her son, saw him pinned to the earth. She was so glad that she cried, she dropped down then, and rolled on the ground; after that she jumped up and danced around his body, danced many times, danced till she was tired.

"Hereafter," said Pakalai Jawichi, "everybody will call you Howichinaipa. You will be a person no longer; you will be only a little bird, with these arrow-marks on both sides of your breast."

He became a little bird then and flew away, the little bird which we call Howichinaipa.

Next morning after the second hunt Jupka heard loud shouting in the east; a great Mapchemaina had thrust his head above the edge of the sky. This person had beautiful feathers waving on his head. Jupka had made him shout, and he said to him, —

" Every time you rise up and show yourself to the people of Jigulmatu you must shout in that way."

This great person in the east had two dogs; they were small, but very strong. " Which of you is coming with me? " asked he that morning. " I want a good dog; I am always afraid when I travel in the daytime."

" I will give you a name now," said Jupka to this person in the east. " All people will call you here-after by the name which I give now. The name which I give you is Tuina. You will be known always by this name. And your name," said he to the dog, " will be Machperkami."

When Tuina was ready to start, he made his small dog still smaller, very small; put him under the hair on the top of his head, and tied him in there.

When all dressed and ready, with the dog fast-ened in his hair, Tuina became as full of light as he is in our time. Before he was dressed and armed and had his dog on his head Tuina had no bright-ness, but when he started he filled this whole world with light, as he does now in the daytime.

Bohkuina had made a road for Tuina to travel

on ; he had made this road in the sky, and Tuina
went straight along to the west by it, till he reached
the great water.   When he was ready to plunge into
the water, a hatenna (grizzly bear) of the water was
coming out and saw him.   Tuina put his hands out
and motioned with his arms as if they were wings,
motioned as if to jump in.

"Tuina is coming!" said the grizzly bear of the
water.   "It will be too hot here if he comes.   Let
us make ready and go to high mountains.   We
cannot stay here if Tuina comes."

A great crowd of water grizzlies came out of the
ocean and went away to the mountains.   Tuina
jumped into the water, and it rose on all sides, boiled
up, rolled away over the shore, every kind of shell
of the ocean went to land at the same time.

Tuina went far into the water, way down to the
bottom ; he went through the bottom, deep under
the water and the ground, and returned to the east.

Long before that Jupka had made a road under
the earth for Tuina to travel on, a road back to the
east.   Jupka turned the earth bottom upward, and
made this road right through from west to east; and
before Tuina started Jupka said to him, —

"I have made a road, a straight road under the
earth for you, a good road ; there are no rocks on
it, all is smooth.   Bohkuina made the road on the
sky, the road from east to west for you to run on ;
I made the road down below, the road under the
earth from west to east.   When you reach the east,
you will rest a while, rise in the morning, come up
and go west again on the road which Bohkuina

made; you will do this every day without failing; you will do this all the time."

When Jupka stopped talking, Tuina went west, went back in the night on Jupka's road; and so he does always.

The day after Jupka had talked with Tuina, given him his name and his work, he said, " I will make Yana now, and I will give them a good country to live in."

He took buckeye-sticks, broke off a large number; he wished to lay them down on the top of Jigulmatu and make Yana. He put down the first stick and said, " I will call this one Iwilau Yana" (Yana of the middle place).

When he had said these words, a man rose up before him, a Yana.

" You will stay here in this middle country," said Jupka. " You will be chief."

Jupka put down another buckeye-stick, and it became a Yana woman at Jupka's word. He put down a third stick, which became a boy.

" This is an orphan without father or mother," said Jupka; and he called the boy Hurskiyupa.

Jupka put other buckeye-sticks, a large number of them, around the first Yana, the chief, and made common people. They all stood around the chief and Jupka said to them, —

" This is your chief; he will tell you what to do; you must obey him and do what he commands."

" Now," said Jupka, " what will the people of the middle country eat? what shall I give them?" and he thought a while. " You will eat clover," said he, "and roots.   I will give you sticks to dig these roots.   You will eat fish, too, and venison.   Eat and be strong, be good Yana people.   When the chief wants a deer, he will call you together and say, 'I wish to eat venison; I want you to go out, I want you to hunt deer and bring home venison to eat.'   You must obey the chief always."

NOTES

THE following notes are put in as condensed a form as possible. They are confined to explanations of the actors or characters in the myths, and to information concerning the meaning of names of persons and places.

The myths from one to nine inclusive are Wintu, from ten to the end Yana. These two nations, though neighbors, are not related ; their languages are radically different.

NOTES

IN 1895 I made a journey to California in consequence of an arrangement with the late Charles A. Dana, editor of "The Sun." According to this arrangement, Mr. Dana was to publish on consecutive Sundays such myth-tales as I might think of sufficient value to appear in his paper. Those myths were to be found by me in California, Mexico, and Guatemala.

I began at the source of the Sacramento River, and worked down to the mouth, my last stopping-place being the extensive hop-fields in the lower valley.

In San Francisco I wrote the following short account of the Wintus. That done, I set out for Mexico.

In the city of Guadalajara I copied the myths obtained in California and sent them to "The Sun." After that I worked at "Quo Vadis," the greater part of which I translated in Guadalajara.

All the myths in this volume were published in "The Sun," and appeared as a part of a series pertaining to Indians in California, Mexico, and Guatemala.

Only the California part has been published thus far.

After leaving Guadalajara I spent almost a year in Guatemala and Chiapas, the southernmost state of Mexico. Among the last places which I visited was Palenque. A view of one part of the ruins of this remarkable and mysterious city appears as a frontispiece to the present volume.

THE WINTUS

THE Wintus are a nation or stock of Indians who before the coming of white men owned and occupied all that part of California situated on the right bank of the Sacramento, from its source near the foot of Mount Shasta to its mouth at the northern shore of San Francisco Bay.

These Indians extended into Trinity County on the west, and still farther to the mountain slope which lies toward the Pacific. Only a small number of them, however, were on the western declivity. The great body of the nation lived on the eastern slope of the Coast Range and in the Sacramento Valley. Some of their finest mental productions are connected with the upper course of the Sacramento and with the MacCloud River, or Wini Mem.

It is difficult to determine what the Wintu population was half a century ago, but, judging from the number of houses in villages, the names and positions of which have been given me by old men, I should say that it could not have been less than 10,000, and might easily have been double that number. At present there are not more than 500 Wintus in existence.

The Wintus have suffered grievously ; great numbers have been killed by white men, others have perished by diseases brought in by strangers ; but those who remain are strong and are more likely to increase than diminish. Times of violence have passed, and the present Wintus are willing and able to adapt themselves to modern conditions.

It may be of interest to readers of these myth tales to know something of the present condition of the Wintus.

In 1889, when I was in California, commissioned by Major Powell for the second time to make linguistic investigations among various tribes of the Pacific coast, a few Wintus came to me in Redding, California, and complained of their wretched condition. There was not a spot of land, they said, where they could build a hut without danger of being ordered away from it. " This country was ours once," added they, " but the white man has taken all of it." I told them to bring their people together, and invite also the Yanas, who had suffered more than all other people of that region, and then explain to me what was needed.

The two peoples met on a little stony field in a brushy waste outside the inhabited part of Redding. There they made speeches and discussed matters for three hours the first day and as many the second. They gave me all the points of what they wanted, which was simply that the United States should give each man of them a piece of land, with help to begin life on it. I jotted down in brief form what they had told me, read it to them, and they were satisfied. Next day the paper was copied in the form of a petition from the two nations to President Harrison. They signed the petition before a Redding notary, and gave it to me with a request to lay it before the President.

Early in 1890 I was in Washington. Anxious to win the case of my poor Indian friends, — or " Diggers," as some men are pleased to call them contemptuously, — I looked around for a Congressman of influence to go with me to support the petition before the President. I found no suitable person till I met my classmate and friend, Governor Greenhalge of Massachusetts, at that time a member of Congress. When he heard the tale of the Yana massacre and realized the sad plight of the Wintus, he offered at once to cooperate with me. He went to the President and explained the affair to him. Two or three days later he accompanied me to the White House. I gave the petition to President Harrison, who promised to favor it with his executive initiative. He did this so earnestly and with such emphasis that an agent was appointed very soon to find land for those Indians. The agent found land for them in various places, but within the radius of their former possessions. The condition of the Wintus at present is this : They have lands which are described, but in most cases the boundaries are not indicated by any material mark, or at least very few of them are ; white men are trespassing, and it is impossible for the Indians to protect themselves till their boundaries are fixed tangibly. They will not have the means to begin serious work till they receive assistance. They are waiting now in hope that the Commissioner of Indian Affairs will have their lands surveyed, and that Congress will make a small appropriation for their benefit. This is the extent of their hopes and wishes. They are very glad to have land, and the majority of them will make fairly good use of it. When I met them in 1895, they were very grateful for the part which I had taken in settling them in life, adding that they could not have settled themselves unassisted. As to me, I cannot but make an emphatic acknowledgment of the generous and effective aid given by Governor Greenhalge.

"Olelbis," the first myth published in "The Sun" (March 29, 1896), was preceded by the following brief introduction : —

The Wintus, with whose creation-myths I begin this series, are a very interesting people. Their language is remarkably harmonious, rich, and flexible. It has great power of describing the physical features of the country in which it is spoken, as well as the beliefs and ideas of the Wintus themselves.

The picture of Olelbis, a being who lives in the highest and sees everything, is drawn more distinctly and with more realism than any character in other American religious systems, so far as I know.

The theory of creation evolved by the Indians of North America is complete, simple, and symmetrical. I have referred to it somewhat in the introduction to "Hero Tales of Ireland," in "Myths and Folk-lore of Ireland," and in "Myths and Folk-tales of the Russians, Western Slavs, and Magyars." This theory is in brief as follows : —

There was a people in existence before the present race of men ; in speaking of the present race of men, the tales have in view Indians only. This first people lived in harmony for a period of indefinite, unimaginable duration, without division or dissension, — undifferentiated, so to speak. This was the golden age of existence, a Nirvana preliminary to life as we know it at present, a Nirvana of the gods, as the Buddhist extinction of self is to be the Nirvana of just men when all shall be one in all and one in one. At last a time came when character appeared, and with it differences and conflicts. When the conflicts were past and the battles fought out, the majority of the first people were turned into all the animated things, walking, creeping, crawling, swimming, flying, that have ever been seen on the earth, in the water, or in the air. They were turned also into trees and plants of every kind, — some into heavenly bodies, others into remarkable stones and rocks, just as, in the Bible, Lot's wife was turned into a pillar of salt.

According to this theory, every individual existence which we see in the world around us is a transformed or fallen god. Every beast, bird, reptile, fish, insect, or plant was at one time a divinity of high or low degree, an uncreated person who had lived in harmony with his fellows from the beginning till the time when variety

of character, or individuality, appeared and brought with it diffi-
culties, or perhaps we might say, penalty. With individuality
came conflicts; when those conflicts were over, creation was
finished.

At the end of each particular conflict the victor turned by means
of a word the vanquished into that which embodied and expressed
his character. The vanquished on his part had a similar compel-
ling word, and changed his opponent into the beast, bird, or other
existence which described him ; in other terms, he gave his opponent the physical form, the outward personality, which corresponded
to the nature of his hidden or at least his unapparent character.
Besides these metamorphosed or fallen divinities, there is in the
Indian mythologies a group, a small minority, which was not
changed, but left this world going out under the sky at the west to
live in harmony and delight ; and they live in that way to this moment. Sometimes this group, or a part of it, went to live above
the sky.

The Indian Creation-myths all relate to the adventures and ex-
ploits of the "first people," — the gods ; none relate to human
beings, and none touch on anything done since man appeared on
earth. They are the accounts of what took place when there was
an order different from the present, and explain how the present
order rose from the first.

Such, in substance, is the foundation of American religious systems, and the method of all of them, so far as examined. The
Wintu is different from many others in its methods and details, but
the result is the same in all cases. Olelbis, with few exceptions,
disposes of the first people, retains with himself whomsoever he
likes, sends to the earth and transforms those whom he thinks more
useful below than above, and gives the example of a single ruling
divinity which, without being represented as all-powerful or all-wise,
manages through the knowledge and services of others to bear rule
over all things.

OLELBIS

THIS myth contains a complete statement concerning the beginnings of Wintu belief. Olelbis occupies the first place in the estimation of Wintus. To understand the Wintu mind, it is indispensable to begin with Olelbis. Other myths illustrate this one, explain parts of the Wintu system, and help to explain the mental life of the people; but this tale of Creation is to Indians of the western half of the Sacramento valley what their sacred books are to historic races.

No Wintu has been converted to Christianity; hence the faith of the nation is undimmed, and its adherence to primitive religion unweakened. I cannot explain their position better than by giving the words of one of the most intelligent Wintus whom I have met. After I had collected all that I could find, and had received needful explanations as far as was possible, I spoke some time with this man. Referring to their religion and ideas, he said : " When I talk of these things, I am afraid, I feel kind of scart" (scared).

That explains their position perfectly. Their faith is of the firmest; they are full of awe; they believe that Olelbis is up there now in the "Central Blue," in his marvellous Panti Hlut, the most beautiful structure in the universe, and from there sees everything that happens. That heavenly house is framed of living oaktrees, which bear acorns continually, the Indian bread of life, — that house which has in and around it all the flowers that have ever bloomed, flowers whose roots can never die.

Winishuyat, mentioned in "Olelbis" and in other tales, is one of the most interesting personages in Wintu mythology. He is described as a little man, about the size of a thumb, and is always placed on the top of the head by the person whom he accompanies and aids. This person never fails to tie his own hair over Winishuyat, and thus conceals him from every stranger. Winis means "he sees;" the literal significance of huyat I have not been able to get at satisfactorily thus far. The essential meaning of the whole word is that he sees in mind the approaching danger before it is evident to the physical eye. Winishuyat means, therefore, the prescience of danger, — seeing danger while it is yet at some distance ; not necessarily distance geographically, for the danger may be present, but concealed in the breast of a dissembling enemy, and some time, short or long, may be between it and actual happening.

The peculiar thing in the case is that foresight is separated from the hero, and is made the distinguishing quality of his little thumb-sized attendant, just as if each power had to be connected with a person, — no person having more than one great trait of character.

In the Yana mythology there is no name corresponding to Winishuyat, but the same office is filled by a maternal uncle.

In the tale of "Juiwaiyu," Jupka, the uncle of the hero, makes himself as small as a thumb, and is tied in under the hair of his nephew. In the winning of Paiowa, at the house of Tuina, Igupatopa performs for his sister's son the same kind of service rendered by Winishuyat, — with this difference, that he is more active ; he is not merely an adviser, he is a helper, a strengthener ; he gives counsel to make his nephew wise, and then enters into his heart to fortify him, to render him brave and strong.

It is curious and instructive to note in European Folk-tales the survival of Winishuyat and his approximate equivalent, the Yana uncle. In Slav tales this person is the mangy, miserable, neglected little colt which, when taken outside the town, shakes itself and becomes a marvellous magic steed, golden-haired, untiring, and wise, faithful to its master as the sun to his course in the sky.

This steed knows what is coming, knows exactly what to do, knows the mistakes that his master is sure to commit, knows how to correct them ; and the cumulative effect of these corrections increases immensely the momentum of the final triumph.

The Tom Thumb of nursery tales, the mentor of his big brothers, gives also a striking reminder of Winishuyat.

MEM LOIMIS

T<small>HIS</small> beautiful myth, in which wind and water are the moving characters, needs little if any explanation, save in one point, that relating to the Hlahi, commonly called doctor by white men. The word Shaman used in Siberia describes his position accurately. He is not the master of spirits exactly, but he is the favorite and friend of one or of more spirits ; that is, of such spirits as promised him their co-operation at the time when he became a Hlahi. If this person observes the rules of life that are always imposed on him who enjoys the friendship of this or that spirit (these rules refer mainly to food agreeable to the spirit), and does what is needful when the spirit is invoked (the needful, in this case, includes smoking and dancing), together with chanting the song of this spirit (every spirit has its own song), the spirit will come at his call.

Sanihas Yupchi smokes and dances ; the Tsudi girls sing or chant. The name Sanihas Yupchi means the archer of Sanihas ; Sanihas means daylight or the entire light of day from dawn till darkness, — in other words, all the light that Sas the sun gives between one night and another, — though Sanihas, daylight, is always represented as a person, and not the product of Sas's activity. This Sanihas Yupchi, the archer of daylight, the usher of the dawn, is no other than Tsaroki Sakahl, who has a white stripe on his back, the messenger who was sent by Torihas to invite Katkatchila to the hunt which caused the burning of the world in "Olelbis." He appears also as the envoy who ran in darkness on the gleaming sand trail to invite Hawt to Waida Dikit's green and red house, where the world concert was held, at which Hawt proved to be the greatest musician in existence.

In the note to "Kol Tibichi" will be found an account of how the Hlahi receives the aid and co-operation of spirits.

Most interesting beliefs are connected with Wokwuk, the son of Olelbis and Mem Loimis. The Wintus believe Wokwuk to be the greatest source of power and wealth.

According to "Olelbis," different bits of Wokwuk came down to the earth and were turned into elk and various valuable creatures ; the tip of Wokwuk's little finger became the earthly Wokwuk.

Wintus told me that if a man were to see the earthly Wokwuk, who was made from the tip of Wokwuk's little finger, he would grow immensely rich from the good luck which the sight would bring him. The last Wokwuk seen appeared a little over a hundred years ago. The story of its appearance is as follows : —

One day an old woman at a village called Tsarken, about twenty miles north of Redding, went for wood. Soon she ran home almost breathless, leaving her basket behind.

"Oh, my grandson," cried she to the chief, "I am frightened. My grandfather and grandmother used to say to me when I was a girl, 'You will see a wonderful thing some day.' I have just seen something wonderful on the hill. I believe it is a Wokwuk. Old people told me that if a Wokwuk is seen he will stay in one place a long time. I think this Wokwuk will stay, and wants us to see him."

The chief made a beautiful shed of small fir-trees, covered it with fir branches, and placed sweetly smelling herbs in it ; he sent for neighboring chiefs, and next day all went in their best array to the Wokwuk, bearing water in the finest basket of the village, and carrying a large oak slab and a rope. They found the Wokwuk facing north, and went near him. The chief lighted his pipe, blew the smoke toward every side, and said to the Wokwuk, —

"You have come to see us ; we have come to salute you. You have come to show yourself. You are a great person, and all the Wintus in the country will hear of you ; all the chiefs in every place will speak of you. I am glad that you are here. I am glad that you have come to my country."

He talked more to the Wokwuk ; spoke very nicely. Next he took water in his mouth and blew it around in every direction. After that the chief smoked a fragrant root instead of tobacco, blowing the smoke toward the Wokwuk, speaking to him with great respect.

"Now we will take you home with us," said the chief. They carried the oak slab to the Wokwuk ; he did not stir. They pushed him onto the slab, tied one leg to it, then took him home, placed the slab in the shed, and untied the Wokwuk. He remained two months there, never ate anything, never tried to escape.

Every morning they talked to the Wokwuk. During two months no one went to hunt, no one ate venison or sucker fish. Finally, all the Wintus were invited and all the Yanas, — a great assembly. They saluted the Wokwuk, each chief addressed him; last of all came a chief from Wini Mem, named Tópitot, leading a black bear. This bear walked erect like a man. He had bands of porcupine quills around his fore and hind legs, and a buckskin band covered with the red scalps of woodpeckers around his head. The bear bowed down to the Wokwuk, and the chief addressed him. When other chiefs spoke to the Wokwuk during the two previous months, he never raised his head or gave a sign of answer; but when Tópitot had finished, he raised his head and gave out a sound which was loud and long.

Next morning the chief of the village wished good luck to all, then he brought a rope, hung Wokwuk to a tree, and took his life. He plucked him, gave the quills to the chiefs, including himself, cut off the head, kept it; the body he carried to an ant-hill; when the ants had taken all the flesh, the bones were separated from each other and given to each chief.

When the chiefs went home, they spoke to the quills and bones as if praying, at first every morning, then once a week, then once a month, and continued this for a long time. After that each put away his bone or his quill in a triple covering. The bone or feather was wrapped first in a cover of the red scalps of woodpeckers sewed together; outside that were two mats made of reeds.

The owner of a Wokwuk bone or quill does not show it to any one, not even to his wife or children. When he dies he leaves it to a son, or, if he has no son, to a daughter. The possession of Wokwuk relics gives luck, but the owner must never eat venison or sucker; these are offensive to Wokwuk.

Five years after the quills were put away only the stems of them were left; five years later they were as fresh as if just plucked. If the quills were to be exposed before people, the people would all die; if to one person, that person would perish.

The owner of a quill or bone unwraps it occasionally, places water near it, and talks to it, saying: " Give us good luck ; make us well. I give you water, you give us strength." If he points the relic and mentions a person's name, saying, " Make him sick," that man will die surely.

If the owner of a Wokwuk relic dies without heirs, the bone or quill is sunk in a sacred spring ; if it were buried with the owner, all would get sick and die.

Both feathers and bones grow old in appearance, and later on they are as fresh looking and perfect as ever.

NORWAN

NEXT to " Olelbis " stands " Norwan," both for value and interest. This remarkable myth recalls forcibly the Helen of Troy tale, both in its general plan and in many particulars.

The great war among the first people is caused by the woman Norwan. Norbis Kiemila, who claims to be her husband, is descended from the heavenly white oak which forms part of Olelpanti Hlut, the divine mansion in the " Central Blue."

Norwan's full name is Pom Norwan en Pitchen, that is, daughter of the land on the southern border. She has another name : Hluyuk Tikimit, which means the dancing porcupine. Her residence, or hlut, was Norwan Buli, Norwan Mountain. The Yana name of this mountain is Wahkanopa, which means the son of Wahkalu. Wahkalu is Mount Shasta, and Wahkanopa Lassen's Butte.

Norwan, or Hluyuk Tikimit, the dancing porcupine, has still a third name, Bastepomas pokte, the food-giving or food-producing woman. In her quality of producer she occupies a position in Wintu mythology similar to that of the divine descendant of the earth and the sun in the Algonkin religious system. This Algonkin myth is one of the most beautiful and significant, not among creation, but among action myths. And here I beg to call attention again to the distinction which I make between the two classes of myths.

Creation myths relate always to what was done among the "first people in the world which preceded this," while creation was going on, or more correctly, perhaps, during the time of those transformations or metamorphoses from which resulted the present world and the order of things contained therein.

Action myths relate to ever-recurrent processes in nature which began as soon as the sun had his course marked out for him and the physical world around us received its present form and fashion; this happened before all the "first people" were metamorphosed. The vast majority had received the physical bodies which they have at present, but a few were left, and they remained in various places till they saw or heard the new race, the Indians. Action myths, therefore, relate to various processes in nature which never cease. For us the most important are those involved in the relations between the sun and the earth.

The great Algonkin sun and earth myth which has many variants and vast wealth of detail, describes those relations more profoundly and broadly than any other Indian myth devoted to the same subject.

The Algonkin myth in its most extended form describes the earth maiden as becoming a mother through being looked at by the sun. She gives birth to a daughter who is called Wakos ikwe, the fox woman; this daughter becomes the mother of a great hero, the highest benefactor of aboriginal man in America. He is the giver of food and of every good gift by which life is supported.

Of this myth there is a shorter version in which the hero is born of the earth directly; he is her son, not her grandson.

This benefactor and food-giver is no other than that warm air which we see dancing and quivering above the earth in fine weather. Descended from the sun and the earth, this warm air supports all things that have vegetable or animal existence.

This myth in its more extended form, the one to which I have referred first, is similar to that which Schoolcraft pieced together and which Longfellow took as the foundation of his beautiful poem "Hiawatha," though not identical with it.

Schoolcraft, with his amazing propensity to make mistakes, with his remarkable genius for missing the truth and confusing everything with which he came in contact, gave the name Hiawatha to his patchwork.

Hiawatha is an Iroquois name connected with Central New York. The Iroquois were mortal enemies of the Algonkins, and the feud between these two stocks was the most inveterate and far reaching of any in America. It was, in fact, the only Indian tribal hatred that rose to historical importance, and it was by the adherence of the Iroquois, the "Five Nations" of New York, that English dominion in North America was established.

The Algonkin force of America was on the French side, but the Iroquois held all water communication between Lake Erie and Ontario, the greatest strategic position on the continent at that period. They cut the Algonkins in two, and prevented France from receiving their undivided assistance.

Had the whole Algonkin power aided the French, they would have had great chances of victory. Had the Iroquois been friends of the Algonkins and acted with them, there could have been no doubt of the triumph of France at that juncture. But the Algonkins and Iroquois were mortal enemies ; the Algonkins were friendly to the French, the Iroquois to the English.

In the face of all this Schoolcraft makes Hiawatha, who is peculiarly Iroquois, the leading personage in his Algonkin conglomerate ; Hiawatha being an Iroquois character of Central New York (he is connected more particularly with the region about Schenectady), while the actions to which Schoolcraft relates him pertain to the Algonkin Chippewas near Lake Superior.

It is as if Europeans of some future age were to have placed before them a great epic narrative of French heroic adventure in which Prince Bismarck would appear as the chief and central Gallic figure in the glory and triumph of France. The error and absurdity would be, as the Germans say, *colossál*, but not greater or more towering than in Schoolcraft's Hiawatha. Longfellow, of course, could not free himself from the error contained in his material ; but the error, which was not his own and which he had no means of correcting at that time, did not prevent him from giving his work that peculiar charm which is inseparable from everything which he did.

In the original Algonkin myth the hero to which Hiawatha has been accommodated was a child of the sun and the earth. Whatever his names in the numerous versions found in the twenty-eight languages of this richest and most varied Indian stock of North America, he is always the bounteous benefactor of man, the kindest of all divine powers that have ever appeared upon earth. He is always in reality that warm light which dances and quivers before us in fine weather, and through which every man, beast, reptile, insect, fish, bird, and plant lives and flourishes.

This myth has received on the Pacific coast, or more correctly on parts of it, a different treatment from that given it east of the Rocky Mountains. There the benefactor is a female, a daughter of the earth. Nothing is said as to who her father was. It is significant that she dances all day, that she is called the quivering porcupine and the food-producing woman.

In Indian myths from New York to California the porcupine is ever connected with light; in some cases it is the sun himself. In "Tulchuherris" of this volume, Sas (the sun) carries a porcupine quiver, and is advised never to lay it aside, for as long as he keeps it on his shoulder he is safe from his children the grizzlies (the clouds) who wish to kill him.

In California Norwan, daughter of the earth, occupies in part the place of the Algonkin hero, the child of the sun and the earth. Her usual life is of the housekeeping order; she has great supplies of food in her hlut, or residence, and she goes on dancing each day until evening. The great and characteristic event of her life, her departure from the dance with her partner, is of the same scope and meaning as the last journey of Hiawatha when he sails to the west and vanishes in the regions of sunset. The hero of the Algonkin myth must go, he cannot stay; he must vanish in the ruddy glow of evening because he is the warm dancing air of the daytime. He must go whether he will or not. Before he goes, however, he cheers all whom he leaves behind by telling them that another will come from the east to take his place and comfort them. Next morning, of course, the comforter comes, for the life career of the Algonkin hero is included in the compass of a single day, and a successor is bound to come as surely as he himself is bound to go.

Norwan dances, and then goes away with her partner, to the desperate vexation of Norbis Kiemila, her would-be husband, who wishes to have her to himself exclusively. She dances, as she says, without knowing it and goes away unconsciously. She dances with this partner because she cannot help it, and departs imperceptibly to herself.

Who are the rivals for her person?

Norbis means "living in the south;" he lives in the southeast, the land of greatest productiveness, in the region of Hlihli Piu Hlut Ton, that most beautiful of houses on earth, and second only to the divine mansion in the "Central Blue." He is descended from one of the white oaks in the heavenly house.

The person who was metamorphosed afterward into the red wiu bird (Tede Wiu) is his rival, the person with whom Norwan left the dance, thus causing the first war in the world. Was this person the red of evening which became Tede Wiu afterward? If we acknowledge that he was, and if we are willing to admit Norbis as the representative of all people living east of the west, we have at once the two parties to an irreconcilable rivalry in the most vital of questions, the possession of warm sunlight, and that most vital of questions is embodied in the person of a woman. That was the cause of the first war in the world and of fell strife. A story substantially the same as this was, we may think, the ultimate basis of the Iliad. The mythic origin of the particular tale from which Homer constructed his epic had been forgotten, that may be granted, but there is little doubt that in rustic Greece men might have found a similar tale which was mythologic beyond peradventure; and the Helen of that tale, or her equivalent, was a person like Norwan. With the materials at our command even now, we have enough to indicate this, for was not Helen the daughter of Leda and the divine swan, a person to be fought for with all available energy in the world at that period, and to be fought for in a war which surpassed in importance all that have ever succeeded it?

Helen of Troy, the daughter of Leda and of Zeus, the overarching heaven, with all its light; Norwan, daughter of the earth, with Lassen's Butte, California, for her residence; and the Algonkin hero whose place is taken by Hiawatha, are all different representatives of the same person, different expressions for the same phenomenon ; and that person or phenomenon is the warm air which dances above the earth in fine weather. This air, in one case noted here, is conceived as the greatest benefactor of man, that being who gives the choicest and most necessary gifts to all, and, in the other two cases, as a priceless treasure, in the form of a woman who is to be fought for with all the valor that can possibly be summoned, and in a manner that in Helen's case inspired the noblest epic known to the world thus far.

These three cases show clearly the methods of mythology, and prove the absolute need of knowing that we must deal (to borrow mathematical language) with constants and variables taken together, — knowing clearly, meanwhile, which are constants, — and not with variables only, supposing them to be constants, or with constants and variables mixed together without being able to distinguish which belong to one class and which to the other. Were some writer to deal with the prehensile capacity in animated creatures, and describe how it is exercised, he would find a variety in the organs used for grasping things which would represent very well the variety of methods employed by primitive man in mythology to represent the same phenomenon or force in nature.

If man be considered as standing on his hind feet, his fore feet (the hands) are his grasping instruments. With the elephant the nose is prehensile ; with some monkeys the tail performs this office, in part at least. With tigers and lions, dogs and cats, the mouth and teeth are prehensile instruments of great force and precision. With the bear the forepaws are almost hands. The two feet with their talons, which correspond to the hind feet in quadrupeds, are the graspers with birds of prey, working instruments with domestic fowl, and weapons with some other birds, as, for instance, the ostrich.

Take another case, the teeth, one office of which is to reduce food to fine particles ; with all mammals they serve this purpose, and, in many cases, others also. Birds have no teeth, but they have a substitute in the gizzard, which they line with gravel and other hard particles ; and this second stomach, by contraction, grinds to pulp grain and other food already softened in the crop or first stomach. The boa-constrictor has no teeth and no second stomach; it chews by crushing between its body and a tree the beast which it is to swallow. The chewing mouth of the boa has for one jaw the tree, for the other its own body; between those two jaws it reduces to a soft mass the carcass of the creature to be swallowed.

In considering the various personages in mythology, it is all important to discover, first of all, what they are, and, next, what they do. The office filled by a certain personage in a group of myths belonging to a given race or tribe may be filled by an entirely different kind of character in a similar set of myths of another tribe. This results sometimes from different geographic and climatic conditions, and sometimes from looking at the phenomenon or process of nature in another way. There is as much variety in the treatment of one subject by various tribes as there is variety in prehensile members and the use of them among grasping creatures, or as there is difference in the manner of reducing food to fineness among quadrupeds, birds, and boa-constrictors.

TULCHUHERRIS

TULCHUHERRIS resembles certain European tales more than any other in this collection. Apart from other merits, the value of such a tale in comparative mythology is evident.

The old woman, Nomhawena, is an earthworm now; the Indian tale-teller says that there is no doubt on that point. Pom Pokaila, her second name (Pom, earth; Pokalia, old woman) admits of two translations, — old woman of the earth, or old woman Earth. In the first case it would apply to Nomhawena, who digs the earth always, is a woman of the earth; in the second, it would mean the earth itself. The earth is, in fact, Tulchuherris's mother. Nomhawena is his grandmother, in a titular sense at least. In more countries of the world than one, grandmother is the title of a midwife; and the office of midwife was performed by Nomhawena at the birth of Tulchuherris.

We may picture to ourselves the scenes and circumstances of Tulchuherris's birth. Root Flat is one of those level places where innumerable little piles of fine soil are brought to the surface by the labor of earthworms. Over this valley, as over so many others on the Pacific coast, fog is spread after sunrise, — fog which comes up from the earth dug in every direction by Nomhawena's people. In this fog is Tulchuherris, the mighty son of the earth ; in other words, lightning, electricity, that son of the earth who comes to maturity so speedily.

Kulitek Herit, brother of Tulchuherris, for whom Nomhawena mourned so deeply, is now the white feather which appears sometimes in the black tail of the black vulture. Komos Kulit is the Wintu name of this vulture. There were three great feathers among the Wintus, transformations of three great persons among the first people. The first of these is the white feather just mentioned, which is the metamorphosed Kulitek ; the second is the longest black tail-feather of the black vulture, which is the present form of Hamam Herit, who fought in the Norwan struggle ; the third is the longest wing-feather of the same vulture. This feather is the metamorphosed Tubalus Herit.

The first two feathers are used on great occasions in war ; the third feather, only by doctors or Hlahis.

In Indian mythology there is a subtle, but close and firm, connection between the sunflower and the sun, which is illustrated strikingly in this story. The old woman, by her magic art, burns great piles of big trees in two or three minutes, while a handful of sunflower roots is beyond her power and keeps the fire alive for years. This illustration, in the material world, of the Indians, reminds one of the still, small voice in the spiritual world of the Hebrews. The sunflower root in this Tulchuherris tale is invincible from its connection with the sun, the one source of light and heat ; the still, small voice is considered almighty because of its connection with the whole moral life and light that exists in the universe.

The two obsidian knives in Sas's house are an interesting reminder of the Damocles sword.

In the case of Tichelis, now ground squirrel, and Hawt, the

present lamprey eel, we have cases of personal collision resulting in transformation. In the Wintu mythology this is exceptional, and in this instance one-sided, for the vanquished make no attempt to transform Tulchuherris.

SEDIT AND THE TWO BROTHERS HUS

SEDIT was in favor of death for men, and gives his reasons. It cannot be said that he brought death into the world, but he stopped the work which would have kept it out.

His discourse with the Hus brothers is curious ; it represents the immortality and goodness of a weak and limited creature like man as barren and monotonous. The comparison of this conversation with the account of Adam and Eve before and after the Fall is not without interest.

The critical, unbelieving, disobedient Sedit, who is so willing to make life in the world varied and interesting through death, so long as the question stands apart from his own immortality, and his great concern and anxiety when he thinks that he must himself die, is brought out in good relief.

The earnest and honest Hus brothers stand in strong contrast to the sneering Sedit. The Hus character is a lofty one in Wintu mythology. This may seem strange to a new student of Indian ideas, when he remembers what a foul creature the turkey buzzard is.

The buzzard is considered as a purifier on earth, and surely in regions like Central America the service rendered by the bird in this regard is memorable. The buzzard is everywhere the most frequent and striking figure in Guatemala and Southern Mexico, both in city and country. In California there is a fine of five dollars for killing one.

The original Hus character is conceived by the Wintus as striving toward religious purification as strenuously as the earthly buzzard works at cleaning the earth of carrion of various descriptions.

The following remarks accompanied this tale when published in
"The Sun" : —

This tale of Sedit and the Hus brothers is a splendid bit of aboriginal American philosophy, and touches on topics which have
exercised many minds besides those of primitive America.   The
subject of life and death is treated here so simply, and at the same
time so well, that I believe few readers would ask for explanation
or comment.

Some statements, however, touching Sedit are not out of place,
I think.   The coyote is very prominent in the mythology of every
region where he is found.   The basis of his character is the same
in all myths that I have collected.   He is a tremendous glutton,
boastful, talkative, cunning, exceptionally inclined to the other sex,
full of curiosity, a liar, a trickster, deceiving most adroitly, and is
deceived himself at times.   He comes to grief frequently because
of his passions and peculiar qualities.   He is an artful dodger, who
has points in common with the devil of European folk-lore, being
in many cases an American counterpart of this curious and interesting personage.

Of Northern Pacific coast tribes in the United States, the Modocs
have given most distinction to the coyote.   Among them the chief
coyote is a trickster on the grandest scale, and has obtained possession of the indestructible disk of the sun, through which he is immortal, or, at least, is renewed every day to carry that luminary.
Because of his vanity and boastfulness, the coyote undertakes
various enterprises in which he fails through his passions.

Sacred springs and small lakes in the mountains are very prominent in the Modoc religion.   A young man who hopes to be a
magician or a doctor goes to these mountain springs before he is
married or knows woman.   There he fasts and watches a week or
longer until he is nearly exhausted.   If he is to be a magician or
doctor, spirits appear to him in this interval.   A coyote went to
those mountains (in the time before men were on earth, of course),
hoping to gain great magic power, but on the way he ate various
kinds of food hateful to the spirits of the springs.   These spirits
were disgusted with the odor of food that came from him, struck
him with mange, drove him away, made him hungry, foul, and

wretched forever.   He ran away, howling and lamenting, without hope of pardon.   From this coyote are descended an especially bad breed of coyotes in Oregon.   They are all foul and hungry to this day.   In dark windy nights the mangy descendants of that glutton are heard bewailing the fault of their ancestor, their own fallen state and lost happiness.

The Shasta Indians have a long tale of a coyote whose fond grandmother tried to make him a great sorcerer.   When the time came, she sent him to the sacred mountain and gave every instruction.   He was not to stop, eat, or drink on the road, or to speak to any one.   When about two-thirds of the distance, he passed near a house ; inside was loud thumping and hammering ; a frog woman was pounding seeds and singing ; her house was full of food ; coyote caught the odor of it, stopped, could not resist the temptation to go in.   He went in, ate and drank everything put before him.   In Indian mythology frog women are not vestals ; so breaking his fast and gluttony were not his only offences.   He had fallen past redemption.   On leaving the frog woman's house he went through a series of unmentionable adventures, at the end of which there was nothing left but his head, which was in a pool by the wayside, and just as much alive as ever.

Two sisters, afterwards ducks, who were going that way, found and pitied the unfortunate.   It was not easy to carry him, but the younger promised to do so if he would shut his eyes and not open them till she set him down on his grandmother's threshold.   This condition was to prevent him from seeing how she carried him. When half-way home, curiosity overcame him.   Though only a head, he opened his eyes and fell to the ground.

The duck woman had pity again, and took him to his grandmother.   Loud was her wailing at sight of her lost and ruined grandson.

Sedit came to grief through peculiarities of character.

HAWT

THIS myth of Hawt is very curious and subtle; it is one of the best told tales that I have found anywhere. There is a largeness about it, and, at the same time, a perfectly firm grasp on the part of Waida Dikit, the master of the assembly, that produce a grand effect.

Though the story is long, it needs, I think, no explanation beyond what is stated in the introduction and in preceding notes, except some remarks touching the character of Hawt.

Hawt, the great musician, is identified with water; he is, as it were, the spirit of water made visible.

In this myth, only the musical powers of Hawt are exhibited; but in the Yana Tirukala, which means the same thing as Hawt (lamprey eel), we see the active side of the same personage, we see him as a worker. Original is Hawt indeed, — a living flute fingering his own body as he would an instrument; inhaling air and blowing it out through the apertures in his sides.

The present lamprey eel has marks, as it were, of holes in his sides.

NORWANCHAKUS AND KERIHA

THIS tale contains actions and a number of personages difficult to identify, because their names are merely epithets. Eltuluma means "he swims in;" but who it is that swims in we know not. Keriha seems connected with ducks, from the fact that he wore a duck-skin all his life on earth, and, when he threw off this skin, all ducks were produced from it.

Norwanchakus means the southern end of that staff or stick to which was attached the net with which these two brothers dragged Pui Mem and Bohema Mem, and named each place from the thing which came into the net in front of it.

Nodal Monoko (the little man who ate so many salmon and sturgeons, and carried so many away in his bag) means "sweet in the south." He has another name, Nodal Wehlinmuk, which means "salt in the south." At first he is hostile to grizzly bears, but later has intimate relations with them and marries one. His acts point strongly toward electricity or lightning. His bag, in which the whole world could be put away, may well have been a cloud bag.

Norwinte means "seen in the south;" but, again, we have no knowledge of the person seen. Poni Norwanen Pitchen, the full name of Norwan, is also an epithet meaning "daughter of the land on the southern border," and would convey no information if it stood alone; but as Norwan, in addition to many other details, is also the dancing porcupine and the food-producing woman, we know who she is.

The existence of Puriwa and Sanihas (darkness and daylight) before the sun was in the world, is most interesting. This is one of many proofs that every phenomenon was considered to be independent. Daylight is a personage quite apart from the sun, who is merely that old Sas who fought with Tulchuherris, and who travels through the sky every day from east to west in utter loneliness. He carries that glowing torch which we see as he moves on his way through the sky; but the light of day is a separate personage. Similar considerations apply to Puriwa, darkness or night, who is also a distinct and independent entity.

The struggle between Keriha and Hubit has much charm for Wintus; they laugh heartily at the recital of it.

KELE AND SEDIT

OLD Kele, the mountain wolf, is evidently one of the first people sent down from the sky by Olelbis; not in part, but in person. His sons and daughters were not his children, but his creation; he made them from sticks, just as Jupka made the Yanas at Jigulmatu.

In the note to "Kol Tibichi" is a Wintu account of the character and actions of Kele's sons and daughters. A very interesting and valuable account this is; it explains the werewolf idea perfectly. The wolf man of Northern Europe, the *Lykanthropos* of the Greeks, must have been just such a person as Kele's sons and daughters, who were people apparently when they went forth to harm Indians, but who turned into wolves when they were discovered and rebuked. At home, in their great sweat-house, those people are wolves; but when they go out on their travels up and down through the world, they are exactly like Wintus, save only the hairy foot.

KOL TIBICHI

IN connection with this tale I add the following remarks about one of the two modes of making doctors, and about certain spirits. These remarks are given, as nearly as possible, in the form of the original Wintu narrative.

I have added, besides, the songs of four great existences, or gods. Every individual existence in Indian mythology has its own song. This song refers to what is most notable in the actions or character of that existence. The given song is sung by a doctor immediately after its spirit of that existence has entered him.

Kol Tibichi's yapaitu (yapaitu is another name for one of the first people), the rainbow, would not leave him till he used a woman's red apron as a headband, because the rainbow is connected with the catamenial periods of Sanihas (daylight).

The yapaitu dokos (yapaitu missile), mentioned further on, is a projection of the spirit itself of the yapaitu. Sometimes it flees from the patient; the duty of the doctor, in such a case, is to find the dokos. If he does not, it may return to the sick man after the doctor has gone; and in that case the last condition of the patient is worse than the first. Generally, however, it waits to be cast out.

THE MAKING OF DOCTORS AMONG
THE WINTUS

THE chief assists always in this ceremony, because a doctor can be made only in a sweat-house. Two chiefs may consult together and agree with old doctors in this matter, or one chief may do so if it suits him. If doctors begin, they must consult the chief, be-.cause he owns the sweat-house. The doctors and the chief or chiefs agree upon the time, and then give out the news that on a certain night they are going to create doctors. Young persons who wish to be doctors go to the sweat-house ; most of the old people stay at home.

The men heat the sweat-house, shut it up closely, and sit down. Sweat pours from them like rain. When they have sweated suffi-ciently, all go to the river and swim. After that the people, men and women, go into the sweat-house. One doctor or two will be-gin to sing. Young unmarried men or women who are candidates present themselves. The doctors suck out of these all that is bad in them, all that is impure, unclean. They suck the forehead, breast, back, arms. At times they suck out blood ; at times some-thing sharp like a fine bone comes out. They suck out every-thing that is evil. When they have finished sucking, the doctor sings again, and puts a yellowhammer's feather into each ear of the candidate. The feather may go in out of sight, or the doctor puts it on the person's head, and the feather may sink through his skull. Now the people dance, and especially the candidates for the dignity of doctor. The chief goes out, stands on the housetop, and calls to all the yapaitu in the rocks, in the water, in Olelpanti, in the trees, in bathing springs, to come. " We are going to make doc-tors," says the chief ; " you must come and help my people."

After this the chief goes in, and they close every hole, every chink in the sweat-house ; close them all safely. There is no fire, no light, inside. When they have begun to talk in the sweat-house, one doctor calls to all the spirits of yapaitu in the east, west, north, south to come. Pretty soon a spirit may be heard on the housetop; spirits make a whistling noise when they come. That moment a man or woman falls down, and all know that the spirit has gone into that person's head.

Now the doctor calls, " One more; one more ! "

In a moment another whistling may be heard as the spirit touches the housetop and goes in. Another man or woman falls; the spirit has entered that one. The persons into whom spirits have entered know nothing. They become as if crazy, as if they had lost their wits. They try to go to the housetop. Some try to climb the central pole ; some want to leave the sweat-house ; they know nothing for half an hour perhaps.

One doctor keeps on calling spirits, and they come one at a time. Many doctors may be made in one night, or a few, or none. There are always many people in the sweat-house to whom spirits will not come. The spirits never go into people unless they like them. The spirit looks straight through a man and knows him immediately.

The people dance all night. There is no light in the sweat-house; the place is very hot, though there is no fire there. Next day those to whom spirits have come tell the doctors and chief what spirits are with them. If not, the chief may give them food offensive to the spirits, and the spirits would kill them if they ate. Some spirits may stay two or three days with a person, who would then sit inside all the time. The old doctors have to ask this spirit what it wishes, and make it go away for a time, so that the person possessed may eat something. Each spirit has its own kind of food. If we give a man something that the spirit has never eaten, it will kill him right away if he eats. The old doctors ask his spirit what it wants, and it tells. The salmon spirit, for instance, likes leaves or water ; a sucker of the mountains would eat mountain pine nuts, but a valley sucker needs nuts off the digger pine. If strange food is placed before a spirit, it is afraid ; and if the man possessed eats this food, the spirit will kill him. Some spirits don't like buckskin, and the man to whom they have come must not wear it.

The bad spirits are numerous ; the sucker is one of these, and so is Kele (the mountain wolf). This wolf is dangerous; it may hurt you in this way : you may think that you see a good-looking man or woman on the mountain or in the woods. If you go toward this person or this person comes toward you, comes near you, speaks to you, and you agree with it, the next thing you know this strange man or woman turns into a wolf, runs away, and your mind is gone; the wolf has taken it. The sucker does the same, but disappears before your eyes or turns into something ugly.

There are three causes of sickness. The first is when a good yapaitu spirit is angry with a man and strikes him with his spirit point; second, when a bad spirit puts his missile in a man and makes him sick (the spirit in this case does it at his own instance); third, when an evil spirit sends his missile into a man at the request or prayer of a doctor.

When the dokos or missile that has been sent into a man is drawn out by the spirit which assists the curing doctor, the doctor forces the dokos to tell what yapaitu sent it, and at the prayer of what doctor. But the dokos does not tell the truth in every case, and sometimes accuses the wrong person. It is very difficult, therefore, to know surely what doctor is guilty of making a man sick. A doctor, if the spirit is in him when he comes to see a sick man, is able to look right through the body of the patient and see where the dokos lies. Sometimes he is not able to draw it out; he can see where the dokos is, that is all; but if his spirit were stronger than the one who put it there, he could draw it out and cure the patient.

There is danger, however, in drawing out a very powerful dokos by sucking, for when it is coming out of the sick man's body it may be sent down through the mouth of the doctor into his body by the spirit who owns it, and the doctor is killed in this way.

A doctor may have twenty or thirty spirits, but he rarely calls on more than two or three, and it is seldom that any great number are fitted to work together in a given case.

The office of doctor is very dangerous, especially if the doctor is powerful. If he has many spirits to help him, each has to be pleased in its own special way; each has its own food, prefers certain kinds, and dislikes others. The doctor must not eat food hateful to his spirits: if he does, he is liable to be killed. A man who has twenty or thirty spirits is greatly limited, therefore, in his manner of living.

Some spirits do not like venison, others do not eat fish; the doctor who commands these spirits must eat neither venison nor fish, and so with other kinds of food in the case of other spirits.

The man who seeks to be a doctor cannot choose his spirits; they come to him; he cannot refuse to receive them, and must live in a way to please them.

Every dokos can be extracted from a sick man's body by the aid of a spirit stronger than the one who put it in.

Among other spirits, doctors have the spirit of the sun, the spirits of stars and the clouds to help them. These are good spirits. Sedit's spirit cannot help doctors much. They call it sometimes, but it does n't do much; it has not the power. Suku (dog) is very powerful and bad. If Suku wants to kill a man, he does it quickly. A doctor who has the Suku spirit in his service is great. If a man has been made sick by Suku, he will vomit blood, or bleed from his nostrils all the time. The Suku spirit is a good one to send to kill people. Chir (the sucker fish) is an evil spirit too. When Chir wants to kill a man, it makes him giddy and crazy right away. He becomes senseless and dies, unless some doctor cures him, and generally doctors can do nothing against Chir. The Chir sickness is the worst that spirits bring. It is called chiruntowi, sickness from the sucker. The man who has it dies; he cannot tell where he is troubled; he grows dizzy and senseless. No one can cure him unless by great luck. Something tried by some doctor may save him — just by chance, just because it happens so. Kele is also an evil spirit. He has a song, the same which his two daughters sang on the mountain top (see the tale "Kele and Sedit"), and which Sedit heard far away in the west. This is a poison song, and draws people after it. Kele is here now, suppose, in Cottonwood or in Tehama, and sees a man up at Yreka. Kele sings, and the song goes as straight as a string to the man. It draws him and draws him; he is drawn as water is when people pump it. The man must follow the song; he has got to do so, he cannot help himself, he is sick; his sickness is called lubeluntowi (sickness from lubelis). The man will keep going and going and going ; he will not know what makes him go. Suppose I am listening to Kele's song. I go, and it is the song that draws me. I hear it ; but nobody else does. The spirits of the Kele girls drew Sedit to them; he could n't help himself, he could n't stop ; he had to go, and he never went home again ; he had to stay up at Kele's. The spirits of Chir and Kele always make people crazy.

Many Wintu women lose their minds, and are killed by Kele's sons. Many Wintu men have been lost through Kele's daughters. Suppose I am out here in the wood, I see a woman coming, a nice woman. She stops and talks ; I talk to her. If I have sense in me, I look at her toes to see if she is one of those Kele women. If she is, she has a bunch of hair on the tip of her foot, and if I see it, I say right there, " You are a Kele ! " At these words she will leave me and run. When ten feet away, she will turn to a mountain wolf, and I shall see that Kele running away very fast.

Suppose some woman is out in the woods. She is thinking of some man that she likes, and right away she sees the very man she is thinking of. He is coming to meet her. He comes up and asks, " Where are you going ? " The woman is glad to see him. She tells. He carries her to the mountain, and never again will that woman be seen by her friends or by others. It was one of Kele's sons who took the form of the man she was thinking of, so as to entice her away and destroy her. If the woman has sense she will look down at the foot of the stranger, see the tuft of hair, and say, " You are Kele ; go off." He turns to a wolf on the spot, and runs away to the mountain. All Wintus went barefoot in old times, and this tuft could be seen, if a person had sense enough left to look for it. As every one wears shoes or moccasins now, it might not be easy to find it. But to this day the Keles lead people astray. All the Wintus know them, and are afraid.

They live on Wenempuidal, a high mountain near the left bank of the Little Sacramento. Dekipuiwakut, a small creek, comes down from Kele's Mountain and falls into the Sacramento. White men call it Hazel Creek. The Keles live at the head of this creek. The whole mountain is their sweat-house. They are up

there now, and almost any night you may hear them howling on
the mountain when the evil brothers are going home.

The following four spirit songs are from my Wintu collection.
Two I give in the original, with literal translation ; the other two,
in translation only.   The lightning song, by referring to the connection between lightning and the sucker, which has one of the
most formidable spirits, enables us to suspect why the sucker is so
much feared by Wintus.   In the Olelbis song, the great one above
is the cloud-compeller, as in classic mythology.   The tanning is
described in "Olelbis."   In the Hau song, the celestial Hau is described as travelling along the Milky Way.   This is the Wintu
comment on the text.   Many readers will agree, I think, that the
Polar Star song, the fourth, is composed on a scale truly immense.
The lightning song sounds wonderfully like an extract from the
Sanscrit, "Rig Veda."

SONGS OF SPIRITS.

1. Walokin tsawi, Lightning's Song.

> Mínom tóror wéril chirchákum sáia
> Dúne wérem winwar dún bohémum.
> I bear the sucker-torch to the western tree-ridge.
> Look at me first born (and) greatest.

2. Olelben tsawi, the Song of Olelbis.

> Olél bohéma ni tsulúli káhum síka nı.
> I am great above.   I tan the black cloud (there).

3. Song of Hau (red fox).

> " On the stone ridge east I go.
> On the white road I, Hau, crouching go.
> I, Hau, whistle on the road of stars."

4. Song of Waida Werris (the Polar Star).

> " The circuit of earth which you see,
> The scattering of stars in the sky which you see,
> All that is the place for my hair." [1]

[1] Hair in Indian mythology, as in other mythologies, is the equivalent of rays of
light when connected with the sun and with planet luminaries.

THE YANAS

As a preface to the few myths of the Yanas which have survived, I beg to offer the following words touching this ill-fated people :

Previous to August, 1864, the Yanas numbered about three thousand, as I have been informed on the sound authority of reliable white men. Taking the names and population of villages given me by surviving Indians, I should say that this estimate is not too large.

During the second half of August, 1864, the Yanas were massacred, with the exception of a small remnant.

The Indians of California, and especially those of Sacramento Valley, were among the most harmless of human beings. Instead of being dangerous to settlers, they worked for them in return for fair wages. The Yanas were distinguished beyond others for readiness to earn money. White men occupied in tilling land knew their value, and employed them every season in haymaking and harvesting.

At the present day the Wintus, and the few Yanas that are left, go down the valley and labor during the season in hop-fields and vineyards.

Why were the Yanas killed ?

The answer is as follows: Certain Indians lived, or rather lurked, around Mill Creek, in wild places somewhat east of Tehama and north of Chico. These Mill Creek Indians were fugitives ; outlaws from various tribes, among others from the Yanas. To injure the latter, they went to the Yana country about the middle of August, 1864, and killed two white women, Mrs. Allen and Mrs. Jones. Four children also were left for dead by them, but the children recovered. After the murders the Mill Creeks returned home unnoticed, carrying various plundered articles with them.

Two parties of white men were formed at once to avenge the women and four children. Without trying in any way to learn who the guilty were, they fell upon the Yanas immediately, sparing neither sex nor age. They had resolved to exterminate the whole nation. The following few details will show the character of their work : —

At Millville, twelve miles east of Redding, white men seized two Yana girls and a man. These they shot about fifty yards from the village hotel. At another place they came to the house of a white woman who had a Yana girl, seven or eight years of age. They seized this child, in spite of the woman, and shot her through the head. "We must kill them, big and little," said the leader ; "nits will be lice."

A few miles north of Millville lived a Yana girl named Eliza, industrious and much liked by those who knew her. She was working for a farmer at the time. The party stopped before this house, and three of the men entered it. "Eliza, come out," said one of them ; "we are going to kill you." She begged for her life. To the spokesman, who had worked for her employer some time before, she said : "Don't kill me ; when you were here I cooked for you, I washed for you, I was kind to you ; I never asked pay of you ; don't kill me now."

Her prayers were vain. They took Eliza, with her aunt and uncle, a short distance from the house and shot the three. My informant counted eleven bullets in Eliza's breast.

After this murder the party took a drink and started ; but the leader, in killing Eliza, said, "I don't think that little squaw is dead yet." So he turned back and smashed in her skull with his musket. The man who counted the bullet holes in her bosom, himself a white man, saw her after the skull was broken. He knew the girl well, and gave me these details.

Another party went to a farm on Little Cow Creek where they found three Yana men threshing hayseed in a barn. The farmer was not at home. They killed the three Indians, and went to the house. The three wives of the men killed in the barn were there and began to scream. The farmer's wife hurried out with a quilt, threw it around the three women, and stood in front of them, holding the ends of the quilt. "If you kill them you will kill me," said she, facing the party. The woman was undaunted, and, as it happened, was big with child. To kill, or attempt to kill, under those conditions, would be a deed too ghastly for even such

heroes; so they went away, swearing that they would kill the
"squaws" later. These three Indian women were saved and
taken beyond the reach of danger by two white men.

And so the "avengers" of Mrs. Allen and Mrs. Jones continued. At one place they killed an Indian woman and her infant,
at another three women. In the town of Cottonwood they killed
twenty Yanas of both sexes. The most terrible slaughter in any
place was near the head of Oak Run, where three hundred Yanas
had met at a religious dance. These were attacked in force, and
not a soul escaped. The slaughter went on day after day till the
entire land of the Yanas was cleared. The few who escaped were
those who happened to be away from home, outside their country,
and about twelve who were saved by Mr. Oliver and Mr. Disselhorst, both of Redding. The whole number of surviving Yanas
of pure and mixed blood was not far from fifty.

Some time after the bloody work was done it was discovered
that the Mill Creek outlaws had killed Mrs. Allen and Mrs. Jones,
and that the Yanas were innocent. The Mill Creeks were left
unpunished.

My inquiries as to how civilized men could commit such atro-
cities found the following answers : —

In 1864 there was a large floating and mining population in
Northern California, which "had no use for Indians," and was
ready to kill them on slight provocation. In distinction to these
people was a small number of settlers who lived among the Yanas
in friendship, and hired them to work on land. The killing was
done by men who did not know the Yanas. Those settlers who
did know the Yanas were overawed, and were unable to save them,
except secretly, as in the case of the two men who rescued the
three women on Little Cow Creek by conveying them beyond
danger. Oliver and Disselhorst, who saved twelve, were at the
edge of Redding, where support was possible. At first the rage
of the killing parties was boundless ; they swore that white women
would not be murdered again in that country, and that not an
Indian should be left alive in it. An intense feeling of indignation
at the murder, coupled with an unspeakable contempt for Indians,
was the motive in the breasts of most of the white men. Had

they looked on the Yanas with ordinary feelings of justice, they would have tried to find the guilty instead of slaughtering a whole nation. There was another element among the slayers of the Indians, — a vile one, an element which strives to attach itself to every movement, good or bad in all places — a plundering element. That year the Yanas had worked a good deal, and it was not uncommon for single persons of them to have from $40 to $60. One informant told me that a man showed a friend of his $400 which he had taken from murdered Indians. Money and everything of value that the Yanas had was snatched up by these robbers.

Nearly all the men who killed the Yanas have gone out of the country or are dead. A few are in Northern California yet, and the children of some of the dead ones are living there now. Though one's indignation at the deeds of 1864 be great, there is no use in mentioning names at this hour. All that is left is to do for the poor remnant of an interesting people that which we have done for Indians in other parts: give them land properly surveyed and the means to begin life on it.

THE WINNING OF HALAI AUNA

THE Yanas were fond of astronomical myths, or myths of the upper world. The morning star and the moon appear in them frequently. The great sweat-house of the sun is the dome of heaven.

The name of the mysterious and mighty old uncle, Igupa Topa, seems to me to be derived from Iguna, chief sweat-house, and Tuina or Toina, the sun. Tuina is the prevailing pronunciation, but Toina is used also. Igupa is the regular form of son of Iguna, as is Topa of Toina. He is a person whose strength is well known to the sun, who has evidently a clear perception of how dangerous a person he is.

The shooting of Wakara into the sky is a curious variant of the tree-bending by Tulchuherris and Sas in the Wintu myth.

THE HAKAS AND THE TENNAS

THIS myth describes a deadly feud between the people who were turned into flint, that is, fire, presumably lightning, and the grizzlies or cloud people. After I had prevailed on him to give me the story, the narrator told it with unfeigned delight. His sympathy with the old woman Tsuwalkai was great, and his enthusiasm for Tsawandi Kamshupa, who rose from the spittle of Tsawandi Kamshu, evident and striking. The origin of Ilhataina in this myth and in the following called "Ilhataina," which is the usual name for lightning, strengthens my view that the Wintu Tulchuherris, a name which is merely an epithet, meaning "dug up," is the same person as Ilhataina of the Yanas. The regular acknowledged lightning of the Wintus is called Walokit, who is a child of Wima Loimis, grizzly-bear maiden, and the sun.

ILHATAINA

IN this myth lightning is "dug up," as in the preceding one. Electricity is one of the earth's children.

The putting on of Gowila's skin by Ilhataina is one of the curious acts frequent in Indian mythology. In the Aztec worship of Mexico, in Montezuma's time, the sacrificing priest put on the skin of the victim as far as the waist.

The wish of Ilhataina to get the old rabbit-skin robe is worthy of attention.

HITCHINNA

AMONG the Iroquois the cyclone was represented as a great head, the name of which in Seneca is Dagwa Noenyent. This head would pass through a forest and tear up the greatest trees by the roots.

The method used by the deceitful Metsi to rid the world of Hitchinna might remind one of the way of cooking oysters at the waterside in Virginia near the places where they are taken.

TIRUKALA

I HAVE referred to Tirukala in the Wintu myth "Hawt." The battle described in this myth and the child which rises from the spittle of Burnt Face and reaches maturity in one day, are very striking.

Tirukala gives the active, the working side of water as a personage, the widener of valleys, the pusher apart of mountains, the maker of all streams and rivers. Tirukala works without ceasing, he sings as he labors, and never eats food of any kind.

Hawt (in the Wintu myth) gives the artistic, the poetic side of the same person, whose voice is that of Niagara and the raging ocean at its loudest, that of the tiniest rivulet or of the raindrop at its gentlest.

SUKONIA'S WIVES AND THE ICHPUL SISTERS

IT is noteworthy that in Indian myths whenever two sisters are sent somewhere, as in the present case, and warned by father or mother against some deceiver who is likely to meet them on the way, the elder sister is generally ready to become a victim, the younger is the wise and obedient one, as in this myth.

We have again a case of putting on the skin of a slain person to become like him or her.

The test of bringing water was perfect, since no one who was not of the household could know where it was.

THE FINDING OF FIRE

In this, as in all Indian myths of the bringing of fire, it is procured by stealing. The pursuit in all cases is most strenuous.

In one myth relays are posted along the road at short intervals; these deliver the fire to one another in great haste. At last the pursuers are very near, when the fire is given to him who afterward becomes the turtle; he places the treasure in his mouth and rolls into a deep river, where he hides till the baffled masters of fire turn homeward sorrowing.

HAIKA KAINA

Here we find another myth of a flint people.

In the Hakas and Tennas we have a struggle between the lightning and the clouds. In Haka Kaina the myth represents the advance of spring to colder regions. The swan-maidens go north with the early lightning of the year. Hence Haka Kaina, the war chief of Wahkalu, the great residence of Jupka, is represented as stealing them. In another myth, of which, unfortunately, I have only a fragment, these same swan-maidens are borne away north by Haka Kaina with great pomp and circumstance. The chief is attended by an immense escort, in which all the personages are phenomena of springtime. His regular force, his trusty warriors do not migrate; they stay all the year at Wahkalu, unless when absent on some expedition. The most characteristic person in the escort is a species of poplar-tree, the leaves of which tremble like those of an aspen. This hero dances all the time from his point of starting in the south till he reaches Mount Shasta. This gives a fine picture of that kind of tree putting forth leaves which quiver with gladness at the approach of the swan-maidens.

The marshalling by Haka Kaina of forces so numerous that they surround the immense base of Mount Shasta, the enormous dust

which they raise, dust which goes up to the sun, their death by fire
at the hands of the Mini Aunas, their resurrection and return home
with the swan-maidens and all the spoils of Hwipajusi's people, are
conceived on a scale truly grand.

TITINDI MAUPA AND PAIOWA THE
YOUNGEST DAUGHTER OF WAKARA

PAIOWA is the evening star.   Wakara's most interesting daughters
are always Halaia, or Halai Auna, and Paiowa.   The first is the
morning, the second the evening star.

Halaia's sister, Pahnino, in this myth became afterward a shell,
or rather a creature which lives in a shell, as did also her mother.
I do not know which kind of shell Pahnino is ; it has bright colors.

The increase and decrease of food, the magic power of weapons,
the jealousy and hostility of the husbands of other sisters, are usual
in Yana myths of this kind.

THE TWO SISTERS HAKA LASI AND
TSORE JOWA

LOVE of this sort, of a sister for a brother, is found in European
lore occasionally, and is, of course, a survival from a very remote
past.   In this myth it is the love of one of the first people, a
female, afterward turned into a loon, for her brother, who was
afterward turned into a wildcat.

Bringing to life is one of the most familiar performances in
American mythology as well as in Keltic.   In Yana it is done
by kicking or turning over a corpse with the foot ; by boiling in
water, sometimes one hair, sometimes the heart ; or by striking the
corpse with a twig of the red rosebush.   In Keltic it is most
frequently done by the stroke of a Druidic or magic switch, which
resembles the Yana method with the rose twig.   The red rose has

significance, no doubt. In Keltic we are not told the kind of wood from which the Druidic switch was taken.

In Seneca myths raising from the dead was very impressive. Sometimes the dry, fleshless bones of hundreds and hundreds of the first people were found lying in a heap or close together. The hero, another of the first people, pushes a hickory-tree as if to throw it on them, crying at the same time, " Rise up! or the tree will fall on you." That moment all the dry bones sprang up, took on flesh, and assumed their old forms immediately. Indian humor creeps out sometimes by giving us two lame people of the uprisen company. In the hurry and rush, while the dry bones are arranging themselves, two legs get astray ; two personages have each one leg which is his own and one which belongs to his neighbor.

JUIWAIYU

THIS myth has many and very valuable elements, — the importance of dreams, the stopping or slackening the course of the sun, the music of Juiwaiyu as he moves, the choice of the right road, the storm of vermin, Jupka as monitor and helper, the summons to send Damhauja's daughters to meet him, the inexhaustible venison no larger than a walnut, Juiwaiyu's marvellous music on the mountain, the bringing home of countless deer in the body of a fawn, the race with Damhauja's sons-in-law, the meeting with the poison spider, the rattlesnake and the grizzly bear, the storm, the drowning of Damhauja and his resurrection, — make this one of the richest of Yana tales.

Playing with two bones was very much like playing ball. Near both ends of the field barriers were set up, and each side had to put the bones past the barrier toward which they faced.

The starting-point was in the middle of the field, at an equal distance from both barriers. At the opening of the game all the players gathered at this middle point ; the bones were thrown up, and all struggled for them. Whoever caught the bones on his stick either hurled them toward the barrier beyond which he wished to put them, or he ran toward it, bearing them on the point of his stick. If there were swifter runners than he, they took the bones from him, or if he hurled them ahead, they ran and threw them or carried them toward one barrier or another. The bones were fastened together by a string some inches long.

In Yana tales, Damhauja, the moon during the last quarter, plays or rather played, a great part. I say played, since, unfortunately, we have but a fragment of Yana lore left after the events of 1864. Damhauja's sons-in-law on the west side of the river, in this tale, were various Mapchemaina people, — that is, beings who somewhat later became beasts, birds, plants, rocks, and insects on earth. All the stars were his children. His daughters, stars, were married to Mapchemaina people, except the two of whom Juiwaiyu had dreamed. His sons, stars also, lived near him, and were at enmity with his sons-in-law.

THE FLIGHT OF TSANUNEWA AND DEFEAT OF HEHKU

IT is not so easy to decide who Hehku is. Her most usual, if not her regular and normal, form is that of a horned serpent ; but she changes herself into various forms. When angry, or rather when raging, she becomes a Putokya, — that is, a skull person, like Hitchinna. These Putokyas seem to be the cyclone or tremendous wind which moves in a narrow path and makes a clean sweep of everything.

The gambling scene in Jupka's sweat-house is good. Hehku has easy work till she meets the master, who to his incomparable power adds deceit.

The game, connected here with Jupka's sweat-house, is played by two persons sitting opposite each other. One of these holds a small "Jupaiauna" bone or stick in one of his closed hands, and the other guesses which hand it is in. The process of playing is as follows : —

Each person has ten little sticks or counters at the opening of the game. One holds the "Jupaiauna," and begins action by placing his hands behind his back and deciding in which hand to hold the bone for that time; next, he closes his hands firmly, and brings them out before his breast. He holds them back downward, the little finger of each hand touching that of the other. The person sitting opposite guesses where the bone is; the other opens both hands then, and shows his palms. If this bone is in the hand indicated by the guesser, he wins; if not, he loses. A game is finished when one side holds the twenty counters; that is, when one side has won the ten little sticks given to the other at the opening of the game.

As Hehku sat with her back to the west, her right hand was south and her left north. When her opponent guessed south, if the bone was in her right hand she sang it into her left (the north), — literally, enchanted it north. If the bone was in her left hand, she let it stay there, and thus she won in every case.

Jupka, by limiting the game to one guess, and by his quibble of words, proved himself a keener trickster than Hehku, whose predicament is described fairly well by the Russian saying, "Kosá nashlá na kámen," the scythe met a stone; or the biter bitten, as we might say.

THE FIRST BATTLE IN THE WORLD AND THE MAKING OF THE YANAS

THE beginning of this myth is somewhat similar to that of "Olelbis." A messenger is sent to invite the Master of Flint to come and show the Mapchemaina, or first people, how to kill deer. Kaltsauna, the owner of flint, is like Katkatchila of the Wintus; he is transformed later into a lizard. In character he is different, being old and testy though liberal, while Katkatchila is affable, but wonderfully tenacious of his weapon, and prizing it so highly that when the flint is stolen he does not hesitate to set the whole world on fire.

Kaltsauna put the various kinds of flint in places where they are found to this day, and taught the first people how to make arrow points.

These hunts of the first people or gods are, for the Yanas, the great prototypes of hunting. To this day all sorts of game are under the control of certain spirits of the first people, whose favor is essential to success in hunting.

The story of Howichinaipa's change into a little bird gives a good case of forced metamorphosis, and also a good picture of the stern spirit of Indian vengeance inherited from the first people.

Vengeance is a sacred duty which they were not free to neglect under any consideration. "Vengeance is mine, saith the Lord, and I will have it."

Machperkami, the tiny dog in the hair of Tuina (the sun), is an exact substitute for Winishuyat of the Wintus.

The descent of Tuina to the lower side of the earth, his night journey from west to east on the road made by Jupka, is described with clear and precise brevity. There is no doubt as to the nature of the water grizzlies who rise out of the ocean and go to the mountains at the approach of Tuina.

The account of the creation of the Yanas is as concise as possible, and at the same time complete.

WINTU PLACES MENTIONED IN THE MYTHS

Bohema Měm	Great water, Sacramento River.
Bohěm Bŭli	Great mountain, Bald Mountain.
Bohěm Puyuk	Great peak, Mount Shasta.
Bohěm Těhil	Great Tehil.
Bŭlibok Puyuk	Bulibok peak.
Bŭli Puiwăkat	Eastern mountain slope.
Dokŏs Hleï Púriton.	
Dau Paki Olěl	Upper side of the dam, above the dam.
Ělitsarauton	Root flat.
Ěl Hakam	In the elbow.
Halat Pom	Grapevine land.
Han Bŭli	Fox mountain.
Hïn Pom	Owl land, now Slate Creek.
Hlïhlï Puihlut Ton	Acorn eastern sweat-house place.
Kahi Bŭli	Wind mountain.
Kaisansi Haraston	The road place of Kaisus.
Kawikěn	Down in Kawi.
Kěri Bŭli	Acorn mountain.
Kïlïtcěpïn Kenharas . . .	Arrow straightener's down-road.
Kïnwïnïs Pom	Looking down land.
Lasan Holŏk	Spider's house (or den).
Lorŭs Pom	Sandstone land.
Miol Tapa	Tree on the island.
Měmnom Kalai	Southern water divide.
Nomkěn Kobalus Waiměmton	Northern shell water place.
Nomlopi	Southern Lopi.
Nophlut	Deer's sweat-house.
Nŏrken Měm	Water down south, now Little Sacramento.
Nŏrpat Kodiheril	Kodi village stand southward.
Nŏrpuikěn	Down southeast.

Nŏrwan Bŭli	Norwan mountain.
Nŏrwanbulihlut	Norwan mountain sweat-house.
Nŏrwĭnte	Seen in the south.
Olpŭhlchĭton	Blowing upward, *i. e.* wishing, place.
Pantĭ Tsarau	Upper sand flat, now Fall River.
Pas Puisono	Nose (promontory) sticking out eastward, now Redding.
Pĕnĕl Kĕntĕ.	
Pokaitĭn Mĕm	Woman's talk water.
Pom Wai Hudi Pom . . .	Land in the north, rumbling land.
Puidal Pom	Land far east.
Puidal Wĭnnĕm	Winnem far east.
Pui Mĕm	Eastern water, now Pit River.
Puitiĕl Ton	In the eastern side (region) place.
Pui Torŏr	Eastern ridge.
Saskĕwĭl	Sas's dwelling.
Sonŏmyai	At the stones.
Sawal Pom	The bathing-place land.
Sudi Sawal	The Sudi bathing-place.
Tayám Norél	Waiting in the south, now Trinity Centre.
Tcanahl Puyuk	White peak.
Tĕdĕ Puyuk	Red peak.
Tĕhi Bŭli	Tehi mountain.
Tidŏk Waisono	Ant northern nose (nose-promontory).
Tóriham Pui Torŏr	Eastern crane place.
Tókŭston	Rock ridge place.
Tsarau Hĕril	Sandflat village, now Stillwater.
Tsĭk Tĕpji	White oak whirling-place.
Waikĕn Pom Pui Humŏk Pom	The land down north, the eastern silent land.
Waihola Puyuk	Northern pipe place.
Waikĭdi Pom	Northern Kidi land.
Wĭni Mĕm	Middle water, now MacCloud River.

YANA PLACES MENTIONED IN THE MYTHS

Chupïskoto . . . . . . Red rocks.
Daha . . . . Great water, Sacramento River.
Hakachímatu . . . . . . Blue and white flint place, Pole-
                               cat Spring.
Hakamatu . . . . . . Flint place, Buzzard's Roost.
Hwitalmauna . . . . . Whistling-place, Little Flat.
Iwïljami . . . . Montgomery creek.
Jamahdi
Jidjïlpa . . . . Cedar creek.
Jigŭlmatu . . . . . . Round place, Round Mountain.
Juka Mapti.
Kamshumatu . . . . . Clover place.
Kĕtmatu . . . . . . Poison place.
Kurulsa Mauna.
Motiri Mauna.
Oáimatu . . . . A hollow mountain northeast of
                               Round Mountain.
Pawi . . . . Clover creek.
Pulshu Aina.
Wahkalú . . . . Mount Shasta.
Wahkanopa . . . . . . Lassen's Butte.
Wajami.
Wakaruwa . . . . . . Wakara's (moon's) dwelling.
Wamarawi . . . . . . A round mountain at Ball Creek.
Wewauna . . . . Round place.

VALUE OF LETTERS IN THE LIST OF PLACES AND IN THE NAMES OF PERSONS THROUGHOUT THE VOLUME

A long = a in hate	I short = i in bit
A short = o " not	O long = o " note
Ai = i " bite	O short = o " not
Au = ow " now	U long = oo " boot
E long = ai " bait	U short = u " bull
E short = e " bet	J = our J
I long = ee " beet	H = German ch

All other consonants have the same value as ours.

All short vowels are marked with ◡; the long are unmarked.

When the Indian meaning of names is known, I have given it before the present name of the place given by white men. When the name given by white men stands alone, it indicates that the Indian meaning is uncertain or unknown.

Names accented on the penult have no accents printed on them; all others have printed accents.